Caciques and Cemí Idols

CARIBBEAN ARCHAEOLOGY AND ETHNOHISTORY
L. Antonio Curet, Series Editor

Caciques and Cemí Idols

The Web Spun by Taíno Rulers Between Hispaniola and Puerto Rico

José R. Oliver

THE UNIVERSITY OF ALABAMA PRESS

Tuscaloosa

Typeface: AGaramond

∞

The paper on which this book is printed meets the minimum requirements of American National Standard for Information Sciences-Permanence of Paper for Printed Library Materials, ANSI Z39.48-1984.

Library of Congress Cataloging-in-Publication Data

Oliver, José R.
    Caciques and Cemi idols : the web spun by Taino rulers between Hispaniola and Puerto Rico / Jose R. Oliver.
        p.   cm. — (Caribbean archaeology and ethnohistory)
    Includes bibliographical references and index.
    ISBN 978-0-8173-1636-5 (cloth : alk. paper) — ISBN 978-0-8173-5515-9 (pbk. : alk. paper) — ISBN 978-0-8173-8117-2 (electronic) 1. Taino Indians—Religion. 2. Taino Indians—Implements. 3. Taino Indians—Colonization. 4. Indians of the West Indies—First contact with Europeans—Hispaniola. 5. Stone implements—Hispaniola—History. 6. Icons—Hispaniola—History. 7. Christianity and culture—Hispaniola. 8. Christianity and other religions—Hispaniola. 9. Religious syncretism—Hispaniola. 10. Spain—Colonies—America. 11. Hispaniola—Colonization. 12. Hispaniola—Antiquities. I. Title.
    F1619.2.T3O55 2009
    972.9′02—dc22
                                                                                2008038785

Special Credits

Front Cover Illustration: A close-up of the face of a cemí idol recovered from a cave site in Carpenters Mountain, Jamaica (Cat. AM 1977. Q1). For this portraiture the head was cropped to highlight the personage's facial features; the gold sheet eye and lachrymal inlays and the shell-denture inlays were digitally added to render a likely interpretation of what the face might have looked like had the inlays been preserved. Photograph and digital additions with Adobe Photoshop by José R. Oliver. ©The Trustees of the British Museum.

Back Cover Illustrations: A three-pointed stone cemí from Puerto Rico. ©Museo de Historia, Arte y Antropología–Universidad de Puerto Rico. Author's photo (inset back cover). Photograph of the author at the Bateyes de Viví (U-1) site, Barrio Viví Arriba, Utuado, Puerto Rico (2005).

To my daughter, Juliana,
for the joy she brings to my life,
and
to my wife, Kim,
my guardian angel

Contents

List of Illustrations and Tables

List of Illustrations

Note: Figures in the present text are referred to as "Figure x," with the word "figure" capitalized and spelled out. Figures in cited text are referred to as "fig. x," with the word "figure" lowercased and abbreviated.

List of Tables

Note: Tables in the present text are referred to as "Table x," with the word "table" capitalized and spelled out. Tables in cited text are referred to as "table x," with the word "table" lowercased.

Preface

The arguments presented in this book were essentially written in a rather short, intense period of just under five months, from early November 2006 to early March 2007. Yet the ideas and insights took much longer to gestate. My interest in this topic began in the early 1970s as a teenager, with my curiosity in trying to understand the potential meanings that could be elicited from rock art and iconography, most particularly the petroglyphs that so frequently are found engraved in stone-demarcated plazas or precincts (*bateyes*), but are also painted or carved in caves and on rock boulders found in rivers and dotted throughout the land. From these rather naïve initial efforts, my thinking eventually matured and led to an in-depth analysis of the iconography of the civic-ceremonial center of Caguana, Puerto Rico (Oliver 1980, 1992, 1998, 2005). It was while writing the Caguana papers and the book in the 1980s and '90s that I became increasingly concerned not so much with the *objets d'art* per se, but with the relationships that they may have had with the native peoples who created and used them. In these papers and the 1998 book, I had taken an overtly structuralist and linguistic approach, influenced by an R. Tom Zuidema and Donald W. Lathrap brand of structuralism and linguistics, ultimately all of it deriving inspiration from Claude Lévi-Strauss's ouvre. Linguistic theory, nurtured by Professor Rudolph Troike during my graduate school years at the University of Illinois at Urbana-Champaign, was central to my analysis of the iconography of Caguana. My purpose, then, was principally to provide the ritual and ceremonial scenarios where humans interacted with and "decoded" the icons in order to elicit their potential meanings and functions.

Because my book on Caguana's iconography was written in Spanish, many Anglophones (for better or worse, it *is* the international language of academia) were unable to read it. In 2003 Peter Siegel offered me an opportunity to write a chapter on Caguana's iconography in English. It appeared in his edited book *Ancient Borinquen: Archaeology and Ethnohistory of Native Puerto Rico,* published by The University of Alabama Press in 2005 (Oliver 2005:230–284). Reworking and synthesizing the original 1998 book into an article-length essay rekindled my fascination with the nature of the relationship of the *cemí* icons and the ancient natives. Although it was a synthesis that still followed the structural approach of the 1998 book, I also began to pay more attention to the processes that rendered these icons into active agents rather than passive entities—that is, cemí petroglyphs as persons. The roles of the *behiques* (shamans) and of the *caciques* (chiefs, who were also shamans) became more prominent focusing on their relationships with these monumental (petroglyph) cemí icons. Shamanistic and altered states of consciousness theories, such as those presented by G. Reichel-Dolmatoff (1978) for the Desana of the northwest Amazon and David Lewis-Williams (2002) for the "explosion" of Upper Paleolithic cave art in Western Europe, were put into, I hope, good use.

As a result of the 2005 publication, I was invited by Warren DeBoer to contribute a paper in the 71st Annual Meeting of the Society for American Archaeology, for the symposium "Enduring Motives: Religious Traditions in the Americas" (see *71st SAA Abstracts,* 2006:304). In writing this paper, titled "Cemís and Human Agency; or, Religion and the Making of Taíno Political History," I wanted to provide a different perspective to my previous publications on cemí iconography and to get away from just considering the petroglyph art of Caguana (and similar sites), where the iconography is monumental and thus "fixed" in space, and instead focus on *portable* cemí icons. The time constraints for oral presentations at the SAA meeting forced me to rigorously focus on human-cemí agency and interaction, their mobility and circulation, and on specific insights regarding the religious tradition centered on *cemiism.* Since the 71st SAA meeting was held, of all places, in San Juan, Puerto Rico, I was also invited to present a paper in the plenary session, devoted to the topic of "Islands in the Stream: Interisland and Continental Interaction in the Caribbean," organized by my colleague L. Antonio Curet (Field Museum of Natural History). My contribution was titled "Taíno Interaction and Variability between the Provinces of Higüey, Eastern Hispaniola, and Otoao, Puerto Rico," providing yet another opportunity to focus on aspects of the exchange (gift giving/gift taking) of objects imbued with cemí potency, on their mobility or circulation across islands, and their implications. It was while preparing this paper that I became painfully aware that I needed to develop a much more theoretically rigorous argument to address the questions of "who is" (person, personhood) and "what is" about a cemí idol that can be given, taken, exchanged, stolen, mobilized, and even mutilated or destroyed, before I could delve into the larger questions of native inter-insular politics. This led me to study a corpus of archaeological and anthropological literature concerned with personhood, and in particular the phenomenon of the partibility of persons (and other nonhuman beings and things), which, of course, is essential if one wishes to completely understand the character of the entities (cemís) being circulated, including the human persons involved in the circulation of cemí objects.

Not long after the SAA meetings concluded in April 2006, I received an invitation from Antonio Curet to contribute a chapter in a book based on the papers that had been presented in the plenary session. I started writing with this objective in mind, but it soon became evident that I would be unable to justify my conclusions;

more words were needed. A discussion and evaluation of the anthropological and archaeological theories on human agency and personhood and on mobility and gift exchange had to be made explicit if my arguments about Taíno caciques and their cemí idols could be sustained. With Curet's gracious blessing, I abandoned the idea of writing a chapter-length version as soon as I figured out how to provide an adequate ending to a book of this kind. The topic—an examination of the social webs spun by Taíno rulers and the role of the idols as nonhuman persons imbued with motility and action—did not easily lend itself to a solid finish, one that provided a satisfying closure, both from an academic and a literary (narrative) sense. So, one might ask, what if the caciques and idols were related in these or those ways, and under such-and-such contexts? Or why would it be relevant to dwell on the history of a particular distribution of cemí idols between and within Hispaniola and Puerto Rico?

Eventually I found an answer to these questions. I realized that the religious beliefs about the cemí idols were at the very core of the conflicts between the Spanish conquerors and the natives, that what happened to these idols and what humans and cemís did as actors (agents) was a decisive turning point in the history of ancient Caribbean natives and a crucial crossroads for what was to follow during the rest of the sixteenth century under the Spanish colonial dominance. The outcomes of the clashes in Hispaniola and Puerto Rico—veritable bloody wars and rebellions of natives against the Spanish Christians—offered a sense of finality and yet also of a new beginning. In the Cuba of 1511 there are the first well-documented examples of what can only be described as the initial phase toward syncretism between aboriginal and Christian religions where icons, once again, were at center stage: the Virgin Mary, adopted as a cemí, confronted rival native cemís in combat. As the next centuries unfolded, the numinous cemí icons of old were gradually replaced by a Marian devotion, yet it is an advocation that still today has some echoes of the ancient religion of cemíism, such as in the cults surrounding the Vírgen de la Caridad del Cobre and the Vírgen de Guadalupe de El Caney that arose in Cuba in the early 1600s (Portuondo Zúñiga 1995; Pérez Fernández 1999). The indigenous elements of the Marian cult were conjoined ("swamped" is the word) with contributions from the diverse Old and New World populations arriving in the Caribbean. The resulting syncretic palette of the early Indian-Spanish-Marian "cemíistic" cults would be further enriched by voodoo (or *vodou*) in Hispaniola, *La Regla de Ocha* and *Lucumí* in Cuba, and by Puerto Rican spiritualism (grouped under the misnomer of "*Santería*"; see Alegría Pons 1993; Brown 2003; Deive 1979; Métraux 1972; Pérez y Mena 1998). The following three long colonial centuries saw new regional and national identities being forged, among them the "Indio." During these centuries of colonialism, significant populations that recognized themselves as Indios (in contrast to Criollos, Mestizos, whites, Africans, mulattos, etc.) were largely excised from official history by the dominant (white peninsular and Criollo) oligarchy. Syncretism, transculturation, and acculturation are concepts that need to be reappropriated by archaeologists once again (albeit anthropologists in the Caribbean have never really forgotten them). I am gratified that independently Samuel Wilson's (2007) new book has paid attention to these three sociohistoric processes. But this latter (post-1520–1530s) history of the Caribbean is a matter that will not be pursued at great length here. Its proper analysis deserves another book or two.

The final shape this book has taken owes a huge debt to Tim Insoll (Manchester University), who taught me to think of religion not just as rituals or ceremonies (my 1998 and 2005 writings) but as an all-encompassing way of living and thinking about one's life; that religion must be as fully integrated in the archeological analysis as much as economics or politics are. Tim also pointed the way in my search for approaches regarding identity in archaeology. Chris Fowler (Newcastle University) prodded me with numerous stimulating questions I had neglected to raise or had given short shrift. His book *The Archaeology of Personhood* (2004) was a magnificent source, forcing me to think hard on questions about the partibility of persons and stimulating me to search deeper into the corpus of Maussian theories of gift exchange and reciprocity. Both Insoll's and Fowler's work pushed me to look into Oceania (Melanesia, Polynesia) for inspiration on the issues of personhood and the circulation of idols, and also to Africa, where there are, of course, remarkable and fascinating parallels with the Caribbean in the ways in which potent idols are used, such as the Ba-Kongo peoples' (Congo Basin) complex relations with the *minkisi* idols (e.g., Anderson and Peek 2002; MacGaffey 1993; Voguel 1997). Unfortunately, for reasons of space, an in-depth comparative analysis of African and Caribbean idols will have to remain a project for the future. Fowler and Insoll, as British scholars, less familiar with the Caribbean, also encouraged me to discuss what is or is not known about Taíno kinship, descent, and inheritance to better appreciate the matter of the circulation of cemí objects. This resulted in the addition of a new section to this book.

A very special debt of gratitude is due to my colleague and long-time friend Jeff Walker, archaeologist of the Caribbean National Forest, whose excellent research and writing on stone collars, three-pointed stones, and other cemí artifacts marked a path to follow and scrutinize in this book. Walker's work is a source of inspiration that, in my view, should be taken full advantage of by Caribbean archaeologists.

Lively conversations over the years with my colleagues at Leiden University (The Netherlands), Corinne Hofman, Arie Boomert, Menno Hoogland, and their graduate students Angus Mol and Alice Samson have also contributed in rekindling my interest in researching the theoretical issues surrounding exchange and mobility, forcing me to review the literature stemming from Marcel Mauss's concepts of the gift. Clearly the nature of the webs or networks of interactions in which humans and their potent cemí icons circulated can be most fruitfully informed through theories of the gift. In doing so I have relied primarily on the literature about Melanesian-Oceanian social anthropology and ethnography for three reasons: First is the fact that the theories of gift exchange and, equally important, of personhood (identity, dividuality, fractality, and so forth) are not only mature but also have been richly researched for a much longer time there than elsewhere. Second, Melanesia and Oceania, like the Caribbean, involve maritime societies and islands. Third, I am much more familiar with the literature of this region than that of other regions of the world.

Antonio Curet (Field Museum), Samuel Wilson (University of Texas–Austin), and Reniel Rodríguez Ramos (University of Puerto Rico–Utuado) insisted that I had to change or at least explain my use of the term "Taíno." This term is hugely powerful; it is so embedded in our minds that it would be foolhardy and pretentious of me to eradicate it. Although reading various papers published by Curet (see References Cited) made me aware that my use of "Taíno" in previous works was inadequate (Oliver 2005:281–282n1), it was while reading and commenting on Rodríguez Ramos's recent Ph.D. thesis (2007) that I realized I could no longer let it pass with just a warning footnote. The standard Rousean normative definition of Taíno peoples and cultures (Rouse 1992) is thus given a substantial facelift in this book. This revised view also found further stimulus in the 71st SAA Annual Meeting, where I collaborated with Rodríguez Ramos and Joshua Torres in a paper (Rodríguez Ramos et al. 2008) that demonstrated the inadequacies of the cultural scheme developed by Irving "Ben" Rouse (1992). This review is important because the Rousean normative model still remains a dominant cultural-historic paradigm throughout the Caribbean and, more important, has contributed to the newfound native heritage among modern Caribbean groups (more visibly among the "Hispanic" Antilles and the United States) who define themselves as direct heirs of the Taínos. In this regard, I lament that Wilson's excellent new book, *The Archaeology of the Caribbean* (Cambridge University Press, 2007), had reached my hands too late to include or comment upon his insights here. Its publication marks fifteen years since the last Caribbean-wide synthesis was published by Rouse. Nonetheless, I mention it here to encourage the reader to consult Wilson's work, alongside this book, especially his chapters 4, "The Taino," and 5, "The Caribbean in the Eve of Contact."

Joanna Ostapkowicz (Liverpool Museum) also contributed insightful comments and shared her expert knowledge on Taíno wooden icons. Her warnings about my sleight of hand in the use of gender in my text were most welcome. Although I write in English, my brain also operates in Spanish and Catalan, Romance languages that have marked gender biases in their semantics and lexicon. Cuban archaeologists Jorge Ulloa Hung and Lourdes Domínguez were crucial in helping me understand the issues of syncretism surrounding the Marian cult in Oriente and furnishing hard-to-find literature on this topic. Needless to say, there are other colleagues and institutions that have contributed in the making of this book, and they will be duly noted in the Photo Credits and Copyrights section. In sum, while I have to claim responsibility for what you are about to read, the bare truth is that this book is the product of collegiality and cooperation—a meeting of minds, if you will—but distilled through my thoughts and penmanship. And thus, I am solely to blame should I have failed to do justice to their comments and critiques, or have misinterpreted their published work.

Finally, the staff at The University of Alabama Press, and Jill R. Hughes, my copyeditor, are to be commended for their superb job in turning the original manuscript into a proper, readable book.

Here are some pointers for make the reading easier. Native words are italized and their English gloss is provided in parenthesis or in the surrounding text at their first mention, or where it is most relevant. Italics were also reserved for words that I wish to emphasize and for Linnaean taxonomic nomenclature. I have also translated into English all the Spanish texts that have been quoted in the text. Some translations, especially Old Castilian, may have an awkward English syntax in order to render as closely as possible the original text, the reading of which is nevertheless still comprehensible in English. This book is divided into twenty-two sections that one might call chapters (I do not). To make it easier to navigate, I divided the twenty-two sections of the book into six parts, as follows: part I: Introduction and Theoretical Premises (sections 1–5); part II: The Form, Personhood, Identity, and Potency of Cemí Idols (sections 6–8); part III: The Social Relations and Circulation of Cemí Idols and Human Beings (sections 9–14); part IV: Stone Collars, Elbow Stones, Three-Pointers, Stone Heads, and Guaízas (sections 15–18); part V: The Battles for the Cemís in Hispaniola, Boriquén, and Cuba (sections 19–21); and part VI: Conclusions (section 22).

Caciques and Cemí Idols

PART I

Introduction and Theoretical Premises

1   Introduction

In this book I will be exploring the underlying social significance of the spatial distribution of a class of religious portable artifacts—*cemís*—that the Taínos and other natives of the Greater Antilles (ca. A.D. 1000–1650) regarded as numinous beings and believed to have supernatural, magic powers. (A more precise definition of *cemí* will be provided later.) To understand the distribution of cemí idols requires a close look at the relationship between human beings and other (non-human) beings that are imbued with cemí power. I will be exploring interisland interaction through the web of human and cemí idol relationships that was spun within the Taíno cultural sphere, most specifically between Puerto Rico and Hispaniola (Figure 1). I will explore not only the inter-insular relationships in which cemís and humans acted but also where all interaction begins: at the personal, face-to-face level between persons and cemí idols. The material evidence comes from a selection of archaeological artifacts largely held in museum collections. The evidence for the interpretation of human and cemí interactions emerges from a critical review of the sixteenth-century Spanish ethnohistoric documents and, most particularly, from the famous *Relación Acerca de las Antigüedades de los Indios* written by Fray (Friar) Ramón Pané in 1497–1498, on orders of Christopher Columbus (Pané 1974 [1497–1498], 1990, 1999).

Although objects imbued with cemí potency are quite diverse in material, form, and style, I will be focusing on four broad formal categories: (1) the large, highly decorated three-pointed stone sculptures, (2) the large stone heads, (3) stone collars, and (4) elbow stones (see Figures 2, 3). A fifth category, the *guaízas,* or "face masks," will also be highlighted, as they provide a fascinating contrast to the other four categories, especially the stone heads. The first four classes of iconic artifacts are endogenous Caribbean creations for which there are no firmly established homologues or antecedents in the American continents (see Oliver 1998; Walker 1993:450–451). They are of interest because their spatial distribution is restricted to southeastern Hispaniola, Mona Island, Puerto Rico, Vieques Island, and the Virgin Islands (García Arévalo 2005), although a few rare *large* three-pointers did spread farther south into the Lesser Antilles, as far as the Grenadine Islands (Crock and Petersen 2004; Kaye et al. 2004; Knippenberg 2004). In contrast, the spatial distribution of the guaízas extends beyond the frontier of the so-called Classic

Taíno culture area. As Jeffrey Walker (1993:378–392) pointed out, there seems to be a codependent relationship between the massive and decorated three-pointers, stone collars, and elbow stones, so it is possible that these three artifacts may have spread as a set rather than as separate items.

The geographical distribution of all four objects is much more restricted than the maximum regional extent of what has been called the "Classic Taíno" culture area—that is, by the archaeologically and normatively defined distribution of the late Chican Ostionoid (ca. A.D. 1000–1500) series of cultures (Rouse 1992: figs. 2, 3). Various other portable and powerful artifacts have a wider distribution throughout the Antilles than the four classes mentioned, such as the guaízas worn on the chest, belt, arm, or forehead; *duhos* (seats or benches); wooden figures or statuettes; inhalators (for hallucinogen snuffing); and, above all, a myriad of elaborate pendants and plaques for body adornment (on Taíno wood artifacts, see Oliver et al. 2008; Ostapkowicz 1999; Saunders and Gray 1996). The geographical circumscription of the aforementioned four classes of cemí artifacts, centered between east-southeastern Hispaniola and Puerto Rico, suggests two things: (1) that there existed a shared tradition in each island region of manufacturing these particular classes of cemí icons, and (2) that there existed a tight, reinforced, socially driven web or network through which these icons circulated and were inherited. This distribution of artifacts also suggests that the so-called Classic Taíno natives did not all share or construct in the same way their identity, or their "Taínoness." As will be argued shortly, Taíno is best approached as a spectrum or mosaic of social groups with diverse expressions of Taínoness (Rodríguez Ramos 2007), not all of whom were Taíno peoples in the conventional or standard sense provided by Irving Rouse (1965, 1992) and others. In this book I will analyze the political-religious significance of the cemí objects and their distribution. I will also focus on the relationships between the icons and human beings and the various contexts in which these relationships were enacted. In doing so, the scale at which interactions take place is also considered, ranging from the intimate, face-to-face or person-to-person relationships to the broader regional, inter-insular relationships of human interaction.

The diverse cemí idols were central to the exercise of native political power and as such were seen as a direct threat to the hegemony of the Spanish conquerors. At the same time, however, these potent objects were literally allies in the resistance put up by the native leadership against the onslaught of Christendom with their icons of saints and virgins. The struggle of the Antillean natives was in many ways a battle for the rule and survival of cemí idols. The war of the region of Higüey in Hispaniola (1503–1504) and the Rebellion of the Caciques (chiefs) in Puerto Rico (1511–1519) provide the contexts in which to analyze the intertwined human and cemí relations, offering valuable insights on the consequences of Spanish colonization. Yet, at the same time the significance of appropriation and empowerment with regard to cemís will also be studied. This is the case of a Cuban cacique with the adopted (Spanish) name of Comendador, who appropriated a Catholic icon and used it as he would have used a cemí in order to engage in a ritualized combat against the rival cacique who was "protected" by his own cemí icon—an example of the initial process of Catholic syncretism with echoes of Taínoness that survived into the eighteenth century in the cult of the Vírgen de la Caridad del Cobre and the Vírgen de Guadalupe (Pérez Fernández 1999; Portuondo Zúñiga 1995). These and other accounts dealing with resistance and syncretism will be explored in part V of this book. Before the iconoclastic conflicts can be discussed, and before the relationships between cemí idols and natives can be analyzed, it is imperative to provide a critical review of what is meant here by *Taíno* (singular), since it is given as *the* culture and language of the natives in the Greater Antilles, and to also re-examine what is implied by *Taínos* (plural), since it refers to the individuals and the people who created, gave meaning, and used the cemí idols.

2   Believers of Cemíism

Who Were the Taínos and Where Did They Come From?

This section serves as a background on Greater Antillean archaeology so as to contextualize, in broad strokes, the potent cemí objects and to identify, again in broad strokes, the peoples who interacted with them. It is not an easy section to write, because in the last few years our understanding of who the Taínos and their historical antecedents were have changed and continue to change dramatically—so much so that the 2008 annual meeting of the Society of American Archaeology in Vancouver is devoting a whole symposium to this topic, aiming at reaching some consensus on the matter. This section is also difficult to write because if "Taíno" is, in essence, an inoperative term that refers to nothing of real substance, then what term should archaeologists use, in colloquial speech, to refer to this spectrum of "peoples" inhabiting most of the Greater Antilles? It will not do to forward a long phrase or sentence, full of conditional statements, to replace the term "Taíno."

The native informants encountered by Fray Ramón Pané in Hispaniola spoke two distinct languages: the Macorix language (about which we know only a few words) and the widely spoken, dominant, and elegant Taíno language. The latter is a member of the northern Maipuran subfamily that in turn is grouped in the vast Arawakan linguistic stock spread throughout lowland South America.

The natives inhabiting most of the Greater Antilles have been and are still labeled as "Taínos" ever since the term was first coined by Constantine Samuel Rafinesque in 1836. The Taínos are assumed to have shared a homogeneous culture and language. The term *nitaíno,* from which "Taíno" derived, refers to an elite stratum or class and not to an ethnic group. Moreover, not a single sixteenth-century Spanish document ever used this noun to refer to the tribal or ethnic affiliation of the natives of the Greater Antilles. True, the term *tayno* (meaning "good" or "prudent") was mentioned twice in a short account of Columbus's second voyage by his physician, Dr. Álvarez Chanca, in a very specific context, while in Guadaloupe (Chanca, in Navarrete 1922:218–219). This was a response to the Spaniards from natives of Boriquén who had been captured by the so-called Caribes of Guadeloupe, and who wished to escape on Spanish ships in order to return home to Puerto Rico. In other words, with this term they were effectively saying something like "we are the good, prudent guys," unlike those others. After this singular mention, the term was not to be used again until the end of the nineteenth century, first by Daniel Brinton (1871), but only to refer to a linguistic classification and then, as noted, by Rafinesque in a broader, cultural sense.

The Spanish simply referred to them as *Indios, Indios de estas Indias Occidentales* (Indians of these West Indies). In the *repartimiento* and *encomienda* systems (forms of forced labor and slavery) the natives were listed as being such-and-such (personal names or titles) who belonged to this or that place (toponyms; e.g., Juanillo de Caguana, cacique de Caguas), or who belonged to this or that cacique (e.g., Isabel Cayaguax de Humacao). Besides "Indios" there are very few other terms written by the Spaniards that refer to collectivities. There is, of course, the name "Lucayo" for the Indians of the Bahamas. This term is a compound of *luku* or *loko* (meaning "person," in singular) and *kayo* ("island"). Thus, in answer to Christopher Columbus's question, the Bahamian native in effect said he was a "person-[of-the-]island,"—that is, "an islander"; an excellent self-designation, but hardly an identification of membership in a given polity or larger ethnic group. Other designations were given by natives to other natives: such as *Cigüayo* (in Hispaniola), which makes reference to their peculiar hairstyle, gathered at the back of the head in a pony-tail fashion, or *Ciboney,* a term that the Spaniards claimed was given to a people from central to eastern Cuba who, to the Spaniards' eyes, were less developed than those originating from Hispaniola. Another term, *Macorix* (plural, *Macoriges*), was given to natives who inhabited a region of that name in northeastern Hispaniola who spoke a non-Taíno language and who also had a "Cigüayo-like" hairstyle.

In sum, the terms of reference and self-designation that natives used relative to ever higher levels of inclusion (from person to household and from local place level to larger social aggregates and polities) remain unknown. What is clear, though, is that a plurality of social groupings existed, crosscutting both linguistic boundaries and political allegiances, and originating from diverse traditions and places.

A. Rouse's Standard Culture History: A Brief Overview

The late Irving Rouse (b. 1913–d. 2006; Keegan 2007a) is recognized as one of the leading figures in the development of culture history in archaeology in the Americas (Willey and Sabloff 1974), and has had a lasting international impact on how scholars and the general public perceive the pre-Columbian history of the Caribbean and of the Taínos of the Spanish contact period. As Reniel Rodríguez Ramos, Joshua Torres, and I (2008) noted recently, most archaeologists working in the Caribbean "have assumed [the] premises [of Rouse's model] in a *quasi*-religious fashion, merging culture and society into a single domain and considering that these have changed concomitantly along a unilinear temporal vector." Because it is Rouse's vision of what the Taínos are and how they emerged that prevails in the Caribbean, this section focuses on a critique of his assumptions.

Within a classic culture-historic paradigm, Rouse (1992) defined three Taíno culture areas based on the distribution of diagnostic features (Figure 4): the Western Taíno, which encompasses most of Cuba, Jamaica, and the Bahamas; the Classic or Central Taíno, covering Hispaniola and Puerto Rico; and the Eastern Taíno, extending from the Virgin Islands and those north of Guadeloupe. This core-periphery spatial model is in many ways impressionistic. It is based on what Rouse regards to be manifestations of high-level, elaborate artistic achievements at the core (Classic or Central) versus the much more impoverished achievements of peripheral Taínos (Eastern and Western). Earlier, Rouse (e.g., 1942:165) had used the term "Sub-Taíno" to express the notion of underdevelopment or marginality. The more politically correct geographical designations, Eastern and Western, cannot hide that these variants of Taíno are still grounded on notions of substandard achievements in comparison to the core area.

For Rouse (1992:32–33), the "Taíno people who greeted Columbus" were the culmination of a process of continuous historic divergence from a single phylum, from a common ancestral culture. For Rouse, all closely related styles (that shared a set of ceramic norms or a modal complex) are indicative of a common ancestral style and hence form a series of styles. In principle, all of the norms shared between closely related styles would be elicited from the set of diagnostic modes characterizing the posited ancestral style, much in the same way that historical linguists (e.g., Noble 1965; Payne 1991) reconstruct protolanguages on the basis of a shared or cognate lexicon (phonemes, morphemes, words) found in a set of living or recorded languages. Rouse's "series" is archaeology's analogue of the linguists' protolanguage (see Raymond Gordon's *Ethnologue* [2005] for the latest Arawakan family tree classification).

By 1980 Rouse introduced the subseries (Figure 5), an intermediate taxonomic level between style and series. This taxon was introduced by Rouse (via a suggestion from the late Gary S. Vescelius) to acknowledge that within a series, a subset of styles appears to share more norms (modal complex) among themselves than with other member styles of that same series; thus, their divergence from the posited ancestral style (series) was more recent. To distinguish a series from a subseries, Rouse added the suffix "-oid" (e.g., Ostion*oid*) to the former and "-an" (e.g., Ostion*an*) to the latter. Differences between styles of the same subseries and series were primarily the result of cultural divergence (or fission), a process that Rouse (1989, 1992) identified as analogous to biology's founder's effect: after fission, daughter communities will carry only a part of the parental genetic stock (i.e., a part of the parental norms and modes that make up a style). Rouse, like Gordon R. Willey, was a great synthesizer. His description of the entire developmental history of the Taínos takes but one paragraph:

> All the Historic-age Taínos made pottery belonging to a single Ostionoid series [A.D. 600–1500] of local styles. The ancestry of the Classic Taínos can be traced back into prehistory through a Chican Ostionoid subseries, the ancestry of the Western Taínos through a Meillacan Ostionoid subseries, and

the ancestry of the Eastern Taínos through an Elenan Ostionoid subseries. The three ancestries converge in the Cedrosan Saladoid subseries of Puerto Rico and the Lesser Antilles. From there the trail leads back to similar deposits on the Guianan and Venezuelan coasts [Rouse 1992:32–33].

In other words, the cultural traits of the Taíno peoples and their regional variants (Western, Eastern, Classic or Central) all derived from the spread of the Saladoid series of peoples, and their ceramic styles, from their original homeland in the Orinoco Valley (2300–900 B.C.), reaching the West Indies between ca. 400–250 B.C. In Rouse's model the Lesser Antillean Ortoiroid series of cultures (Archaic age) were either quickly decimated or rapidly acculturated to the civilizing forces of the advancing Cedrosan Saladoids, who brought and imposed a sedentary lifeway, ceramic technology, and a subsistence based on agricultural production to the "hapless" nomadic bands of hunter-gatherers. Even in Hispaniola, where Rouse (1992) recognized a greater degree of interaction between the Archaic populations (El Porvenir and Courí cultures) and the early Ostionoid cultures (Anadel and Macady cultures) spreading out of Puerto Rico, the effect was the same: the Archaic hunter-gatherer groups became very rapidly "Ostionized" (i.e., Rouse's Meillacan subseries). The presence of non-Saladoid (and non-Ostionoid) pottery in Archaic sites such as El Caimito and El Porvenir in southern Hispaniola and of Caimanes III in Cuba, for Rouse, were essentially a brief instance of copying Saladoid ceramic technology (not the style) even when the dates cited (ca. 400–300 B.C.) are more than three centuries older than the earliest Saladoid presence in Hispaniola or Meillacan in Cuba (Figure 5). In any event, the Archaic cultures with pottery in Hispaniola were also to perish under the weight of colonization by the early Ostionoids—that is, the direct descendants of the Saladoids. These were the early Ostionan Ostionoid cultures (Ostiones to Arroyo del Palo) that spread from Puerto Rico westward into Hispaniola, the Bahamas, eastern-central Cuba, and Jamaica, starting around A.D. 600. Only the westernmost region of Cuba was spared. Rouse argued that at the time of Spanish contact, western Cuba was entirely inhabited by hunter-gatherer bands designated as Guanahatabeyes or Guanahacabibes. In the sixteenth century these bands were described as troglodytes (cave dwellers), who lacked agriculture and settled village lifestyles, a description that fostered the illusory image of a surviving Archaic population that remained culturally ossified in time (Rodríguez Ramos 2006).

The implication of Rouse's developmental scheme is that the Taíno religious ideology and ritual paraphernalia were, in effect, the result of inheritance and subsequent local innovations from this single ancestral Cedrosan Saladoid source (Rouse 1982:52–54). The Archaic hunter-gatherers had nothing of substance to contribute to the emergence and coalescence of the later Taíno culture. This view has also resulted in the use of ethnohistoric analogy and archaeological compari-

sons with northeastern South America to the exclusion of other areas of continental America, such as the Isthmian region of Panama and Colombia or the southeastern United States (Gulf Coast). Julian Steward's (1948) original definition of
a circum-Caribbean culture area was reduced to the Caribbean islands and northeastern South America by Rouse.

Rouse treated religion and its paraphernalia in the same typological fashion as
he did ceramics and other artifacts. In his last synthesis, Rouse's (1992) approach
to religious artifacts had not changed much from his earlier writings (see Rouse
1948). In his only explicit paper on the development of religion in the Greater
Antilles, Rouse wrote in the mid-1980s: "the ceremonial artifacts of the Greater
Antilles are as complex and variable in their stylistic attributes as the pottery. . . .
These objects were presumably used to worship the deities that the historic Taíno
Indians called zemis [sic]. They are representative of a religion called zemiism.
Until recently, religious objects were found only in sites dating from Periods IIIb
[A.D. 900–1200] and IV [A.D. 1200–1524]. Now, however, similar ceremonial
objects are turning up with Hacienda Grande, the earliest Saladoid style [in Puerto
Rico]" (Rouse 1985:52).

For Rouse, the Taíno ceremonial artifacts are related to the "worship of the
deities"—that is, cemí icons (who are not deities anyway). He argued that cemí
objects developed from a single ancestral Saladoid source, and thereafter religious
art went through a "dark age" only to undergo a revival later: "It is beginning to
look as though we may distinguish two climaxes of religious art in the Antilles,
one known as Igneri [from the Island Carib word eyeri, meaning "man/husband"]
during Period IIa [A.D. 300 B.C.–A.D. 400] and the other known as Taíno during Period IV [A.D. 1200–1524]. The two are comparable to the Classic and Post-
Classic stages in Nuclear America. They are separated by a dark age, like that between Classic and Renaissance art in Italy" (Rouse 1985:52).

Rouse goes on to argue that the spatial distribution of Taíno art supports his
hypothesis of a religious revival out of the preceding "dark ages," the latter represented by the Elenan Ostionoid and Ostionan Ostionoid cultures and styles. This
purported Taíno renaissance "reached its highest development in the Mona Passage
area and is much the same on both sides," on the eastern Dominican Republic and
western Puerto Rico (Rouse 1985:52). However, Rouse says, "the art objects became simpler and less typical as one proceeds through the Windward Passage area
into the Western Periphery [Western Taíno] and through the Vieques Sound Area
into the Lesser Antilles [Eastern Taíno]," and he concludes that "the development
of ceramic styles parallels that in ceremonial art" (Rouse 1985:52). Although in
this article Rouse did not include a discussion of the Archaic age, it is clear from his
1992 synthesis book that the entire corpus of cemiism and the religious or ceremonial artifacts (and hence, ideology and practice) evolved from the Cedrosan Saladoid or "Igneri" art (Rouse 1992). It is striking that after reading Rouse's 1992

book, one comes to the conclusion that the diverse Archaic cultures, whose ancestors had been inhabiting the Caribbean islands since around 5000–4000 B.C., have contributed very little, if anything, to the emergence of Taíno culture, especially regarding religious beliefs and practices.

B. From a Unilinear Ancestry to Multiple Authors and Ancestries

Needless to say, Rouse's (1992) unilinear developmental culture history is seriously flawed. The following critique focuses on Puerto Rico, as it is here where Rouse (1952) first began, in 1937, his construction of the cultural-chronological model and is also where the archaeological data is denser and better documented. To begin with, the diverse Archaic populations substantially contributed to the cultural patterns and social configurations, not to mention the material culture, of the societies and cultures that Europeans encountered from 1492 onward. The two Archaic series noted by Rouse are likely to have originated from two different continental regions: the Casimiroid (and all of its variants, such as Seboruco) are said to have come from the southern Yucatan Peninsula (especially Belize) in Central America and spread through Cuba eastward, while the Ortoiroid (others call it Banwaroid) originated in the Trinidad–Paria Peninsula (Venezuela) region and spread northward through the Lesser Antilles (Wilson et al. 1998). Surely, the groups from each of these two different continental regions brought with them different bodies of knowledge and material culture to the Caribbean. Maritime voyages back and forth from the Caribbean islands to the homeland and also from and to various other continental areas in the circum-Caribbean, like the Isthmus of Panama and Colombia, continued to be undertaken long after the initial colonization (see Rodríguez Ramos and Pagán Jiménez 2006).

Rouse (1992) recognized only a single Archaic culture for Puerto Rico: Coroso (Ortoiroid series). He admitted, however, that there were Casimiroid contacts between the Dominican Republic (e.g., Courí) and Puerto Rico (e.g., Cerrillos site, in Cabo Rojo). It is clear now that a growing number of Archaic complexes do not neatly fit a single Coroso cultural pattern or are merely Coroso with some influences from Hispaniola (Rodríguez Ramos 2007). A suite of sixty absolute dates related to Archaic or pre-Arawak sites not only shows an initial occupation around 4000 B.C. (Angostura site, Vega Baja), much earlier than Rouse admitted (i.e., Coroso complex at 1000 B.C.), but also persisted for much longer, until at least A.D. 400 (Rodríguez Ramos et al. 2008:fig. 2). This implies that the later Archaic populations coexisted with the so-called Hacienda Grande (i.e., Cedrosan Saladoid) and La Hueca cultures for some eight centuries (400 B.C.–A.D. 400), more than ample time for all kinds of social interaction and exchanges to develop. Detailed analyses of Archaic lithic complexes undertaken by Rodríguez Ramos (2006, 2007) demonstrate that the reduction protocols to produce a variety of implements were quite different from those of Hacienda Grande (Cedrosan Saladoid). On the other hand, the reduction sequences recorded for the (non-Saladoid) La Hueca and Punta Candelero (Huecoid) complexes are essentially derived from the Archaic assemblages (Rodríguez Ramos 2001, 2005b). The protocols of reduction, and the resulting functional and formal tool types, developed by the Archaic over several millennia were adopted by the non-Saladoid La Hueca and Punta Candelero groups in Puerto Rico but not by groups producing and using Hacienda Grande–style pottery. As was first proposed by Luis Chanlatte Baik, it was from the Archaic and Huecoid that the early Ostionoid populations (see Figure 5: Monserrate and Santa Elena) inherited a lithic technology that would continue evolving until the Spanish contact period (Rodríguez Ramos 2005a). The differences in lithic technology between the Saladoid and Huecoid point to significant differences in how these populations interacted with the contemporaneous Archaic populations.

The La Hueca culture, first found on Vieques Island, presented a serious problem to the cultural-chronological edifice erected by Rouse (Chanlatte Baik and Narganes Storde 1984; see Oliver 1999 for a detailed appraisal). In essence, Rouse interpreted La Hueca and other related complexes (mainly Punta Candelero on Puerto Rico, Hope Estate-1 in St. Martin, and possibly Morel-1 in Guadeloupe) as cultures that diverged from a common Saladoid background, and thus placed them in a different subseries: the Huecan Saladoid. A careful reanalysis of all the data, however, indicates that La Hueca, Punta Candelero, Hope Estate-1, and Morel-1 (and others found in Puerto Rico) are best treated as separate and distinct from the Saladoid complexes (Oliver 1999; Rodríguez Ramos 2001, 2007). Differences are found not only in the decoration of their ceramics (e.g., emphasis in zoned incised decoration as opposed to white on red) but also in their respective vessel form sets. As Rodríguez Ramos (2001) demonstrated, the lithic reduction protocols of the La Hueca and Punta Candelero assemblages are also very different from those of Hacienda Grande and other Cedrosan Saladoid lithic assemblages. If anything, Rouse should have placed the La Hueca and related complexes in a separate, Huecoid series rather than within a Huecan subseries of the Saladoid series. The distinctiveness of the Huecoid styles points to a separate ancestry or developmental history from that of the Cedrosan Saladoid. Its origin is still debated; some suggest a Colombian-Isthmian, others a northeastern Venezuelan homeland (Rodríguez Ramos and Pagán Jiménez 2006). Regardless, the key points to emphasize are that (a) the Huecoid and Cedrosan Saladoid material cultures indicate different degrees of social interactions with contemporaneous Archaic groups; (b) the Huecoid has a separate origin from that of the Saladoid; and (c) the subsequent Ostionoid societies of Puerto Rico emerged as a result of such culturally and socially plural interactions.

Among the artifacts found in Archaic contexts are what can only be regarded as the oldest known prototypes of the three-pointed icons. This prototype would later in post-Saladoid/Huecoid times (after A.D. 700) evolve into the large, highly decorated iconic trigonoliths (cemí icons) found in Puerto Rico and southeastern Hispaniola. The small three-pointed icons were found at Puerto Ferro on Vieques Island, a site dated between 2330 B.C. and 460 B.C. (Chanlatte Baik 1991; Rodríguez Ramos 2007:81). They were made from the horn of the *Strombus spp.*, a marine conch (Rodríguez Ramos 2007:110–111, fig. 4–9). These small, simple three-pointers (made not only of shell, but also of coral) have also been reported for a number of the Cedrosan Saladoid (400 B.C.–A.D. 400) sites throughout the Lesser Antilles, not just Puerto Rico. Interestingly, La Hueca and other related sites (e.g., Hope Estate-1 in St. Martin, Morel-1 in Guadeloupe [see Hofman and Hoogland 1999]), which Rouse grudgingly and incorrectly grouped in a Huecan Saladoid subseries, have yet to yield three-pointed artifacts. Again this points to significant differences in how the Huecoid and Cedrosan Saladoid interacted with the Archaic groups. The La Hueca–related artisans adopted Archaic protocols of lithic reduction, whereas the Cedrosan Saladoid adopted an artifact that would become one of the most ubiquitous religious icons of the Greater Antilles.

The radical differences between Huecoid and Cedrosan Saladoid material cultures noted above do not imply that there were no commonalities between them. One refers to the paraphernalia used in religious rituals involving hallucinogens. It would appear that both the La Hueca and Hacienda Grande were already conducting rituals involving the inhalation of hallucinogens, possibly *Anadenanthera peregrina*. Sadly, there is no *direct* archaeobotanical evidence as yet available to support this inference, and equally important, there is no evidence that can help determine when and which psychotropic plants (such as evening primrose, a mild hallucinogen; see Newsom and Wing 2004) first reached the Caribbean islands. Attempts by Quetta Kaye at the Institute of Archaeology to extract residues from drug inhalers have failed to produce results (personal communication 2007). The available evidence is indirect. Hacienda Grande style includes a small bowl with two spouts that were probably used for inhaling hallucinogenic powder (Figure 6: B, C). This bowl type is invariably decorated with zoned incised-crosshatch designs. The La Hueca–style vessel set also includes a bowl type with a pair of spouts for inhaling the hallucinogenic powder and is also decorated with zoned incised-crosshatched designs, some filled with white or red pigment (as is almost all of the La Hueca–style decorated pottery). Some of the latter are effigy bowls (Figure 6: A) depicting, for example, turtles (see Chanlatte Baik and Narganes Storde 2005:10), something that is absent in Hacienda Grande inhaling bowls. Although there are differences in zoned incised-crosshatching techniques between the Hacienda Grande (Saladoid) and La Hueca, they both have a vessel type that fulfills the same function: to inhale the hallucinogenic powder. In terms of material culture, this is one of the few artifacts that *are* shared between the Huecoid and Saladoid. In just about everything else they could not be further apart (Chanlatte Baik and Narganes Storde 2005; Oliver 1999).

It is assumed that the drug involved is *cohoba*, the seeds that come from the *cohóbana* tree (*Anadenanthera peregrina*), on the basis of (a) Spanish ethnohistoric documents describing cohoba and its psychotropic effects among natives in the Greater Antilles, and (b) the paraphernalia used for inhaling the drug require spouts or tubes for inhalation, also described by the Spaniards. This tree can still be found today in Puerto Rico and other islands. Other species of the genus *Anadenanthera* are found from Central America to northern Argentina, and are still used in rituals by natives inhabiting Venezuela and the Guyanas. For now, I adopt the view that *A. peregrina* is the most likely source of hallucinogen used by Huecoid and Cedrosan Saladoid groups, and leave the door open that the plant's source may have entered into the Caribbean in Archaic times from northeastern South America (Ortoiroid) or perhaps from Central America (Casimiroid). As Jeff Walker commented (personal communication 2006), it is very important to establish when the cohóbana tree reached the Caribbean, because it makes a world of difference whether natives perceive their surrounding world through hallucinogenic experiences—in contrast to those using other means to achieve varying degrees of altered states of consciousness (e.g., via tobacco, alcohol, dreams, or even music, as in voodoo ceremonies), or to others who simply do not use any kind of stimulants. No doubt that the use of psychotropic drugs has profound effects in the religious art styles of the natives (Reichel-Dolmatoff 1978).

The Saladoid and Huecoid (400 B.C.–A.D. 500) spouted ceramic bowls for inhaling were apparently discontinued by early Period IIIa in Puerto Rico and elsewhere. During Period IIIa it seems only the Y-shaped snuffing tubes made of bird bones were in use. These were probably used much earlier, but thus far, because of their fragility, none have survived. It is clear that by later Ostionoid times (Period IIIb–IV; Figure 7: D) the piece holding the three inhaling tubes had become highly elaborated in some specimens. These tube holders depicting anthropomorphic and zoomorphic personages were sculptured in manatee bone, marine shell, or wood (Figure 7: A, B, C, F). Another variant of the standard Y-shaped inhaling device consists of a combined spatula (for inducing vomit) and inhaler and bears perforations indicating that it was also used as a necklace pendant (Figure 7: E). The two spatulas projecting from each side of the inhaler (tube holder) represent the wings, with the tube holder at the center most frequently depicting a bat personage.

Both the Cedrosan Saladoid (400 B.C.–A.D. 500) and La Hueca (190 B.C.–A.D. 500) have yielded the earliest known Macorís-type stone-head prototypes. The Saladoid sample is made of shell, not stone (Chanlatte Baik and Narganes Storde 1984:77, fig. 46), whereas the La Hueca sample is made of serpentinite

(Chanlatte Baik and Narganes Storde 2005:38, lower right); thus far, proto-Macorís heads are absent from pre-Arawak contexts. Still, its presence in early Saladoid and Huecoid contexts, like the miniature three-pointed stones, indicate just how old these icons turned out to be. In time, the miniatures would evolve into the large Macorís stone heads.

To summarize, the evidence strongly indicates that Rouse's early Ostionoid styles in Puerto Rico were not merely the result of a single line of development out of a Cedrosan Saladoid ancestry, but stemmed from much more complex forms of interactions and exchanges between the Archaic groups (Coroso and others), Cedrosan Saladoid, and Huecoid (see Rodríguez Ramos and Pagán Jiménez 2006). The comparative examples discussed provide a flavor of the variable and selective nature of the adoption, mimicry, or transmission of techniques of tool manufacture, ceramic style and technology, and religious paraphernalia (three-pointers, inhaling tubes) among these three blocks of populations. This can be further amplified by briefly reviewing settlement patterns, sedentism, and food procurement and production.

Rouse's characterization of *all* Archaic-age subsistence economy as exclusively based on wild food procurement has recently been proven incorrect. The Archaic-age ground stone tools, including the distinctive "cobble edge-grinder," sampled from Maruca (Rodríguez López 1997, 2004) and Puerto Ferro (Chanlatte Baik 1991) sites have been subjected to starch residue analyses by Jaime Pagán Jiménez (Pagán Jiménez et al. 2005), with fascinating results. The stone tools analyzed from Maruca (Ponce) date between 1295 B.C. and 395 B.C.; the ones from Puerto Ferro (Vieques) date around 700 B.C. The starch residues indicate that three domesticated and several other cultivated and wild plants were processed at either or both sites. The domesticated plants are maize (*Zea mays*), common bean or *frijol* (Leguminosae: *Phaseolus vulgaris?*), and manioc or *yuca* (*Manihot esculenta*). The cultivated plants are the sweet potato (*Ipomoea batatas*) and two kinds of arrowroot or *yautía* (*Xanthosoma sagittifolium, X. violaceum*), while the wild edibles are the *corozo* palm (*Acrocomia media*), canavalia bean (*Canavalia sp.*), *gruya* or *achira* (*Canna sp.*; cf. *indica?*), yam or *ñame* (*Dioscorea spp.*), and the *marunguey* (*Zamia portoricensis*). The latter is a close relative of the *guáyiga* (*Zamia amblyphyllidia*), described by Fray Bartolomé de Las Casas (in the 1500s) as the principal staple of the natives of Higüey in eastern Hispaniola and, surprisingly, has turned out to be an important staple in Puerto Rico from Archaic times until Spanish contact (Pagán Jiménez and Oliver 2008). Like manioc, *Zamia* requires a complex set of procedures to eliminate the toxins, but unlike manioc (a root crop), the starch is concentrated in the trunk, which is mostly subterranean. At least some, if not many, of the Archaic groups were, in effect, gardeners or horticulturists who maintained a broad-spectrum diet, including domesticated plants, and who also managed forest resources, such as *corozo* palm trees and possibly the *marunguey*. Some of these plants, as noted by Pagán Jiménez and his colleagues (2005), like avocado and maize, probably came from Mesoamerica; others, like *marunguey* and *guáyiga,* seem to have come from contacts with the Isthmian region of Panama and Colombia; still others, like manioc, seem to come from northern South America: the sources and implied contacts are thus circum-Caribbean and not just limited to the northeastern lowlands of South America (Newsom and Wing 2004; Rodríguez Ramos and Pagán Jiménez 2006).

In sum, the Archaic societies were not the simple roaming bands of hunter-gatherers or foragers described by Rouse (1992:58). As Lee Newsom and Elizabeth Wing (2004) noted, the agricultural Saladoid populations migrating into the Caribbean around 400 B.C. would encounter an already developed Archaic cultivation (at least house gardens) system in place. The cultivars in use by Archaic groups were most likely incorporated into the Cedrosan Saladoid suite of plants, and with these a variety of food recipes (perhaps even food taboos and restrictions) and other farming techniques. And one might also expect that the late Archaic gardeners would have also adopted farming techniques and cultivars from the Saladoids. The Archaic populations were thus cultivators of domesticated plants, even though a substantial part of their diet still consisted of fishing, hunting and gathering, and managing wild plants. It is for all of the above reasons that Rodríguez Ramos (2007) prefers to group these diverse groups as pre-Arawak rather than Archaic, doing away with its connotations of antiquity (age) and their pre-ceramic, nonagricultural status.

In Puerto Rico there is also evidence of postholes that suggest at least semi-permanent pre-Arawak dwelling structures; these posthole features are not unlike those found that are associated with permanent Saladoid and post-Saladoid residential structures in Puerto Rico. If one adds that some pre-Arawak sites were deep, dense, and quite large in area and showed continuous refuse accumulation, then they are far more sedentary than has been assumed by many until recently. Some sites, like Maruca, Ortíz, and Paso del Indio, also have burial grounds, which is suggestive of a higher degree of sedentism and territoriality. Angostura, on the margins of the Manatí River floodplain, clearly shows a semicircular distribution of four large, mounded midden deposits surrounding a clear (low debris) central area, probably the community's plaza (Rodríguez Ramos 2007:121–127, figs. 4–13; see also Siegel 1996, 1999). The same description applies to the Guayabo Blanco site in western Cuba. This is a pattern that parallels that of many, if not the vast majority, of the later Cedrosan Saladoid right up to Chican Ostionoid village settlements on coastal and broad valley areas of Puerto Rico. My own experience visiting pre-Arawak sites on the southern coast of Hispaniola is that if anything, some of the sites are even larger in area than, say, Angostura, although a lot more archaeology needs to be done to confirm or refute their status as fairly sedentary villages.

In Cuba and Hispaniola, pre-Arawak sites had independently developed ceramic technology. Cuban archaeologists grouped a number of such pre-Arawak sites with pottery under the label of *proto-agrícola* (Ulloa Hung 2005; Ulloa Hung and Valcárcel Rojas 2002; Veloz Maggiolo et al. 1974), all of which Rouse had incorrectly labeled as Meillacan Ostionoid (Figure 5: Arroyo del Palo). These pre-Arawak groups with pottery predate by several centuries the appearance of late Cedrosan Saladoid (in eastern Hispaniola) or early Ostionoid in the rest of Hispaniola and eastern-central Cuba. Indeed, the decorations of the pre-Arawak stone vessels of Hispaniola (e.g., Courí, El Porvenir) do resemble some of the decorative elements of their pottery (called El Caimito style) and seem to have been implicated in the transfer of some designs to the so-called Meillacan ceramic styles. It is even conceivable that a lot of what is now classified (following Rouse) as Meillacan in Hispaniola and Cuba is in fact a direct development from pre-Arawak ceramic styles. In Puerto Rico, too, Rodríguez Ramos (2007:119–120) reports finding pre-Saladoid/Huecoid pottery at Paso del Indio associated with the local pre-Arawak component, with one context dated between 600–450 B.C. and another to A.D. 90.

To summarize, the pre-Arawak societies were neither the simple, highly mobile bands subsisting on fishing, hunting, and gathering wild plants, nor did they vanish under the weight of the culturally advanced agricultural Cedrosan Saladoid populations. The rise of what Rouse called the Ostionoid series of cultures owes its diverse character not to a single source but to a plurality of sources (it is multiauthored) that resulted from different interactions between the original pre-Arawak residents, the Arawakan-speaking Cedrosan Saladoid, and the (as yet linguistically unknown) Huecoid newcomers. The Ostionoid of Puerto Rico was the product of more than eight hundred years of Saladoid, Huecoid, and pre-Arawak coexistence.

The early styles of the Ostionoid series in Puerto Rico (Figure 5) according to Rouse (1992) developed entirely from a Cedrosan Saladoid ancestry. Yet when one examines the full range of absolute dates (Figure 8), it becomes clear that the late Saladoid culture, represented by Cuevas style, completely overlaps with the range of dates assigned to Rouse's purported later developments: the "pure" Ostiones and Monserrate styles (Rodríguez Ramos et al. 2008). Cuevas-style ceramics can in fact be found in varying proportions mixed in the same context with Ostiones or Monserrate styles at some sites, while in other sites only one or the other style is present. This is not always the result of mechanical admixtures or post-depositional factors, as Rouse (1952) invariably assumed, but rather is a reflection that plurality predominates (Rodríguez Ramos and Pagán Jiménez 2006). The same phenomenon can be noted between the modified Ostiones and the Santa Elena styles; their dates also overlap to a certain extent with the dates of purportedly earlier Ostiones and Monserrate styles.

The situation in the neighboring Dominican Republic has not been well studied, partly because of a lack of sufficient radiocarbon dates, but my experience at the El Cabo site in the Higüey region (eastern Dominican Republic) suggests that much of the same is going on there as well (Hofman et al. 2007). The so-called Estilo Intermedio (also named Macao, Punta, or Atajadizo) has been found in association with either or both the Anadel and Boca Chica styles (see Figure 5), with the latter being the immediate precursor of the historic Taíno pottery. In northwestern Hispaniola the presumably earlier Meillac style (Meillacan Ostionoid series) has been found in the same stratigraphic contexts as the later Boca Chica/Carrier styles, and at contact period sites, such as around La Isabela (Deagan and Cruxent 2002). If Meillac ceramics prove to have a "pre-Arawak with pottery" ancestry, then its more Taínoan designs and forms, along with diagnostic Boca Chica–style pottery found in the same contexts, are indicative again that complex processes of social interaction are at work in the creation of Meillac. These situations strongly suggest that instead of homogeneity there is a plurality of styles that are variably used and deployed by different social groups within and between different localities at any one time. The range of chronological overlap in the production and use of potteries of different styles at a site suggests that other social phenomena are at work rather than only continuous divergence from a single ancestral line.

In Puerto Rico, and most likely also in the neighboring islands, marked changes began to take place in settlement patterns, demography, and material culture around A.D. 500–700 (Curet 2005:95–143; Curet et al. 2004; Torres 2005).

[There were] marked shifts in the configuration of the regional interaction spheres observed in previous times, from ones that promoted the production and trade of shiny raw materials (both semi-precious stones and nacreous shells) and finished personal adornments [i.e., Saladoid, Huecoid, contemporary pre-Arawak] to the circulation of other emblems of social hierarchy and/or ethnic identity within the island and in surrounding regions [i.e., Ostionoid]. These changes signal marked alterations in the ideological and economic structures upon which those interactions were articulated previously in Puerto Rico, the Antilles, and the Greater Caribbean [Rodríguez Ramos 2007:233].

Around A.D. 500, "new identities began to be forged within the island [Puerto Rico] and reformulated in a context thus characterized by cultural and social plurality rather than homogeneity" (Rodríguez Ramos 2007:233). This was a time span when village fission began to intensify on the long-established semicircular settlements of the coastal plains and when new avant-garde daughter settlements were established not only on the coastal plains and large interior valleys, but also in the interior high mountainous region (Curet 2005; Curet et al. 2004).

It is during Period III (Figure 5; ca. A.D. 700–1200) that the ubiquitous lithic collars and probably the large three-pointed icons begin to appear in the archaeological record of Puerto Rico, eastern Hispaniola, and the Virgin Islands. It is possible that the elbow stones and the large Macorís-type stone heads also began at this time, although this is yet to be confirmed. Not only these but other features indicate considerable changes taking place in all spheres of society and culture. These include what seems to be a ranked order of settlements: some sites redefined their public space from an unmarked circular or semicircular central plaza to a quadrangular or rectangular space marked by monoliths. In some instances another rectangular court area near the settlement was constructed. Presumably the latter were dedicated to the Antillean rubber-ball game (see Oliver 1998; Siegel 1996, 1999; Torres 2005). The plazas (bateyes) were demarcated with limestone slabs or metavolcanic monoliths that were often decorated with petroglyphs that are nothing more and nothing less than monumental cemí icons (Oliver 2005; see Figures 9, 12: b, g). Ball courts, however, either lack petroglyphs or may have only one or two as terminal monuments. Plazas generally show an ensemble of petroglyphs (Oliver 1998, 2005). Sites that had only a single stone-demarcated court, however, may have fulfilled a variety of functions, including ball games.

The earliest known multi-court civic-ceremonial site is found near Ponce, in southern Puerto Rico. This site, Tibes, is found at the edge between the broad coastal plains and the limestone hill area north of Ponce, adjacent to the Portugués River. Tibes began during Cedrosan Saladoid times (250 B.C.–A.D. 600) as a settlement with an unmarked, perhaps round, central plaza within which a burial ground was found. Its semicircular configuration, based on the spatial distribution of Cedrosan ceramics, is not as clear as I once believed (Oliver 1998). Ongoing research directed by Antonio Curet has revealed that the Cedrosan Saladoid–period semicircular midden distribution is in part the result of redeposition that took place when the precincts demarcated with stones were being constructed. Nevertheless, the central area, where the main quadrangular precinct is located today, seems to have always been a plaza and not a residential area. Radiocarbon dates suggest that the period of intense construction of plazas and ball courts occurred between A.D. 1000 and A.D. 1200 (Curet et al. 2006:34). During this time a large quadrangular plaza demarcated with stones was built, surrounded by a star-shaped precinct, a large rectangular court, and six other smaller rectangular precincts, all framed by monoliths. Only the main plaza contains petroglyphs. Shortly after A.D. 1200, for reasons as yet unknown, the site was essentially abandoned, although it apparently was visited by later groups, since Chican Ostionoid ceramics have been found there in small numbers.

One key change at Tibes was the abandonment of the burial ground at the center of the unmarked plaza when it was redefined as a quadrangular plaza framed by monoliths. This change suggests that the various ceremonial activities in the central plaza were no longer linked with the ancestors' remains buried underneath; rather, the focus shifted to the iconographic personages engraved on several monoliths framing the central plaza (Oliver 1998, 2005). It has been hypothesized that this shift in mortuary practices is linked to a change from an egalitarian society to a stratified society (Curet et al. 2006; Curet and Oliver 1998; Torres 2005). After A.D. 1200, when Chican Ostionoid ceramic styles were in full bloom, multiple court sites proliferated all over Puerto Rico.

Tibes seems to have been replaced by, or perhaps even competed with (at least for some time), another multiple court site known as Jácana (PO-29), located in the Barayama sector, just four kilometers up the Portugués River. Jácana is a recent discovery that will substantially contribute to our understanding of Puerto Rican pre-Columbian history. In 2006–2007 New South Associates performed archaeological work to mitigate any adverse impact of a planned dam and flood-control project undertaken by the U.S. Army Corps of Engineers (ACOE) in a property managed by the Department of Natural Resources and Environment–Puerto Rico (Espenshade and Siegel 2007). At the time of this writing there is a strong public critique of the excavation methods and site management procedures (Betancourt 2007a, 2007b; Joseph 2007). Nevertheless, given the site's importance and uniqueness, the ACOE had finally agreed to preserve it for future research. Preliminarily, what is known thus far is that this site has one and likely multiple courts demarcated by monoliths. The main central plaza displays a complex iconography—as complex and elaborate as that of Caguana (Utu-10) in Utuado. While Caguana has a limited residential occupation (i.e., it is *not* a nucleated village), Jácana shows a permanent and much longer occupation, with at least five mounded middens (Espenshade and Siegel 2007:figs. 6, 21).

The occupation at Jácana probably began sometime between A.D. 400 and A.D. 700, based purely on the presence of deposits with early Cuevas/Monserrate– and Santa Elena–style ceramics, and continued into Period IV (A.D. 1200–1500), based on Capá-style ceramics (Espenshade and Siegel, personal communication 2007). If so, its early occupation overlapped with that of the early Elenan-period occupation at Tibes, but Jácana seems to have continued to be occupied after Tibes' decline or abandonment. At PO-29 there is a partially uncovered main plaza, measuring 40 x 50 m (2000 m²). Erect monoliths seem to enclose all four sides of the plaza, as is the case with a few other batey sites in Puerto Rico (e.g., Bateyes de Viví in Utuado; Oliver and Rivera Fontán 2006). Most unusually, seven monoliths found in the northern row displayed elaborately carved petroglyphs, whereas in all other well-known batey sites, including Tibes and Caguana, the petroglyphs are found only on the eastern and western monolith rows. In the northern row there is one particular petroglyph that is reminiscent of the two high-ranked anthro-pomorphic personages of Caguana, but whose head has been depicted sideward, as if detached from the body (perhaps decapitated?), and resting on its shoulders (Figure 9). This personage is accompanied by a rounded face that is turned upside down and engraved below the main personage's body. The latter petroglyph head was clearly hidden from view, as it would lie below the floor level of the court. Several others depict two pairs of opposing heads, with one pair above ground, the other pair hidden under the plaza's floor (i.e., they are inverted heads looking up toward the surface). Near the center of this plaza an excavated 121-m^2-block area yielded 26 human burials, with a *predicted* maximum of 430 interments for the plaza yet to be excavated (Joseph 2007). I would predict that this burial ground most likely predates the erection of monoliths around the plaza if indeed this site followed the same pattern noted for Tibes. Unlike Tibes, the pattern of midden deposits appears not to be arranged as a semicircle around the plaza; however, this may be due to a lack of intensive archaeological tests to the southwest of the site, across a tributary creek.

The physical proximity between Jácana and Tibes is particularly intriguing, and raises key questions about the nature of political religious power and territoriality (i.e., *cacicazgos*) in Puerto Rico. For example, if the two sites overlapped during the time period when *both* had already constructed their multiple courts (ca. A.D. 1000–1200), then it is possible that the political leaders controlling each site were in competition for the allegiance of the surrounding communities, not to mention economic resources. With only four kilometers separating the sites, it is hard to envision both being at the *center* of a hierarchically ordered polity, or a major chiefdom. This would beg the question of precisely what Caribbean archaeologists, including myself, mean by the word "center" in the term "civic-ceremonial *center*." In other words, if these two sites are contemporaneous, then they ought to be regarded as non-centers of a polity, or of adjacent peer polities. However, it is just as possible—given the iconographic style of the monumental cemí petroglyphs sculptured in a Taínoan art style—that Jácana arose as a civic-ceremonial center as a consequence of Tibes' decline (ca. A.D. 1200), and it may have been implicated in the declining fortune and eventual demise of Tibes. Tibes' iconography does stylistically antecede the style depicted in Caguana and hence that of Jácana (Oliver 1998, 2005). After the decline of Tibes, other civic-ceremonial sites besides Jácana emerged elsewhere in Puerto Rico, not only on the coast (see Torres 2005), but also farther up in the highlands, such as at Palo Hincado, Bateyes de Viví, and Caguana, and on the north coast (e.g., Tierras Nuevas). Civic-ceremonial sites with bateyes also sprung up in southern and easternmost Hispaniola and in some of the Virgin Islands, such as St. Croix and Virgin Gorda (Drewett 2000; Drewett and Bates 2001; Faber Morse 2004).

As populations moved from the coastal plains into the mountains of Puerto

Rico (starting around A.D. 500–700), the settlement pattern no longer adhered to the ancestral semicircular villages of the coast. In the region of Caguana, Utuado, for example, the pattern developing from Period IIIb (A.D. 900–1300) to Period IV (A.D. 1300–1500) is one of dispersed farmsteads or homesteads, each with its own "front-yard" batey or multifunctional plaza marked with monoliths and petroglyphs (Oliver et al. 1999). These small homesteads were linked together through vacant courts located in possibly neutral areas between homesteads. Presumably these vacant courts are where the Antillean ball games were held. The Antillean ball game, let us not forget, was not just a competitive sporting event but was also, on solemn occasions, a highly charged religious-ritual performance, as we shall see in part V of this book. Moreover, ball games were particularly important to the economy: natives could bet large amounts of goods on the outcome of the game. On occasions, a human life could also be at stake and put up for betting (winners would gain the right to kill the person), as several captive Spaniards would find out (see section 19). Such bets, if dependent on pure chance, imply that they are not instances of reciprocal economic exchanges (winners get all), although it is probable, as game theory teaches, that in the end it can all even out: one could win as much as one could lose in the long run. It could well be that betting could only be done in favor of one's home team rather than on hedging the odds on a team with a better winning record. Sadly, the rules of betting in these times are unknown.

In the midst of the dispersed farmsteads, on the broader alluvial terrace of the Tanamá River, the large multiple court site of Caguana had emerged around A.D. 1200, just about when Tibes had declined and, I suspect, when Jácana was in ascendancy on the southern coast. Such multiple precinct sites were able to hold much larger crowds for ritual performances and other public activities in their large central plazas and the surrounding smaller precincts. Multiple precinct sites thus appear to have functioned as civic-ceremonial centers integrating or linking a network of dispersed farmsteads, in the case of the highlands, or surrounding nucleated villages, in the case of coastal plains and broad interior valleys (Oliver 1998, 2005; Oliver et al. 1999).

The ups and downs, the rise and decline of these multiple court civic-ceremonial sites, are probably linked to shifting political alliances (see Curet 2005). I would argue that the shift in focus from buried individuals to iconographic representations (of, probably, cemified ancestor personages) was a factor in changing the dynamics of allegiances that groups had to a site where ancestors "resided." The practice of burying ancestors in the plaza was discontinued precisely to sever direct links between the actual buried persons and the living humans, and was purposefully replaced by other means of constructing genealogical links to the civic-ceremonial center. It would seem that ceasing to gather ancestors under the plaza would make it easier for surrounding community members to forward claims for membership in a given civic-ceremonial site that no longer required physical proof by pointing to actual buried individuals: "My relative is buried there, hence I belong." Instead, a symbolic, possibly fictitious, kinship connection could be established to the site via the icons of ancestors or their avatars (i.e., cemí-petroglyphs of bats, souls of the dead, etc.) displayed in the plaza's monoliths.

True, descent reckoning can be politically manipulated to assert claims of membership to such-and-such site of "origin" (and to other key features of landscape, like burial caves) without any reference to burials or iconography, but physicality is important; to be able to point to the tombs of one's ancestors matters, as it can be wielded as a forceful material evidence. The change from a focus on buried skeletons or bones of humans to ancestors and souls of the dead in iconographic form certainly marks a new way, though not the only way, of reckoning descent. It must be emphasized that it is not the only way, because burials were still conducted, but in many sites these were placed within midden deposits (i.e., behind and under houses) or in cave locations, but the deceased ancestors were no longer congregated as a "community" under the central plaza area (see Curet and Oliver 1998). By removing the remains from the plaza and placing them under the house or in the household's funeral cave, the message seems to be one of appropriating the dead, of placing them under the control or care of a specific family and lineage of a given household. The *society* of dead ancestors is thus fissioned, segmented, and taken from the shared communal space of the site to the periphery of individual domestic residences, and beyond to funeral caves. This is in sharp contrast to the earlier Saladoid period, communally shared burial "residence" of the society of deceased ancestors (under the plaza) (Curet and Oliver 1998).

Elsewhere in Hispaniola (except the southeast), eastern Cuba, and Jamaica, the public spaces were expressed differently, as none were stone-demarcated rectangular or quadrangular bateyes displaying a concentration of petroglyphs of ancestors and other potent personages; instead, earth embankments were used at some sites (Alegría 1983), such as the En Bas Saline site in Haiti. Here, the settlement sprung up around a huge, C-shaped central plaza marked with earth ridges, within which an elite structure (possibly, a chief's *caney*) was erected on a mounded platform (Deagan 2004). It follows that the way in which social groups in these areas materially identified with or claimed adherence to a given civic-ceremonial site (and its leader or cacique) differed considerably from that of southeastern Hispaniola, Puerto Rico, or the Virgin Islands, where smaller-scale and stone-demarcated bateyes predominate (for a detailed discussion, see Oliver 2008b:153–158).

The above discussion provides only a glimpse of the complexity of social and cultural interactions that started around A.D. 500 and became even more complex from A.D. 1200 onward. The rise and decline of civic-ceremonial centers, and the implied demographic shifts (see Curet 2005), cannot be explained solely in terms of stylistic typologies or merely by pointing to divergence from a homogeneous ancestral culture or people. In Rouse's 1992 book, all of these diverse and complex manifestations are summed up as "Classic Taíno," but such classification obscures what are substantial and significant differences in how peoples construct their group or ethnic identities and claim membership to a place. That the phenomenon of stone-demarcated plazas (with its symbolic replacement of skeletons by monumental petroglyph cemís) is tightly circumscribed to Puerto Rico, the Virgin Islands, and southeastern Hispaniola and is not a key feature for the rest of what Rouse called "Classic Taínos" (or Chican Ostionoid) is a strong argument to drop this classificatory concept. The daily affairs of sociality, politics, religion, economics, and so on were enacted and expressed differently in, say, Puerto Rico than in the northwestern Dominican Republic or eastern Cuba. This is not a matter, as Rouse proposed, of a progressive degradation or simplification (via diffusion or migration) of the Taíno culture, as one moves away from the core and into the eastern or western peripheries, but primordially of complex processes that create and re-create new identities within and between villages, regions, and islands—identities and allegiances reformulated in an environment characterized by cultural and social plurality, not homogeneity.

I do not yet have enough evidence, but I have a strong suspicion that the coresidence of two fairly differentiated ceramic styles (e.g., Santa Elena and "modified" Ostiones or Capá and Esperanza) found in some, if not many, archaeological sites of Puerto Rico and the Virgin Islands may be a reflection of the shifting allegiances to civic-ceremonial centers. When centers are in decline, for whatever reason (e.g., death of its ruler, military conquest, or even the theft of a chief's powerful set of cemí idols by competitors), the surrounding population will ultimately shift its allegiance, and often its residence, elsewhere, to a more promising, ascending civic-ceremonial center and to a leadership they would trust or risk trusting. To ease a new claim of membership to an emerging civic-ceremonial center where one actually has no buried ancestors, changing how one reckons ancestry to iconographic representations of ancestors seems to be an effective means of recruiting new members by the emerging leadership.

The demographic and settlement pattern shifts documented by Antonio Curet (2005, Curet et al. 2004) and Joshua Torres (2005) for Puerto Rico have less to do with population pressures on economic resources and much more to do with the changing winds of native political and social relations, of which the rise and decline of civic-ceremonial sites is its most visible symptom. However, the rise of new centers does not necessarily entail that they will exhibit a greater degree of complexity in linking settlements than those that preceded it or those that are in decline. The temporal cycling between more centralized and expansive polities and decentralized and less expansive ones is something noted in other areas of the New World, such as the southeastern United States (Anderson 1994; Pauketat 1994). As I will discuss later, the ensembles of numinous icons imbued with cemí potency (e.g., from portable three-pointed stones to fixed, monumental petroglyphs) that were "owned" by caciques and other political elites are at the heart of these shifts and changes of allegiance: religion is not just a passive supra-structural ideology to justify the status quo of leaders, but is rather actively involved in conditioning human actions, decisions, and certainly causally implicated in the shifting allegiances from one declining civic-ceremonial center to an ascending one as much as in maintaining alliances between peer (but potentially competitive) civic-ceremonial centers.

Most scholars, myself included, agree that Period III (Figure 5: A.D. 600–1300) signals the development of complex, stratified societies, but beyond that there is little consensus as to their specific character: some would have single- to multiple-tiered hierarchical chiefdoms developing throughout the Greater Antilles and into Rouse's Eastern Taíno area (Crock and Petersen 2004; Redmond and Spencer 1994; Rouse 1992); others suggest that paramount chiefdoms existed only in Hispaniola and then were applicable to only one or another of the Hispaniola polities (Wilson 1990). Still others argue for polities resembling something more like the "big men" or "great big men" Melanesian models (Moscoso 1986), that all caciques were "local." Certainly, the ethnohistoric data points to substantial differences in levels of sociopolitical organization within and between eastern Cuba, Hispaniola, the Bahamas, Jamaica, Puerto Rico, and the Virgin Islands (Curet 2002, 2003, 2006; Curet et al. 2004; Keegan 2006; Keegan et al. 1998; Siegel 1996, 1999). What is clearer is that Hispaniola's chiefdoms (whether or not this is the appropriate term) were more complex and centralized than in Puerto Rico, at least by the time of Spanish contact.

The Spanish did refer to the native political entities as *cacicazgos,* a word that has been co-opted by scholars in order to refer to chiefdoms in the classic sense of Elman Service or Julian Steward. But the term *cacique* (*ka-sikua-ri* [*-li*]) among the Lokono (Guyana Arawak speakers) simply translates as a male or female head of the house (Bennett 1989:23, 40). It equally refers to the head of a family, a lineage, or a coresidential group as much as it refers to an apical leader of an entire polity: they are all caciques. In Hispaniola, Bishop Las Casas (1929 [3]:555) identified degrees of seniority among caciques through a set of three words of deference used when addressing a senior leader. *Matunherí* was reserved for the highest-ranking cacique, akin to saying "your highness"; *baharí* was used for second-ranking caciques, akin to saying "your lordship," while *guaoxerí* (*waherí*) was used to address the third-ranking persons, perhaps local caciques or nitaínos. A fourth term also used to address high-ranked persons was *guamiquina* (*wamikina*) or *guamahehi* (*wama-herí*). This term is recorded for both Hispaniola and Puerto Rico (Oliver 1998:66). *Wamikina* is a compound of "our lord" (*w-ama*) and "principal" or "first" (*iki-ni,* which derives from the word for number one: *h-eke-tí*). This term was also used when addressing strangers of high rank, such as Christopher Columbus (see Oliver 1998:66). Such distinctions of deference and rank do not necessarily translate directly into a three-tiered hierarchical political structure consisting of paramount caciques and chiefdoms and second- and third-tiered caciques and their smaller, subordinated cacicazgos. As Wilson (1990) deftly argued, although a few caciques were principal lords in Hispaniola (e.g., Behechio of Bainoa-Xaraguá or Guarionex in Maguá-Caiabó), their political power and authority were hardly those of an absolute ruler or despot; thus the subordination of other caciques seems to be more a matter of contestation and political wheeling and dealing than is generally recognized. The complex nature of relations among chiefs and their rank vis-à-vis other caciques, with varying degrees of centralized authority, will be addressed later in this book when we analyze how human political power is brokered through the deployment of powerful cemí icons. Suffice it to say that the classic definitions of hierarchically ranked chiefdoms are inadequate for describing the diverse nature of the cacicazgos in the Greater Antilles. Probably heterarchy should be considered more seriously. I think there are some useful insights to be drawn from how hierarchical and heterarchical powers operate among Xinguano polities in Brazil (Heckenberger 2005), and how heterarchy in particular might also work to explain the cases of "peer" cacicazgos in, for example, Puerto Rico.

There is some consensus that the more complex polities at the time of Spanish contact, those that seem to suggest a centralized power and a hierarchical organization, apply only to some, not all, of the cacicazgos of Hispaniola (e.g., Wilson 1990; Curet 2003). In Puerto Rico (including Mona, Vieques, Culebra, St. Croix islands) it is generally acknowledged that the cacicazgos there were rather smaller and best seen as peer polities—that is, there was either an absence of or far less emphasis (or instability) on the centralization and hierarchical organization or subordination to a paramount cacique (see Curet 2003, 2005). Eastern Cuba and Jamaica are regarded in a similar way, but there are dissenting voices; for example, Roberto Cassá (1974) argues against the presence of hierarchical chiefdoms in Hispaniola, whereas John Crock and James Petersen (2004) see classic chiefdoms even in the small outlying island group of Anguilla–St. Martin, in the northeastern Lesser Antilles. If one reads the discussions of chiefly descent rules by William Keegan (Keegan et al. 1998; Keegan and Maclachlan 1989) or the comparative study of Oaxaca-Taíno chiefdoms by Elsa Redmond and Charles Spencer (1994), it is evident that they assume the Taíno cacicazgo fits into the classic description of a chiefdom type (à la Service or Steward).

If I have not discussed in any depth the archaeological evidence to evaluate the nature of pre–Spanish-contact Caribbean chiefdoms, it is simply because there is not much to put one's hands on. The various existing arguments on the nature, complexity, and diversity of chiefdoms, or even whether there was any chiefdom at all, almost entirely rest on how the sixteenth-century Spanish documents were interpreted. Furthermore, to extract useful data from the Spanish chronicles, only the brief periods between A.D. 1492 and 1504 for Hispaniola and between A.D.

1508 and the 1510s for Cuba, Puerto Rico, and Jamaica would be useful to gain some sense of native political organization before the onslaught of the Spanish conquest (see Curet 2002, 2003). After these dates the native political structures were no longer operational. Moreover, the evidence required to assess social stratification has not been archaeologically documented, and yet such data are, at least for me, the minimal precondition to even consider questions about complex polities, including chiefdoms. No one has yet produced data on the composition of a household, of household economy, or whether different houses and households in a village have access to more resources than others.

As I see the situation now, what we have is like a large one-hundred-thousand-piece puzzle of which only a number of bits here and there are in place, still without having the foggiest idea of what the final picture looks like. This is not to say that in the Caribbean archaeologists are not designing and conducting archaeological projects toward this end, but that the results at the necessary temporal and spatial scales to peek into the changing structures and processes of sociopolitical formations have yet to come.

C. From Taíno Peoples to the Taínoness of Peoples

If, as has been argued to this point, the Rousean concept of a Taíno people is fraught with contradictions and unsustainable assumptions, what is the alternative? This is important because there has to be some consensus as to the identity of the people who created and used the potent icons and artifacts that are the central subjects of this book. In agreement with Rodríguez Ramos, I suggest that instead of a normative "Taíno people,"

> what existed was a spectrum of Taínoness whose diverse representations resulted from the variable negotiations in which at least some of the indigenous peoples of the islands engaged in order to facilitate their interactions while retaining their differences. In some cases, some of the elements of such Taínoness show variable syncretism of the ideological narratives that might have been derived from the different ancestral histories of each of the different groups that inhabited the islands where this spectrum was manifested. The mosaic of syncretism observed at this time is thus the result of the myriad of interactions and negotiations in which those different people were engaged within the islands and with the inhabitants of the surrounding continental regions with which they were interacting [Rodríguez Ramos 2007:312–313].

However, the term "Taíno" has become so ingrained in both popular and academic circles that it is virtually impossible, even foolhardy, to try to eradicate it. In this book I purport to use the term "Taíno" or "Taínoan" to refer to this spectrum or mosaic of social groups who express, negotiate, and contest in various ways their "Taínoness" and who participate with various degrees of intensity in becoming and being "Taínoan." Used in this sense, the terms "Taíno," "Taínoan," or "Taíno-ness" also acknowledge that the natives' religious concepts and associated material culture had multiple ancestral sources. Being multiauthored/multisourced means that in every generation aspects or elements, even bodies, of theological and philo-sophical concepts that inform attitudes and ways of engaging socially, and the ma-terials that mediate within and between humans, are selectively appropriated via mimicry, synthesis, or syncretism, and made "their own" by social groups. Such bodies of knowledge and materials are acquired from a broad reservoir that has had different historical origins.

The issue of how much Taínoness is needed to be identified as being and be-coming Taínoan (as a material object or as a person, social group, and further up the scale) is a matter of identity formation and social relations and of what is avail-able in the reservoir of ideas, materials, and practices that can be co-opted for various ends that are, of course, historically contingent. Philip Leis (2002) and oth-ers (Anderson and Peek 2002) have dealt with precisely the same issues when exam-ining the plurality of peoples and ethnicities of the Niger Delta in western Africa, especially in relation to art and iconography. The material cultures of the peoples of the Niger Delta, says Leis (2002:15), "were critical in the historical processes of both defining and being defined by the Delta populations," much in the same way that objects of political-religious art (cemí icons) that we shall examine in this book were defining and being defined by the societies inhabiting this region from eastern Cuba, the Bahamas, Hispaniola, Jamaica, Puerto Rico, and the Virgin Islands.

Leis also speaks of the complex mosaic of languages, cultures, and ethnicities of the Delta inhabitants, of their diverse points of origin, and the complex ways of interaction within and between social groups that are constantly deconstructing and reconstructing identities. Leis observed that "notions of primordiality and cul-tural conservatism on the one hand and of inventiveness and cultural convergence on the other are two major ways of thinking about identity formation." In the case of the former pair (primoridality, conservatism), with their stress on descent, the ethnic boundaries are defined in reference to blood ties leading to a common an-cestry and to an "innate shared tradition of customs and beliefs" (Leis 2002:18). On the other hand, as Leis noted, inventiveness and cultural convergence stress "collaterality," where "boundaries are more [reliant] on opposition to surrounding populations, and the cultural differences within a population are fused within a re-created history"—that is, a given ethnic group often discovers and rediscovers it-self "by assimilating past populations with an eye toward legitimizing its history on par with that of present-day neighbors. A newly defined ethnic group may, by the very nature of the opposition that creates it, quickly arrive at a self-definition that insists on its primordial status" (Leis 2002:18)—that is, to insist on their cultural and even temporal priority among all Delta populations, even if in fact they were not the first. If in theory cultural identities are formed in many different ways, "in practice the processes blend and can be hotly contested" (Leis 2002:18). These are the kinds of processes that I would argue are also operating in the contestation of being more or less Taínoan, on the various configurations that Taínoness can be or become. Moreover, Leis observed for the Niger Delta what he calls a remarkable feature of cultural identity formation, which ought to at least be considered with regard to the Taínoness of the natives being studied here: "[S]eemingly, similar peoples see themselves as being different, and conversely, peoples defining themselves as having one culture may be more different from each other than they are from those that they see as belonging to other ethnic groups. We have no simple answer as to why this occurs, particularly where populations are in intimate contact with each other, even intermarrying. The Delta people provide us a good example of how conservatism and cultural change can operate at the same time and thus suggest one type of resolution" (Leis 2002:18).

This observation is also echoed by Martha Anderson and Philip Peek (2002:33), who note that "contiguous ethnic groups are never as different from each other as they believe themselves to be. Nevertheless, as is readily observed, the Igbo are clearly more Igbo than the Yoruba," and then ask "what accounts for this difference?" The authors start with the premise that the arts "reflect ethnic identity and that both content and form will be used to demonstrate change, affiliation, and difference. A cultural complex of a myriad of elements, any and all of which may be altered" (Anderson and Peek 2002:33). Like these authors, this book also intends to contribute to questions of cultural identity as it is negotiated and contested (webs of social relations among rulers) through the means of what must be regarded as a religious art that has serious personal and political consequences in how natives interact and display Taínoness. Identity, as intimated in the quote above by Rodríguez Ramos (2007:312–313), is always in the state of becoming, of being negotiated and contested (see Gillespie 2001; Insoll, ed. 2006; Joyce 2005). The kind of Taínoness on which I am focusing from here on involves peoples who interact through a basic matrix of religious beliefs and practices—enshrined in cemíism—that inform their behaviors (values, attitudes, and motivations) to themselves and to "Others," including strangers, and that, importantly, also implicate the action of formally specific and potent (art) objects (beings) imbued with supernatural power. It is a web of social relations engaging humans and their potent objects that creates diverse forms and contexts defining the Taínoness of native actors. These cemí objects can be deployed, as Anderson and Peek (2002) suggest for the Delta peoples, as personal as well as ethnic markers of sorts, but more than that they also elicit constructed memories that constantly recapitulate their cultural priority (primordiality) and conservatism and at once motivate cultural inventiveness and convergence. The interesting thing occurs when "Others," the opposites, enter into relationships with different understandings of Taínoness or of what it is to be or become Taínoan. That is precisely where this book culminates, with the natives' sense of identity grounded in Taínoness and the Spaniards' own sense of identity, each probing and adjusting, and each reacting and battling their mutual (mis)conceptions of "Castilianess" and Taínoness. In the Hispaniolan and Cuban cases discussed in part V, convergence (assimilation) and difference (resistance), syncretism and antisyncretism, will be treated in detail. However, there is a road to be traveled before reaching that juncture. Next, it is useful to discuss the above noted webs of interaction from the perspective of what is known about descent, inheritance, and succession among sixteenth-century natives of the Greater Antilles.

D. Descent, Inheritance, and Succession in the Sixteenth-Century Greater Antilles

Webs of social relationships are, of course, extremely diverse and reticulate in any society, ranging from those established by blood and affine relations to those between trading or ritual partners (e.g., godparents-godchildren), between total strangers, and between the living and their deceased relatives. Among the natives, particularly in Hispaniola and Puerto Rico, ritual exchanges of names to cement friendships, pacts, and alliances (*guaitiao*) were frequently reported by the Spaniards and did extend to total strangers. Natives and Spaniards exchanged names with each other for a variety of reasons, as we shall see later in parts IV and V. Moreover, kinship and descent also apply to numinous icons imbued with cemí potency, making the network of social relations among and between human and nonhuman beings that much richer. This section intends to provide a summary of what is known thus far about kinship, descent, inheritance, and succession among the ethnohistoric natives in the time of Columbus. There is no question that these are the key building blocks of sociality, of what Rodríguez Ramos (2007) and I call "Taínoness."

Sadly, the Spaniards never bothered to collect or write about native kinship terminology. Not surprisingly, most of the available information has to do with the inheritance of the office or estate of a *cacique* (male chief) or *cacica* (female chief, chieftess). Inheritance of the estate usually refers to the right to rule, and only in one case is there an explicit and specific reference (from Hispaniola) to the bequest of material goods or heirlooms upon the death of a chief. This is important because the heir to the office is not necessarily also the beneficiary of the deceased's wealth. The Spaniards' comments on rules of inheritance and succession were mostly restricted to the political elite (the caciques and nitaínos, or "nobles"); next to nothing is really known about the "common" person (*naboría*). To date, the best and most recent analyses on succession are those of Curet (2002), Keegan (2007b:95–121; Keegan et al. 1998; Keegan and Maclachlan 1989); and Jalil Sued Badillo (1979, 1985). However, there is still considerable dispute on how the sixteenth-century chronicles are to be assessed and interpreted, as exemplified in the recent exchange between Keegan (2006) and Curet (2006) in the *Ethnohistory* journal.

Curet (2002:260–263) makes the plausible argument that the rules of succession among the natives of Hispaniola and Puerto Rico were most likely to be based on customary law. He makes the critical observation that the transmission of office is not automatic or enshrined in law, but is flexible and adapting to existing social and political conditions. "The manipulation of the automatic rules can happen mainly under three circumstances: when there are a number of political factions struggling for power, when the automatic successor is not fit for the position under normal circumstances and where one candidate is better positioned to deal with the situation" (Curet 2002:263).

The key sources of ethnohistoric data are Pedro Mártir de Anglería (1989), Bartolomé de Las Casas (1929), and Gonzalo Fernández de Oviedo y Valdés (1944), all of whom wrote early in the sixteenth century and furnished versions of the rules of succession. Las Casas, who arrived in Hispaniola in 1502, noted that the chief's sister was to inherit the office, because the sister's children shared the chief's own blood line, whereas this could not be demonstrated with his own children (Curet 2002:264; Keegan 2006:384; Las Casas 1929 [2]:562–563; Vega 1980: 20). Hence, it would seem that descent is congruent with matrilineality. Although Mártir (1989) never set foot in the Caribbean, he was not only the earliest chronicler (1492–1525) but was also in an advantageous position to interview ocular witnesses or their written communiqués to the Spanish court. Mártir provided a somewhat more complicated scenario than Las Casas. He noted that (a) the preferred candidate for succession was the firstborn son of the eldest sister of the cacique; (b) failing that, the office would go to the son of the next eldest sister, and so on down to the son of the youngest sister; (c) if the cacique had no sister or sister's children, then the office passed to the cacique's brothers; (d) in the absence of brothers, the office would be inherited by the cacique's sons; (e) and failing all of the above, the office would pass to the person who had the reputation of being the most powerful (Curet 2002:264; Keegan 2006:385–386). The first two rules suggest a preferential matrilineal succession. The alternative route "c" still retains the office within the cacique's family/lineage, although the heirs' own children would not belong to their father's matriline. Alternative "d" also retains the office within the cacique's family, but inheritance suggests patrilineality. Finally, alternative "e" suggests that there was a way for a stranger (outside any line of descent) to achieve the office of cacique.

Oviedo (1944 [1]:247; also in Curet 2002:264; Keegan 2006:384) presents a different, seemingly contradictory, account. The cacicazgo was to be inherited by

(a) the eldest son (primogeniture) of any of the cacique's wives; (b) if, after inheriting the office, the son had no children of his own the estate would pass on to the cacique's sister's daughter or son, "since this child would be more certainly a true descendant of the family line" (Oviedo 1944; trans. Curet 2002:264, or Keegan 2006:384). However, Oviedo also added two further options: (c) if the cacique had no offspring, his sister's son would *not* inherit the estate if he had a brother by the same father; or instead (d) if the cacique had no offspring, then "the relative closest to the mother would inherit holdings derived from the chief's mother (Oviedo 1944; trans. Curet 2002:264, or Keegan 2006:384). Contrary to Las Casas and Mártir, the first rule suggests patrilineal inheritance, while the second suggests matrilineal inheritance. The latter two options (c, d), as Keegan (2006:385) would say, keep the office within the cacique's family. In addition, as Curet (2002:264) noted, inheritance rules "c" and "d," while suggestive of ambilineal inheritance—the estates were inherited from both sides and kept separate—cannot account for "why there are two versions of what happened when the chief had no sons."

The discrepancies among these three chroniclers' accounts partially have to do with differences in the timing and the situations in which these data were recorded (Curet 2002:265). Unusually, Mártir identified his source: Andrés Morales, an experienced navigation pilot who was ordered by Governor Nicolás de Ovando to reconnoiter Hispaniola. In 1508 Morales drafted the first map identifying some topographic features, toponyms delineating native regions and Spanish towns (which form the basis for the map reproduced in Figure 26), and then published it in 1516. Mártir had used the map's information for his first three volumes of the *De Orbe Novo Decades* published in 1514 (Vega 1980:19–20; Vega 1997:29–30; for a large color version of the map, see Oliver 2008a:72–73). However, it is not known from whom Morales obtained the information and where in Hispaniola.

Bartolomé de Las Casas, who arrived on the Hispaniolan scene early enough (1502), is generally regarded as the chronicler most knowledgeable and sympathetic to the natives' ways of life and cultures; he was a firsthand participant in and witness to many of the historic events in both Cuba and Hispaniola. Still, of the three chroniclers under consideration, Las Casas wrote the least on the matter of succession or inheritance. Perhaps the reason for this is because Las Casas wrote *Historia de Las Indias* (1552–1561) when he was an elderly man, in his late seventies and early eighties, thus relying on documents and fading memories. Oviedo, on the other hand, arrived at Santo Domingo in 1523 (Myers 2007:15–23), exactly twenty years after the collapse of the last cacicazgo in the Higüey region of Hispaniola, almost a decade after the Rebellion of the Caciques of Puerto Rico (1510–1511), and after the severe famine of 1495–1496 and the devastating smallpox epidemic of January 1519 (see Wilson 1990:91–97). By 1523 it is more than likely that the native customs of inheritance of the office, not to mention the estate, had adjusted to the new and radically changed circumstances. Indians native to Yucatan, the Lesser Antilles, the northern coast of South America, and the Isthmian region (Panama-Colombia) had been captured as slaves or held in *encomienda* (assignment) and resettled in the Greater Antilles, as were African slaves raised in the Iberian Peninsula or captured in western Africa, all of this adding to the multicultural mix of potential influences in the Greater Antilles (see Deive 1979:45–101). In sum, Oviedo's account must be taken very cautiously, not the least because he was arguably the most racist and Hispano-centric of all the major Spanish chroniclers (but see Myers 2007).

Another problem was the tendency of some chroniclers to extrapolate what they learned from a given locale to a whole island, to groups of islands, and even to the entire West Indies (Curet 2002:265). Furthermore, the sources of the information regularly remained anonymous; Mártir's revelation of his source (Andrés Morales) is exceptional. Were the informants from the same ethnic group, the same polity, or were the accounts synthesized from diverse sociocultural groups? Were the rules described based on ideals or actual practices? I agree with Curet (2002:266) that it is likely the Spaniards translated what in effect were customary laws into a set sequential order of preferences based on "strict laws à la European style" that are "not characteristic of most chiefdoms" in the Americas. On the other hand, this does not imply that the chroniclers were incapable of comprehending complex succession rules; in theory, royal successions in the fifteenth-century Iberian Peninsula were as complex and could be as mind-boggling, being twisted and manipulated to fit the purpose, as anything they could have heard from native Hispaniolans. It is interesting to note, as Keegan (2006) observed, that only Oviedo described primogeniture in Hispaniola—also a common succession rule among European monarchs. Yet, I hasten to add, even in the Iberian Peninsula exceptions abound: the future Queen Isabella of Castile inherited her crown against the will of her reigning half brother, Enrique, or Henry, IV, who instead preferred his bastard daughter, Juana "La Beltraneja." After Enrique IV's death in 1474, a war of succession ensued, and Isabella, supported by her faction of nobles, was recognized as the Queen of Castile and León in 1479 (Covarrubias [ca. 1611] 2001:216–217).

Let us turn to modern scholarly interpretations. On the basis of the above chroniclers, especially Mártir, Rouse (1948:231, 529) concluded that the office of cacique was inherited matrilineally, and that the population generally practiced a patrilocal residence pattern "despite the matrilineal inheritance." Roberto Cassá (1974:144–145), a historian from the Dominican Republic, concluded that the pattern of succession and inheritance reflected a transition from matrilineal to patrilineal that ultimately created a bilineal (or ambilineal) pattern of succession. He argued that these patterns applied to caciques, leaving open the possibility that the rule could be different for the commoners. As Curet (2006:267) noted, Cassá's arguments relied far more on ethnographic analogies to modern South American

Indians than to sixteenth-century Spanish documents. Puerto Rican ethnohistorian Jalil Sued Badillo (1979, 1985; see also 2003), like Cassá, also concluded that the different succession rules described by the chroniclers reflect a transition from matrilineality to patrilineality, the latter resulting from Hispanic influence. Francisco Moscoso (1986:267), another Puerto Rican historian, concludes that there was a strong "emphasis" on matrilineal succession. All of these scholars, except Curet, ascribe patrilineality and primogeniture to European influence and argue that the original, pre-Columbian succession rule was matrilineal.

William Keegan (2007b; Keegan et al. 1998; Keegan and Maclachlan 1989) also concluded that the Taíno chiefs exhibited matrilineality, that descent was traced through the maternal line. Keegan and Morgan D. Maclachlan (1989:618) believed that the chroniclers' references to patrilineality were "an exceptional practice that may have been brought about by the Spanish disruption of the indigenous social system." Furthermore, attempts by Keegan (2006; Keegan et al. 1998; Keegan and Maclachlan 1989) to resolve the paradox of having a matrilineal descent while also practicing patrilocal postmarital residence are dealt with by suggesting that the Taíno chiefdoms were characterized by viri-avunculocality (i.e., after marriage, the husband and his wife set up permanent residence with his maternal uncle). This practice, according to Keegan, would apply mostly to the elite. Keegan and Maclachlan (1989) then use this premise to account for the archaeological pattern of establishing new settlements in several of the islands of the southern Bahamian Archipelago. This is a distinct possibility, but it hinges on a hypothesis that cannot be tested. The pattern of establishing new settlements does correlate with viri-avunculocality, but a correlation does not necessarily entail causality. Keegan's argument is essentially circular: viri-avunculocality explains the pattern of establishing new settlements that are, in turn, explained by viri-avunculocality. Other explanations can compete with viri-avunculocality to account for the observed archaeological settlement pattern. In a recent paper, a reply to Curet's (2006) critique, Keegan (2006; see also Keegan 2007b:93–123) stands firm by his matrilineal descent and viri-avunculocal postmarital residence thesis, but without really adding any new data to further his position. Somewhat less dogmatic is the view of Samuel Wilson (1990:34, 117). Although he thought that the native system was predominantly matrilineal, he was conscious that kinship, succession, inheritance, and postmarital residential patterns among the natives of Hispaniola were much more complex than had previously been understood.

Curet (2006:268), on the other hand, argued that all of these scholars were extrapolating to all "Taínoland" rules of succession that most likely were applied in only some areas of Hispaniola. He rightly questions the assumed equivalency between rules of succession of office and the rule of (matri-/patri-/ambi-) lineal descent. And as I noted earlier, I would also add that inheritance of the office is a different matter than the inheritance (bequest) of goods and heirlooms, as we shall examine in detail later in this book. Curet (2002, 2006) further objects to the extrapolation of rules that are applicable to the chiefly elite to the rest of the population, and goes on to discuss with examples why his critique is well grounded.

In his reply to Keegan, Curet (2006:397) did "not deny that some matrilineal, idealized rules of succession may have been present among some Caribbean polities." Rather, his key points were: "(1) rules of succession should not be equated a priori with rules of descent without the appropriate evidence; (2) [cultural, social] variability existed in the Caribbean, and we have to determine the appropriateness of these rules for our case study; and (3) rules of succession are not strict, but flexible, open to manipulation, and we should not expect that they were always followed as the chroniclers suggest. Additionally, rules of succession are not ahistorical . . . but they are heavily influenced by individuals, [competing] factions, and historical conditions" (Curet 2006:397; 2002). In short, Curet takes a much more relativistic position in contrast to the more normative, rule-of-law perspective taken by Keegan and others mentioned above.

There is one thing that cannot be emphasized enough. The chroniclers were recording the information about the various alternative routes of succession for caciques (mostly from Hispaniola) at a time of heightened strife and stress, not just political but all around (economics, health, social relations, religion, etc.). I strongly suspect that most of the rules the Spaniards were writing down from native informants in Hispaniola were not just the preferred routes of succession established by customary law, but also others (such as Oviedo's discrepant rules) that were being implemented ad hoc. New or rarely invoked succession routes would make sense in the face of the brutal imprisonment, killing, and execution not just of the ruling caciques but also of many of the preferred heirs. Even by the time Morales obtained the information relayed by Mártir, shortly before 1508, all five of the most important cacicazgos had already collapsed under Spanish military conquest. Even the Caiçimú chiefdom (or more likely, several peer polities of the Higüey region) in the east of the island had collapsed in 1504, when the last battle of Higüey concluded. It is in this context that I believe the rules of succession should be analyzed: a period of sustained, repeated, severe crises; a time of native chaos brought about by a power vacuum; a time when many, if not most, of the heirs were simply unavailable to fulfill their inheritance. Such circumstances also provided unique opportunities for traditionally competing political factions (from within and without a polity) to create ad hoc rules or to twist, amend, or work around traditional customary law. This is not to say that all the rules noted by the chroniclers were ad hoc and without reference to tradition, but merely to point out that when the Spanish were taking that information from natives, it is quite possible that they were explaining not only traditional rules from the past, but also any and all rules that were at that moment being invoked as a result of the power vacuums created by the Spanish conquistadors. The corollary to this assertion is that whenever such circumstances of severe political crises arose, including those in pre-Columbian times, it would be expected that traditional or customary inheritance and succession laws would be severely tested and very likely revised.

All the scholars have brought to view sufficient cases from Hispaniola and Puerto Rico to suggest that succession through the maternal line did take place. But exceptions to this just as often imply that matrilineality was neither the dominant nor the only form; as Curet (2002, 2006) insists, rules of succession were far more flexible than assumed. There are only a handful of actual cases of succession involving specific individuals that illustrate the variety of practices in place—keeping in mind that most of these were recorded at a time when polities, entire cacicazgos, had collapsed or were collapsing all around.

In Hispaniola, a man named Guarionex succeeded his father as the principal chief of Caiabó, a chiefdom found in the Maguá (meaning "Large Valley") region that the Spanish labeled La Vega Real (see Cassá 1974:144; also see Figure 26). Guarionex's father was already dead, presumably long before the Spanish arrived and hence a pre-contact customary law. Here I agree with Curet (2006:396) that it is unlikely that Guarionex had inherited the chiefdom from his father, because the Spanish had simply assumed that the Hispanic-style rule of primogeniture applied to this case, as Keegan (2006) suggested.

Another instance is the cacique of the Caiçimú region in southeastern Hispaniola. This cacique, Cayacoa, was succeeded by his wife, later baptized in the Spanish style as Inés de Cayacoa (with the preposition "*de*" meaning belonging or married to), before the first battle of Higüey took place (in 1503). In this instance the choice was to keep the office within the cacique's immediate family. But this choice is not an instance of matrilineal inheritance.

Cacique Caonabó is an entirely different case. He accessed the office of principal cacique of the region of Maguana, or "Not Large," Valley (encompassing the Cibao Mountains), through personal achievement. Caonabó was, as Keegan (2006:387; see also 2007b) noted, a *stranger* cacique; his birthplace was in the Lucayo Islands (Bahamas). Chronicler Las Casas, in his *Apologética Historia*, specifically wrote:

> The fourth king [of Hispaniola] was Caonabó, last syllable stressed, who ruled the province called Maguana, coterminous or sharing its borders with Xaraguá . . . he was a most valorous and *esforzado* [backed by the force of "law"], who had *gravitas* and authority and who, as those of us who came there [Hispaniola] at the beginning understood, belonged to the Lucayo nation, a natural [born in] of the Islands of the Lucayos, who migrated from there to here [Hispaniola]. *And because he was singled out as a man of war and peace, [he] had become king of that province, and was highly esteemed by all* [Las Casas 1929 (3):554, my translation; my emphasis].

It seems to me unwarranted to interpret this passage as anything other than what it states. Caonabó achieved this status for exactly what Las Casas and other chroniclers said: he was a "noble man in war and in times of peace" (Las Casas, in Curet 2002:274).

Oviedo (1944 [1]:133) added that "Caonabó married Anacaona, sister of *cacique* Behechio; being a *principal caribe,* he came to this island [Hispaniola] as an adventurer captain, and being the person that he was [a principal], he married [Anacaona,] making his principal residence where now is the [Spanish] village of San Juan de La Maguana." Oviedo labeled him a "Carib," not in the sense of ethnic or linguistic affiliation but rather for actively and militarily conspiring against the Spanish. Such a label brought about all the connotations of uncivilized savagery that gave the Spaniards a legal justification to wield a "just war" and, thus, the right to enslave him or to carry a summary execution (but see Keegan 2007b:18–50).

Cacique Behechio was, by most contemporary accounts, the most powerful of all caciques at that time, ruling the large cacicazgo of Bainoa in southwestern Hispaniola. He resided in a province (or perhaps a village) known as Jaraguá, near today's Lake Enriquillo in Haiti. Although part of Caonabó's newfound chiefly power resulted from becoming Behechio's brother-in-law, the reason that such a high-powered marriage was arranged in the first place had to be because Caonabó's achieved reputation made him a most desirable asset. Like Curet (2006:396), but unlike Keegan (2006:387; 2007b), I do not see any documentary evidence to suggest that Caonabó was one of a set of "matrilineal nephews of the chief" who succeeded to office by competing against other nephew candidates for the job, and determined to be the "best fit." I concur with Curet (2006:396) that Keegan's interpretations "would all sound adequate were it not for the lack of hard evidence." Keegan's (2006, 2007b) is a plausible hypothesis but one that is not testable, unless new ethnohistoric documents emerge to support it.

Behechio himself was succeeded by his sister Anacaona (Curet 2002:274; Oviedo 1944 [1]:244–245), who, in turn, may have been succeeded by her nephew, Guaorocuyá. As Curet noted, Behechio and Anacaona were on relatively good terms with the Spanish for some time. When Behechio died (probably of natural causes), Anacaona inherited the chiefdom of Bainoa and took up residence in Jaraguá. This occurred just after the Spanish armies had destroyed her husband's (Caonabó's) chiefdom of Maguana, and after Caonabó had died, along with all hands, in a ship that sank at La Isabela Bay, during a hurricane. Anacaona's accession is not an option in the rules provided by the chroniclers summarized above (i.e., inheritance by the chief's sister rather than by her offspring). In this instance the office (and presumably part of the estate) would remain, as Keegan (2006) likes to say, "in the family" of the chief, but it is still possible that she inherited the position because she may have been perceived as the best or most fit option given the circumstances. Her rule was not to last, however. In 1503 Governor Nicolás de

Ovando had surreptitiously given orders to burn the caney (the cacique's temple house), where between forty and eighty subordinated or allied caciques loyal to Anacaona were assembled, with the pretext that new negotiations of their tributary conditions would ensue (Las Casas 1929 [2]:166; Oviedo 1944 [1]:172).

Anacaona herself was imprisoned for three months and then hanged to death. Cacique Guaorocaya (or Guaorocuyá), a nephew of Anacaona, who perhaps inherited her office, rose to arms in the nearby Baoruco highlands and led a losing battle against Governor Ovando's forces (Las Casas 1929 [2]:168; Oviedo 1944 [1]:173). He too was executed by hanging. The natives' rebellion continued to spread to other areas in the Bainoa region, to Guahaba on the north, to Sabana de Hanyguayaba to the west, and to the peninsula of Guacayarima in southwestern Haiti.

Let us examine two other examples of succession through matrilineal routes, both from Puerto Rico. One of the more influential caciques when Juan Ponce de León began the colonization of Puerto Rico in 1508 was Agüeybana I, nicknamed "El Grande" (The Great One) by the Spanish. Agüeybana ruled in the southwestern region of the island, which came to be known as Guaynía (Oviedo 1944 [3]:192–194). His mother was identified as a chieftess and noblewoman (cacica, doña) and as having much sway on Agüeybana's decision making and negotiations with Ponce de León. As Sued Badillo (1979:62) noted, the Spaniards fairly consistently applied the titles of "Don" (male) and "Doña" (female) to those natives who were of chiefly descent or high noble status (probably nitaínos with connections to chiefly lines); the nitaínos or lesser, subordinated chiefs were identified as *capitanes* (captains). Agüeybana's mother was baptized Doña Inés. Oviedo, however, used both titles to refer to her: "*caçica Doña* Inés," which raises the issue of whether she was given the title of cacica by the Spanish just because she was the mother of a legitimate chief, or because she was a legitimate cacica who delegated public political power to her son. In any event, Agüeybana I's mother was a highly influential political figure. Oviedo said that Agüeybana was "very obedient to his mother," and that she was a woman who was "prudent, [in] counseling [Agüeybana] and the Indians that they be good friends with the Christians if they did all not want to die in their hands" (Oviedo 1944 [3]:193). Doña Inés was well informed of the Spanish victories over the powerful cacicazgos of Hispaniola, the last one (Caiçimú-Higüey) defeated just four years earlier.

When Ponce de León met Inés, she was married to Don Francisco, who was *not* identified as a cacique. Don Francisco was also the stepfather, not the biological father, of Agüeybana I. Doña Inés had a brother, identified as a *hidalgo* (a knight or nobleman) named Luis de Añasco, who in other documents is identified as a cacique. Añasco was either his surname or, more likely, referred to the region where he ruled. In 1510 Doña Inés and Agüeybana I both died of natural causes. Oviedo (1944 [3]:194) wrote that "*heredó el señorío un hermano suyo*" ["the estate was inherited by a brother of his"], also named Agüeybana. From whom Agüeybana I inherited the office is not mentioned and remains unknown. But it is clear that his brother, Agüeybana II, inherited the office of chief. This was the chief whom later (part V) we will meet as the leader of the 1511 Rebellion of the Caciques of Puerto Rico.

The final example is the most detailed and has been well researched by Sued Badillo (1979:24–25; 1985:61–69). It refers to a group of related chiefs and chieftesses of the adjacent Caguas and Turabo Valleys in Puerto Rico who had performed labor and services in a large estate privately owned by the Crown and in partnership with Ponce de León, the Royal Hacienda of Toa. This estate was on the Toa Valley where La Plata River flows, in what is today the western edge of metropolitan San Juan. The caciques and cacicas of Caguas appear in the *demora* (work period) lists for the Royal Hacienda between 1513 and 1519; further unpublished documents located by Sued Badillo (1979) in the Archives of the Indies in Seville trace some of their descendants up to 1543. During a work period, each chief would come with his retinue of nitaínos and contingent of naboría laborers. During these early years the cacique of Caguas, for example, would have up to two thousand naborías (Sued Badillo 1979, 1985). Alongside the caciques and cacicas of Caguas, chiefs from other regions would also fulfill the demora. Each cacique, however, retained control of his or her subjects. Along with the natives, there is also mention of a few black African slaves residing in the Royal Hacienda, since 1513.

Because each cacique and cacica had his or her own retinue of naborías, Sued Badillo (1979) infers that probably each one ruled a particular dominion or population (*población*) in the Caguas-Turabo Valley region. The demora lists mentioned a "*cacique de Caguas*" (or Caguax), who was an early ally of Ponce de León (since 1509) and who loyally continued to provide service and labor at the Royal Hacienda until his death in 1519 (Sued Badillo 1979:61; Tanodi 1971:82–125). As Sued Badillo noted, this cacique of Caguas—the one who maintained a steadfast alliance with Juan Ponce de León till his death—is none other than Francisco de Guaybanex (in one instance spelled Cayguanex). Oddly, in the first demora list of 1513, Guaybanex appears among Cacica Catalina's retinue as being only a "*capitán de la dicha cacica*" ["captain of the said chieftess"] (Sued Badillo 1979:61). Catalina was thus the chieftess (of Caguas), according to the 1513 demora list. She was accompanied by her mother, a very old woman, judging by her name, Yayo, and the nickname given by the Spanish, "*cacica vieja*." Catalina also had a sister named Doña María, with the title "Doña" indicative of her status as a noblewoman. Assuming that Yayo was a legitimate cacica, it is nevertheless her (eldest?) daughter who clearly was exercising the power to order and command the workforce; if so, it is possible that Yayo may have delegated or relinquished her office in favor of Catalina (perhaps because of infirmity). On the other hand, and perhaps more likely, it could also be that Catalina inherited her office from a cacique or cacica on her mother's side rather than directly from her mother. This matrilineal emphasis seems to be supported, as Catalina had two daughters who also were to become cacicas later. Their husbands are not even mentioned in the list. In any event, it was Catalina, the cacica of Caguas, who was in full authority, while Francisco de Guaybanex was listed in a subordinated position.

After 1514 Catalina of Caguas is not mentioned again in the demora lists and is presumed dead (Sued Badillo 1979:62). Instead it is Francisco de Guaybanex who is mentioned as the cacique of Caguas. It is clear that Guaybanex had "replaced her, politically" (Sued Badillo 1979:62–63) and that he remained the key chief of Caguas until his death in 1519. What is not clear is whether Guaybanex was related to Yayo (and thus Catalina and María) and, if so, in what way. Interestingly, however, members of Catalina's family appear mentioned among Guaybanex's demora group, including old chieftess Yayo, the mother of Catalina. At this time, in 1514, Yayo is described as cacica—that is, she bears the same rank as cacique Guaybanex.

In the demora list of 1515, Francisco de Guaybanex is once again mentioned as the cacique of Caguas. Interestingly, Yayo, the old chieftess, is mentioned not at the head of the demora list, as would befit her status, but is embedded with the rest of the women. Sued Badillo (1979:63) correctly infers that by this time "the cacique of Caguas had become the most important chiefly figure, in fact, for the Spaniards, although we do not know the mechanisms and avenues that were used to achieve this." In 1516 the only chief leading the naboría work group at the Royal Hacienda of Toa was Guaybanex.

The following year, 1517, a new chieftess, Doña Isabel de Cayaguax, enters the scene in the Royal Hacienda of Toa and forms part of Guaybanex's retinue. Sued Badillo (1979:63; 1985:24) uncovered documents demonstrating that she was none other than cacique Guaybanex's sister. Doña Isabel of Cayaguax is mentioned along with her two children, Juanico ("little John") de Comerío and Doña María. The latter is a different María, unrelated (as far as can be ascertained) to the Yayo–Catalina de Caguas line. To distinguish her from the other María, she will be called María Cayaguax. Sued Badillo (1985:24) calls her María de Caguas, but this is confusing because the other María is also from Caguas. Juanico de Comerío had already appeared before in earlier demora lists as one of the captains under cacique Guaybanex's retinue. María Cayaguax would eventually inherit her uncle's (cacique Guaybanex) office after his death in 1519, when she was only nine years old (Sued Badillo (1979:63; 1985:24). In this case, her status as a minor did not affect inheriting the office.

The data of Catalina de Caguas as a chieftess receiving her office from or through her mother, Yayo, and seemingly passing it down to her daughters suggest to Sued Badillo a *probable* matrilineal descent. But it is the other chiefly branch descending from cacique Francisco Guaybanex to his nine-year-old niece María Cayaguax that fits the "preferred rule" of matrilineal descent noted by both Mártir and Las Casas. The case of Catalina is much more difficult to assess, because it depends on how one interprets Yayo's status as cacica. Also, because Yayo appears as part of Guaybanex's retinue in the following work periods, the assumption is that in one way or another these two chiefly lines were related, but it is impossible to prove.

Cacica María Cayaguax's mother, Doña Isabel de Cayaguax, was first mentioned in the 1513 demora list as being in command of fifty workers exploiting the salt mines of Abey (or Yabey), in southeastern Puerto Rico. She was first married to the cacique of Cayey, and after his death she married the cacique of Humacao (eastern Puerto Rico), and hence was also known as Isabel Cayaguax of Humacao (Sued Badillo 1985:24). Through his sister's marriages, Guaybanex of Caguas had affine relationships with caciques (brothers-in-law) who governed a good part of southeastern Puerto Rico. Interestingly, however, the caciques of Humacao and Abey were to remain rebellious against Spanish rule; their cacicazgos were the last areas of guerrilla-style resistance, long after the island-wide rebellion of caciques in 1511 (which Guaybanex did not join). It is clear that neither Guaybanex nor María Cayaguax had the political muscle to force the caciques of Abey and Humacao to join them in a political alliance with the Spanish forces, despite their affine relationships.

The end to the story of Isabel's daughter, cacica María Cayaguax, is a sad one (Sued Badillo 1979:63–69). As the heir of the influential cacique of Caguas (Guaybanex), María was the victim of abuses by successive administrators of the Hacienda of Toa (no longer belonging to the Crown), particularly the very powerful treasurer Don Blás Villasante and the wily majordomo Diego Muriél. They (and probably others, too) were all currying her favor because of her command over a large native workforce at a time (late 1520s) when the native demography was collapsing. As noted, in the early days cacique Guaybanex commanded around two thousand naborías in the hacienda; by 1528 there were less than three hundred (Sued Badillo 1979). In the attempt to gain her favors, the situation reached scandalous proportions (read sexual exploitation), so much so that the bishop of Santo Domingo was called in to resolve the situation in 1528. The end result was that to quell all the sexual improprieties, the bishop arranged for María Cayaguax to marry the majordomo Muriél. He accepted the offer in exchange for a suspension of the tax debts he had incurred against the Crown. This marriage produced three mestizo children. In 1548 Muriél placed María Cayaguax and the children on board a vessel destined for Spain. Tragically, the ship sank and with it the last of the chiefs of Caguas.

These accounts of the chiefs of Hispaniola and Puerto Rico offer a glimpse of the social and political conditions in which some of the informants of the chroniclers were immersed. It shows that various alternate modes of accession to the office were in play. It is, as Curet (2002, 2006) argued, not crystal clear that the dominant descent and inheritance rule is matrilineal; other routes existed. No doubt the Spaniards had a serious impact on matters of succession, but I am inclined to think that the various alternative routes described by the chroniclers were options that arose from tradition (customary law) as well as from the political crises confronting the native elites. I accept that there are instances that strongly suggest matrilineal succession, but clearly there were important exceptions within and between Hispaniola and Puerto Rico.

This overview has focused on descent and inheritance among chiefs, taking into consideration only the relationships among human beings. What it has not considered are the social relationships that the chiefs had with nonhuman beings and other "things" imbued with cemí vitality. With broad strokes, this topic is explored in the next section.

3 Webs of Interaction
Human Beings, Other Beings, and Many Things

All webs of sociocultural interaction, whether between oceanic islands or between islands and continents, begin with face-to-face relationships between at least two human beings or nonhuman beings and other "things" who are embedded and act in a given social and cultural milieu. Relationships between human actors begin at home, within the residential compound of the household. As individuals mature and grow to assume increased responsibility in society, their network or web of relationships will expand beyond the confines of the homestead or village and, for some individuals, into far-flung regions, not to mention those who will leave their natal settlement for good.

Throughout their life cycle, humans will keep changing their web of social relations; thus their personal identities will also change accordingly. Ideas and perceptions about self in relation to other beings and things—native philosophies of "being" in the cosmos—lead to distinct ways in which persons are constructed and thus condition the ways in which interactions are effected (Fowler 2004). Personhood as a state of being, therefore, becomes an important frame of reference, a theoretical approach to explore and inform about the nature of interactions between human beings and other things in the cosmos—in particular, the cemí icons.

In any face-to-face social interaction between human actors, some ties or interconnections are strongly developed, maintained, and encouraged to persist, if not expand, over the long run, whereas others are weakly developed, ephemeral, and may contract, dissipate, or disappear over time. The motivations driving human actors toward particular kinds of face-to-face relationships are, as might be expected, tremendously diverse. Humans place different values on things and on relationships and rank them accordingly. These ranked values are thus what motivate different behaviors and social relations (Graeber 2001). The motivation that rests on such a set of values, however fugitive a concept it might be, is nevertheless the driving force that propels humans into action (or inaction) toward (or away from) establishing and maintaining, expanding, or even closing the webs of relations. What forces and circumstances motivate the spread of highly valued cemí artifacts is one of the fundamental questions to be addressed in later sections of this book. How the humans and other beings and things are *valued*, as David Graeber (2001) has eloquently elaborated in his book *Toward an Anthropological Theory of Value*, is what motivates attitudes and behaviors in all social relationships, most particularly in the Maussian context of giving and receiving and in the Marxist context of production and consumption (i.e., inalienable or alienable things or acts rooted in values). Motivation, whether voluntary or coercive, occasional or persistent, drives positive *and* negative relationships, be these spurred by kin-based gift reciprocity (or avoidance), by descent and martial alliances, by perceived economic gains, by advantageous political maneuverings, or by threats of conflict and aggression.

Graeber said that value is:

> the way people represent the importance of their own actions to themselves: normally, as reflected in one or another socially recognized form. But it is not the forms [structures] themselves that are the source of values. Compare, again, [Marilyn] Strathern. Because of her Sassurean starting point, she sees value as a matter of "making visible": social relations take on value in the process of being recognized by someone else. According to [Nancy] Munn's approach, the value in question is ultimately the power to *create* social relations; the "making visible" is simply an act of recognition of a value that already exists in potential. Hence, where Strathern stresses visibility, Munn's language is all about "potencies," "transformative potential," human capacities that are ultimately generic and invisible. Rather than value being the process of recognition itself, already suspended in social relations, it is the way people who *could* do almost anything (including creating entirely new sorts of social relation) . . . assess the importance of what they do, in fact, when they are doing it. This is necessarily a social process; but it is always rooted in generic human capacities [Graeber 2001:47].

By virtue of their power to act, objects imbued with cemí, especially those with legendary status, were highly valued and thus motivated human beings to act and react to, and with them to achieve determined, desired goals. More important, these cemís, as iconic beings, are essential in *creating* certain kinds of social relations that could not exist in human society without their participation.

Social relations and interactions are set on a landscape (and a "seascape") that is both naturally and culturally constructed. Of particular relevance in addressing socially driven webs—such as implied by humans and their cemí artifacts—is that the meanings and values elicited are relational and contextual; that is, *perspectival* (Descola 1996; Fowler 2004; Viveiros de Castro 1996). Interaction requires an understanding of where human beings situate themselves and how they perceive themselves vis-à-vis other nonhuman beings, physical entities, and other phenomena that populate and constitute the landscape and cosmos. In this regard, the *multinatural, animistic* perspective of the cosmos by native societies is a crucial framework in which to situate the relational analysis and interpretation of human beings and cemí beings. It will be demonstrated later that cemí icons are not merely indivisible, inert objects circulating along with human beings in a web of social relations. They are instead animated beings—persons—with different, changing natures and who are as much agents as they are patients in their relations with human beings (Gell 1998). In short, the cemí icons shared the center stage in human interpersonal and intergroup relationships. Together with human beings, cemís (as objectified forms), artifacts, goods, information, knowledge, and so on are the "things" that circulated or were transported throughout the web's pathways, whether by sea, land, or both. And which "things" were circulated, or not, is in large measure predicated on the values attached or bestowed to them by all the parties involved (e.g., desirable, not desirable; can be gifted or not given).

A web is, of course, a metaphor, a human-constructed spatial model that purports to describe the properties and dynamics of pattern formation resulting from, in this case, social interactions between human and nonhuman beings (i.e., cemí). Archaeologists are supposed to tease out the principles that constrain or govern the processes (e.g., gift exchange, reciprocity, redistribution) that produce a given web pattern (e.g., dendritic, hexagonal, orthogonal, radial; see Ball 1999). However, since the vast majority of these cemí icons lack detailed provenience data, the pattern of pathways connecting different sites between and within islands cannot be specified, and thus the configuration of the web (nodes and pathways or vectors) remains vague. At best what can be observed is the sphere or area of interaction (as depicted in Figure 1).

By definition, a strong, persistent socially driven web that extends between islands denies the assumed (or conventional) idea that islands—in the Latin sense of *insula*—are uniquely suited "laboratories" to study evolution and historical development because of their presumed relative isolation, and thus treatable as closed systems. Some, perhaps most, archaeologists working in oceanic islands would now likely argue that whether particular islands or archipelagic groups are more open or more closed social systems is for archaeology to demonstrate, and that what ought to be rigorously defined and analyzed is precisely the varying kinds and degrees of social connectivity between islands and sets of islands. Oceans are not inherently barriers or negative space, a point made by Donald Lathrap for the Caribbean more than two decades ago (Lathrap and Oliver 1984). Ultimately, socially driven webs can and do transcend physical, geographic boundaries.

It may be argued that if there is anything at all that distinguishes island from continental archaeologies, it is to be found in the one inescapable constraint imposed on a human-driven web of interaction: the key nodes of interaction—the starting, staging, and ending points for the flow of humans and material culture through the web—*cannot* be placed on oceans for obvious reasons. Among nonwestern, preindustrial societies these nodes must be land-based or at least very near land-based (wetlands). In contrast, in "islands-in-continents," surrounded by sea-sonal freshwater oceans, humans have choices as to where to situate and build land-based islands for settlement and gardening. Often these artificially engineered continental islands are also connected by raised causeways, analogues to the canoeing lanes in the Caribbean Sea. It is striking, though, that during the high flood season the ancient peoples inhabiting the savannas of Mompox (Colombia), Llanos de Bení-Bauré (Bolivia), and Llanos del Orinoco (Venezuela), would engage in a lifestyle and a pattern of travel, intercommunity visitation, and exchange (by canoes) far more similar to that of Caribbean seafaring natives than that of their own continental lifestyle during the drier summer season (Mann 2000; Morey 1975, 1976; Plazas et al. 1993). In short, in oceanic islands humans have no choice of where to locate dryland-based islands, but at the same time and in terms of life-styles, there are many parallels to be found between islands in continents and islands in oceans.

As Paul Rainbird (2007) has argued, it pays off to intellectually decenter the land from "is-land" in favor of an archaeology of the sea, and more specifically, focusing on maritime society. He addresses the fundamental question of whether there is something special about island archaeology in terms of approach, method, and interpretation that sets it apart from continental archaeology, to which he answered "a qualified 'yes,' but for the most part 'no.' It is mostly negative because . . . we have been asking the wrong questions and therefore debating the wrong issues" (Rainbird 2007:2). He argues that a fruitful approach to an archaeology of islands must have "at its heart a requirement to conceptualize coastal peoples, whether living in an island, boat or continent as *members of maritime societies*" (Rainbird 2007:3; my emphasis; see also Hofman et al. 2007).

The effectiveness and the ability to engage in interisland social interaction depend, of course, on seafaring technology (Callaghan 1995, 2003, 2008; Callaghan and Bray 2007). In the Caribbean, such technological know-how is a given precondition, since it is clear that the first human colonization of oceanic islands from the continent was "not accomplished by swimming" (Lathrap and Oliver 1984); the potential for interisland connectivity, and thus interaction, in the Caribbean was there since the first arrival of human groups some six thousand years ago (Rodríguez Ramos et al. 2008; Wilson et al. 1998). Technological improvements, however, can affect the properties of the web system—for example, increased efficiency because of less energy expended in propelling the vessel; less travel time; larger vessels with larger, heavier loads; and so forth.

The web pattern is thus a model, a two- or three-dimensional spatial configuration of nodes interconnected by pathways or vectors. Nodes, at a macro scale, are land-based islands; at a smaller scale these nodes are the coastal settlements, the ports of departure or destination, with intermediate staging points, in the flow of people and goods (and cemí icons) between islands and in the to-and-fro movements between the coast and various points inland. Such nodes, particularly seaport sites, can be envisioned as *attractors* of humans and other things flowing through the web system. It is of interest to know what is attractive or repellent and why. Some might see portable artifacts flowing in a web exclusively as autonomous, indivisible entities mediating between humans, as the things through which interaction is further qualified into transactions, negotiations, and gift exchanges between human beings. And this is so, but I will also argue that the pre-Columbian natives of the Caribbean understood the interaction between objects and humans, and also the exchange of objects between human beings, in a rather different light than contemporary, postindustrial Caribbean islanders and westerners do. Here the native's perspective of a multinatural cultural and animistic world (a feature of Taínoness) contrasts with that of our current understanding of cosmos as a multicultural natural domain (Viveiros de Castro 1996). While contemporary people might consider an object as an indivisible entity *and* as having an individual nature, the Taínoan societies and other Caribbean natives most likely perceived these objects as having multiple natures for which there was a unique, integrated cultural interpretation. It matters, then, that we sort out what are the intrinsic characteristics or properties of the entities (i.e., people, cemí icons) flowing through a web, because these will condition and define where and how interaction takes place (contexts), what the transactions or exchanges entail (relations), and how they are effected (causality, agency).

4 Personhood and the Animistic Amerindian Perspective

Before proceeding to flesh out the contexts and relationships between human beings who express Taínoness and these other things imbued with cemí power, it is useful to first discuss what is meant by the terms "person" and "personhood," especially because these have not yet been contemplated in analyses of Caribbean material culture. Here I follow very closely the notions of person and personhood discussed by Chris Fowler in his excellent book *The Archaeology of Personhood.* Fowler (2004:124–125, table 5.1) produced a very useful table in which he compares the animistic, totemic, and naturalistic worldview perspectives, each with its own particular modes of personhood construction. This table should be consulted as I develop the arguments to follow below. (For copyright reasons, it is not reproduced here.)

A *person* is "any entity human or otherwise that may be conceptualized and treated as a person," while *personhood* refers to the "condition or state of being of a person as it is understood in any specific context. Persons are constituted or constructed, de-constituted, maintained, altered, and transformed in social practices through life and death" (Fowler 2004:7). Fowler goes on to say that "exactly who or what may or may not be a person is contextually variable," and, of course, what each person *is,* is very much dependent on the interrelationships with other human beings and with other beings and things. "Personhood is attained and maintained through relationships not only with human beings but with things, places, animals and the spiritual features of the cosmos. Some of these may also emerge as persons through this engagement. People's own social interpretations of personhood and the social practices through which personhood is realized shape their intentions [and I would add motivations] in a reflexive way, but personhood remains a mutually constituted condition" (Fowler 2004:7).

Personhood is not, therefore, a cumulative set of fixed, distinguishing personality traits. Rather, as Fowler noted, the life and afterlife of a person is an ongoing process where "personhood of different kinds is sought, struggled with, and attained" (Fowler, personal communication 2007). Personhood is in effect the state of being rather than the process per se, but "the process of becoming a person is vital to the state of being of a person," and thus "personhood deals with that process" (Fowler 2004:7). And in an animistic world, persons and personhood include not just human but also other beings and things. Persons are constantly evolving

and changing; one might detect particular phases of changes in personhood status, such as those captured in Arnold van Gennep's famous *rites de passage* (for a
review of religion from an archaeologist's perspective, see Insoll 2005). The broad
and flexible definitions of person and personhood set up a framework in which to
approach the analysis of the interaction between iconic artifacts imbued with cemí
and the Taíno human beings that socially engaged them.

Following Fowler and others (Descola 1996; Gell 1998; Viveiros de Castro
1996), there are three basic modes or fields of personhood: animism, totemism,
and naturalism (Fowler 2004:table 5.1). These refer to the forms that person and
personhood relationships "are supposed to take" (Fowler 2004:7). But in order to
address these fields or modes in relation to person and personhood, it is necessary
to first define several key concepts that, in Fowler's words: "describe the overarching
logic of being a person within any social context and in the specific long-term
trends in the practices that support that logic. . . . People actively engage with these
trends, and with that particular concept [mode] of personhood, when they pursue
strategies of interaction. As a result of these interactions, each person is constructed
in a specific way" (Fowler 2004:7).

The first set of features of personhood that need to be defined relate to the con-
trastive notions of individual, individuality, and indivisibility on the one hand,
and of dividuals and dividuality on the other. As might be intuitively guessed, *individuality* refers to the common concept of personal uniqueness that all persons
have (Fowler 2004:7–9). As Fowler noted, in common usage, "all people are individuals," but it does not follow that individuals have an indivisible nature. *Indivisibility* refers to a state of being indivisible, whole—a unitary person. This state of indivisibility is the prevalent, contemporary "western mode" of personhood identity,
where "individuality lies at the core of a fixed and constant sense of self," a sense of
personal identity, and where the individuality is "stressed over relational identities"
(Fowler 2004:8; Strathern 1998).

Persons can alternatively be conceived as dividual rather than individual persons. *Dividuality* refers to a state where the person (and its body), the *dividual,* is
acknowledged to be "composite and multi-authored," where persons engaged in
social relationships with other beings and things "owe parts of themselves to others," and where the person is composed of traits or features that may have different
origins or authorships, such as the mind, soul, and body (Fowler 2004:8). Some of
these features that make up personhood are not necessarily fixed in the body; they
can also, for example, temporarily or permanently enter or exit or pass through the
body (see also Joyce 1998, 2005). Changes in the different elements that constitute a body thus change its balance and "alter the disposition of the person" (Fowler
2004:9).

Partibility is one formal expression of the dividual person and personhood. As
the term implies, it refers to the reconfiguration of the dividual person such that

one part or element can be subtracted and given to another person or entity, to which it is owed (Fowler 2004:9). Being a "multiply constituted" person, composed of diverse relations, makes him, her, or it "a partible entity: an agent [that] can dispose of parts or act as a part. Thus, [e.g., Melanesian] women move in marriage as parts of clans; thus 'men' circulate objectified parts of themselves among themselves" (Strathern 1988:324–325; cited in Fowler 2004:48–49). *Permeability* is another formal expression of the dividual person, and refers to a state whereby the person can be suffused or "permeated by qualities that influence the internal composition of the person" (Fowler 2004:9). Melanesian societies are often cited as prime examples of partible persons, while Hindu societies are exemplars of permeable persons (Fowler 2004; Strathern 1998; Weiner 1992). In the last decade or so, other examples of dividuality have also emerged. For the ancient Maya, there are analyses of the various modes of constructing and conceptualizing persons and personhood, and research ranges from topics such as the performance of the body and mortuary rituals (Gillespie 2001; Joyce 1998, 2001, 2005) to illuminating cross-comparisons of "embodied lives" between Maya and Egyptian civilizations and their different ways of constructing self (and others) through theories of embodiment (Meskell and Joyce 2003).

The dividual and partible character of persons among natives engaged in expressing their Taínoness is sufficiently documented by the sixteenth-century Spanish chroniclers. To take one example among many, Fray Ramón Pané details how the *behiques* (shamans) in Hispaniola cured illness from the body of a patient whose sickness was suspected by all to be the result of neglecting his duties to the cemí (Pané 1999:22–23). The key act during the ritual involved sucking on selected parts of the patient's body, after which the shaman spat the ailment or sickness into his hands. Before sucking, the shaman hid inside his mouth a cotton-wrapped satchel enclosing a piece of meat and some bones (in other instances these were small stones). The satchel of stones was the entity that enabled the shaman's sucking to extract and capture the sickness from the patient's body. The shaman then gave the satchel, with the sickness safely wrapped, to the cured patient and commanded him to take care of "it," and "it" was expressly designated by Pané as a cemí. It is this face-to-face interaction between shaman and patient—mediated through the cemí-imbued satchel of stones—that changed the patient's personhood vis-à-vis the rest of the community: from a socially marginalized, sick ("sinner") person to a once-again healthy, productive member. Sickness was the partible, perhaps even permeable, component of the patient's body and persona that could be extracted and assumed (and neutralized) by the cemí—that is, the satchel of stones—through the sucking action of the shaman. As Fowler pointed out to me, both Susan Rasmussen (1995) and Piers Vitebsky (1993) have dealt even more extensively with the same issues for, respectively, the Tuareg of Africa and the Sora of Eastern India. Both of these authors explored issues of boundaries, of what sickness is, and how it is treated among the Tuareg and the Sora, "both of whom seem to show strong concepts of the permeability of the body" (Fowler, personal communication 2007). There are thus illuminating cross-cultural parallels between the Taínoan, Tuareg, and Sora notions of partibility and permeability in regard to sickness and curing. In the Hispaniolan case, intangible illness permeates from the patient to the satchel of stones by the sucking action of the shaman, who then gives the cemí-imbued stones containing the captive, or perhaps neutralized, sickness to the care of the patient.

Pané (1999:23) then notes that the Hispaniolan natives, in general, "believe it is true that those stones are good [i.e., have supernatural powers], and they help woman give birth, and they keep them very carefully, wrapped in cotton, putting them into small baskets, and they feed them some of what they eat, and they do the same thing with cemís." These "aniconic" cemís with curing as well as protecting powers then assume humanlike qualities, such as having to be fed or prayed to.

By "aniconic" I follow Alfred Gell's (1998:97–98) usage. An icon is defined by the *Concise Oxford Dictionary* (11th edition, electronic version) first as "a devotional painting of Christ or another holy figure, typically on wood, venerated in the Byzantine and other Eastern Churches," and second, but more appropriately in this instance, as "a person or thing regarded as a representative symbol or as worthy of veneration." "Aniconic" thus means that the "thing" or "person" in question is *not* a figure (i.e., formal representation) of the entity in question. Yet, while not formally or anatomically resembling a *figure* of a thing or person, it is still nevertheless regarded as such. Examples of this include a wide range of objects (mostly magical), such as the pebbles noted in Pané's account above, or the crystal-quartz talismans or charms used by shamans in northwestern Amazonia, such as the Desana and Tukano (see Reichel-Dolmatoff 1979, 1988).

Another expression of dividuality is *fractality* (Wagner 1991). The fractal person encapsulates the personhood concepts of partibility and multiple composition that are repeated or replicated at different scales, going from particular persons to larger social groups or collectivities, such as clans and lineages, and extending from the living to a nonliving "family" of beings (e.g., apical, mythological ancestors). Citing Strathern's (1988; see also Mosko 1992) work in highland New Guinea, Melanesia, Fowler (2004:47–52) commented that "just as people combine a diversity of relations, so clans combine a diversity of persons: the composite person exists in the same format at both scales," at the level of person and at the level of clan. In Fowler's words:

> Strathern [1988:14–15] argues that gatherings and ceremonies bring together a whole clan as a dividual person, so that "[t]he bringing together of many persons is just like the bringing together of one". . . . Both clans and individuals move between being one person with many relations (dividual) and or being presented as one of a pair in a relationship (partible). Unlike the single person, the clan is usually fragmented and partible, but becomes

dividual during social gatherings. The clan and the person therefore have parallel compositions and move between parallel conditions of personhood [Fowler 2004:48].

In short, the clan (or sib, phratry, moiety, etc.) is like a person; the clan and its members are each envisioned as a whole person. The dividual and fractal quality of persons and personhood is well attested among Melanesian "Big and Great Men" (Godelier and Strathern 1991; Hage and Mosko 1998; Mosko 1995). "Exchanges between big men are exchanges between clans: clans are equivalent, and so are all the persons within them, including the big men" (Fowler 2004:49). The scale at which fractal personhood is taken beyond single persons into larger and diverse groupings, of course, varies from society to society.

A Taínoan example of a partible person is the famous ancestor cemí idol found in the 1880s in a cave near Maniel, province of Barahona, in Hispaniola (Kerchache 1994:158–160; Vega 1971–1972:88; see Figure 24). This is an anthropomorphic idol made of cotton and vegetable fiber cordage. The idol's head covers an actual human skull fragment (seen only by x-ray) while the thorax-abdomen's cotton fabric is probably wrapped around a *higüero* or calabash (*Crescentia cujete*), or perhaps a block of wood. The human skull is thus embedded within, given a new face, and provided with an outer "skin" and body: part of the deceased human is thus recomposed as a cemíified ancestor—in short, a person. Wrapping and embedding a human skull is not uniquely a Taínoan notion, and is in fact a prevalent mode of personhood presentation throughout Oceania, in societies such as the Maori (see Gell 1993; 1998:109–115). The dead human person's skull being recomposed and reconstituted as a cemíified ancestor idol (i.e., given a new skin, body), among other things, results in a new set of relations between the living descendants and the cemíified ancestors. The clan/lineage is a person as much as the cemíified idol is a person; exchanges between living caciques or nitaínos are exchanges between chiefly clans or lineages (see section 2 D).

One of the four classes of cemí icons noted in this book—the large stone head (Figures 3: e, 25)—is most likely the stone-carved version of the cemíified human skulls of ancestors kept in calabashes or wrapped in cotton idols. The human head cemís (a kind of trophy head) made in stone and shell have a long history in the Caribbean, going back to the Saladoid and Huecoid period, around 400–200 B.C. (see Oliver 1999), but at this early time these trophy heads were limited to personally worn pendants, often made of marine shells or gemstones like serpentinite (see photographs in Chanlatte Baik and Narganes Storde 2005:37–40). Only much later in time would these become large stone heads (no longer to be used for personal adornment) made of what to us westerners seem to be ordinary and fairly abundant rock species (Figures 3: e, 25).

5 Contrasting Animistic and Naturalistic Worldviews

On the basis of available ethnohistoric data, it can be argued that the historic Taínoan construction of personhood is fundamentally dividual and partible, and it operates in the context of an animistic perception of the landscape, of the cosmos. *Animism* entails the belief that beings, things, objects, and so on all can potentially have a life force or energy—a soul, or *anima* (in its ancient Latin sense). Persons and personhood are constituted in terms of social relations and interactions with other human and nonhuman beings, animals, spiritual and physical things, even landscapes, in a particular way that anthropologists long ago labeled animism.

In this animistic view, the cosmos is comprised of beings that have different natures but, along with human beings, share a unified cultural world. Both Philipe Descola (1996) and Eduardo Viveiros de Castro (1996) have eloquently demonstrated that such a multinatural perspective predominates among many Amerindian societies of the South American tropical lowlands. It is a perspective grounded on the continuity of relationships between all things, natural *and* cultural. In this view, the transformation of form is crucial to the interaction between beings, each assuming a form appropriate to the relationships in which it is engaged.

In contrast, the contemporary western *naturalistic* perspective is one whereby human society exists in a natural world; it is perceived as a series of different cultures within a unifying human nature. It is, as Fowler (2004:table 5.1) indicated, a multicultural natural perspective that "creates an alienating discontinuity between what is perceived as a natural versus cultural phenomenon." The identity of persons is fixed by species (e.g., Linnaean taxonomy) rather than as a status of being/s that is negotiable, and where the relationships and interactions between people, animals, and things are dialogic. While in a multinatural cultural (animistic) perspective, transformations of form are vital to interaction between beings, in a multicultural natural (naturalistic) world, forms are propagated identically by natural reproduction from one generation to the next.

In the animistic perspective, nonhumans can be and often are persons who comprise a part of the human world: nature is social and cultural, not just "natural." Instead, in the western naturalistic tradition, species are what constitute different social groups. Moreover, in an animistic perspective, human beings and other beings can also appear in forms other than their own, such as body transformations or transmutations. Thus, animals, objects, places, things, spirits, plants, animals, and even places in the landscape can be persons or parts of persons. This view contrasts with the naturalistic perspective, whereby the human world *is* the social world and diverse societies and cultures belong to, are part of, nature. A naturalistic perspective holds that only humans can be fully construed as persons, whereas animals, plants, objects, and places "can only be thought of as persons in a whimsical or fantastic context"—that is, "the metaphors between non-human and human are merely representational" (Fowler 2004:125).

As shall be seen later, a cemí has multiple natures: it is manifested as, or imbued in, physical things (stone, wood/trees, gold, bones, etc.) and as phenomena displayed in nature (hurricanes, floods), as well as in the created idols and icons (Oliver 2005). By virtue of the cemís being engaged in social relationships with human beings in a variety of contexts, they are construed as persons (anthropomorphism). And like human beings, these cemís have names and titles, roles marked by gender and age, and social rank; they build up reputations and have a history of deeds based on their acts and relationships with human beings and with other beings and things in the cosmos—in other words, they have biographies. It is evident that not all cemí entities were captivated and transformed into iconic/aniconic images (artifacts), but hereafter the focus of this study is on those cemí forces and energies that *were* objectified into icons.

Later in this book I will deal with the question of whether cemí objects can take on only a limited set of forms (archetypes) and characteristics ("personalities") or if they are instead much more ambiguous and able to, for example, change gender, form, and so on, either within a certain range or in a limitless fashion. At this point, I can introduce a teaser: some of these cemí objects are sculptured so that one body integrates or contains two (or multiples of two) persons; thus, personhood changes by changing the perspective of the object relative to the viewer, or vice versa. For example, in one perspective the visible personage may be an anthropomorphic head while the zoomorphic personage remains occult. Again, rotating the cemí icon hides the humanlike head and reveals the froglike personage. The two distinct persons, frog and human, are nevertheless embodied in a single object (Figure 10). Classic art historians label this phenomenon as the Janus mode, and, structurally, it is an expression of dualism. Hence, when a single sculptural piece holds at once different morphologies (human head vs. frog) of persons, this is already an indication of the playful ways in which an icon can take on a specific set of traits but at the same time hold another set of completely different ones. As shall be seen, one interesting and key notion involving the changing personhood of the same cemí icon revolves around the occult and the visible. It does have the same effect as a magician has on us when he pulls a rabbit out of a hat: it is magical. David Graeber (2007:240–251) has discussed the importance that magic, both the visible and the occult, has in order to understand the power and potency of material objects and, particularly, the values attached to them and the performer by an audience. The many and changing natures of cemís—now visible, now occult—are thus not only of a conceptual or mental kind but are also skillfully rendered in a wide range of material objects (e.g., Figures 10, 21). The relative perspectives of the cemí object and the viewer, and how the person displays or holds the icon for contemplation by other humans, thus provide a complex and dynamic environment for engaging in social relations.

What are the relationships that cemís have with human beings, especially cemí icons? What are the social and political-religious implications of these relationships in regard to the spatial distribution (or web) of the large three-pointers, stone collars, stone elbows, and large stone heads? To address these questions, the first step is to define what the concept of cemí refers to so that its material correlates, the cemí as artifact, can be understood.

PART II

The Form, Personhood, Identity, and Potency of Cemí Idols

6 The Cemí Reveals Its Personhood and Its Body Form

The notion of cemí finds similar, though not identical, analogues in other societies around the world, such as among the Ba-Kongo of western Africa, for whom *bilongo* ("medicine") is what animates and confers potency to their magic wooden idols (*minkisi*; see Anderson and Peek 2002; MacGaffey 1993; Voguel 1997). It is also analogous to the paired notions of *mana* and *tapu* (taboo) in Polynesia, or the *hau* and *mauri* couplet among the Maori of New Zealand (Graeber 2001: 170–178). Cemí thus relates to the notion of "vital essence" that Raymond Firth (1959:225) discussed for the Maori long ago. The conceptual dyad *hau/mauri* entails "the assumption that behind any material form is an invisible, dynamic power that makes it what it is" and all at once is "the source of appearance and potential for action, which . . . was for Maori philosophers seen as merely the inner expression of an inner nature" (Graeber 2001:177). David Graeber's definition is applicable to my understanding of what cemí is.

To start with, the Taíno-language term *cemí* refers not to an artifact or object but to an immaterial, numinous, and vital force. Under particular conditions, beings, things, and other phenomena in nature can be imbued with cemí. Cemí is, therefore, a condition of being, not a thing. It is a numinous power, a driving or vital force that compels action; it is the power to cause, to effect, and also denotes a condition or state of being.

Among modern-day Arawakan (Northern Caribbean Maipuran) speakers—the Lokono of Guiana and Surinam—*semehi* means something that is, or tastes and smells, sweet (Bennett 1989:39; Oliver 1998, 2005). The stem "*semel i-*" can also be found in the word *semičiči,* a Lokono noun for "shaman" or "curer." Thus, in Lokono, *seme* is an adjective meaning "sweetness," while *semehi* is the noun for "sweet." Other things, especially fruits, that have the condition of being sweet also carry the "*semel i-*" morpheme: *semeheyo-bali,* a noun, is a sweet sage plant (*Lanta cara*) used by medicine men for curing, while *semetho,* translated as "sweet-one," is a noun for a vine (species unidentified) that yields a sweet, edible fruit. In short, most Lokono words with the morpheme "*seme-*" allude to shamanism or to curing (magical) properties. It is no coincidence that honey, along with the contrasting tobacco, is one of a key pair of opposing elementary concepts widely deployed in Amerindian mythology, famously analyzed by Claude Lévi-Strauss (1974) in one part of his *Mythologiques* trilogy. As there were no honey-making bees in Hispaniola, mythology bestowed the sweet but astringent guava fruit (*Psidium guajava*) with the same role that honey had for continental Amerindians (Oliver 1998:72). But under what conditions does a cemí materialize? Fray Ramón Pané, who was ordered by Christopher Columbus to investigate the religious beliefs and practices of the natives in Hispaniola, provided a detailed description of the context in which an ordinary human being from Hispaniola encounters that which is cemí (Pané 1974, 1990, 1999). His report to Columbus, begun in 1494 and completed by 1498, stated: "The [cemís] of wood are made in this way: when someone is walking along [in the forest], and he sees a tree that is moving its roots, the man very fearfully stops and asks it who it is. And it answers him: 'Summon me a behique and he will tell you who I am.' And when that man goes to the aforesaid physician, he tells him what he had seen" (Pané 1999:25–26).

To an ordinary human being, the cemí is manifested by an unusual or uncommon sign in nature: a tree moves its roots when ordinarily that is not expected to occur. Through a process of abduction (Gell 1998:15), the man reasons that the tree root is displaying a different nature; it is something other than the ordinary root of a tree given the circumstances of the encounter: it unexpectedly moved; therefore, it is cemí. Abduction is a mode of cognitive operation or inference employed in semiotics and logic discourse. Gell (1998:14) defines abduction as "a case of synthetic inference" and cites the definition given by J. Holland and his colleagues: "Abduction is induction in the service of explanation, in which a new empirical rule is created to render predictable what would otherwise be mysterious. . . . [It is] based on the logical fallacy of affirming the antecedent from the consequent ('if p then q; but q therefore p'). Given true premises, it yields conclusions that are not necessarily true." (See Gell [1998:15] for more examples of abduction.)

One can surmise that other such uncanny manifestations in nature would also lead to similar abductive reasoning, such as when a person encounters a rock in a river where there was none the day before, or where one discovers a stone that has an unexpected shape or unusual characteristics for that place and that moment. At this point, however, the cemí manifestation still is pretty much an occult, undefined entity. To unveil its identity—that is, its personhood—requires the specialized religious knowledge of a behique or cacique; the naboría apparently lacks the skills for interpreting the numinous manifestations, though not the ability to recognize its potential presence.

The next and crucial phase relates to the uncovering of the identity, the personhood, of a particular cemí:

> And the sorcerer or wizard runs at once to see the tree [about] which the other man has told him; he sits next to it and prepares a cohoba for it [the tree/root]. . . . Once the cohoba is made [that is, once the ceremony of inhaling hallucinogens is concluded, the shaman] tells it all his titles, as if he

were a great lord, and he asks it: "Tell me who you are, and what you are doing here, and what you wish from me, and why you have had me summoned. Tell me if you want to be cut down [i.e., cut and sculptured], or if you want to come with me, and how you want to be carried, for I will build you a house with land." Then the tree or zemi [cemí], *turned into an idol* or devil, answers him the manner in which he wants it to be done. And he [the shaman] cuts it and fashions it in the manner he has been ordered; he constructs a house with land [*sic*; from Spanish *heredad,* meaning a cultivated garden], and many times during the year he [the shaman] prepares cohoba for it [the idol] [Pané 1999:25–26; my emphasis].

Confirmation of the status and unveiling of the occult nature of this tree root (or stone) is done through the performance of a ceremony that involves the shaman's inhalation of a powerful hallucinogen known as cohoba. It is while in a state of altered consciousness that the cemí in the tree root reveals its true nature, body form, and personhood. The revelation consists of "vocalizing" his names, titles, and genealogical ancestry; its body (idol) form and accoutrements; the specific powers he or she can wield; and, finally, the proper ritual forms and times of veneration.

The cemí's specific body form, whether iconic or aniconic, is revealed to the shaman during a hallucinatory trance, after which the shaman, or more likely a skilled Taíno artisan, sculptures the tree (or rock, bone, etc.) into an idol, already invested with personhood. Henceforth, this particular cemí idol will be housed and revered; cohoba ceremonies will be performed at prescribed times throughout the year, and he or she will receive food offerings from the first harvests (Figure 11). In other words, the sculptured wood idol is thus invested with personhood, and it will henceforth be engaged in social relations with the human being to whom it is entrusted. It is more than likely that three of the four classes of cemí artifacts noted—three-pointed stones, stone collars, and elbow stones—were produced in the same way described by Pané. Once sculptured (unveiled, revealed) into an iconic or aniconic object, the cemí idol is to become linked with a particular human being who becomes its trustee or caretaker and who must ensure compliance with the ritual and ceremonial requirements owed to the cemí. Perhaps one ought to consider, too, that the cemí icon could also be conceived as the trustee or caretaker of its human "partner," although there are no concrete ethnohistoric references supporting this view.

It seems that cemí icons had their own kin relations; they had genealogy and descent lines. Admiral Columbus's son Hernando (or Ferdinand) wrote that "they give a name to this statue, I believe that is that of the father, grandfather or of both, because they have more than one and others more than ten [names] in memory, as I have said, of some of their ancestors" (Colón 1985:203, ch. 60). One legend told of Guarionex, a paramount cacique of Hispaniola, who was entrusted with Yucahú

Guamá Bagua Maorocoti, the highest-ranking of all cemí idols recorded by Pané. This Yucahú had a "mother" named Atabey Yermao Apito Zuimaco, who was the highest-ranking female of all the cemís recorded by Pané (1999:3–4, 30–31; see also Arrom 1975:19–26). A major, distinct class of cemí artifacts (see section 16) refers to those "that contain the bones of their [the Taínos] fathers and mothers and relatives and ancestors; they are made of stone or wood" (Pané 1999:21) and, as noted earlier, are also enclosed in full-bodied cotton idols, or held in calabash bowls or baskets. This class of cemí ancestor idols does have a direct-descent linkage with surviving human beings, as well as, I presume, with other deceased relatives that have also become cemíified. Thus, the cemí idols are in a web of kinship and descent that binds sets of idols among themselves and, in the case of ancestor idols, with living human beings. Therefore, two types of relationships existed: the sort of patron-client relationships between human trustee and the cemí idols, and those binding relationships grounded on kinship. The former type, for example, entails transactions where cemís, the "patrons," deliver favors or goods to their (non-kin) human "clients" in exchange for, for example, ritual food offerings. The latter type is based upon the mutual, reciprocal obligations defined by kinship, such as between ancestors and their descendants, husbands and wives, uncles and nieces, and so forth.

The bodily transformation of the cemí—for example, from amorphous stone to three-pointer—is not restricted to just portable objects. I have argued elsewhere (1998, 2005, 2006) that the petroglyphs carved on monoliths demarcating plazas or ball courts, or carved and painted on the walls of caves, on boulders in rivers, and in other localities in the landscape (rock art), should also be regarded as cemí icons or idols, whose form and personal identities were uncovered and captivated in the same way as described by Pané for the tree root (Figure 12).

These are all fixed in space and for all practical reasons unmovable (Figures 9, 12). Although it may be technically possible for the large batey monoliths to be moved by the natives to other localities, even across islands, I suspect these occasions, if they ever happened at all, would be extremely rare. Spatially fixed cemí icons can be found in open areas that are visible to the public, such as plazas, river boulders, and rock cliffs, and also in closed environments, such as caves. Like the large caney of the cacique, activities taking place in caves are not in view of the general public; both appear to be more intimate, restricted spaces. The immobility of the cemí icons, which are often monumental, declares that the scenario, the landscape—be it a cave, rock cliff, river pool, spring, or plaza—is itself a circumscribed or self-contained sacred domain that is inhabited, guarded, occupied by these cemí personages.

While portable icons could be arranged and rearranged according to the requirements of the ritual, the fixed monumental icons in plazas and in rivers, rock shelters, or caves could not. How such fixed monumental cemí icons differ from portable ones in terms of their meanings, ritual function, and especially in their relationship with human beings is a subject that deserves further study. For example, later, when the giving and theft of cemís is examined (section 12), it will become apparent that nonportable icons cannot be gifted or stolen without relinquishing space itself. Thus, such fixed icons do not circulate through a web; human beings come to them. The focus in this book, however, is on the portable cemí icons, leaving the discussion of monumental, nonportable cemí icons for another time (but see Oliver 2005).

7 Cemí Idols and Taínoan Idolatry

What is striking among the various Spanish chroniclers is that they all coincide in the diversity of forms that both iconic and aniconic objects imbued with cemí could assume and in the varied media from which they were made (Figures 13–15). Fray Ramón Pané (1990:26) makes it clear that the cemí objects/idols came in different shapes and were made of stone, wood, and other materials (e.g., human skulls, bones, and meat bits). Indeed, the chronicler Oviedo, with his characteristic and vulgar ethnocentrism, stated that the natives in Hispaniola and neighboring islands

> venerate the Devil [shaped] in diverse forms and idols . . . [and] as I have said [before], in many things they paint and carve, and sculpture it in wood and clay, and in other materials; they make a demon that they call cemí, so ugly and as scary as the [devil that] Catholics paint at the feet of Archangel Saint Michael or Apostle St. Bartholomew [referring to wood idols]; but [the cemí is] not tied with chains [as St. Bartholomew's devil]; instead [it is] venerated: sometimes [it is seen] seated in a tribunal [probably a duho or seat, but may also be a platform of some sort], other times [it is] standing on its feet, and [we see it] in different manners [poses] [Oviedo 1944 (1):251].

Oviedo further notes:

> I have never found in this generation [of people] such ancient [tradition] painted, sculptured, or carved relief and so highly revered [image] than the abominable and garish Devil—painted [depicted] in many and diverse ways, or sculptured, or de bulto [with volume], with many heads and tails, with deformities, and so scary, and with fierce fangs and dentures [teeth], and with large canine teeth, and disproportionate ears, with burning dragon eyes [a reference to shiny shell or gold inlays], and as a fierce serpent, and in many different forms, to such an extent that the least scary [-looking one] commands fear and admiration. And these [cemí images] are so sociable and commonplace for them that not only [do] they have a place to display them in the house but even more so in the benches where they seat (that they call duhos), meaning that he who sits [a human being] is not alone seating, but

he and his adversary [i.e., the cemí image carved on the man's seat; see Figure 18]. And in wood, and in clay, and in gold and in other things, as many as they can, they sculpture, and carve or paint, snarling and fierce face, as who he is [i.e., the devil] [Oviedo 1944 (1):229–231; see Figure 13].

Most of these idols were subjected to some form of veneration or another. What the Taíno did with these idols, in effect, constituted *idolatry*, but in the sense originally intended by this word, and as reinstated by Alfred Gell. I concur with Gell (1998:97–98) that "all idols, I think, are iconic—including the so-called aniconic ones—whether or not they look like some familiar object, such as a human body." I applaud Gell's reinstatement of the word "idolatry," which "has had a bad press since the rise to world domination of Christianity and Islam, which have both inherited the anti-imagistic strain of Biblical Judaism. Christianity, encumbered by its Greco-Roman inheritance, has had to struggle more actively with recrudescence of *de facto* 'pagan' idolatry, and has experienced cataclysmic episodes of iconoclasm" (Gell 1998:98). Islam has been more consistent and persistent in its iconoclastic posture, but Muslim (as opposed to Islam) art has not always been entirely devoid of religious iconic representations, including the Prophet Muhammad. For example, the Muslim art of Medieval Persia (today's Iran) has such depictions in various mosques and palaces (see Kennedy 2004; Menocal 2002; Ruthven 2000).

The idol's body form (which Gell calls the "index")—even when visualized by the native shaman via hallucinatory revelations given by the cemí spirit—is nevertheless based on Taínoan artistic conventions, on a "prototype" in the sense denoted by Gell (1998:25). Body form and decoration (the "looks") provide the visual cues for recognition by the believers of who a given cemí is. The formal, visual cues emerge from a mental vision of what this cemí looks like, and, conversely, that mental image is the prototype or blueprint that the body of the image or icon materially assumes.

As Gell (1998:25) noted in regard to prototypes, one can take the Goodmanian assertion that "any given icon, given appropriate [symbolic] conventions for reception [e.g., 'dog' means canine animal in English], could function as a representation of any arbitrarily selected depiction or 'referent'," a view that parallels the Sassurean postulate of the arbitrary nature of the sign in linguistic semiotic theory. Gell (1998:25), however, rejects Goodman's view and instead argues that any "iconic representation is based on the actual resemblance in form between depictions and the entities they depict or *are believed to depict*" (my emphasis). He goes on to assert that "a depiction of an imaginary thing (a god, for instance) resembles the picture that believers in that god have in their minds as to the god's appearance [e.g., the three-pointed form of the cemí in our case], which they have derived from other images of the same god, which this image resembles," and concludes by indicating that "what matters to me is only that people believe that . . .

the god, as agent, has caused the image (index), as patient, to assume a particular appearance"; that even in the case of highly schematic representations, "only very few features of the entity being depicted need to be present in order to motivate abductions [by the viewer] from the index [e.g., idol] as to the appearance (in a much more completely specified form) of the entity depicted. 'Recognition' on the basis of a few under-specified cues . . . is not the same as 'not specified at all,' or 'purely conventional'" (Gell 1998:25).

The sculptured cemí idol (Gell's "god"), the shape and form it shows, along with specific cues of style and decoration, is what the natives believe to be the form of that numinous entity, and is revealed by this entity to the shaman through the cohoba hallucination. What matters is that this entity, the cemí, is the agent (e.g., tree root, river rock, cave stalagmite) that causes the idol or icon to assume this particular form and not another. The four classes of stone cemís have distinct sculptural forms: three-pointed shapes, angular (elbow) stones, oval or ring shapes, and humanlike head shapes. Other forms can also be distinguished as distinct classes in the varied corpus of sculptural art, such as "canopied" cohoba idols, duhos, and vomiting spatulas, and made of such diverse materials as cotton, wood, bone, *guanín* (gold-copper alloy), and shell. Each idol's shape is recognized as an index of a given cemí prototype (Figure 13: compare sets a-c and d-f; Figures 2, 14). But the specific *identity* of any singular icon is another matter. Personal identity is no doubt based on subtle but discriminating visual cues recognized by the native believers, but that I, as an uninitiated westerner, may not be able to recognize.

8   Cemís and Personal Identities

Consider the three-pointed idols in discussing the issue of identity and representation. There are many singular icons that assume the elemental three-lobed form (Figures 2, 13: i, 14, 29: a, d, f), but that can be further distinguished on the basis of variations in detail (Walker 1993). Among such differentiating features are details like whether or not they are simple, undecorated icons; whether the carved facial features are human- or animal-like; whether the biomorphic faces are carved on the rising cone or on the lateral prominences; whether they are large, small, or miniature; and so on. Do these idols each represent and embody a different cemí spirit, or are these different versions or aspects of the same cemí "divinity" (e.g., compare Figure 2: m and 14)?

Improving on the typology first proposed by Jesse Walter Fewkes (1907:111–*passim*), Jeff Walker (1993:338–351) defined four basic formal types of three-pointed idols. Of course, such typology is based purely on morphology and does not pretend to reflect an emic classification. Still, questions arise: Are these four types slightly different versions of the *same* cemí prototype? Are they the form recognized by the natives to be the same numinous, unsubstantiated cemí spiritual force or entity? Or is each formal type a manifestation of four (or more) different cemí prototypes? These are unresolved questions. It may be that all three-pointed stones, despite small or large variation in detail, are based on the same prototype; they all embody the same cemí spiritual force that was manifested in nature, visually cued by its basic three-lobed form. The three-lobed form is the identifying criterion (Figures 2: k, 14). Alternatively, the different features and details of three-pointed idols are visual cues that refer to different prototypes—that is, each of these three-pointed icons embodies a different cemí spiritual entity. In this last case, one could reason that the details, rather than overall form, are what matter.

But there might be a third possibility: that the essence of a specific cemí manifestation is visually cued by the three-lobed form; that all three-lobed forms are shapes that signal the same numinous power source—in other words, a specific "sweet" (cemí) spirit. These forms may possibly extend not just to the three-pointed sculptured idols, but also to the perhaps sacred landscape: the three-pointed limestone hill (*mogotes*) clusters that are so prominent in the karst regions of Puerto Rico (Oliver 2005:fig. 7.3). The three-pointed form is totally different from, for example, stone heads, stone collars, duhos, the anthropomorphic cotton ancestor idols, or the actual skulls in baskets of cemíified ancestors, which definitively suggests that such formal categories are based on different prototypes (in Gell's sense). However, in all of these cemí categories, the additional details and features of decoration and style are what provide the visual cues for the recognition of particular, even singular identities.

Given Pané's biographic synopses of the twelve known cemís from Hispaniola, it is clear that each idol was regarded by the natives as a singular, distinct personage (but in the animistic, multinatural tradition), with a specific personhood that included the names, titles, and rank, and coming with a legend attached to that and only that idol (or index). Not all twelve idols were given descriptions of their body forms, but those that were have different iconic shapes, and hence refer to different prototypes. In short, all the evidence points to one conclusion: each singular cemí icon constitutes a distinct, differentiated personage, even when all are three-pointed stones, for example, or all are elbow stones. Recall that the small (some miniature-sized) three-lobed form with barely any decoration begins in pre-Arawak and continues through Saladoid times. Its lack of distinguishing features—it began as a faceless icon—may be indicative of a more generic identity, but by at least A.D. 900 these generic, more homogeneous icons are joined by a suite of large, highly decorated ones with stylistic features—with faces—that allow one to establish their identity. The latter diverged from a small generic or undifferentiated cemí entity to a suite of three-pointers that are stylistically differentiated. They evolved from "faceless things" to distinct "faced beings." In essence this is a process of "anthropomorphization" that makes sense when one realizes that the Taínoan locus of the soul of both the living (*guaíza*) and the dead (*opía*) is in the face of a living human or the head (i.e., skull) of a deceased person, as shall be discussed later (sections 16 and 17). That the "face" is selected for identity is also logical because it is not only where most details of identity are found but is also where emotions are expressed, making us human. The total lack of such details and emotions, as in the case of the head or "face" of a skull, is of course the absence of that which makes us alive: the guaíza. But even the skeletal face of a three-pointed stone or a Macorís-type head has an identity, because it is still fueled by a vital force or cemí, only it is not of the living but the nonliving being, animated by its opía (see also Oliver 2008b).

A legitimate question raised by Fowler (personal communication 2007) is whether the same "originary" cemí *spirit* might proliferate several identical versions of itself (revealed as icons) that then may lead their own lives but that in some way link back to the disembodied cemí (i.e., as spirit accessible via hallucinatory experiences). The ethnohistoric documents do not describe what or who the natives saw during hallucinatory trances, nor do they tell us whether the icons had a specific disembodied, spiritual counterpart in the dreamy hallucinatory world. I would speculate that the same cemí spirit can probably reveal itself (as narrated in the account by Pané) more than once. Perhaps this would explain why, for example, archaeologists can group three-pointers into several types, each of which depicts fairly similar, though not identical, kinds of personages (e.g., beaky birds, bats, high-ranked anthropomorphic beings, etc.). Still, the available evidence is insufficient to take this matter beyond an educated guess.

Once a cemí is objectified, personal identity is established by the fact that the biography/legend imputed to any singular icon can only be so constructed on its de facto relationship with human beings (on identities and archaeology, see Insoll 2006). In other words, in the hypothetical case of, say, two exactly duplicate cemí icons, there is the inescapable fact that through their life history each cemí idol will engage with different humans, be asked to act upon different peoples, beings, and things, under differing circumstances, and their actions would have varying effects, making of each a distinct person, a cemí being with a unique biography (on biography and value, see Graeber 2001:34–37). Legendary tales about each cemí, as told and retold by natives, are the result of specific interactions between a given cemí and the human beings with whom it has related to as agent in many transactions throughout the lifetime of the idol. Even after a cemí idol escapes from his human trustee forever, as was the case of Opiyelguobirán, the legend survived, although his biography ceased to accrue. As Pané (1999:29) noted, "they never saw him again, nor did they hear anything about him." Examples of these cemí legends cum biographies collected by Pané will be examined in the following sections.

All the twelve cemís, for which their legends are known, show certain behaviors that are humanlike. These idols are thus anthropomorphic; however, this doesn't necessarily mean that all are displayed in the physical shape or semblance of a human figure but more that they are imputed with a wide range of behaviors that are normally ascribed to ordinary biological humans, whether these look like living humans and animals (iconic) or not (aniconic). Animals, stones, tree roots, shells, bones, all can potentially be imbued with the animated force of cemí sweetness; their relations with humans are anthropomorphic. A distinction must be made between humanlike behavior and the capacity or power to act. The latter is where an icon has capabilities that are extraordinary, beyond that of mere mortals: it has "sweetness," it is imbued with cemí. The icon or idol is "animated" by cemí. But a human shaman or cacique can also transcend the ordinary and be capable of extraordinary feats, but only through the relations he or she establishes with the cemí and the execution of appropriate rituals, such as the cohoba ceremony. Indeed, the inhalation of the hallucinogen is what changes the ordinary human nature of this human into what the Lokono called *semičiči* (shaman, medicine man), but for which the Taíno provided a lexical innovation: behique.

As Gell (1998:122–124) noted, the attribution of animism (and anthropomorphism) on a wood or stone idol is not the same as attributing it with biological life in order to define "animacy" in terms of volition, intentionality, or sensorial capabilities. In this regard it is worth paraphrasing Alfred Gell (1998:123) in extenso.

He wonders about how "representational indexes" (i.e., idols) can be apprehended as "social others, as repositories of agency and sensibility," which to modern westerners has the appearance of irrational beliefs and practices. Gell points out that it is irrational, if not downright strange, to a westerner that believers speak to, dress and bathe, or feed an idol rather than a living and breathing human being. Just as aware of its strangeness and irrationally as are westerners are those who engage in such behavior—the believers. But in contrast, notes Gell, the latter also hold "that the cult of the idol is religiously efficacious, and will result in benefits for themselves and the masters they serve in their capacity as priests" or shamans (Gell 1998:123). Gell goes on to say that it is not a case where believers and shamans cannot distinguish between "stocks and stones," but rather that in certain contexts these objects are thought to have "unusual, occult properties of which the religiously uninstructed would remain ignorant, and the instructed but skeptical, wrong-headedly incredulous." The attribution of "intentional psychology" or of volition to religious idols survives and prospers precisely because it is "odd and counter-intuitive" (Gell 1998:123). For Gell, the key issue to be considered is the "*unusual occult capacities that the idol possesses according to believers*" (Gell 1998:123, my emphasis). Furthermore,

> What we need to know is how idol-worshipers square the circle between "what they know"—and what we know they know—and what they know about persons and their capacities as intentional agents. They cannot confuse the two, but it remains possible that [human] persons have attributes which can also be possessed by stocks and stones without prejudice to their categorical difference from [human] persons. That is to say, "social agents" can be drawn from categories as different as chalk and cheese . . . because "social agency" is not defined in terms of "basic" biological attributes (such as inanimate thing vs. incarnate person) but is relational—it does not matter, in ascribing "social agent" status, what a thing (or a person) "is" in itself; what matters is where it stands in a network of social relations. All that may be necessary for stocks and stones to be "social agents" in the sense we require, is that there should be actual human/persons "in the neighborhood" of these inert objects, not that they should be biologically human persons themselves [Gell 1998:123].

To follow up on Gell's advice, I will next consider what occult capacities these cemí idols possessed as intentional agents, according to Taínoan believers—that is, from an emic perspective—and "where [they stand] in a network of social relations."

PART III

The Social Relations and Circulation of Cemí Idols and Human Beings

9 The Power and Potency of the Cemís

The cemí artifacts are *social* agents of causality as much as living human beings are. Each cemí icon has specific, definable powers that were either highly beneficial or extremely dangerous for human society. Some examples follow: a cemí icon named Baibrama had the power to cause illness to human beings (Pané 1990:27). Another, a stone idol named Guabancex, had the power to order and unleash violent wind- and rainstorms. This feminine stone cemí idol had two assistants, also made of stone. One was named Coatriquie, who, on Guabancex's orders, "command[ed] all the other cemís from that province to assist in causing a great deal of wind and rain," while the other, Guataubá, gathered all the rainfall "and [let] it run to ravage the country" (Pané 1990:29). Other cemí idols had benign powers, such as the unnamed but explicitly described by Pané as "three-pointed stone" cemís that cause yuca (*Manihot esculenta*) to grow (Pané 1990:26).

Pané (1974:34–35, 43), writing on the different kinds of cemís, noted that some made of stone or wood "contained the bones of his father, and his mother, and relatives"; some others "could speak"; and others could "make the things to eat grow, others that make rain, others that make winds . . . others that are the best for aiding pregnant women give birth" (see also Colón 1985:202–205). One also learns of other kinds of powers possessed by cemís from what caciques, shamans, and others wished to obtain from them:

> [The caciques kept] these diabolical images in their houses [caneyes], in selected dark places and locations that were reserved for prayer. There they entered to pray and ask for what they wished: be it water for their fields and cultivated gardens, for a good harvest, or for victory against their enemies; in sum, in there was the old Indian who answered [what the cemí told him] to his taste [or liking] . . . and he would enter and speak with it, and since he [the shaman] was an ancient astrologer [diviner], he would tell them [the other people present] what day it would rain and other things . . . and when war should be carried or delayed, and without [consultations with] the presence of the Devil [cemí idol], they neither embarked nor did anything that was of importance [Oviedo 1944 (1):251–252].

If one reads carefully the legends (all are quite fragmentary) attached to each of these twelve cemí idols recorded by Pané, several important characteristics of personal identity and personhood emerge. The first is that most, though not all, of these cemí icons are differentiated according to gender principles (masculine, feminine, asexual). Second, each idol has a set of personal names or titles that are indicative of status and rank differences between the known cemís—the more names and titles, the higher the status. Third, they had genealogical ties to other cemí entities or to living human descendants. Fourth, all had specific capabilities and powers to alter or cause future events, some of which were related to weather control. The power of cemís is thus not a generalized or abstract force, but one that had specific immediacy among the living and in nature. Fifth, all cemí idols were entrusted to a living human being. Sixth, in most instances, Pané records that a given cemí idol would circulate through successive human trustees. This was the case of the cemí Corocote, who was first in cacique Guamarete's house, then passed on to another unnamed cacique, and finally ended up with cacique Guatabanex of the Jaraguá region in Hispaniola (Pané 1999:28). Seventh, and finally, in several of the recorded legends, the cemí had the capacity to escape from or abandon its human trustee. This comes very close to free will (see Pink 2004) or volition, a capacity for autonomous decision making and action that is independent of its human trustees. Human "ownership" was not guaranteed; hence, my frequent use of the word "trustee" rather than "owner." This capacity to flee and abandon plays a key role in the making or breaking of caciques. Those leaders who were perceived to be inept, who were unable to control or negotiate the cemís entrusted to them, could potentially be "abandoned" by their cemí idol, temporarily or forever, as happened in the legend of cemí Opiyelguobirán. Thus, one might say that the human and his or her idol are companions of sorts, but I suspect it is a tense, sometimes dangerous relationship, because these idols can do as much good as evil, bringing about gentle, fertilizing rain or destructive floods.

In analogy to their human counterparts, cemí idols were also hierarchically structured; they were ranked and stratified (see Stevens Arroyo 1988:ch. 12, table 7). Cemí Guabancex, as noted earlier, was a high-ranked feminine personage that had two subordinated or auxiliary cemís, named Coatriquie and Guataubá (Pané 1999:29). One of these, Coatriquie, was ordered to "call all other cemís" in the province, meaning that he or she was in charge of putting into effect Guabancex's orders. The interaction between these cemís parallels the human social hierarchical order whereby the cacique is the one who commands; the nitaíno, or elite advisors, are in charge of putting the orders in motion; while the naboría, or commoners, are those who actually implement or execute them. The Guabancex stone idol was "in a country of a great cacique, one of the principal caciques, whose name was Aumatex." It was a living cacique, Aumatex, who was entrusted with the Guabancex cemí idol. Hence, a high-ranked and potent cemí is engaged in social relationships with, most specifically, a human person of similar rank to whom it was entrusted. For example, Guarionex was mentioned earlier (in section 6) as being an important cacique of Hispaniola who was entrusted with Yucahú Guamá Bagua Maorocoti, the highest-ranking of all masculine cemí idols recorded by Pané (1999:3–4, 30–31).

As noted, the cemí idol also had the power to run away from its trustee on its own accord. Two slightly different examples of this will suffice: "The cemí Opiyelguobirán has four feet, like a dog, they say, and is made of wood, and often at night he leaves the house and goes to the jungle. They went to look for him there, and they brought him home, they would tie him with a rope, but he would return to the jungle. And they tell that when the Christians arrived on the island of Hispaniola the cemí escaped and went to a lagoon, but they never saw him again, nor did they hear anything about him" (Pané 1999:29).

In the second example, rather than the idol running away for good from his trustee, it escapes from a conflagration: "They say that when they built the house of Guamarete, who was a preeminent man, they placed the cemí that he kept on top of his house; this cemí was called Corocote. And once when they [the natives] were at war among themselves, Guamarete's enemies burned the house in which the aforementioned cemí Corocote was located. They say he got up and walked the distance of a crossbow shot away from that place, next to some water" (Pané 1999:28). From the moment the shaman in hallucinatory trance exposes who the cemí is and what he or she looks like, it is clear that this entity is already invested with specific powers. Somehow, I do not think the sacred power of the cemí idol will decrease or increase over its lifetime. The "sweetness" force—cemí—is imbued in this idol from its inception. As well, from the start, the rank of the cemí idol is revealed, but it may in time acquire new titles or names as its reputation grows, just as caciques were bestowed titles as their reputation grew (see Oliver 2000:205). I suggest that over the lifetime of the cemí idol, his or her prestige and reputation will grow with the steady accumulation of acts and deeds that can only come with time—the stuff out of which legends and "thick" or long and sedimented biographies are made. Antique, senior cemí idols will be far more reputable, coveted, and valued than newly minted ones (Oliver 2005). Highly prestigious cemí idols cannot be newly sculptured on demand and at the whim of ambitious politicians (caciques, nitaínos); even ordinary people will be aware that such a new icon, even if it were of a high rank and powerful, has yet to demonstrate how effective it is and, likewise, that the cacique has the wherewithal to control and extract benefits from the cemí idol that will lead to a good government. The human trustee's reputation, seniority, and knowledge must be up to the task; the trustee must be able to show people that he or she can control, manipulate, negotiate, and even cajole the cemís to yield and direct their powers to the trustee's (and society's) advantage: a fruitful marriage, victory in war, a great harvest, and so on. The effectiveness of the icon is thus tied to that of the human trustee. A corollary implication is that a cemí icon does not automatically increase prestige throughout its lifetime; that would depend on its relationship with its human trustee and what the latter can accomplish in concert with the given cemí icon.

A newly minted cemí idol, on the other hand, has yet to accrue a biography or legend that enhances the idol's prestige and reputation. A newly minted, high-ranked cemí idol in the hands of a neophyte cacique can potentially be doubly worrisome in the eyes of the community. The heir who has recently come into chiefly office and who will inherit at least some of the cemí idols from the deceased cacique will find him- or herself having to demonstrate whether, as a trustee, he or she will have the ritual knowledge and capabilities to *efficiently* engage with a contingent of powerful cemí idols of different ranks and different accrued reputations. One can only imagine how stressful the death of powerful caciques would be for society.

10 The Display of Cemís
Personal vs. Communal Ownership, Private vs. Public Function

Earlier I described the aniconic cemís (the stones wrapped in a satchel) that shamans extract from patients to capture an illness to be kept by the patient afterward. These and other small cemí objects like this were most likely for personal and private use and devotion, unlike some of the larger cemí idols entrusted to the caciques, and possibly to the nitaíno elite as well. By virtue of their relationship with elite members of society, the sphere of action of the cemí idols, their power, was one that affected the well-being of a polity and of the population at large. These cemí idols have to do with the public affairs of government and not as much with the well-being of any given member of society. This does not preclude the fact that caciques and nitaínos also had these kinds of personal, private, "talismanic," cemí-imbued objects. Like other colleagues, I suspect that many, if not all, of the small (as small as 3 cm) three-pointers (Figures 2: i, k; 29: a) are of this private or personal kind, and that their effects were accordingly limited to one person or perhaps members of a family (Walker 1993:143). To these one might add a wide range of necklace pendants and danglers depicting cemí icons (Figures 13: a-f, h, i; 29: b, d, e).

Following Jeff Walker (1993:145), a distinction must be maintained "between "'communal' (group) ownership and 'personal' (individual) *ownership*," on the one hand, and "'public' (visible to the people) and 'private' (visible to the individual) *use*," on the other (emphasis in the original). The focus in this book is on those cemí icons that were engaged by caciques and political leaders, those whose actions affected the affairs of the state, of the population at large. To use Walker's terms, these are cemí idols meant for public use, *not* to be confused with "used or seen by the public" (for public display). I agree with Walker that the *larger* cemí icons were probably personally "owned" by the cacique and nitaínos, and that their function was public (i.e., personal-public objects). Certainly the monumental cemí petroglyphs carved on the monoliths demarcating plazas (bateyes) were for public use and display, visible to all (Oliver 1998, 2005). I would clarify, though, that the portable objects (perhaps also the monumental cemí petroglyphs; Figures 9, 12) were not owned but rather *entrusted* to the cacique, not because I argue for a community-wide ownership but because from the native's animistic perspective these cemí icons were not inherently or always under the absolute control of the cacique: as animated beings, as persons, cemís could abandon, and did run away from, the cacique. In that sense, no one can own (short of slavery), as property, such cemí personages, just as a cacique did not own the naboría. On the other hand, runaway cemís could be recovered, and others that were stolen could be induced to perform for their human trustee, as there are descriptions in Pané (1999) of these being tied up and placed inside a sack—that is, immobilized (Oliver 2008b:183). Thus the cemí's free will, like the human's, could be curtailed.

Walker (1993:140–147) suggests that the larger, more voluminous icons were also meant for public display, most particularly the large stone collars and elbow stones (Figures 3, 19–23), but also the larger three-pointed stones, some of which were likely to be strapped or tied onto the outer panel of stone collars (see Figure 22: b). Given the meaning of the word *cemí* as "sweetness," as that which is imbued with numinous potency (unknown to Walker at the time), I am reasonably satisfied that this term applies to stone collars and elbow stones as much as it does to the miniature three-pointers. However, like Walker, I strongly suspect that the larger, highly decorated cemís (encompassing the four classes noted) were intended for use in affairs pertaining to the public, the community, and the polity ("public use" and on marked occasions for "display," too).

It is very likely that stone collars, elbow stones, stone heads, three-pointed stones, duhos, wooden idols of various kinds, and the like were also publicly displayed at particular times during the year, as would all the regalia of the caciques and nitaínos, which included the guaíza pectoral, necklace pendant, and guanín plaque with cemí iconography (Oliver 2000; see Figure 27). But more frequently the ceremonies and rituals where these cemí icons were used, invoked, consulted, and negotiated with were those taking place in the privacy of the chief's caney; they were visible to a select group, as we shall see shortly. This does not mean that the community at large did not envision or know what generally went on inside the caney, but they were not ocular witnesses to or active participants in these ceremonial rites.

Walker (1993:147–149) proposed: "If there were many [cemí artifacts available] they were probably personal objects; if they were few, they were probably public objects." Using stone collars as a sample, Walker devised a simple test: He assumed that Hispaniola had four or five paramount chiefs, as Spanish chroniclers suggested, and that the total number of chiefs per generation remained constant in a seven-hundred-year period. Walker further assumed that generations changed every twenty years at a minimum or every fifty years at a maximum, which would translate into a total of 35 (or 14) generations (in seven hundred years) of paramount chiefs. The result would be that a total of between 56 and 140 stone collars "would need to have been made in Hispaniola over the estimated period [between A.D. 800 and A.D. 1500] for them to have been personally owned items by the principal caciques of the island" (Walker 1993:148). If the actual number of stone collars were within the expected estimated range, then it would reflect that these were personally "owned" and used by the principal caciques (one per cacique, per generation), but "many fewer collars in the archaeological record could mean that they were carefully curated, and therefore public property" (Walker 1993:148).

Walker's test was meant to be just a rough indicator. He assumes that only paramount chiefs would have a stone collar and that they would possess only one through their lifetime. He also assumes that rather than the heir inheriting the stone collar as an heirloom from the deceased cacique, a new one would be carved to, for example, commemorate accession to the office. Hispaniola did appear to have four or five chiefs who could be labeled "paramount" (see Wilson 1990), but it is clear that stone collars were never produced, used, or even traded outside the southeastern region of Caiçimú-Higüey; hence, all stone collars in that chiefdom were destined for the one (presumed) paramount chief. The other four or so paramount caciques should not have entered into Walker's calculations. Furthermore, it is still an unresolved matter whether Puerto Rico ever had paramount chiefs as did Hispaniola or whether their cacicazgos were in essence peer polities (also called cacicazgos by the Spaniards). A final point is that over the seven hundred years, the native political systems in both islands had to have changed to some extent or another, even cycled from simple to complex and back to simple as suggested by Timothy Pauketat (1994) and David Anderson (1994) for chiefdoms in the southeastern and midwestern United States.

Rather than arguing as Walker does for personal-public versus communal-public ownership, I suggest that what the fewer than expected samples (relative to numbers of chiefs) would mean is that these lithic collars were curated and maintained in circulation via inheritance, as I will argue later. Walker observed that up to 1993 there were only 182 examples of stone collars, of which between 90 and 106 were complete and provenanced to 22 sites or district areas in Puerto Rico (1993:147, table 3.1). As a result of Sued Badillo's (2001a:72) study, the total has since increased to 465, of which 275 are complete specimens and coming from some 52 sites or district areas. The increase to double the number might mean that these stone collars were not just in the hands of two or three paramount chiefs (if there were ever any such paramount chiefs), but also in those of local or subordinated chiefs in Puerto Rico.

If one looks exclusively at the rates of new stone collar production per year, per generation, and disregards for whom the stone collars were being manufactured, the results ought to give a rough estimate of just how frequently new ones were produced. Table 1 shows that in a seven-hundred-year period, the average production of stone collars ranges between 0.15/yr and 0.26/yr, using Walker's data, or between 0.39/yr and 0.68/yr, using Sued Badillo's data. Both data sets do suggest a low yearly average rate of production. If these data are recalculated in terms of the

Table 1. Estimated Average Production of Stone Collars in Puerto Rico (A.D. 800–1500)

Total Lithic Rings Produced in a 700-yr period	Number of lithic rings produced per year	Number of lithic rings produced per generation (25-yr)*	Number of lithic rings produced per generation (45-yr)**	References
182 (includes fragments)	0.26	6.5	11.7	Walker 1993
102 (excludes fragments)	0.15	3.6	6.5	Walker 1993
475 (includes fragments)	0.68	17.0	30.4	Sued Badillo 2001a
275 (excludes fragments)	0.39	9.8	17.6	Sued Badillo 2001a

*Assumes 25 years for each new generation; in 700 years there are a total of 28 generations.
** Assumes 45 years for each new generation; in 700 years there are a total of 15.6 generations.

number of new stone collars produced per generation, the figures will, of course, increase. Assuming a shorter, twenty-five-year span for a generation turnover, and using the more recent data from Sued Badillo, between 10 and 17 stone collars were produced per generation. Assuming a larger (more unlikely), forty-five-year generation turnover, the average production would be between 17 and 30 per generation. Thus, yearly production rates are low, but in terms of the total new stone collars per generation, the figures are higher. If we assume that *only one* new collar was commissioned for every newly installed cacique (i.e., a new generation), then Sued Badillo's figures (Table 1) suggest that Puerto Rico had between 10 and 17 caciques (assuming a 25-yr/generation) or between 18 and 30 caciques (assuming a 45-yr/generation). The latter figure seems to be somewhat closer to the total number of important caciques known for Puerto Rico during the Spanish contact period (Alegría 1979; Sued Badillo 1985, 1979).

Clearly, the conclusions that can be derived from Table 1 are predicated on far too many shaky assumptions. The most important is the unrealistic assumption of political stability over seven centuries—that is, an unchanging number of successions of caciques per generation—followed by the equally untestable assumption that a new stone collar is to be commissioned every time a new cacique inherits the office. Still, the rates of production are generally small compared to many other kinds of (nonperishable) objects that could qualify as potent or powerful political-religious artifacts. However one looks at the data, the average rate of production per annum can only be described as low. As such, it does make sense to claim that on the average, few individuals would come into possession or control of stone collars. Given these low yearly rates, it is quite possible that the older, existing stone collars would be curated and thus remain in circulation (e.g., kept in the family). This challenges the assumption that in every generation the installment of a new chief would necessarily require the commission of one new lithic ring; chiefs may even have had an incentive to keep the lithic ring that belonged to his or her ancestor chief rather than to commission a new one, as the old stone collar would already have an established reputation. Finally, as Samuel Wilson (personal communication 2007) observed, "Broken fragments may still have power, value, prestige and history," which raises further questions about the issue of stone collar production and replacement rates. And, of course, the same could be said for fragments of other cemí icons, such as three-pointed stones.

For the larger and highly decorated three-pointed idols, the number is higher than stone collars, but certainly these are not run-of-the-mill. Admiral Columbus (Colón 1985:204) did note that in Hispaniola "the majority of the caciques had three [separate] stones to which they and their people had great devotion." At least one of the stones "that is good to cultivate cereals and legumes that they planted" is known to have included the three-lobed form (see Arrom 1975).

The encomienda census led by Alfonso de Alburquerque in Hispaniola in 1514 recorded 401 caciques, with this figure representing only a fraction of what the cacique population would have been in 1492 (Moya Pons 1987: 110). Like Hispaniola, Puerto Rico at the time of Spanish contact also had many local caciques, which would account for the larger number of known archaeological three-pointed stone specimens. The much greater number of caciques in Hispaniola in 1514 relative to the number of three-pointed stones, stone collars, and elbow stones suggests that only high-ranked caciques would have them. However, the 1514 statistics for Hispaniola have to be modified to exclude all regions outside the distribution of stone collars and large three-pointers—that is, it should consider only the southeastern region from Santo Domingo to Caiçimú. For Higüey (Caiçimú) the total population was 1,189, of which there were 5 caciques and 2 nitaínos (Moya Pons 1987: 110). Santo Domingo, with a total of 77 caciques out of 7,171 souls, is excluded since it is quite clear that many of the assigned Indians were brought from far away to serve in the capital and work in the Royal Hacienda. The smaller number of chiefs in Higüey seems to correlate with the low numbers of large stone collars recovered in this region. Unfortunately, I do not have figures for the total number of stone collars or of large three-pointed stones thus far known for the Dominican Republic, but all of my colleagues insist they are few in number compared to those found in Puerto Rico.

In the end, lacking statistics, more precise dates, and contextual data (especially provenience) for these objects makes this exercise speculative. What is important, though, is that answers to the questions raised will go a long way in understanding the overall value and importance that these objects had and tell us about how many and how frequently they were in circulation.

The issues of personal versus public use, and, especially, ownership among the Taíno, are all the more relevant when one examines the geographic distribution of the cemí icons in question. What can be given and what cannot—or as Annette Weiner (1985, 1992) and Maurice Godelier (1999; cf. Mauss 1990; Mosko 2000) put it, "giving for keeping" and "keeping for giving"—revolves around the question of who controls the destiny and circulation, and thus, the social relationships, of these objects, keeping also in mind that the aborigines believed that these idols were personages capable of independent motility: they could run away to "other beings" and to other places. The questions of rarity versus abundance, inalienability and alienability, and thus a measure of perceived value, also inhere on resolving questions about how many and how often these things were available for circulation and for inheritance. Because these iconic objects do seem to be fairly rare within an area of maximum geographic distribution, even in Puerto Rico, I suspect that the stone collars and other such prestigious cemís would be curated and passed on, even when new ones were probably entering the arsenal of powerful cemí idols that caciques kept in their caneyes. Walker did not consider that cemís accrued prestige and reputation over time while they changed hands from trustee to trustee. That alone provides a strong incentive to curate cemís rather than to retire them from circulation (e.g., burial, ritual killing), and thus be frequently replacing them with newly minted ones.

11 Face-to-Face Interactions
Cemís, Idols, and the Native Political Elite

When a cacique had to make strategic decisions about policies that affected governance, he usually convened a council meeting in the privacy of the caney attended by a retinue of his closest advisers, probably those of nitaíno status and, on important occasions, by subordinated or allied caciques. He then initiated the cohoba ceremony, invoking the appropriate cemí, or contingent of cemís, in order to consult and divine what they had in store for the future should this or that policy be implemented (Figure 15). Bishop Las Casas narrated one such council gathering conducted behind closed doors, in the caney of the cacique. Las Casas does not tell us when such an event took place (perhaps 1502–1520s). He spoke from personal experience but also as a recollection elicited much later when he was back in Spain. However, his experience is a generalization I am willing to accept as applicable to Hispaniola and Puerto Rico:

> They had the custom of convening cabildos [council meetings] to determine arduous things, such as mobilizing for war or other things that they thought important for performing their cohoba ceremony. I saw them sometimes celebrate their cohoba . . . the first to start was the Señor [cacique], and while he was doing it the rest remained quiet. Having done his cohoba (which is inhaling through the nostrils those powders [Figure 7], as it was said before, and were absorbed while seated on low and well-carved benches they called duhos . . . [Figures 15, 18]) he remained for a while with his head turned sideward and with his arms resting on the knees. Then he raised his face to the sky, speaking his truthful words, which must have been their prayers to the true God, or the one they had for god. All responded almost like when we say "amen," and this they did with great pomp of voices or sound. Then they thanked him, and said flatteries to captivate his benevolence, and begged him to tell them what he had seen [while in his trance]. He would give an account of his vision, telling them that the Cemí spoke to him and certified the good or adverse times [to come], or that they would have children or that they would die, or that they would have conflict or war with their neighbors [Las Casas 1929 (3):546; my translation].

Such hallucinatory encounters entailed praying to (in the Latin sense of *prex precis*: "to obtain by entreaty"), perhaps also negotiating with, the cemí so as to extract a favorable outcome and to divine what the future had in store and therefore find out if or when it would be wise to implement a proposed action or policy. The cacique would then tell the nitaíno advisers of his visions and interaction with the cemí, and then, I assume, it would be roundly discussed and debated by the council members. The agenda set for this kind of cohoba ceremony, as gleaned from Las Casas's quote, is to deal with matters that concern the polity's welfare and security rather than any one individual's needs. The order of access is very clear: the cacique (not the behique, which is not mentioned) has the prerogative to communicate directly with the cemí; the rest of the assembled have to wait for the results of the exchange.

In this instance, the cemí invoked may be in fact the idol or set of idols (Figures 11, 15, 16) present in the cohoba ceremony—which minimally included the duhos (Figure 18) on which the cacique and elite sat, the "canopied" wooden idol holding the tray or platter with the hallucinogen (see Figures 11: a, c; 15: a), and the decorated bifurcated tubes for snuffing the drug (Figure 7)—and who articulated with a central idol, as Columbus noted (Colón 1985:203). These may also be the potent idols that in concert summoned the numinous presence of an unsubstantiated cemí force, apprehended by the cacique through an altered state of consciousness induced by the cohoba drug. For instance, Oviedo (1994 [1]:229–231) explicitly tells us how the cacique seated in a duho is not alone, but rather that it is he and his cemí *"adversario"* (opponent), which Oviedo equated with the devil of Christianity. This may not be a prejudiced misconception by Oviedo. The cemí of the duho could in fact be the cacique's true opponent, since many of the cemís described by Pané do have a "dark side," with powers that are dangerous and capable of untold calamities if not properly controlled by the cacique. When a cacique literally sits on his adversarial companion, he is sending a strong visual signal of his ability, power, and knowledge to control the duho cemí (Oliver 2008b:172–173, 180–181).

Admiral Columbus noted that the Taíno chiefs "had a house for each one, separated from the town, where there is nothing but some of the relief-carved wooden images that they call cemís." Such houses (caneys) were, in effect, temples dedicated to service the cemís, for ceremony and prayer (*"no se trabaja para más efecto que para el servicio de los cemíes, con cierta ceremonia y oración que ellos hacen allí, como nosotros en la iglesia"* ["all the work is done for no other effect (purpose) than to serve the cemís, with certain ceremony and prayer, as (we) do in church"]). He further noted that "they venerate one [cemí] more than the others and I have seen them venerate more and be more reverent to the one than the others" (Colón 1985:203, ch. 62), probably reflecting the pecking order of the cemís on the basis of their seniority, genealogic descent, and reputation accrued through time, as argued earlier (e.g., perhaps icons like those in Figures 11: b, 16, 17).

Thus it is clear that while the cacique engaged the numinous, unsubstantiated cemí *spirit*, he was also surrounded by iconic images and sculptured idols that were themselves cemí. The duho, the canopied cohoba idol, and even the Y-shaped inhaling tubes (Colón 1985:203) were often decorated with carved images of cemís (Figure 7). Also included might be other decorated paraphernalia used in preparation for the hallucinogenic trance, such as vomiting spatulas and effigy pestles to grind cohoba seeds. But one or a few of those legendary, senior idols were the central figures of devotion, as Columbus noted. The cacique and councilors were thus not alone in invoking the cemí as spirit and as idol. The cacique was interacting with a complex network of cemí icons during such divinatory encounters.

The impact that such cemí idols had in the running of earthly political power and on the ordinary folks did not escape Columbus's attention. He told, secondhand, a famous story about a group of Spaniards who, despite the natives' wariness, entered a caney with cemís. As the cohoba ceremony progressed, the Spaniards heard the idol "shout and speak" in the Taíno language, which they could not understand. One of the idols described conforms to the archaeologically known "canopied" idols (Figures 11: a, c; 15: a), but there also was a central idol that spoke. The Spaniards told Columbus that the whole event was a hoax—indeed a lie—carried out by the cacique to subjugate the population to his will. The account goes as follows:

> And it so happened that on one occasion that they were weary of us, the Christians entered with them [the natives] into the said house and suddenly the cemí shouted loudly and spoke in their language. From this it was discovered that it was made with artifice, because it [the idol] being hollow, had fitted, in the lower part, a hollow cane or trumpet that extended [back] into the dark side of the house, covered with foliage, where there was a person that spoke what the cacique wished him to be said, as much as it can be [intelligibly] spoken though a trumpet. As a result, our people, suspecting what it could be, kicked with their feet the cemí, and found it to be as I have said. Realizing that we [the Spaniards] had discovered that [trick], the cacique begged them, with great insistence, not to tell anything to his vassal Indians, nor to others, because with this trick he held them all in obedience. Because of this we can say that there is a shade of idolatry, at least among those who do not know the secret and deception by their caciques, because they believe the cemí is the one that speaks and they all are, in general, so deceived. *Only the cacique knows and conceals such false credulity that he uses to extract from the people all the tributes he wants* [Colón 1985:203–204; my emphasis].

The above cohoba ceremony presents a somewhat different scenario than the council meeting cohoba discussed earlier. In this instance, it is the cemí idol who speaks to an apparently larger audience, Spanish intruders included. The cacique's assistant, perhaps a behique or shaman, verbally relays through the *fotuto* (a Taíno word for trumpet) hidden in the cemí idol whatever transpired during the hallucinogenic visions and consultations that the cacique had with the cemí spirits. Of course, at a simplistic level this is how the political-religious elite held sway over their subjects, as Columbus noted. But at another level, the "trickery" is unlikely to have been perceived as a deception or hoax in a sort of Marxist-Machiavellian (ideological) plot by the cacique to extract tribute from the "ignorant" assembly (on magic tricks, see section 20 E).

I suspect that speaking through the hollow cane transformed ordinary speech into sacred speech: it communicated what was revealed to the cacique and his assistant (in our western view, the actual speaker) during hallucinatory ecstasy. I would be surprised if the natives assembled in this house were not well aware of the hidden fotuto or that a human being was actually speaking through it. If indeed we are dealing with dividuality, partibility, and with extended persons (cf. Gell 1998), both the cemí idol and the speaker are dialogic persons capable of vitality and, not surprisingly, of speech. The Spanish, not understanding what was said through the trumpet, had missed what probably was a speech pattern, a cadence, distorted through the fotuto that in itself was of divine origin. The inner workings of the cemí (its hollowness, the trumpet) and the hidden men are supposed to be secrets, knowable only to the initiated, for those in authority. It is even possible that the cacique, and perhaps also the speaker, were still under the influence of the hallucinogen. That such knowledge was privileged is, of course, a key source of chiefly power. The Spanish were well aware of this, even though the motivations of trickery attributed to the elite and the presumed stupidity of the noninitiated masses are in all probability wrong. The knowledge coming from the visions, and other sensorial experiences, under the hallucinogenic drug are real enough to the cacique and are what believers need to confirm the presence and animacy, via verbal instructions, of the cemí (as idols and as a spiritual force), and it is in that context that the cacique begged the Spaniards not to betray the secrets of the ritual. Ignorance of the natives' multinatural perspective and partibility of persons precluded any reasonable interpretation of this event by sixteenth-century Spaniards.

Bishop Las Casas (1929 [3]:545–546) reported on other cohoba ceremonies that were public in the sense of being more inclusive. He contrasts the two closed-quarter ceremonies described above with those where "all of the principal people of the town gathered, by permission of the behiques, or priests, or by the señores, to conduct this sacrifice that they called cohoba; it was a pleasure to watch them." Unfortunately, other than inhaling the cohoba, there are no descriptions as to what roles, if any, the cemí idols may have played in such public, festive occasions. I suspect that some cemís may have been taken out of the caney or the cave and publicly paraded.

12 Hanging On to and Losing the Power of the Cemí Idols

I would suggest that it is in the ritual context of cohoba divination and ecstasy that a cacique's efficacy as a leader was tested. He had to demonstrate dexterity in controlling, negotiating, extracting, and interpreting the will of all the cemís entrusted to him. As noted earlier, there is solid evidence that even powerful, reputable caciques, during times of crises, could and would lose control of their cemís. The legend from Hispaniola featuring Opiyelguobirán (a four-legged, doglike idol) tells of his *repeated* escapes from a cacique, of the struggles by the latter to keep it in the caney, to the point of needing to tie up the idol with a rope (Pané 1999:28–29). This legend also gives us the specific reason of why Opiyelguobirán finally ran away never to return: the cemí's permanent abandonment was linked to the arrival of the Spanish. In the legend, blame lies squarely on the Spanish conquistadors; the silent implication is that the cacique had lost control of Opiyelguobirán because of his inability to cope with the devastating effects of the Spanish conquest. The cacique's strategies and policies on countering the Spanish failed because he failed to extract support from the cemí: the idol abandoned him. The cacique was powerless to control the unraveling events due to his repeated failings in predicting what was to come. Not even tying up Opiyelguobirán prevented his permanent departure.

The abandonment of any cemí idol would undoubtedly imply a loss of face and prestige for the cacique, and would have the potential to create opportunities among his political rivals to assume, or at least contest, his leadership. For living caciques to govern effectively, they had to maintain control of an appropriately powerful contingent of cemí icons, those with tested reputations and with legendary status. This also means that legendary, powerful cemí idols *could not* be ordered upon demand by a cacique in order to buttress or aggrandize his reputation and power. The implication of theft for the spatial distribution of cemí icons is obvious: there are bound to be cemí idols that did not originate in the settlement, region, and perhaps not even from the same cacicazgo where they were first created.

To effectively rule, caciques had to be locked onto the powerful cemí idols, specifically those that had the greatest reputation and, therefore, antiquity. It is not surprising, therefore, that the caciques strived to both protect and hide these idols from rivals, and that they also boasted having the most powerful, as Columbus noted: "[T]he caciques and their people boasted having a better [i.e., more powerful] cemí, theirs against the others. And when they go to their cemí, and enter the house where it is, they guard it from the Christians, and [the natives] do not let them enter. [Rather,] if they suspect they are about to come, they take the cemí or cemís and hide them in the forests for fear that they would take them" (Colón 1985:203, ch. 62). Yet, bragging about having the best (most reputable, powerful) can only work if in fact the caciques and their cemís could consistently deliver what was required of them. The same quote, however, adds one other interesting observation: "What is even more laughable is that they [the caciques] have the custom of *stealing* the cemís from each other" (Colón 1985:203, ch. 62; my emphasis).

Zealously guarding the cemís and the threat of theft go hand in hand. Theft is likely to be part of the reason why in some of the legends recorded by Pané, the idols "escaped" or are portrayed as difficult to keep in the caney, and thus tied with ropes. Perhaps in some instances, escaping would then masquerade for stealing. In any event, whether by theft or not, the abandonment of a cemí is an indictment of the cacique's incompetence. At times, bragging could have been a genuine boast— that the cacique would indeed have the "best" cemís. But then if a cacique did have them, why was there a need to steal other chiefs' cemís? Let us examine this phenomenon a bit closer.

Las Casas recounted the same story of bragging about and the theft of cemís, but also added that the natives hid them away not only from the Christians but also from "other Indians of other kingdoms and señoríos [fiefdoms]" (Las Casas 1929 [3]:526). But why would the stealing of cemís between caciques or elites be hilarious, laughable to Columbus? It is, I think, because of the paradox of boasting of having the best and most powerful cemí idols and yet constantly stealing those of other competing caciques or lords. This being the case, Columbus wrongly assumed that they blatantly lied or greatly exaggerated the powers of their cemís; hence, for Columbus, that was the motivation for caciques stealing them. Obviously, theft would be no laughable matter for the victim. To begin with, there is a better than average risk of going to war to recover the idol or avenge the aggrieved cacique, not to mention the loss of face by the victim.

The fact remains that caciques *did* steal cemís from other caciques. The question is, why? What circumstances would lead caciques to steal them? I think that Columbus hit the nail on the head: it was because the señores lacked the appropriate cemís; because caciques needed potent cemí idols to rule effectively. Columbus failed to realize, however, that what fueled the exaggerated boasting and the frenzied thievery was the political crisis that the Spaniards generated through battle and conquest. Important chiefs, like Anacaona, Caonabó, Guarionex, Iguanamá, and Mayobanex, were either drowned, hanged, or burned at the stake within the first decade of the arrival of Columbus to Hispaniola (Las Casas 1929 [1]:481; Oliver 2008a; Sued Badillo 2003:281). Not only were principal caciques executed, but often a whole line of preferred heirs and subordinated caciques was wiped out. The most infamous example of this was when chieftess Anacaona, before her own execution by hanging, had to witness eighty of her allied caciques being burned alive inside her large caney in Jaraguá (Las Casas 1929 [2]:165–166). Most probably all the wooden cemí idols stored in this caney were also burned. As Hugh Thomas (2003:192) tersely put it, "all the native rulers encountered by Columbus in his first years were dead" by 1504. This created both a power vacuum among the top ranks of the indigenous leadership and an acute problem of succession throughout Hispaniola by 1503. Puerto Rico would experience the same crisis following the Rebellion of the Caciques of 1511.

I have argued elsewhere (2005; also see section 2 D) that the various contradictory statements made by the chroniclers on the issue of the succession routes to the office of chief exist not just because the Spanish did not fully understand the native system of descent and inheritance, but primarily because the customary or preferred rules could not be applied; whichever way the natives looked, the preferred heirs were, far more often than not, taken out of contention (see Alegría 1979; Curet 2002; Keegan et al. 1989; Sued Badillo 1985, 2003; Wilson 1990). During this particular decade (1493–1503) of severe, sustained crises in Hispaniola, succession to the office and inheritance of the chiefly "estate" included a variety of routes already discussed in section 2 D. I suspect there were other routes as well, but the point is that these all seem to be contested, negotiable, and even ad hoc given that the preferred option(s) could not be implemented. Such a situation allowed ample room for competitors to forward alternate routes, even new ones not tried before, to benefit their chosen candidates. This could have included the possibility of a stranger becoming a cacique, as was the case of Caonabó, who was born in the Lucayo Islands (Bahamian Archipelago), outside the Hispaniolan chiefdom of Maguana (Keegan 2007b; Las Casas 1929 [3]:554). As noted earlier, the increased theft of cemí idols among chiefs is partly a reflection of these problems of succession.

All of this succession maneuvering was taking place amid battles of Spanish and allied caciques against loyalist, anti-Spanish chiefs (see Oliver 2008a; Tavárez María 2001; Wilson 1990). If, indeed, the ability to effectively govern the cacique required a powerful and potent set of cemís, especially those idols with proven reputation and legendary status, it is little wonder that theft was rampant. The proposed heirs—who probably were well down, if not out of, the preferential line of accession—probably did not have the cemís required for making the tough political and military decisions needed to confront the Spanish and their allied caciques. The heirs may have come from nitaíno factions, not in direct line with the deceased or absent cacique (see Moya Pons 1987:106), thus unlikely to have the required set of legendary cemís. The theft of cemí idols from opponent caciques who were militarily allied with the Spanish may have been encouraged as well by "loyalist" caciques.

The two points to be emphasized in this business of theft is that caciques (1) could not effectively rule and garnish military support without cemís that had long-established reputations and legendary prestige, and that (2) those lacking them had to steal them simply because such legendary, reputable, well-tested cemí idols could not be manufactured to order. Even if newly minted cemís became available, and even if they were very powerful (i.e., of high rank and status at conception), they had yet to acquire their reputation for efficacy (always vis-à-vis their human trustee)—these new cemís had yet to show that they could be effectively controlled and manipulated by the cacique in order to bring about good to society or calamities to their enemies. It would appear, then, that excessive bragging and theft of cemís among caciques was a desperate strategy for desperate times. Although this was in response to the Spanish conquest, it is quite likely that such a strategy was also deployed in pre-Columbian times during similar crises.

Given such a scenario, the implications for archaeology of the escape and theft of cemí idols are that any number of these icons would end up far beyond the settlements or areas where they originated from, and very likely in different chiefdoms as well. Many others that remained in the local area would end up being hidden from the Spanish and other enemy caciques. One likely place for hiding would be in caves, many of which were already sanctified abodes where the cohoba ceremony was most likely linked to rituals commemorating buried ancestors or related to the pictograph or petroglyph images carved or painted on the walls (see Figure 12). Not surprisingly, a significant number of the wooden statues, duhos, and other cemí idols held in museums and private collections worldwide have come from caves, rock shelters, or *jagüeyes* (or cenotes; see Cabello Carro 2008; McEwan 2008).

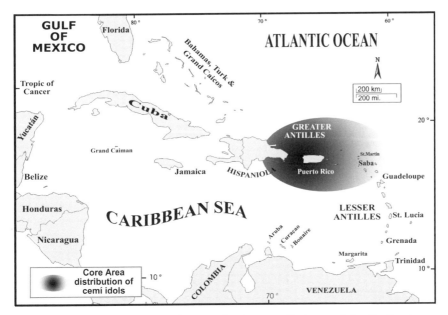

Figure 1. Map of the Caribbean showing the circumscribed area of the distribution of four classes of cemí icons: large three-pointed stones, stone collars, elbow stones, and large stone heads.

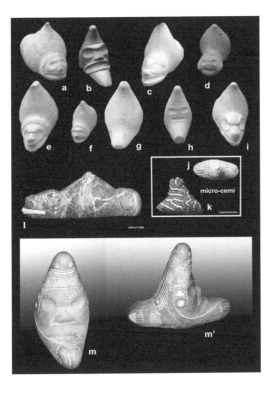

Figure 2. A selection of three-pointed stone cemís from Hispaniola (a-i) and Puerto Rico (j-m). Inset: (j, k) two miniature three-pointers in coral (k) and limestone (j) that first appeared during the Archaic period and continued to be produced until the Spanish contact (Chican Ostionoid) period. Specimens l, m, m': ©Museo de Historia, Antropología y Arte–Universidad de Puerto Rico. Specimens a-i: Museo del Hombre Dominicano; specimens j, k. Fundación Arqueológica Antropológica e Histórica de Puerto Rico (now defunct).

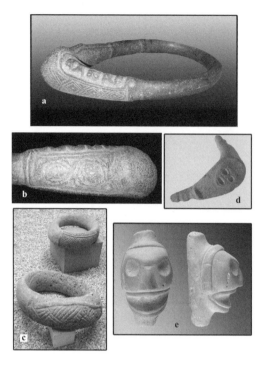

Figure 3. Stone collar, elbow stones, and Macorís stone heads. (a) Slender stone collar from Puerto Rico; (b) slender stone collar detail from La Parguera, Puerto Rico; (c) two coarse stone collars from eastern Hispaniola; (d) elbow stone from Puerto Rico; (e) Macorís-type stone head from Hispaniola (frontal and lateral views). Specimens a, d-e: ©Museo de Historia, Antropología y Arte–Universidad de Puerto Rico. Specimen (c) Museo del Hombre Dominicano. Specimen (b) Peabody Museum of Natural History, Division of Archaeology (courtesy of Prof. Richard Burger).

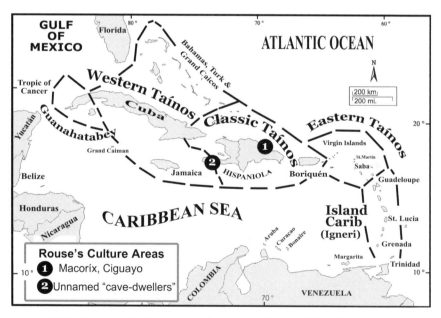

Figure 4. Distribution of cultures and peoples according to Irving Rouse at the time of Columbus (A.D. 1492–1520s) in the Greater Antilles (after Rouse 1992:fig. 3).

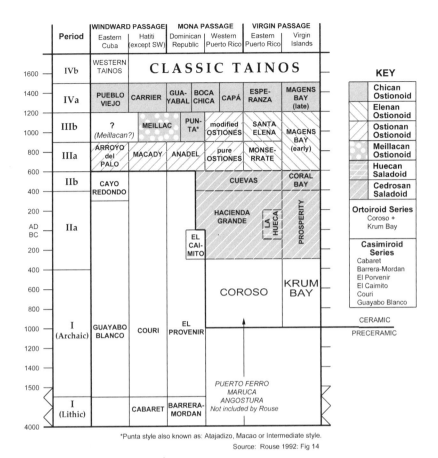

Figure 5. The standard cultural chronology of the Windward Passage, Mona Passage, and Virgin Passage areas in the Greater Antilles (after Rouse 1992: fig. 14).

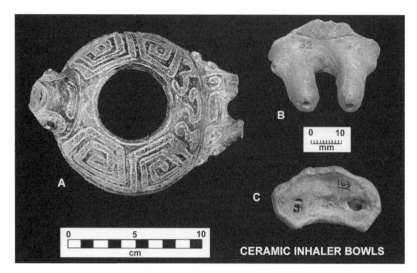

Figure 6. Ceramic bowls used for inhaling hallucinogens. (A) A "turtle" effigy bowl of La Hueca style, with spouts fragmented; (B) exterior view and (C) interior views of a Hacienda Grande–style bowl fragment showing the spouts and orifices for inhalation. ©Colección Museo de Historia, Antropología y Arte–Universidad de Puerto Rico. Specimen C, Centro de Investigaciones Arquelógicas, University of Puerto Rico (courtesy of Luis Chanlatte Baik).

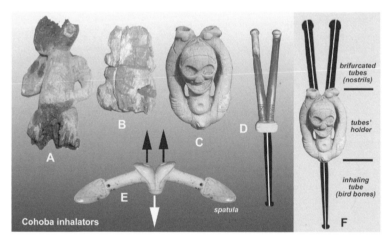

Figure 7. Devices for inhaling hallucinogens (Periods III–IV). (A) A wood anthropomorphic tube holder; (B) a deteriorated *Strombus* shell tube holder; (C) anthropomorphic tube holder made of a manatee rib; (D) a simple Y-shaped tube holder, with inhaling tube missing; (E) reconstruction of a combined spatula and tube holder made of *Strombus* shell; (F) tube holder "C" showing where (bird bone) tubes are inserted. Specimens A and B: Cueva El Faro, Puerto Rico; specimen C: La Cucama, Dominican Republic; specimen D: Coto site (?) Isabela, Puerto Rico; specimen E: Cueva de La Cohoba, Ciales, Puerto Rico. Specimens A, B, C: ©Colección Museo de Historia, Antropología y Arte–Universidad de Puerto Rico. (Note: Specimen E has been reconstructed with Photoshop. The original is slightly more than half complete.)

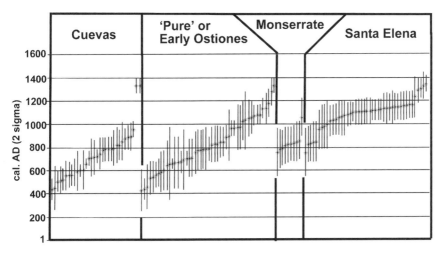

Figure 8. Spread of calibrated radiocarbon dates (2 sigma) associated with Rouse's ceramic styles (Cuevas to Santa Elena). The overlap of dates clearly suggests that instead of these styles succeeding one another, a large degree of contemporaneity existed and that a plurality of styles is the norm for Puerto Rico from about A.D. 400 to 1200 (after Rodríguez Ramos et al. 2008).

Figure 9. The "decapitated" (?) personage found in the main plaza of Jácana (PO-29), Ponce, Puerto Rico. Left, a view *in situ*; center, a frontal perspective; right, a preliminary drawing. Photographs left and center: ©David Deiner and New South Associates, and with permission from the U.S. Army Corps of Engineers, Jacksonville.

Figure 10. An example of the dual natures of a "frog-human" personage modeled in ceramic. It is hanging on and looking into a Santa Elena–style open bowl from the Vacía Talega site, Puerto Rico. Former collection of Dr. Andrés L. Oliver.

Figure 11. Wooden cemí idols involved in cohoba ceremonies. Left: (a) a 39-cm-tall anthropomorphic idol from Carpenters Mountain, Jamaica. Right: (c) a 65.5-cm-tall bird-turtle idol. Both cemí idols show overhead the round platform to place the cohoba (hallucinogen). At the center (b) is a small (ca. L. 39.5 cm) anthropomorphic cemí idol with splayed legs from Jamaica. ©Trustees of the British Museum.

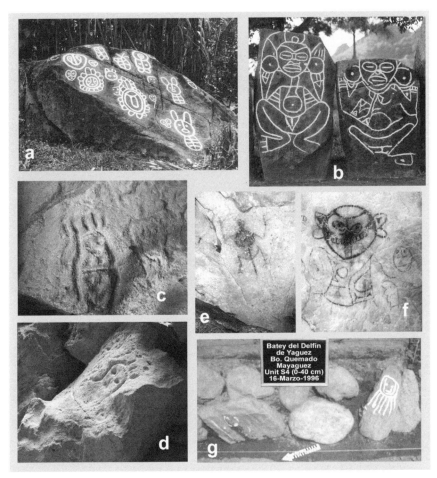

Figure 12. Petroglyphs and pictographs are here interpreted as a class of nonportable cemí icons. (a) Rock boulder from Salto Arriba, Utuado; (b) monolithic slabs framing the central plaza at Caguana; (c-d) petroglyphs at Cueva de Berna, Higüey, Dominican Republic; (e-f) pictographs at Cueva del Lucero, Juana Díaz, Puerto Rico; (g) petroglyphs from the central plaza, at Batey del Delfín de Yagüez, Mayagüez, Puerto Rico; chalk has been added to enhance the design in petroglyphs a, b, and g. Photograph (g) courtesy of Juan Rivera Fontán.

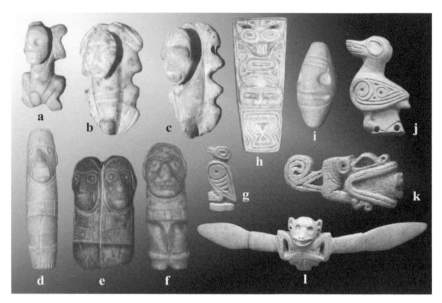

Figure 13. A diverse sample of small cemí artifacts used for body decoration or for personal use from the Dominican Republic. (a-f) stone pendants; (g, j) ornitomorphic vomiting spatula finials; (h) bone plaque/pendant; (i) miniature three-pointed icon; (k) spatula finial depicting a fantastic saurian cemí; (l) pendant cohoba inhaler depicting a bat cemí with spatulas doubling as wings. All specimens from the Museo de La Fundación García Arévalo, Santo Domingo.

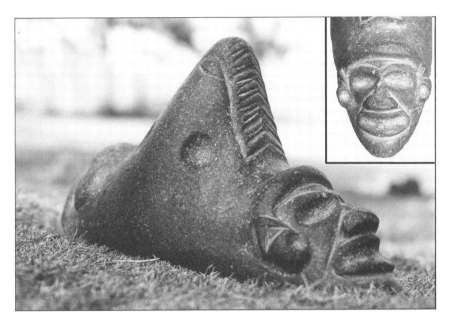

Figure 14. Three-pointed stone cemí with detailed anthropomorphic facial features that lend it identity and personhood from the Turabo Valley, Caguas, Puerto Rico. Courtesy of W. A. Géigel.

Figure 15. (a) A wooden cemí idol with a round platform to hold the hallucinogen and (b) a Boca Chica–style ceramic effigy vessel depicting a shaman or cacique on a duho while under the influence of cohoba. Museo de la Fundación García Arévalo, Santo Domingo.

Figure 16. A bird cemí, 87 cm tall, made of *guayacán* (*Guaiacum officinale*), from Carpenters Mountain, Vere, Jamaica. This sample may represent a woodpecker (*Melanerpes spp.*) given by its "patch" (outline) of feathers on the forehead. It is likely to be one of the central or primary idols for veneration. ©The Trustees of the Irish Museum.

Figure 17. A 104-cm-tall male anthropomorphic cemí idol with splayed legs from Carpenters Mountain, Vere, Jamaica. The broad tear canals on the cheeks probably represent the physiological reaction to the cohoba drug. ©The Trustees of the Irish Museum.

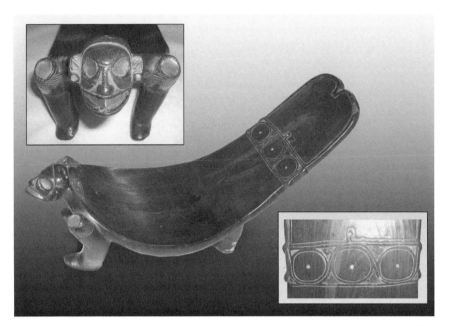

Figure 18. A highly polished guayacán duho, or seat, with gold sheet decorations. The back-seat design (inset) represents the cotton belts used by the Taíno, with the circular designs possibly representing the perforated shell discs sewn into the belt. ©The Trustees of the British Museum.

13 The Inheritance and Reciprocal Exchange of Cemí Icons

If theft was a desperate measure, how were such powerful icons passed on to others under normal, peaceful circumstances? Giving, with the expectation of a future reciprocal gesture, is one way, although the sixteenth-century chroniclers only recorded it for the death of caciques. It is likely that *in life* caciques may have gifted cemí idols to others, although perhaps such idols might have rarely been those regarded with the highest esteem.

Inheritance seems to have been the normal way in which cemí idols changed hands across generations. But inheritance and disposition of the estate of a deceased cacique is a complicated matter. For instance, in addition to the bequest to the heir to the office and, possibly, close relatives, there was also what might be bequeathed to other people, such as political allies and other distant relatives, along with what the deceased would take with him as burial furniture and would thus be permanently taken out of circulation. The first two, inheritance by heirs and gifts to others, are of importance since they would account for the spatial distribution of most cemí idols within and between islands.

Admiral Columbus, as narrated by his son Hernando Colón (1985:204, ch. 60), described various funerary practices reserved for caciques only: in some circumstances the Hispaniolan caciques were burned in the house where they died; in others their bodies were disemboweled and then desiccated over fire, after which the bones (usually a skull) to be buried or enclosed in baskets, calabashes, or cotton idols would be selected. Columbus mentioned that some caciques were also buried in caves along with offerings of cassava bread and a calabash full of water placed over their heads. But Oviedo is the only one to provide some details of what happened with the material wealth of a dead cacique. He wrote about another funeral ritual reserved for caciques in Hispaniola. Funeral *areíto* (dance and chant) performances eulogizing the deceased cacique were organized around feasts that lasted up to twenty days. To these funerary feasts many subjects from within the cacicazgo were invited to participate, as well as other principal caciques coming from regions afar. In such occasions, Oviedo specifically noted that part of the estate of the dead cacique was to be distributed among the invited foreign caciques. In Oviedo's own words:

> after death [the cacique] was tightly fastened from feet to head with very
> long cotton-woven bandages . . . and in a hole they placed him, as in a silo,

and there they placed on him his jewels and those things he valued most . . .
they built a wooden dome, so that the earth would not touch him, and sat
him on a well-carved duho (a small bench [see Figure 18]) and then they
covered it with earth. And the dances-songs that they sang and the Indians
did [areítos], with many others from the *comarca* [neighborhood, region],
and other principal caciques came to honor him, *among whom said foreigners
the belongings of the deceased were distributed* [Oviedo 1994 (1):244; my em-
phasis].

As the funerary feast lasted around two weeks, there is no doubt that the cacique's extended kin would have to outlay great amounts of drink and food. The
length of the feasts most likely depended on the wealth and resources accumulated by the cacique and his kindred. In other words, this was an expensive display
of the cacique and his relatives' wealth and resources. The cacique would then be
buried wrapped in cotton bandages, seated on his duho (see Oliver 2008b:172–
174), and placed in a pit chamber framed by wooden beams and planks so that the
soil would not touch him. The duho, of course, is one of the items of grave furniture that displayed a cemí idol (Figure 15: b). However, Oviedo is not very specific about what else might be buried with the cacique except for a vague mention
of jewelry. The latter seems to indicate the inclusion of selected items of personal
body decoration, such as his stone-bead or *ciba* (pronounced "seebah") necklace.
It is anyone's guess what precisely might be the things "he valued most" and how
many such items would be buried with him. Such things, however, would be permanently taken out of circulation, unavailable for future exchange or as bequests
for descendants.

The meaning of the term "foreign" cacique is tricky to interpret. It most likely
refers to caciques who were *not* direct blood relatives of the deceased cacique and
whose political domain lay outside that of the deceased chief. I suspect that this
category also included those caciques with whom the deceased chief had affine
relationships cemented through marital relationships, although it may also have included caciques with whom political alliances were cemented through means other
than bridal exchange—that is, through the guaitiao ceremonial pact.

The redistribution of wealth to foreign caciques in funeral feasts implies that a
significant portion of his possessions remained in circulation, and I strongly suspect that among these were some cemí idols, perhaps not the most valued or highest ranked, but potent cemí idols nonetheless. To bequest part of this wealth to
foreign caciques appears to be an effective mechanism to ensure reciprocity, to
henceforth obligate these foreign dignitaries to lend their full political, economic,
and military support to the new heir (or heiress), much in the same way they had
when the deceased cacique was alive. It is also likely that there were marital ties between the deceased chief's lineage and the families of caciques from other chief-

doms, pacts that may have been cemented through the guaitiao ritual, which would often include wife exchanges, making the caciques and the recently deceased chief brothers-in-law.

At this point the heir was still a neophyte cacique, an untested individual in the eyes of all concerned. But by virtue of his descent ties to the dead (and, thus, cemíified) cacique, and being the person who was in the ideal position to inherit the office, he had all the support needed to become a competent ruler and leader. The foreign caciques would reciprocate the gifts received during the funerary feast by providing such support, thereby increasing the new cacique's chances of success. However, only time would tell how effective and successful the heir would become, since it would take time to build his reputation as an effective leader and to show that he could control the powers of cemís (as idols and as numinous spirits) he had inherited. The giving of valuables, including cemí icons, could therefore be interpreted as a mechanism to enhance and buttress the new chief's chances to succeed in his new role as cacique.

At the same time, accepting gifts placed the foreign caciques at a disadvantage with respect to the heir cacique and his kindred. As Godelier (1999:11) noted:

> Giving thus seems to establish a difference and an inequality of status between donor and recipient, which can in certain instances become a hierarchy: if this hierarchy exists, then the gift expresses and legitimizes it. . . . *The gift decreases the distance between the protagonists because it is a form of sharing, and it increases the social distance because one is now indebted to the other.* It is easy to see the formidable array of maneuvers and strategies virtually contained in the practice of gift-giving, and [the] gamut of contradictory interests that can be served. By its very nature, gift-giving is an ambivalent practice which . . . is capable of bringing together opposing emotions and forces. It can be an act of generosity or of violence; in the latter case, violence is disguised as a disinterested gesture . . .
>
> . . . of the two components (sharing and debt) contained and combined in gift-giving, it is the second (the [social] distancing) which probably has the greatest impact in social life when it is organized around various forms of competition for access to wealth and power, knowledge, or ritual [Godelier 1999:12; my emphasis].

By accepting the gifts, the foreign caciques became indebted and would reciprocate by lending support to the heir, who at this point was in a fragile position as a neophyte cacique, especially in the eyes of political enemies or even factions within his cacicazgo. I presume that at a future time, upon the death of one of the foreign caciques, the now much more experienced and mature heir cacique would be invited to participate in the funerary feasts and receive gifts bequeathed by the deceased foreign chief, even perhaps expecting the return of the cemí icon that he and his kin gave to the deceased cacique in the funerary feasts conducted years or decades earlier. The net effect of the circulation of such cemí icons among a series of caciques, and across generations, is that their prestige increased as their reputations grew; and thus accumulated deep and "sedimented" biographies and legends built around their relationships as they circulated from one cacique to another. Circulation, in this case, is across a generation of caciques. A few of the cemí idols reported by Pané (1999) had this across-generation exchange process recorded by the list of the caciques who had it in their possession.

The fact that richly furnished burials, with abundant offerings involving objects of wealth and prestige, identifying a cacique are not archaeologically known for the Greater Antilles dovetails with Oviedo's claim that much of the estate of the deceased caciques remained in circulation. There are perhaps less than half a dozen archaeological burials in Hispaniola known to have yielded relatively wealthy burials, such as at La Cucama–Juandolio (near Santo Domingo; see Figure 25; Mañón Arredondo et al. 1971; Morbán Laucer 1979:35–36; Veloz Maggiolo et al. 1973). But the "richest" burial was found by looters: it included thousands of pink coral micro-beads; a richly carved manatee (bone) cohoba inhalator (see Figure 7: C, F); a small statuette with gold inlays in the eyes and mouth; several loose gold sheets; and a Macorís-type stone head that suggests either an important shaman or an elite individual (Morbán Laucer 1979:35–36; Oliver 2005:fig. 7.11). These items are today on display at the Museum of the Fundación García Arévalo, in Santo Domingo. Burial finds such as this one are exceptionally rare in Hispaniola and do not seem to even come close to the description of the material wealth said to be controlled by caciques of the Spanish contact period, such as Anacaona (Las Casas 1929 [1]:463). The exception confirms the rule: the material wealth, the estate of a cacique, remained in circulation and formed part of a reciprocal exchange system involving foreign caciques. I will return to this theme of giving and taking in the next section, where alienable versus inalienable wealth is also discussed.

In Puerto Rico and the adjacent Virgin Islands, despite far greater archaeological activity than in Hispaniola, not a single burial site can yet be regarded as that of an elite, be it cacique or nitaíno. Moreover, Jeff Walker (1993) noted that large, decorated three-pointed cemí idols have not been found in burial contexts except for one possible instance at the Hacienda Grande site in Puerto Rico. Certainly the same can be said of the elbow stones, stone collars, and the large stone heads. In my own research region of Caguana (municipality of Utuado, Puerto Rico), fragments of stone collars were found in association with midden refuse at a farmstead site (U-27). The only large three-pointed cemí (the so-called half-moon type) was a surface find near a batey (site U-20), while two small cemís were respectively uncovered from a midden deposit at site U-44 and underlying a batey in site U-27, both sites being small farmstead settlements with components dating to the

Taíno or Capá period (A.D. 1280–1450). Finally, an unfinished elbow stone along with several spheroliths of unknown function were recovered from a recently destroyed batey site adjacent to the Tanamá River (Rivera and Oliver 2005). While certainly cemí idols, such as the three-pointed stones, have been recovered by peasant farmers from caves and bought by private collectors and museums (e.g., Jesse Fewkes [1907] on behalf of the Smithsonian Institution), I have not yet heard of any informants finding them in association with burials. The conclusion is that most of these large iconic artifacts were not buried with caciques or elites and thus remained in circulation. Of course, this observation refers to imperishable materials; there is always the possibility that some cemís made of perishable materials were buried.

To summarize, the absence of burial sites of the wealthy in both islands lends support to Oviedo's claim that a large part of the estate of the dead cacique would not be buried with him. The cemí idols—iconic and aniconic—were either to be inherited by kin or gifted to foreign political allies, who would later reciprocate in kind. The only other basis to account for the geographic spread of cemí idols is that of stealing by political rivals or enemies in times of crisis. These are the three key processes that propelled the flow of these cemí icons through a web or network consisting of relatives, political allies, and enemies, some from neighboring regions within an island and others from other islands and polities. In this regard, the three-pointed stones, elbow stones, stone collars, and perhaps the stone heads were part of the material wealth that circulated in a web of relationships that was circumscribed to an area encompassing the eastern Dominican Republic and the northern Antilles.

The reader might rightfully raise the question of whether it is reasonable to assume that potent, valuable cemí icons would ever form part of the materials bequeathed by a cacique or his kindred rather than be kept within the chief's family or lineage. Oviedo only noted that a duho (Figure 18) would be buried with the cacique along with his most prized jewels, along with water and cassava. It will never be known for certain, but there are reasons to think that on certain occasions, given the appropriate circumstances, valuable and potent things, those one would normally think of as being inalienable possessions, were in fact gifted.

Evidence in support of the thesis that apparently inalienable things were given comes from Hispaniola. Las Casas gave an account of a celebrated occasion when Guarionex, paramount cacique of the Magua chiefdom, gifted his areíto to Mayobanex, the paramount cacique of the neighboring Cigüayo-Macorix chiefdom of Hiabo (see Figure 26). The areíto was given in exchange for military protection against an impending attack by the Spanish headed by Francisco Roldán and Bartolomé Colón, who was the *adelantado* (a lieutenant governor in charge of territory fronting the enemy) (Wilson 1990:102–108). Giving Guarionex the areíto lyrics and dance choreography meant "that both caciques were to become henceforth symbolically related as Mayobanex [in accepting it] would assume and share the genealogy and numinous power of the ancestors of Guarionex and of the caci-cazgo of Magua" (Oliver 1998:97–98). Even when Mayobanex's people advised him against lending protection to Guarionex so as to avoid certain defeat and death in the hands of the Spanish, in the end all agreed they had no choice but to honor the pact, because Guarionex "had taught him the areíto of the Magua" chiefdom (Las Casas 1929 [1]:478–479). This was not a gift of material wealth but of sym-bolic wealth, one that involved teaching the associated choreography and the lyr-ics of the chants that narrated the great heroic deeds of Guarionex and the cemíi-fied ancestral chiefs of the Magua. It was literally an invaluable gift of the epic history of Guarionex and his ancestors, thereby incorporating Mayobanex into this history.

The caciques also cemented alliances through a ritual exchange of names be-tween two people as, for example, in the cases of Agüeybana "The Elder" and Juan Ponce de León in Puerto Rico, and Cotubanamá and Juan de Esquivel in Hispan-iola. The individuals would henceforth be reciprocally linked as guaitiaos (or guay-tiaos), a Taíno term that the Spanish translated as "friends" or "allies" (Las Casas 1929 [2]:162, 291; Oviedo 1944 [3]:192). The guaitiao pact did not need to be linked to women (wife) exchange, but as I will discuss later, there are strong indi-cations that sometimes, perhaps often, the name exchange was also accompanied with women exchanges (Sued Badillo 2003:261). Thus, names of caciques and of women (brides-to-be) who were controlled by the caciques, along with cemí idols, formed an integral part of the alliance-forming exchange network. In conclusion, immensely valuable, potent gifts such as the areíto support the proposition that presumably inalienable valuables, such as powerful, reputable cemí idols could have been gifted under the right circumstances. The issues of what may be alien-able versus inalienable possessions deserves further discussion.

14 Cemís

Alienable or Inalienable;
To Give or To Keep

Since the original formulations by Bronislav Malinowski (1992 [1922]) and Marcel Mauss (1990 [1925]), grounded on the ethnology of Trobriand islanders, reciprocity has been widely regarded by anthropologists as a central and universal feature of social systems (Mosko 2000; Sykes 2005:38–64). I bring Oceania and Melanesia to the fore in this section because (a) the theory of reciprocity is well developed in this region; (b) I am more familiar with the literature; and also because (c) it involves islands and archipelagos. The central tenet of reciprocity is that a valuable item is exchanged or traded for another one of similar value or worth. Payment in kind for gifts received could be and often was delayed, but the idea is that there is a standing obligation to repay. In 1992, and building on her previous work, Annette Weiner (1985, 1992) proposed that not reciprocity but rather "keeping-while-giving" was the universal principle governing social life; that there are things that *cannot* be given and that must be kept out of circulation—that is, these are inalienable possessions. At the same time, other things regarded as commodities could and would be reciprocally exchanged. The validity of Weiner's (1992) "giving-for-keeping" theory, when confronted with ethnographic data and facts, especially in Oceania, has invited intensive discussions among anthropologists (for an in-depth critique, see Mosko 2000). The specifics of the critiques notwithstanding, there are agreements among anthropologists of the heuristic value in considering both reciprocity and "keeping-for-giving" in analyzing native exchange systems.

The discussion in the previous section about the circulation of cemís through inheritance and especially as gifts to foreign caciques raises questions regarding the nature of the exchange. Theft also arises in this inquiry precisely because it implies coming into possession of something that is not yours to keep. I assumed in this discussion that the principle in operation of gifts from deceased caciques to foreign ones was that of reciprocity, albeit delayed. I noted that a significant portion of a deceased chief's wealth would be gifted to foreigners, and would be repaid at a later date upon their deaths. I suggested that the foreigners were likely allied to the deceased cacique either through marriage or through a guaitiao pact (which not always but often included women/wife exchanges). The Spanish neither recorded the motivations behind such transactions and exchanges, nor offered any details about the notions or ideology that the natives held about the acts of giving, taking, and keeping. What is clear from the sixteenth-century Spanish writings is that (1) a good part of the estate was given away by the surviving kin of the dead cacique, thus keeping them in circulation (alienable), and (2) that some "jewels" and things most valued by the dead cacique would be buried with him, thus permanently taken out of circulation (inalienable). The sixteenth-century chroniclers did not mention what specific things the heir to the office of cacique and, presumably his or her immediate kin, would retain or keep. Other than the duho, a *higüero* (or calabash) water container, and cassava bread with fruits, no other burial items were described by the Spanish, and as already noted, the archaeology of burials in Hispaniola and Puerto Rico has so far failed to recover any rich cacique burials, precisely because of the very few offerings and artifacts interred with them. Oviedo did mention one other burial "accompaniment" regarding one specific cacique. This is where both the principal wife (*athebeane neque*) and a second wife of paramount cacique Behechio of the Jaraguá chiefdom were interred alive with him when he died. But even here Oviedo (1944 [1]:243–244) is clear in stating that such a human sacrifice "was not generalized in the whole island" of Hispaniola.

Despite this poverty of ethnohistoric detail (in contrast to, say, Trobriand, Maori, or Melanesian ethnographies), I think it is quite reasonable to assume that the heir and his or her kindred would indeed *keep* some of those things—things that simply could *not* be gifted. It is a moot question which things that were under the control of the deceased cacique were "his" to bequeath, and which may have been collectively controlled by his family group or lineage and thus for them to decide if and how they would be distributed. I have proposed that among the valuables to be given as well as those to be kept there were cemí idols and other valued artifacts that had cemí iconography. I also suggested that the more highly valued, high-ranked, and high-status idols (e.g., Figures 16, 17) were perhaps not likely to be gifted—that is, they would be inalienable possessions. Am I right to assume that the most senior, potent, and powerful icons could *not* be given under any circumstances? Probably not. But if given, such a gift would be of supreme political importance between two communities. It is thus worth reexamining the issues of alienable (can be given) and inalienable (must be kept) cemí icons, taking into account that singular cemí icons definitively had different values owing to their variable ranks, statuses, and demonstrated powers and efficacy (on value, see Graeber 2001). Annette Weiner explains:

> Much like the Elgin Marbles . . . whatever happens to these objects, they are perceived to belong in an inherent way to their original owners [i.e., the Greek, not the British]. Inalienable possessions are imbued with affective qualities [as is the cemí] that are expressions of the value an object has when it is kept by its owner and inherited within the same family or descent group. Age [antiquity] adds value, as does the ability to keep the object against all

exigencies that might force a person or a group to release it to others. *The primary value of inalienability, however, is expressed through the power these objects have to define who one is in a historical sense.* The object acts as a vehicle for bringing past time into the present, so that the histories of ancestors, titles, or mythological events become an intimate part of a person's [e.g., in our case, the cacique's] present identity. To lose this claim to the past is to lose part of who one is in the present. In its alienability, the object must be seen as more than an economic resource [i.e., commodity] and more than an affirmation of social relations [Weiner 1985:210; my emphasis].

For those unfamiliar, for years now there has been a heated debate about the rightful ownership of the marble sculptures of the Parthenon Frieze, which were lifted by the Earl of Elgin (hence the sobriquet Elgin Marbles) at the beginning of the nineteenth century and bought, on behalf of the British nation, by the British Museum in 1816 (Caygill 2002:22–23). On the one hand the debate revolves around the question of legitimate ownership in a legal sense, and on the other about who has the right to own a people's cultural heritage and history. Despite claims by the Greek government, the British government has refused their return to Greece. The British public, and individual parliamentarians, however, are equally divided in their opinions about ownership, albeit the return-to-Greece advocates among the public seem to be gaining ground. Regardless of the issue of legal ownership, there is an acknowledgment that the Elgin Marbles are "inalienably" linked to their ancient Greek authors and, thus, to modern Greeks.

Following Weiner's arguments, keeping instead of giving inalienable possessions enables the "owners" (e.g., the caciques, heirs, and their kin groups) to validate their rank and hierarchy. As Mosko (2000:379) noted, in adopting Weiner's position the consequence is that "the preponderance of exchanges typically involves alienable possessions, interpreted [by Weiner 1992:37–40] as strategic attempts to avoid [giving, exchanging] the crucial hierarchical-preserving inalienable possessions." In contrast, for Weiner, the inalienable possessions "endure beyond the lives of humans," reaffirming that the latter possessions were "undoubtedly employed in the validation and demonstration of the identity, rank, authority, status of groups rather than individuals" (Weiner, as summarized by Mosko 2000:379). That is, the objects were curated and kept to validate and reinforce the group's (and the chief's) standing. But Weiner (1992:37; see Mosko 2000) also noted a fundamental paradox in her proposition: she found ethnographic evidence in Melanesia that inalienable possessions *can also* be exchanged, lost, or destroyed, in which case, as Mosko (2000:378) noted, it would (or did) undermine the owner's claims to his position and standing in society. Where does this leave the argument for the existence of things that are inalienable?

Mosko's (2000) principal critique of Wiener's (1985, 1992) thesis was that the concepts of Melanesian personhood deployed by her were "isomorphic with long-standing Western presuppositions," where persons and things, subjects, and objects are viewed as unitary or bounded instead of partible or dividual "entities." That the assumed indivisibility and individuality of persons and things is inappropriate becomes especially evident in many native Melanesian (and generally, Oceanic) theories of conception—those involving blood, semen, and other substances—in accounting for the formation and subsequent changes of personhood through the life and afterlife of human beings, where the processes involved are, first, the decomposition of the person followed by his recomposition into another, still dividual, person, which could also have a very different nature (e.g., an ancestor idol, an intangible spirit or soul, etc.). Sadly, the Taínoan notions about procreation and of life-death-rebirth cycles are essentially unknown, though they are indirectly expressed in the language of myth (see Oliver 1997, 2008b). The Spanish did not record any native theories about how bones, blood, semen, and other substances contributed to the composition of personhood, of what parts were contributed by the mother's or father's lineage to ego, and how these substances were decomposed and recomposed in, for example, rites of passage such as birth, puberty, marriage, and funerals. Nevertheless, as I have suggested above for the natives of Hispaniola–Puerto Rico, and as Strathern (1988; also Mosko 1992, 2000) has suggested for Melanesian societies, if the construction of personhood is dividual, partible, or fractal, it would account, I think, for the paradox that things and persons regarded as inalienable in Weiner's logic were in fact being exchanged. As partible and dividual entities, the agency in any exchange is in the relationships elicited or displayed by the parts owned by a person and owed to other persons. This raises the question of whether the mutually exclusive categories of alienable and inalienable are adequate, since some parts or aspects rather than whole units making up personhood could be given or shared and others kept. So to speak, the boundary of a person does not end at the skin of its body, nor is the body a bounded indivisible entity, be it human beings or other beings and things (see sections 3 and 4).

In the Melanesian *kula, mapula,* and *lisaladabu* exchange systems, there were certain items and things that, despite being given, nevertheless still remained "attached" to their original source—that is, the giver or his group. These were, of course, symbolic attachments in the sense that geographic distance and physical separation existed between the giver and taker and the entity ("object") taken. Despite being kept, used, or displayed by the taker, some constitutive parts of items or entities would remain inherently bound to the giver, since subjects and objects are not conceived as indivisible, unitary entities. Commenting on Strathern's (1988) work, Mosko (2000:381–*passim*) further observed:

> Melanesian persons are best understood . . . as dividual or partible agents [and patients] who, in seeming to exchange objects with one another, detach

and attach respective parts of persons: relations or parts of other persons detached and attached in prior exchanges. . . . As there is no absolute distinction
between subjects and objects as persons and the things they exchange in these
contexts, the Western notions of "ownership" or "possession" would seem in-
congruous with indigenous Melanesian precepts. Manufactured objects need
not bear any intrinsic relation of ownership to their makers or possessors; nor
need they be singularly gendered [as either male or female] since people de-
tach and attach different parts or relations of their persons in different contexts of exchange, objects which might be taken as moveable [i.e., alienable]
may, in other circumstances, be seen as immovable [inalienable]. As a result,
it is not paradoxical that sometimes inalienable possessions can be or are exchanged, destroyed, or lost; and it is not necessarily the case that relinquish-
ment of certain parts of persons (supposedly inalienable possessions) results
in the loss of hierarchical standing [Mosko 2000:380–381].

Thus, in the Melanesian case, agents and actors (persons) can keep certain parts of
themselves while simultaneously giving other parts of them in each transaction: "it
is the giving and mutual elicitation both within and between groups where agency
and sociality lie" (Strathern, as commented by Mosko 2000:381). Unlike Weiner,
for Strathern and Mosko, inalienability is a central aspect of the concept of gift exchange rather than a substitute.

Weiner's theory of "keeping-while-giving" also intended to account for "the
temporal aspects of the movements of persons and possessions and the cultural
configurations that limit or expand the reproduction or dissipation of social and
political relationships through time," asserting that "social value must be created
and recreated to prevent or overcome dissipation or loss" (Weiner, in Mosko 2000:
383). Mosko, however, shows that there is abundant Melanesian ethnographic
counterevidence suggesting instead that "a dual or cyclical process" is at stake,
"consisting of the 'need,' first, to affect dissipation and loss through intentional
disintegration of persons and relationship, characteristically enacted in mortuary
rituals, as a preliminary [and], second, to the expansive creation of new persons
or relations through new or additional exchanges" (Mosko 2000; see also Mosko
1992). Fundamentally, Weiner's portrayal of the inalienable possession of social
reproduction is presented as a "perpetual or unidirectional trajectory of creating
and recreating social values so as to prevent or limit loss and decay" or dissipation
(in Mosko 2000:383), whereas for Mosko: "Social reproduction consists in the
countervailing trajectories of both social reduction and social expansion, where
the dissipation of social values must not be prevented but deliberately affected—
'decomposed,' 'deconceived'—before they can be recreated in the production of
new persons and relations. And . . . this process of alternating personal and social
contraction and expansion is an inherently temporal one" (Mosko 2000:383).

The strength of the anthropological debate about the nature of gift exchange lies in the rich corpus of ethnographic evidence that is available in Melanesia (and generally in the Pacific) to evaluate these competing positions, which in turn provide invaluable ammunition and insights for archaeological research in the region (for Europe, see Chapman 2000). By comparison, the data available for the sixteenth-century Taíno and other Greater Antillean natives is far more limited and incomplete. Although natives did not entirely disappear from the large islands, such as in Cuba and Hispaniola, by the seventeenth century a very different native ethnic social order—Indios—emerged (see sections 20 and 21). But just because such richness of evidence is lacking in the Caribbean does not mean these theoretical approaches should be ignored. They ought to be considered and discussed even if they remain just theoretical propositions and even if there is a danger of overinterpretation. After all, both theoretical formulations (reciprocity and "keeping-while-giving") are meant to have universal application. The fact remains that a great deal of the discussion about trade and exchange in the pre-Columbian and initial Spanish contact period in the Caribbean has been made under the western assumption of the indivisibility and unity of persons and the things exchanged, and where exchanges are also based on western notions of economics. Such assumptions have spilled onto the methods by which archaeologists and ethnohistorians have generally categorized aboriginal material culture (artifacts in particular; but see Oliver 2000). Most, if not all, of the classification and tabulation of artifacts in archaeological reports is based on the principle that even when fragmented, these artifacts represent indivisible units (ideal types) or individuals (as in minimum number of individuals). This is fine to address any number of research questions, but I think it is inappropriate when, for example, one wishes to address questions of sociality and meanings involved in trade and exchange.

The agent-patient relationships I have thus far noted between cemí as idols (and as spirits) and human beings strongly suggest that, like in Melanesia, these relationships are based on notions of partible and dividual personhoods. Further, there is some evidence already presented to suggest that these idols are dividual persons, given the animistic and multinaturalistic perspective of the natives and other neighboring cultures participating in Taínoness. If so, then it seems likely that the "subjects-objects" in the exchange relation involving highly valued cemí idols could be gifted, given appropriate circumstances, as these gifts will still have a part of their personhood attached to the donor. The case of the gift of the areíto is a good indication that immensely valuable and seemingly inalienable things were in fact given in exchange for military protection, and that what was given through sacred words and dances was the history of deeds and genealogical connections held by the donor cacique to the other cacique. Thus this gift was so valuable that it would be dishonorable to refuse it. It would make sense (although it is impossible to prove or disprove with the available ethnohistoric evidence) that in this case, the donor cacique will always be inherently (inalienably) attached to this areíto gift, while the receiving cacique would now share in the past glories and heroic history commemorated by the sacred texts and dances given by the "foreign" cacique of Magua. It is also a logical conclusion that the precious gift of areíto would not be given in most other circumstances. What was at stake in this areíto exchange was the very survival of the cacique and his cacicazgo. The sacred text and dance choreography of an areíto can be conceptualized as parts that define and constitute the personhood of the cacique; the gift thus involves giving away that which defines the person who is to be assumed and internalized by the receiving cacique. In other momentous occasions, such as the marriage or death of caciques, other equivalent valuables, such as potent cemí idols, would be similarly exchanged, entailing new social relations between the exchange parties, and parts of persons being given recompose the personhood of others. To use Mosko's terminology, these potent cemís and areítos (and other like materials and things) are thus "movable." Or to use Gell's (1998) expression, the gifts (e.g., cemís) comprise the giver's *distributed person.*

In the case of giving cemí idols as bequests among foreign caciques, the result is a cross-generational circulation and redistribution of these objects. From the perspective of the gifted cemí idol (rather than the human beings in the exchange web), their relationships with different generations of deceased caciques signify that the parts of the idol's personhood that make up its legend or biography will always be "attached" to a string or series of former human trustees, including deceased ones, in addition to the current human cacique trustee. The one thing that is constant and unchanging is their condition of being sweet and potent, which makes cemí idols different from any ordinary living human being. Humans can benefit from or feel the adverse effects of cemí agency, but I doubt that any living human could have the condition of being cemí, except in the afterlife. On the other hand, reciprocal relations between living humans and cemí idols exist: cemís are cared for, venerated, and given houses for prayer and gardens to cultivate the food that will be offered in exchange for their favorable intervention in making things and events happen.

A human cacique giving cemí idols and other things (e.g., areíto), which at first glance seem to be inalienable "possessions," to foreign caciques does not mean that his heirs, his lineage group will lose strength and dissipate power, rank, or status. The social relationship that the giver has held with the cemí idols, and which defined their mutual personhoods while the relationship lasted, will be attached to the cemí and its new owner, and preserved in the biography and legend of the idol long after the death of the caciques. Aside from all other relationships that define the cacique in life, part of his personhood is defined by the reciprocal exchanges he had engaged in with the cemí idol (e.g., food offering or observing taboos for a favorable cemí intervention). Much the same could be said if some highly valued cemís were gifted in life, perhaps as bride or groom price, or in exchange for political pacts, such as the areíto example described earlier. Relinquishing powerful cemís, like giving away wives and areítos, would not dissipate power but would redefine and strengthen relations of power among caciques. Reciprocity, then, is the key principle behind the circulation of valuable, potent objects and things.

The reciprocal exchange system thus seems to ensure that the network of mutual chiefly alliances and relations is maintained and reproduced, if not expanded. Social—or more accurately, sociopolitical—reproduction in the case of the Taíno chiefs depends on giving these valuables for precisely "keeping" power. Thus, reciprocity is fundamental: it works because the heir of the dead cacique who had to give away a valued cemí idol (and any other valuables) knows that his turn will come to receive in kind. For a neophyte cacique, such support is crucial in the face of enemy chiefs, competing factions within his polity, and to win the confidence of skeptical communities within his chiefdom. More important, one of the ways in which cemí idols accrue reputation and attain legendary status is by changing hands, thus adding to their biography new relationships with powerful humans. The more powerful the human trustee, the more effective will be the transformation of cemí potency into action. This can only occur in two ways: (1) cemís are inherited by heirs and kept "in house," or (2) they are gifted to foreign caciques. The first instance has the advantage that the powerful cemí idols are kept under the direct control of the new chief and his lineage, thus ensuring the concentration of political-religious power. The disadvantage of "keeping" is that the new heir's abilities and power to control and negotiate the cemí idols is as yet untested. They are likely to be mismatched initially. In the second instance, the advantage of "giving" is that the "taker" is likely to already be a senior reputable and well-tested cacique, and thus the relationship with the acquired cemí idol will be more evenly matched. In turn, the cemí idol's reputation, given a more effective negotiating control by the cacique, would increase its reputation and thus become even more valuable. The disadvantage is that the "giver" no longer has direct, physical access to this icon in order to negotiate or extract from the cemí idol what it needs to rule. The delayed reciprocal exchange of the valued cemí idols ensures that every time a cacique dies, a valued cemí idol with increased reputation will be received by someone who can "handle" it. Large three-pointed stones, elbow stones, or stone collars, as well as necklaces, pendants, and other artifacts of chiefly regalia with cemí iconography, will pass on as heirlooms; others will be given to allies; and still others will be newly created to, perhaps, commemorate accession to the office. For a newly minted cemí to become legendary will depend on the abilities of the cacique to control it and deliver the "goods"; this takes time and maturation as a political-religious leader.

There is one last observation to be made: to rule and to engage the cemís as idols (and also cemís as spirits) in the council house requires the *physical* presence of the idols. Proof of this is the necessity to steal cemí idols between competing caciques: a physical proximity to the cemí idols is required in order to control and rule. It is for this reason that I am quite certain that even when valuable cemí idols would be gifted or bequeathed, many of the cacique's arsenal of cemí idols—or at least those that Columbus noted—were the central figures of veneration and would have been gifted only in exceptional circumstances. This is as far as one can argue the issue of which cemí idols could or could not be given, based on the available data from ethnohistoric documents.

To borrow Weiner's (1985:210) phrase, the cemí idols, especially those with a thick biography and legendary status, "have the power to define who one is in a historical sense." They are enmeshed in a network of reciprocal exchanges that define and redefine them as persons. As persons, the cemis are engaged in webs of social relationships with human beings that also define and redefine who they are. The personal histories and identities of the caciques participating in this exchange are as much defined and redefined by what they give as by what they take and keep. If there is one artifact of choice that exemplifies the complex nature of the reciprocal interactions between caciques and idols, then this must be the stone collar.

PART IV

Stone Collars, Elbow Stones, Three-Pointers, Stone Heads, and Guaízas

15 Stone Collars, Elbow Stones, and Caciques

The stone collars and elbow stones are visually complex artifacts, and when the lateral and upper panels are decorated, they truly display the virtuosity of Taínoan craftsmanship (Figures 3, 19–22). Like many of the other cemí idols, iconic or otherwise, both elbow stones and collars appear to have pre-Taínoan roots (i.e., the Ostionan and Elenan Ostionoid periods), possibly as early as A.D. 600 or A.D. 700 (Walker 1997:80). Because elbow stones have the same size and dimensions as the "elbow" portion of the monolithic stone collar, several other archaeologists—for instance, Ricardo Alegría (1986:37)—have suggested that these were essentially collars that were made of part stone (the elbow), with the rest of the arch or ring made from other materials, most likely wood or *henequén* (fiber cordage; Figure 19); others have suggested that they may be salvaged stone collars (Fewkes, in Walker 1997:80). This led them to propose that the composite cordage/wood and stone elbow is the antecedent for the all-stone collars. As we shall see, stone collars were also combined with three-pointed stone cemís to form a single yet compound object (Walker 1997:87).

The narrow, slender ring part of the stone collar is clearly a stone-sculptured rendition of another object made of bent wood that was tied to the two distal ends of the elbow part, visible as a knot or notch in the all-lithic version (see Figure 19: a, b). Logic would dictate that it was the wood-and-stone elbow that gave rise to the all-stone version. But contrary to conventional wisdom, Walker has persuasively argued that the monolithic collars were *not* derived from the elbow stones, but quite the contrary. Jeff Walker (1993, 1997) is very persuasive in showing, through stylistic "generative grammar" and technological analyses, why the reverse is more likely (Walker 1993:286–336). Stone collars evolved from the massive bench type to the slender frame type along with increasing decorative complexity over time. In parallel, the ancient miniature three-pointed stones also evolved into increasingly larger and more richly decorated forms. Late in the sequence, elbow stones appeared. The key feature of elbow stones is the frame forming the undecorated panels, which is linked to the later slender collars and not the earlier massive collars. Walker (1997:87) concludes that "the elbow stone must have come into being during the final decline of massive collars, when they began to evolve in slender forms." Walker further argues that these elbow stones were "abbreviated forms" of the all-stone collars: "I suggest that they were an economical version of the combined stone collar/three-pointer form. The most labor-intensive part of making both of these artifacts was the first stage of shaping, particularly the initial hollowing out of both sides of the stone slab to form the ring of the collar, and the subsequent shaping and engraving of the exterior designs. Abbreviating the ring portion—in essence by making an elbow stone—would have saved a great deal of time and labor. With faced elbow stones, only one artifact, an elbow stone, needs to be shaped" (Walker 1997:89–90).

Walker (1997:90) observed that labor and time saving was further enhanced by the fact that many of the elbow stones were made of softer rock materials, such as limestone, that would have been relatively easier to work with than the igneous materials used for all-stone collars. Moreover, given that the decorated panel in some elbow stones depicts a two-dimensional iconographic version (Figures 3: d; 19: d) of the three-dimensional three-pointed stone cemí, this "faced elbow stone was designed to be used as an economical substitute" for the all-stone collar and its attached sculptured three-pointer.

The function and meaning of the all-stone collars and the elbow stones—that is, the composite wood/fiber plus the elbow stone—are clouded in mystery, because the Spanish chroniclers never mentioned or described them and because so very few specimens have been found in secure archaeological contexts. Thus, before going into a discussion of function and meaning, it is worth first discussing their formal attributes, a task made infinitely easier thanks to Walker's doctoral research on these objects (Walker 1993; see also 1997). The next few pages will endeavor to address the questions of how they were used (human-object interaction) and by whom, what the meanings of the iconographic motifs were, whether they were imbued with cemí and, finally, to evaluate whether they were alienable or inalienable "possessions."

A. Formal Attributes

Conventionally, the all-stone collars have been classed in terms of the relative cross-section thickness as either *slender* or *massive* (Fewkes 1907; in addition to the stone collars illustrated in this book, see Bercht et al. 1997; Fewkes 1922; Kerchache 1994; Oliver et al. 2008; and the catalogs of the Museo del Hombre Dominicano [MHD 1977], the Museo de Historia, Antropología y Arte, of the University of Puerto Rico [MHAA-UPR 2006], and of the Altos de Chavón catalog [n.d.].) Generally, the slender stone collars present highly polished surfaces, whereas the massive ones usually have a coarser surface finish. There a number of either type that bear no decoration, but most of them, particularly the slender monolithic collars, are decorated. The iconography and the decorative motifs of both types of collars are visually complex; this is in large measure because of the physical limitations imposed by the curved, relatively narrow decorative fields (Figures 21, 22). The motifs and icons to be carved must therefore be arranged so as to fit these decorative fields.

Viewed from above, the shape of the stone collar varies from moderately to markedly oval and eccentric, with two modal tendencies. One is the bench mode, which is somewhat more circular in outline (see Figures 3: c; 20: a, b, d, f, g), whereas the other is the frame mode (Figures 3: a; 20: c, e; 22). The bench mode is associated with massive collars, while the frame is associated with slender collars (Figure 20). The slender collars thicken toward the distal end (Figure 21: C), whereas the proximal end (the ring) tends to be very thin and slender. On one side the slender collar segment links to the lower panel by a protuberance or projection. But it is the distal section that bears all the decoration, when present. There are two relatively broad panels on each side toward the apex of the collar (Figures 21, 22). One is a lateral, lower panel, which is frequently decorated (Figures 3: a, b; 21: B; 22: c). The other panel is on the opposite side, also placed laterally, and is undecorated, although it may have an oval concavity (as in Figure 21: D; 22: b). Both massive and slender collars have these lower lateral panels. There is also a decorated upper panel found only on slender collars (Walker 1993:314–315) that bears iconography, sculptured in relief (Figure 21: A; 22: a). This panel often displays what Walker has called a "central figure" (1993: 316–*passim*; Figure 23: q, r).

Walker (1993:326–336, figs. 5–11) has proposed a seriation or progression of design development based on the reasonable premise that the massive bench type of stone collar was the earlier form. This form gradually evolved into the slender frame type. One of the early dominant motifs is the "Headless-Fish" (Figures 3: c; 20: a-d).

> [It] is a clear and lone design at the beginning of the sequence, [but] by its mid-point this design has become substantially stylized, and some of its key elements serve supporting roles for more recently introduced designs, e.g., the fins become the Bird-Frog beaks, and only in outline [do] they retain their original form and meaning. By the end of the sequence the Headless-Fish has become so *passé* it is relegated to the role of a border or frame for newer motifs, and occasionally previously critical elements almost disappear, e.g., the tail becomes less and less defined throughout the sequence, and at least in one example it is all but absent [Walker 1993:335].

The serial progression begins with an image or icon that is displayed in the lateral panel and is visually cued by the knob shape of the distal portion of the collar. Walker labeled this iconic motif the "Headless-Fish." This image indeed evokes the headless body of a fish, with its tail fin being the key visual cue and, hence, less likely to be that of a saurian (lizard, iguana, or snake). The absent head, however, is visually insinuated in some specimens by the protruding knob (as a "head") at the distal end of the collar (Walker 1997:85, fig. 1 b). The second motif in the proposed sequence involves what Walker identifies as the "Bird-Frog Twin," an image that emerges when viewing the upper and lateral decorated panels from a *lateral* perspective (Figure 21: A, *e*). The wing elements and the nose of the bird strongly suggest to me that the biological model is a bat rather than generic birds (Figure 23: J-R). When looking at the upper panel from the top with the collar resting flat on the ground, the twin icons that emerge are in essence the head (with eyes and mouth, sometimes also nostrils marked) and upper torso of two personages that may or not be frogs. Invariably, as Walker noted, these two personages are presented opposing each other. If one focuses the view on the lateral profile of the collar and stands it vertical, yet another image emerges: the head–upper torso personage instead appears in profile and kneeling (Figure 21: *e, f*), more humanlike. The revelation of different images depending on the viewer's perspective relative to the collar's position is anatropic: as one rotates the object, new images become salient and others become hidden (Oliver 2008b: 163–*passim*). Yet the visible and hidden personages are always comprised within a single "body," visually cued by the design elements of the panel (Figures 21: B; 22: c). This is another excellent example of two key features of Taínoness: multinatural perspectivism and dividuality. The stone collars embody different identities and personages that are visible only from different focal points, but at the same time they are articulated into a single entity. This scenario is made even more complex by the proposed attachment of three-pointed cemí idols on the lateral undecorated panel of slender collars (Figure 21: B), most likely those cemí idols that have the head designs sculptured in the apex rather than on either of the lateral protuberances.

The third iconic theme is an elaboration of the former, which may have developed after or at the same time as Walker's "Bird-Frog Twin" motif of the upper decorated panel. Instead of a single pair of opposing personages there are four (compare Figure 23: K, M-P with J, L). Walker named this motif the "Double-Twin Bird-Frog." When looking at the upper decorated panel from a lateral perspective and with the collar resting on the ground (horizontal) and at the lower lateral decorated panel, what emerges is a bicephalous creature (two heads, four pairs of eyes) united by a single body with a design that is "Classic Taíno" (Chican Ostionoid): the central circle and dot depicting the abdomen, framed by triangular-shaped feet that appear to suggest that the legs are crossed (Figures 26: B; 27: c). The same abdomen-feet features are also displayed by the central anthropo-zoomorphic cemí petroglyphs of Caguana (Oliver 1998, 2005; Figure 12: b). The hands in the stone collar are also triangular in shape but rest on the abdominal area, a posture that is also adopted in many Taínoan anthropo-zoomorphic icons and idols executed in various media. Although the shape of the hands and feet are suggestive of frogs, these formal conventions are not limited to just frogs, but may also be portrayed in humanlike figures and in combined animal-human figures, again an indication of the multiple authorship of the identities and personhood of the personage portrayed. Thus, this is a single-bodied personage characterized by a "fantastic" double head (when seen in lateral view, Figure 21: B). Finally, when one looks at the stone collar set in a vertical position (Figure 21: *f;* 23: J-P) and focuses on the two pairs of opposing twins, the personages are kneeling (bent lower legs), a posture that is much more suggestive of a human rather than an animal-like being. This alterity between humanlike and froglike personages in Chican Ostionoid icons has earlier antecedents in Elenan Ostionoid ceramics (see Figure 10).

The last addition in Walker's proposed sequence of stone collars is what he calls the "Central Figure." This icon is always, or almost always, that of a bat personage, which is placed at the center of the decorated panel and can straddle into the upper decorated panel (Figure 23: Q-R). The bat icon is, however, only visible to the viewer when the stone collar is positioned laterally; as soon as one views it from the top, the bat personage disappears and the simple or double-twin personages emerge.

The elbow stones, like their all-stone counterparts, also have an undecorated panel for attaching three-pointed cemís. Presumably, as Walker noted, at a late point in the sequence the three-dimensional cemí icon, particularly the three-pointer type bearing facial motifs on the apex rather than lateral prominences (Bercht et al. 1997:figs. 68, 80; Kerchache 1994:226–227), was replaced by a two-dimensional rendition directly on the panel of the elbow (i.e., Walker's "faced elbow" subtype; see Oliver et al. 2008:118–119, cat. 33). These faced elbow stones invariably depict anthropomorphic personages, sometimes full-bodied but most often showing only the head portion (compare figures 65 with 59 and 66, in Walker 1997). Accepting that three-pointed stones are cemí, there is little question that the faced elbow stones (Figure 19: b) and stone collars with attached three-pointed stones (Figure 22) must therefore also be cemí. This is a composite comprising several cemí beings in close articulation with one another, and with the human "owner."

This relation between human beings and animal entities may not be just about an animistic perspective but also seems to suggest elements of totemism at work. There seems to be a special relationship between the social group and animals (see Ingold 2000). In the Caribbean examples (e.g., the stone collars or in ceramic lugs, Figures 13, 27) the concept of multiple natures is important: there are frogs as frogs, and then there are froglike beings in alterity *and* in synthesis with humanlike beings. An analysis of the Hispaniolan myths collected by Ramón Pané (1999) leads me to think that the concept of animals being humanlike, and vice versa, goes back to notions of a primordial time in the cosmos when that state of being and of sociality (i.e., "paradise") was the modus vivendi for all beings and things. But all that was lost to humanity at some point in time. Yet ordinary humans in the present world regained access to this primordial domain, thanks to Deminán Caracaracol and his three identical brothers, the culture heroes who revealed to humans the "secrets" of cohoba, tobacco, medicines, religious ceremonies, and so on (see Oliver 1997; Stevens Arroyo 1988). Only through ritual performances, especially the cohoba, could an ordinary being once again experience, at least for a while, that primordial, original state of being and commune with the numinous (mythical) beings, with "man-frogs," "bat-men," and so forth. It is a mistake, I think, to assume that the natives thought of this primordial, mythical cosmos as a thing of the deep past (*in illio tempore*). Rather, this primordial domain is omnipresent, in the here and now, but only accessible through proper ritual preparation (e.g., fasting, vomiting) and execution (cohoba, areítos, funerary feasts, etc.).

To summarize, I suspect that the "utopian" ideal of total Taínoness for an ordinary human may well have been to permanently regain that primordial state of being. I get the feeling that the natives' sense of "paradise in afterlife" would be precisely to return to the ways things ought to be: in communion with all primordial beings. In a sense, these mythical animal- and humanlike beings were the ancestral community of personages of the ordinary human society. If this is a correct interpretation, then this special relationship with animals besides plants and other numinous things in nature is suggestive of some elements of totemism. All of this would also relate to Alfred Gell's (1998) idea of the distributed person as it applies to human beings and their objects of art and their outward manifestations of "divinity" (i.e., totems). The issue of how well developed or central totemism is as an element of Taínoness needs further research, which I will leave for a future opportunity. Overall, I think that the animistic perspective more comfortably fits the data available.

B. Known Archaeological Contexts

It goes without saying that stone collars and elbow stones were expensive to produce in terms of invested time and labor. I have already commented earlier that on average there were between ten and seventeen of these items completed per year over a stretch of seven hundred years or so (see Table 1). In short, they are rare, infrequent items and a finite archaeological resource. Sadly, the advent of intensive collectionism toward the end of the nineteenth century (e.g., see Cabello Carro 2008; Fewkes 1907; McEwan 2008) means that theoretically very few stone collars and elbow stones—particularly complete specimens—remain for archaeologists to recover today.

Jeff Walker (1993:449–*passim*) and others (Alegría 1986; Oliver 1998; Sued Badillo 2001a) have noted a high concentration of blanks, or remnants, of the initial shaping of the stone collars that are found piled up at the civic-ceremonial center of Caguana in Puerto Rico. Although these look like *metates,* or milling stones, they undoubtedly represent the early stages of the manufacture of collars;

they show concave depressions on *both* sides, some showing the beginnings of the central perforation of the ring (Walker 1997:fig. 67). Most of these unfinished stone collars or elbow stones are not from Caguana (Utu-10) itself but come from its immediate vicinity, a region characterized by dispersed farmstead settlements sprinkled between the karst hills and small valleys (dolines).

Research in this 15–20 km^2 area to date (1996–2005) has yielded the following data (Rivera and Oliver 2005; Oliver 2005; Oliver et al. 1999). An unfinished elbow stone was found in a batey site (Cag-04), just 2.5 km north of Caguana (Oliver, unpublished field notes). Another fragment of a massive, bench-type limestone collar (undecorated) along with a large "half-moon" type of three-pointed stone were recovered in 1996 on the surface of another single batey site (Utu-20) located only 1.5 km east of Cag-3. These two items were piled together in what was once the edge of the batey, along with a few loose batey stones, the result of clearing for modern farming activities right on top of the batey. At the Vega de Nelo Vargas site (Utu-27), just 1.5 km east of Caguana, two mended fragments of the lower panel were found in a domestic refuse midden next to a small batey. The panel's surface is still rough, which suggests that it was never finished. Possibly it fractured during manufacture, or the material was defective and thus discarded. In any event, it seems that the farmstead sites were producing and/or domestically using slender and massive stone collars, and there is a good chance (but not yet proven) that a part of the farmstead production was controlled or demanded by the cacique of Caguana. This pile of unfinished stone collars represents the highest known concentration of partly worked blanks in Puerto Rico, if not the Caribbean (Walker 1993:447).

Pedro Alvarado (personal communication 2005) also informs me that a complete slender stone collar was found at the top of a mountain peak that forms the dome of Cueva del Lucero, a cave replete with pictographs and petroglyphs, located near Juana Díaz, Puerto Rico. At the base of the mountain there is also an occupation site, with scattered surface materials that include both "modified" Ostiones and Capá ceramic styles (see Figure 5: ca. A.D. 900 onward). Neither the cave nor the site below has been archaeologically excavated yet, albeit most of the pictographic art found at the Lucero cave is in the Chican Ostionoid styles (e.g., see Figure 12: e, f). Also in Puerto Rico, Reniel Rodríguez Ramos (2007:283) reported a panel portion of a possible slender collar fragment at the Río Tanamá site, near Arecibo, associated with Cuevas/Ostiones–style (A.D. 440–850) ceramics, as well as other fragments found at the sites of Tibes (Ponce), Cagüitas (Caguas), and Tierras Nuevas (Manatí) associated with Monserrate/Ostiones/Santa Elena styles. At the Sorcé site, on Vieques Island, a coarse fragment was found in association with what appears to be a Cuevas/pure Ostiones deposit. In short, stone collars predate A.D. 1200–1300, the time when the Chican Ostionoid styles of Capá and Esperanza (i.e., Taínoan styles) developed in Puerto Rico (see section 2).

In the eastern Dominican Republic, slender and massive stone collar fragments have been recovered from a number of sites between Santo Domingo and Punta Macao; however, most have neither contextual data nor published reports. Punta Macao (Altagracia, Higüey) is typical. Based on my conversations in 2004 with Gabriel Atiles, who directed extensive salvage work there at the end of the 1990s, I am aware that several stone collar fragments were found during excavations, but no report has been forthcoming and it is unlikely one will ever be published. The one site where good data exists is at the El Cabo site (Cabo de San Rafael, Higüey) where a limestone collar fragment was found during preliminary tests conducted by Elpidio Ortega (1978) in a midden deposit and possibly related to the earlier Ostionan Ostionoid assemblage (Anadel and "Transicional" ceramic styles). In the latest excavations conducted in 2005 and 2006, the Anglo-Dutch team found two slender stone collar fragments, both made of imported igneous rock. The nearest possible igneous source is in the Cordillera Oriental, around El Seibo, to the northwest. Both specimens were located in a domestic context, within a few centimeters of the basal coralliferous limestone bedrock and associated with Boca Chica (Taínoan) pottery and other artifacts. The 300 m² excavated domestic area is perforated with several hundred post- and pit holes from which at least three clear, round structures (*bohíos*) have been defined. It is the clearest evidence thus far published of slender stone collars in association with houses in Hispaniola (Hofman et al. 2007:95–106).

Walker (1993) has found indications that in some instances stone collars and three-pointed cemís were acquired or donated to museums together as a set, that both were found together. He (1993:380) cites Samuel K. Lothrop's comment that a stone collar and a three-pointer were found together on an unspecified site in the Manatí region, which he could not verify, although he suggests that these are likely two specimens (UPR #301 and #305) now at the Museo de Historia, Antropología y Arte, University of Puerto Rico. Another stone collar of the slender type (UPR #11,009) and a three-pointer were found by workmen digging holes for a water pump station at Los Indios, near the town of Santa Isabel (south coast of Puerto Rico). These two specimens, acquired by Dr. Montalvo Guenard—a prolific private collector in Puerto Rico in the 1930s—were said to have been found "near a metate," which Walker (1993:380) argues was more likely to be a *turén* (stone seat) or perhaps a stone collar blank. Walker found three, three-pointed cemís from Los Indios (formerly Guenard's collection), one of which is almost certainly the one found along with the slender collar. In another instance, an elbow stone and a three-pointer (UPR #11,155 and #11,149) were found at a site "on the property of Domingo Mundo, near the market place of Salinas" on the south coast of Puerto Rico. To these one can add the samples from site Utu-20, already mentioned above. In sum, although these are tentative associations, I agree with Walker's reasons—based on morphological and technological attributes relating both artifacts—for considering the pairing of cemís and stone collars a probable rather than improbable correlation.

To conclude, the immense majority of the elbow stones and stone collars do not come from archaeologically controlled contexts. But the above samples of known contexts suggest that these artifacts—evincing different stages of production rather than as finished products—are found in a broad range of contexts, from civic-ceremonial centers to domestic habitation and midden refuse. It must be kept in mind that the samples with known contexts are all fragmentary, some having faults and being discarded, and others left unfinished for whatever reasons.

Walker's (1993:447–451) study on the museum samples of elbow stones and collars in Puerto Rico shows that they were often found in association with sites that have or once had stone-demarcated precincts (plazas, ball courts), while specimens held at the University of Puerto Rico suggest that at least some stone collars and elbow stones were probably found together as a set. Given these diverse contexts, the next subsection addresses the questions of the functions of stone collars and elbow stones, how they were used, and who might have controlled or used them. In Walker's words: "What is not at issue is that stone collars are found at ceremonial 'ball court' sites—the archaeological evidence indicates that stone collars are associated with these types of sites. What *is* still at issue is whether the stone collar was: (1) worn at all or used as a non-corporeal sacred object; (2) worn diagonally across the chest like a bandolier; (3) worn by all players during games of *batey*; and (4) whether ball games were ever played at the ceremonial site" (Walker 1993:448).

C. Function and Use of Stone Collars and Elbow Stones

Jesse Fewkes (1922:160) had long ago proposed that stone collars and elbow stones could be: (a) an insignia of office, worn on the person; (b) a sacrificial object; (c) idols for animal worship, such as serpents and lizards; (d) idols for tree or plant worship, especially manioc; or (e) a collar for men or women dragging canoes (see Walker 1993: 160–161). One of the most popular theories was, and for many still is, that the stone collars were used around the belt by players engaged in the Antillean ball game or that they were "ceremonial" stone replicas of the actual belts used (Alegría 1983, 1986; Ekholm 1961). The "collar" label came from the Puerto Rican peasants, who also called them *yugos* in analogy to the yokes worn by beasts of burden. The collar idea that was picked up by J. B. Holder in 1875 and Otis Mason in 1877 (Walker 1993:158–159) has stuck as a name regardless of whether they were functionally collars or not.

However, I favor Jeff Walker's view that these objects were items associated with chiefly power and regalia (Walker 1993:449) and that they were likely a combination of heraldic and emblematic objects used by caciques in ritual theater. They were among the personal possessions of a cacique and most likely meant for public display only during particular ceremonial events. Figuring out if and how they might have been worn by a human being would point to some of their possible uses and functions. Walker, who has extensively researched stone collars and elbow stones, concluded:

> On the first point, whether the stone rings were worn, I believe they were. There is uniformity to the interior of the collars. Whatever their exterior shapes, be they massive or slender, the interior shape and size are about the same, a consistency which far exceeds the exterior of these collars. This is fairly conclusive evidence that uniformity was intentionally sought for some purpose, and I see no other reasons for this being the case, other than to wear them. On the second and third points, I do not think they were worn around the waist. Rather, they appear to have been worn over one shoulder and across the chest, like a gunslinger's bandolier; this is because I believe stone collars and three pointers were important props in Taíno public ceremony. . . . On the fourth point, whether stone collars were used by ball players, I feel the evidence is rather tenuous. . . . I am more inclined to think that they were worn in other types of public ceremonies . . . they may have been used in ritual theater [Walker 1993:449].

If such stone rings were used like a gunslinger's bandolier, or hung over one shoulder, they could only be worn for brief periods, as they could weigh up to eighty pounds. Given their weight and bulk, it is most unlikely that they were used in ball games, where agility is essential. Furthermore, the attachment of yet another icon, the three-pointed cemí, to the stone collar certainly rules out their actual use in ball games. In sum, like Walker, I think that because the three-pointed stones were tied to stone collars (as in Figure 22: b), they were more likely to be used and displayed in ritual theater and ceremonial activities rather than mere stone representations of the pads and other belt paraphernalia used by ball players.

I am mystified by the fact that not one single Spaniard ever mentioned these collars, as they are certainly of unusual shape and visually arresting, and at odds with anything the Spaniards would have been familiar with back in the Mediterranean. I can only guess that their function was so obvious to the Spanish that it did not require further comment or, more likely, that these collars were of such central value and importance to the native elite that the natives admirably succeeded in hiding them from public view.

D. Who Are the Personages in the Stone Collars and Elbow Stones?

There is no question that the three-pointer is one of the cemí icons that was first objectified from an encounter with a cemí manifestation in nature, as Pané's (1999) narrative indicated. Whether the stone collars were also manifested and objectified in the same manner as three-pointers is debatable. The three-pointers were subject to veneration and consultation in the cohoba ceremonies conducted in the temple house. Attaching these three-pointers to an iconographically loaded collar is, in effect, a recomposition of *all* the icons into a different bounded entity and should thus be perceived in a different light than if they were to be engaged as separate entities. Obviously, whatever the iconography of the collars meant, and whichever personages or beings were depicted in collars and elbow stones, they could only be a part of the meaning and only part of the cast of beings engaged with the cacique who, along with the attached three-pointed personage, was the third entity involved in this relationship. It is not known whether the same collar would always have the same three-pointed cemí idol attached or whether different ones could be selected for different kinds of ceremonial events. It is likely, though, given the greater number of three-pointers relative to collars, that a larger number of the latter would remain detached from the collars for longer periods, housed, consulted, and venerated in the cacique's caney. In any case, the symbolic content of a stone collar adds to and modifies the personhood of the three-pointed cemí idol, as it provides the latter with yet other images with which to interact. But there is more, because as already noted for the three-pointer-and-collar combination, the images are visually emerging and hiding depending on the perspective of the viewer relative to the position of the collar (and its attached three-pointer). Walker argued: "I suggest that the meshing of several figures can be interpreted as a mechanism used to link various mythical personalities in a single work, very much like telling a story with different characters, or presenting a drama with different actors [agent-patient relationships]. This combining-meshing is seen as a form of relating myths. . . . Thus, a knowledgeable person can 'read' the myth by observing the figures portrayed" (Walker 1993:399).

Furthermore, argues Walker (1993:399), "in Taíno/Chicoid art, there seems to be a deliberate attempt to be ambiguous," in that in most cases "the artist has intentionally not represented a complete animal or person, and only shows one, or a few parts . . . without presenting the whole body," such as the Headless-Fish motif in collars or just head and feet in three-pointed stones. He goes on to argue that this ambiguity is "one way of expressing the omnipotence of the spirit being" (Walker 1993:399). Thus, in this view, "gods (*cemí*) are powerful because they have the properties of *many* different, earthly lesser beings"; they are "a *combination* of many different beings"; they are also "from *part* of many different beings"; and "certain specific parts of many beings specifically relate or refer to a god" (a cemí), such as the fin of a fish, and "it is that part that holds the power."

However, the suggestion of visual ambiguity is true from our western perspective of indivisible persons and the individuality of personhood. It would, of course, *not* be as ambiguous to the natives, whose sense of personhood is fundamentally dividual and partible, even potentially fractal. Note that Walker speaks of parts of (or composite) beings combining and recombining to create other distinctive beings and relations with yet another being (three-pointed cemí). The visible part always would evoke the invisible, hidden part or parts, and rather than just saying that the visible part is what holds power, I would qualify this by stating that the visible cue is what matters to evoke the whole by a process of abduction in the viewer's mind (as argued by Gell 1998).

I regard the all-stone and the partly stone collars (i.e., elbow stones) as having the quality or condition of cemí. This does not necessarily mean that these two entities were engaged by or articulated with the cacique during a cohoba ceremony in the same manner as the other cemí idols (and cemís as spirits) discussed earlier—that is, to pray, venerate, and ask or beg them for support and favors under the influence of cohoba. But just like the cemís portrayed in duhos, inhaling tubes, and other ritual or ceremonial paraphernalia, they are part of the "equipment" required by caciques to achieve a state of potency and knowledge during cohoba ceremonies so as to engage the cemís as spirits (or as hallucinations, visions, from our western perspective). But who are the personages evoked by the stone collars and elbow stones? Are they mythical characters of a remote, primordial past, or are they the sorts of nonhuman, potent beings actively engaged with humans here and now? Walker put forth the thesis that they are personages emerging from or relating to mythology and mythical time, and in that sense they are different from or unlike the twelve cemís described by Pané (see sections 4 and 5). Let us examine this more closely, and specifically in relation to the stone collars and elbow stones and, for now, deprived of the attached three-pointers.

Walker (1993) conducted a detailed analysis of the iconography and the designs of a large sample of collars and three-pointers with plausible interpretations about the kinds of personages displayed and ideas evoked by both types of artifacts. He did so with reference to comparative Taíno and South American mythology. Walker's detailed (1993:284–336) "generative grammar" and modal analysis of the stone collar designs and iconography resulted in the identification of several frequently repeated iconic motifs (Figure 23). Walker's research came up with the following repeated iconographic themes: (1) the Headless-Fish and the related Fish and Water "Jaguars" (i.e., sharks); (2) Frog- or Man-on-the-face's-back; and (3) the Simple Twin and the related Double-Twin Bird-Frog themes (Walker 1993:393–432), themes that seem to allude to the various myth cycles collected by Pané.

The early and dominant iconic form, seen in massive stone collars, is the Headless-Fish personage (Figures 3: c; 20: a-d, f, g). If it is indeed a fish rather than a snake or some other creature, then the personage depicted is undoubtedly related to or comes from bodies of water. What little we know about "water beings" in Taínoan religion comes from the myth cycle that has to do with the genesis of *bagua* (ocean) and waters contained in the Oedipus-like myth of Yaya, the "Supreme Spirit" or "Spirit of Spirits" in Taíno religion (Pané 1999:13–14). In one version of this myth, the defiance of Yayael ("Son of Yaya") by returning to his father's house, despite Yaya's having banished him for eternity, resulted in the son's death by the hands of Yaya, who placed his son's bones inside a calabash (higüero) and hung it from the roof of the house. Later, wishing to see his son, Yaya ordered an unnamed woman (perhaps his wife) to take down the higüero, from which Yayael's bones, now transformed into fish, and water poured out (see Oliver 1997; Pané 1990:13). Being hungry, Yaya then proceeded to catch the fish and eat them. This is an act of endocannibalism: the father (Yaya) "ate" his own son's (Yayael) bones turned into fish (and, thus, food). This myth is not just about the creation of oceans, rivers, and aquatic life (fish as food), but it also lays down two cultural rules: (1) that sons, competitors of the chief/father, have to leave the natal home and establish their own house; and (2) that upon death, selected bones of the deceased will be consumed by the surviving relatives as a proper or ideal funerary ritual (but in reverse, as the father consumes the son). It indicates that Yaya, the Spirit of Spirits, is the ultimate seminal agency in the creation of the ocean and rivers and of aquatic life (as food resources). It also suggests that the sacrificial death of one's own kin is what it takes to stock and replenish the oceans and rivers with fish (food). The calabash is, of course, a uterine symbol, where the bones (as a seminal force) mixed with the "amniotic" fluid gestated life; upon overturning the calabash, the amniotic fluid gushed out with fish, thus populating the oceans and rivers. This myth could also allude to native notions implicated in ancestor veneration and of the partibility of a person: by consuming certain parts of a deceased person (such as mashed bones of a relative) his or her potent vitality will be passed on to or live on in the next generation.

Given the role of Yayael as fish, it is possible that the fish iconography seen in the massive stone collars, as well as in the monoliths of the civic-ceremonial centers of El Bronce, Caguana, and Batey del Delfín de Yagüez (Puerto Rico), refer or relate to this myth and that the fish personage is either Yayael or those descended from him (Oliver 1998:figs. 25, 44; 2005:figs. 7–17; Rivera Fontán 2002, 2005). As Walker suggested, Yayael's transformed nature, or his "other" nature as a fish, could be the character that is captivated and sculptured in the Headless-Fish personage seen in the massive stone collars (Figures 3: c; 20; 23: a, b, d, f, g). If, however, this icon is more than just a mnemonic device sculptured in stone to recall a mythical event and is *also* a cemí idol, an animate fish-person, whose active engagement with the bearer of the stone collar (the cacique) causes things to happen and has effects on future events, then this fish-person is a cemí in that sense of potency and with the kind of identity and dividuality already discussed for the other named cemí idols. I suspect that like other idols, each "fish-cemí" would have a name, title, and rank, and would be fed and venerated. The fish-persons in the stone collars do not have to be specifically or uniquely a direct reference to (or actually be) Yayael, but all may ultimately be derived from or generated by Yaya's acts in the primordial past.

Thus the fish-persons-cemís that *are* the stone collars worn and deployed by the cacique could each be any of the many fish personages descended from Yayael, and ultimately Yaya (who is, in effect, the Supreme Being), each "child" of Yayael having its own ranking, status, name, like cohoba idols did. And, of course, because of the particular relationship that each stone collar has developed with the cacique (the "owner") and with the string of heirs of the cacique who will likely inherit it, they will also accrue reputations, legends, and biographies that are distinct from other Headless-Fish stone collars owned by other caciques and their heirs. This view does not require a total disassociation of the Headless-Fish personages seen in the collars from Yayael and the myth related to him, but it allows for each of the Headless-Fish personages to retain, through mythical kinship, some quality or part of its ultimate originator, and yet simultaneously have its particular identity and personhood. Thus, dividuality and partibility, and the construction and deconstruction of personhood, are the critical concepts for approaching the meaning and symbolism of these artifacts.

I suggest that the fish-cemís depicted in stone collars, as well as in the large monoliths framing the plazas of Caguana and El Bronce, are cemís who have the powers relating to the stocking and restocking of marine or freshwater resources. In the cohoba ceremonies the Headless-Fish collars could be part of the contingent of cemís deployed by the cacique in making decisions and policies regarding fishing rights, scheduling of fishing expeditions, the distribution of fish, and so on. In the Hispaniolan myth it is clear that fishing was regarded as an eminently masculine task that carried high prestige in contrast to cultivation or agriculture (see Oliver 2000). As Walker (1993, 1997) noted, over time, the fish scale designs (Figure 23: chain A mode) of the massive collars lost some of their specificity as "fish," and as in the slender collars, the upper panel became a more prominent decorative field.

Pairing the Headless-Fish cemí of the stone collar with, for example, one of the three-pointed stone cemís that José Juan Arrom (1975:23–29) proposed caused manioc (and presumably other crops) to mature and grow would mean that the cacique holding the composite object would have control and power over the two key subsistence resources of the natives: crops (carbohydrates) and fish (proteins). In both public display and ritual theater the cacique would be framed by, or be one with, the two key personages that have agency over the subsistence economy. If the Headless-Fish personage is paired, for example, with another three-pointed icon whose potency relates to a specific weather phenomenon (such as storms), a different kind of message is evoked, as the relationship of the Headless-Fish personage is with another being. Perhaps this would explain why the three-pointers were *not* permanently attached to a given all-stone, wood-stone, or fiber-stone (elbow) collar. Physical detachment allows for flexibility, permitting the cacique to pair the appropriate three-pointed cemí to the collar for the appropriate ceremonial occasion.

The other repeated theme is exemplified by what Walker labels as the Simple-Twin and Double-Twin personages registered in the decorated upper panel of slender stone collars (Figures 21; 22: a; 23: J-P). These personages are visible and sa-lient when the viewer looks toward the top of the upper panel (Figures 21: A, e; 23: M). The figure that emerges shows the head—with eyes, nose, and sometimes a mouth, too—and torso of a personage that is placed in an inverse position (torso adjacent to torso) to another identical figure. These are the twin personages, whose morphology is very roughly anthropomorphic (Figure 21: e). Often, though, the pair of opposing twins is doubled, with two pairs of opposing twins (Figures 21: A; 23: L). When the collar is standing vertical and the viewer focuses on the deco-rated upper panel, the two opposing twins or the two pairs of twins appear in pro-file as personages kneeling (Figures 21: B, f; 23: M, m', O), with feet against the feet of the other twin (Figure 22: a).

The organization of motifs and iconographic designs in terms of simple (1 vs. 1) dual oppositions is a canonical rule of art design that can then be further elabo-rated as (1 vs. 1) [vs.] (1 vs. 1). In other words, elements are organized into two op-posing sets of pairs to obtain completeness (4 = [1 vs. 1] vs. [1 vs. 1] = 1, or com-pleteness). It was Arrom (1975) who first drew attention to this by pointing out that four is a number that has special significance in Taínoan oral literature: four months was the length of Yayael's banishment; four moons was the time it took a real, flesh-and-blood native to complete a journey; and four twin siblings were the total number of culture heroes of mythology. Dual opposites and the derived quad-ripartite dualism thus express a general principle of structural organization in art, and probably in other things as well. The twin pairs of opposed elements require four parts to complete a whole or a unit; when referring to time units, four is what it takes to complete all time (i.e., forever).

This notion of double twins as paired opposites in a four-field structure (in the decorated upper panel) as a requirement for completeness is precisely underscored by the artist's manipulation of the decorated, lateral *lower* panel of slender collars (Figures 21: B; 22: c; 23: M). When viewed laterally, the simple-twin personages are hidden from the viewer and what emerges in the upper register of the panel is a stylized face with a nose often shaped as a triangle or a circle (Figure 23: K, M) and a pair of eyes. If instead the upper panel has double twins, the lateral view would show a bicephalous image with two pairs of eyes (Figures 21: B; 23: J, L-P). In both examples, the single or double head of the upper panel is underlain by a panel that shows the features of a single body: arms, legs, feet, and abdomen (Figure 21: B), or in the case of bats (Figure 23: M), folded wings. Thus what in one perspective shows opposing twins or pairs of twins and, in total, two or four beings dissolves in lateral perspective into one complete being, one body. Four is what it takes to make a complete whole and to indicate timelessness. The theme of unity/completeness versus partibility/segregation—echoing at once the individuality and dividuality of the entities or personages—is thus elegantly and dynamically rendered (via anat-ropy) in the stone collar. In the examples shown here, the lower panel shows typical

Taínoan (Chican Ostionoid) conventions for feet and legs as triangles and the abdomen and navel as a circle (or oval) and a central dot (see Figures 21: B; 22: c; compare with Figures 9; 12: b). This interplay between dual (quadripartite) structures with anatropy, now hiding, now displaying two/four personages or a single individual, is meant to emphasize the dynamic multiple natures and dividuality of these personages captivated in the stone collars.

Because of the feet form and the squatted position of the personages seen in some stone collars and other anthropomorphic icons, such objects have been described as froglike beings (Figures 12: b; 21; 22: c). Three-pointers also have the same kind of leg/feet forms (in the lateral, distal prominence) depicted, and in the case of full-bodied petroglyphs, such as at Jácana (Figure 9), the shape of their lower extremities as a whole are even more suggestive of the legs of a frog. Frogs in Taínoan iconography appear to be suggestive of fecundity and fertility, announcing the rainy season. In fact, not fiction, the BBC-Bristol team (Reddish 1996) has filmed real *coquí* frogs (*Eleutherodactylus sp.*) raining down from the sky in the cloud forests of El Yunque (Puerto Rico)—that is, dropping down from the canopy to spawn near the puddles below on the ground (Oliver 1998:151–154), a feat of nature that captures the very essence of the "fantastic realism" literary genre of the likes of Alejo Carpentier or Gabriel García Márquez.

The rendering of the legs and feet in the otherwise skeletal anthropomorphic, full-bodied personages, such as seen in Caguana (Figure 12: b) or Jácana (Figure 9), points to the fecundity that all ancestor personages have—that despite their departure from the living, their seminal fecundity is still a paramount condition for the continuation of human life on earth. In anthropomorphic three-pointed cemís, the head, located in one lateral prominence (the face), is where all the signs of power and rank concentrate: large ear spools, elaborate headdress, even the guaíza plaque or mask may be depicted. The other lateral prominence is often provided with froglike legs. In the famous Jamaican wood cohoba idol housed at the British Museum (Figure 11: a), the hands of the personage are rendered with three fingers and their dactyl cups, a feature typical of several species of frogs, including the *coquí*. This feature suggests that part of their nature (as multinatural beings) incorporates the frog quality of fecundity.

Who are the four twin personages so frequently seen in the collars? They could be, as Walker argues, a representation of the four twin culture heroes (led by a being named Deminán Caracaracol) of the Macorix or Magua natives, the personages of mythology that provided humanity with key knowledge and artifacts that were lost to them as they became removed further in time and space from their original state in the primordial world and time. It may also be that these twin personages are the constituent and enabling parts that were required to produce a complete, whole being. The two or four twin beings are indeed miniature idols, suggestively anthropomorphic in outline, as knee-bending or squatting is a posture seen only in anthropomorphic personages, never in zoomorphic beings in Taínoan art (MHD Catalog 1977). Mythology tells us that two twin pairs are involved in completing culture and humanity with their gifts of culture and knowledge, and that these four personages resolve into a single yet potent dividual personage, which appears to allude to frogs. Embedding the four twins into a froglike body would seem to suggest that this "completed" personage (seen laterally) is involved in holding and releasing the knowledge and secrets of the supernatural domain handed down by him or them from primordial times. Not surprisingly, conjoined twins also appear in pendants that are typical of Hispaniola (Figure 13: e).

The last theme refers to the later development in collars of a central figure that to my knowledge is invariably modeled after a bat. The bat figure is, again, only visibly salient when viewing the collar laterally. It is depicted on the lower decorated panel (Figure 23: R), and as well in the upper panel when viewed laterally (Figure 23: Q). A shorthand version of the latter is also visible laterally in the upper panel (Figure 23: M). In one stone collar, viewing the upper and lower panels combined, one can appreciate the two elements that form the body of the bat personage: while the upper half shows the head (eyes and triangular nose motifs), the lower panel registers the pair of folded wings (Figure 23: M). On rotating the upper panel of the bat personage (Figure 23: M-O), one can appreciate the profile view of the twin personages (Figure 23: m') by isolating it from the rest of the design. In Taínoan religion bats are always associated with the dead, and with the non-living souls (*opía*) who at night leave their domain to roam the forests. The bat personage, animated by opía is likely to be just that—the soul of a dead yet animated being, perhaps an ancestor or relative of the cacique who wears the stone collar.

The "bicephalous personage" appears to us westerners as a fantastic creature. It is held together by a froglike body in two other slender collars (Figure 22: c; 23: B) when viewed laterally. To the Single Twins/Double Twins as bat-persons (or as bicepahalous-frog persons) rendered in the collar one must also add the three-pointed cemí idols attached to the undecorated panel. As noted above, there seems to be a choice of any number of three-pointed personages that could be articulated with this stone collar. One might think that the three-pointers with the skeletal-like face or heads carved in the central prominence (both Fewke's and Walker's Type 3) would be a likely choice given the theme of death and souls of the nonliving. The so-called Macorís heads, as Walker (1993, 1997) and others (Fewkes 1907) have noted, are frequently portrayed as skeletal or emaciated heads or as heads of bats (see Figure 25). The Macorís-type stone heads in many instances retain the base or show a vestigial base of the standard three-pointed stones, but much reduced and obscured by the prominence and volume of the head (Figure 25: d-g). In some samples the skeletal stone head also shows bat features, most specifically indicated by the "leaf-nose" motif (Figure 25: b). These stone heads with vestigial bases suggest that they could also be attached to stone collars. This type of stone-head icon may well have developed along with or subsequent to the other three-pointed types. More on these Macorís heads will be discussed in the following section. The point here is that the all-stone collars and the derivative elbow stones with fiber or wood rings form a composite dynamic set of potent icons that articulate with one another in various ways and whose meanings are salient or hidden depending on perspective and also in relation to who is the attached three-pointed idol. This, again, illustrates Eduardo Vivieros de Castro's (1996) concept of multinatural perspectivism.

One question remains unanswered: is the composite personage of a stone collar a cemí icon, like those discussed earlier (e.g., three-pointers or cohoba idols), whom the natives rendered cult and consulted to divine and affect the future? I am inclined to follow Walker's view that some of the icons and personages represented allude to mythological personages (e.g., four culture heroes, bats, or opías, Yayael's "fishy" descendants), but perhaps more specifically to the *roles* of these personages and not necessarily to a sculptured version of the actual named characters of the myth (e.g., Deminán Caracaracol). I also agree with Walker that these personages provide the scenario to "read" both the attached three-pointer and the cacique. The presentation of two or four twins in structural opposition would certainly evoke the culture heroes' roles, with their ability to gift (even if at a "price") their knowledge of cultural secrets, and this may well be the central concept of the two or four icons that overlie the central figure, usually the bat-personage. One knows that the two or four twins are always there accompanying or being a part of the bat personage (or bicephalous frog-person), whether the latter is visible or not. And the reverse is also true; whether visible or not, the two or four twin characters always accompany the bat personage. The latter alludes to the world of the nonliving, but as a deceased person it is also the source for the living natives, linking the spirit, supernatural domain with the ordinary world. What was early in the sequence a Headless-Fish personage that had power over the marine or freshwater subsistence stock had evolved into personages concerned with the culture-giving or knowledge-giving and at once with the world of the dead and ancestors. In some sense these are two opposite yet complementary directions of life-giving: the ancestors are the raison d'être of the living, whereas the four twins make civilized, cultured life on earth possible through their release of primordial secrets. And to this one must also add the three-pointed cemí idol, which we know to have been manifested in nature and then sculptured, and that they had names, status, rank, specific identity, and would be engaged in council meetings for divination. If and when the three-pointer cemí is attached to the stone collar, then it seems at least logical to conclude that the entire apparatus is cemí. I am much less sure of whether the personages represented in the collar alone are allusions to the other forms of the three-pointed cemí and whether the former (the fish, bat, etc.) are *just* a supporting cast included so as to contextualize the nature of the attached cemí (and the person wearing the collar). Instead, I think these allude to the multiple authorship and natures of the depicted personage.

It is of significance that the abridged and later version of the slender collar, the wood/fiber and elbow or stone collar, with the faced anthropomorphic personage seems to have collapsed the removable- and exchangeable-faced three-pointed stone to one single object. The face—and sometimes the entire body—is thus engraved in the panel of the elbow stone (Figures 3: d; 19: d). Therefore, this must be a cemí idol as much as it was when it had the detachable three-lobed form.

The cacique, when wearing the collar with a cemí three-pointer attached, would hence define and legitimize his person and status as cacique and be linked with a contingent of potent personages. If I am right about the view of the bat personages and their articulation with Single-Twin and Double-Twin personages as givers, as agents (the three-pointer that makes rain and the twin personages that gift secrets for civilization), then being displayed by and attached to the cacique makes him quite a potent and powerful personage. Like the twin personages and the bat opía displayed in the collar, he has the power to cause, to give, and to take.

E. The Circulation of Collars and Their Inalienability and Alienability

According to Walker (1993), these collars were very likely worn by caciques as sashes or bandoliers and, as he noted (taking a cue from Peter Roe), were publicly displayed "in ritual theater." There is nothing in the Spanish documentary data to eliminate the likelihood that they could have also been used by the cacique in nonpublic ceremonies, such as the council meetings summoning the cemís inside the privacy of the caney. The cacique, for example, may have worn the stone collar while explaining to the assembled nitaínos or caciques the results of his vision quest into the world of cemís. Or, like his duho, inhaling tubes, canopied cemí idols, and the central idol, the presence of the collar in the caney, whether actually worn or not, formed part of the contingent of potent icons and personages that enabled and joined the cacique to make the hallucinogenic journey. In either context, as public theater or as private ceremony, the collar-and-three-pointer-cemí ensemble defined who the cacique was in a historical sense.

Walker (1993) suggests that the all-stone and wood-and-stone collars were corporately owned by the cacique's kindred or clan, although it was the cacique, the one wearing and using it, who was entrusted with it. These objects, as already pointed out, are exceedingly rare; perhaps at most a new one was commissioned about every two years or so (see section 10, Table 1). The simple arithmetic test performed by Walker (1993:147–149) on the production of stone collars suggests that there would be few new ones added for each succeeding generation of caciques, with the implication that most of these would be kept and passed on to the new heir to the office.

Although secure archaeological contexts for stone collars and elbow stones are very few, and are mostly fragments discarded at different stages of manufacture (or perhaps broken by use), there is as yet not one single report of any stone collar found—fragmentary or otherwise—that can be associated with human burials. The safest assumption and conclusion is that stone collars were curated.

Were these items part of the estate of the cacique (or his family)? Absolutely! However, whether they could form part of the bequest of the deceased to foreign caciques cannot yet be ascertained. Doing so would require a very detailed provenience analysis of the objects themselves and of the quarry sources from which they were extracted, data that is in many cases impossible to obtain (i.e., the collar's provenience is vague or unknown). Given that these collars are clearly symbols of power and authority that make and define the person of the cacique, and given that it is possible that the ensemble (three-pointer plus collar) of icons are potent, causal agents in conjuring the cemís as spirits for consultation, it would seem unlikely that they would be gifted to foreign or ally chiefs. They seem to be inalienable objects possessed by the cacique or his family, and, to use Weiner's phrase, these are things that must be kept. On the other hand, being potent objects that were necessarily engaged in the exercise of chiefly power, they would also be likely targets to be stolen by enemy caciques. It would seem that it is the ensemble rather than either object on its own that would make the collars potent items. And like other cemí idols, I would expect that their prestige would be enhanced over their lifetime and always in relation to the human caciques. The older the stone collar and the more generations of great caciques to have held it, the greater its reputation. Although it is still possible that on occasion a stone collar/three-pointer could be gifted in funerary feasts to foreign caciques, my inclination is to think that this would be an exceedingly rare event, considering how few of them were available. Thus, the two possibilities accounting for their geographic distribution are through theft and through inheritance after the death of a cacique, remaining in the local region.

16 Ancestor Cemís and the Cemíification of the Caciques

Another class of cemí objects that is difficult to determine if they were or were not gifted to foreign caciques or political allies consists of the idols and other receptacles, such as baskets and calabashes, that contain the actual skull or bones of a deceased cacique (Figure 24). Like those idols made of stone, wood, and other media, these cemís were undoubtedly subjected to veneration; they were also imbued with cemí potency. Unlike others, however, these ancestor cemís *did* contain real human bones, usually a skull, selected from the skeleton at some point after the desiccation of the body.

Upon death, the personhood of a cacique would undergo a process of decomposition (literally and figuratively) and deconstruction before being recomposed to emerge as a new person and with a new set of social relations in the afterlife (see Mosko 1992). The deceased cacique can, for example, be transformed into a cemíified ancestor, provided with a new body, made of fiber and cotton (Figure 24; see Kerchache 1994:158–161). This very process of deconstruction and reconstruction (decomposition, death; recomposition, rebirth) of the cacique's person in the form of a cemí idol is precisely what is meant by "cemíification." These ancestor cemís are not the kind that manifested their presence in nature (see section 5) and revealed their personhood to a shaman; rather, they are the product of bodily and personhood transformations of the cacique upon death.

The cemí idol, as a cemíified ancestor, defines the relationships (duties, obligations, modes of social conduct) among the surviving, living descendants. The living cacique heir and relatives entrusted with such an icon would have direct access to this and all other cemíified ancestors by virtue of their direct kinship and descent relations with the set of cemíified ancestor idols. The relationships between the cemíified ancestor idol and the living relatives are fundamentally different than they were when the ancestor was among the living: the dead cacique is now imbued with cemí power and vested with seminal potency and fecundity. The ancestor cemí has the potency to promote the production and reproduction of the cacique heir and his lineage, if not the community at large. Such idols and objects of veneration, like the stone, shell, or wood cemí idols that were first manifested in nature (as discussed earlier), would henceforth be consulted and invoked in cohoba ceremonies, offered food, and kept in the caney.

Admiral Columbus (Colón 1985:204, ch. 60; see also Crespo 2000:127–139) described several ways in which the body of a dead cacique would be prepared for a funeral. Disemboweling and then slowly desiccating the body with indirect fire lit under the hammock of the deceased would be the first stage. Afterward, the skull—and perhaps other bones, too—would be selected and curated, while the remaining bones would be buried as secondary interments in a burial ground or, for example, deposited in a cave. Columbus also mentioned setting fire to the house with the cacique's body inside it. Depending on the temperature achieved, the remnant cremated bones would be collected, curated, or buried.

In any event, the skull or head was *the* key part of the human anatomy (Crespo 2000:129), and the symbolic repository of the dead cacique's potency and power, as is attested by the notorious example of the cotton cemí idol held in the Museum of Ethnography of Turin, Italy (Figure 24), whose cotton head wraps the front part of a human skull. As shall be seen, in life the head of a human being was the repository of his living soul (*goeíza* or *guaíza*). Thus, upon death the head of the deceased, revealed after defleshing as a skull, is most likely to be the repository of his soul in the afterlife: the opía (or *operito*; Pané 1999). The eyes of the ancestor cemí idols, as well as many other cemí icons, were covered with gold sheets (or mother of pearl or other shiny materials), because these are the liminal orifices—windows to the soul—allowing the soul to "see" the world outside and vice versa, for the outside world to reach the inner soul (Oliver 2000).

Two sites with cemeteries, La Caleta and Nisibón, belonging to the Ostionan Ostionoid subseries (i.e., so-called Anadel or Transicional style or period, A.D. 600–900 or 1000) in the Dominican Republic have each yielded one full-bodied, flexed, primary burial with the skull missing (Morbán Laucer 1979:89, 135). The headless bodies not only confirm the practice of curating skulls that was noted by Columbus, but also indicate that it was an ancient custom. Michele de Cuneo, who accompanied Columbus on his second voyage, while in Hispaniola, made one further observation about the process of curation of human skulls (see Sued Badillo 1978:46): "We heard that when the father of someone falls ill, the son goes to the temple, and tells the idol that his father is sick and asks him if he will be cured or not. He remains there until it [the cemí idol] responds: yes or no. If it says no, the son returns to the house, cuts the head off his father and boils it: I do not think that they ate it but rather when it turned white [perhaps meaning defleshed] they placed it [the skull] in the temple. This is done only by the *señores* [lords]" [Cuneo 1983 (1495):249].

The curation of ancestors' bones is also reported for eastern Cuba, along the eastern coast, near modern-day Baracoa (see Figure 28). Admiral Columbus recorded in his journal on November 29, 1492:

[C]ertain mariners in a house of that village, or some other village there, found the head of a man; it had to be a skull, placed inside a basket and covered by another basket and hung from a post of the house, and [it was seen in] the same way in another village. . . . it must be that these [skulls] were from some principal men of the lineage, because . . . those houses were such that they could accommodate in them many people in a single one, and that they [the dwellers] had to be [speculates Columbus] relatives descending of the single one [the skull] [Las Casas 1929 (1):246].

While in some areas of Cuba and Hispaniola the curation of ancestors' skulls was done by placing them in higüeros (*Crescentia spp.*) or baskets, in Hispaniola some skulls were further modified (i.e., cutting and keeping the frontal skull and mandible) and placed within cotton-and-fiber figurines (see Kerchache 1994:158–161). In both cases the focus is the human skull; in both cases the skull is wrapped and given a new body or skin (calabash or idol); in both of these, ancestor cemís were subject to ancestor cult and veneration.

But since in Hispaniola there were also ethnohistoric instances of primary (full-bodied) burials of caciques, it follows that not all were cremated and their skulls detached. One would expect regional variations on the specific treatments. A cacique who was not cremated was Behechio of Jaraguá, the most powerful paramount chief in Hispaniola at the time of Spanish contact (1492–1496/1497). Thus, having a high status among chiefs is not a sufficient criterion for a cacique to be recomposed as a cemí idol. The reasons for the different postmortem funerary practices among caciques in Hispaniola are not known. Many variables besides status enter into play when deciding the manner in which the body of the deceased cacique will be treated. For example, the cause and circumstance of death, where it took place, at what time, and what sort of illness was responsible, or whether it was from violent death or old age, and so on, will determine the funerary protocol to be followed. In the case of direct, primary burials, perhaps the cemíification of the cacique was accomplished through a different process of transformation and materially expressed in a different manner. Perhaps the large stone-head cemís (veritable portraits) were such cemíified ancestor caciques that were buried in full. The actual skulls are largely hidden from view in the cotton idols or the baskets and dressed up with a new head; stone heads directly display the head with strong visual hints of a skeletal facial structure (Figure 3: e).

There are other interesting implications for body treatment after death. Since it is only a part of the dead cacique (the skull) that would be selected and recomposed as a cemí idol, this means the other parts of the skeletal body (apparently minor bones of the deceased, such as ulna and radius, vertebrae, and ribs) were deposited or buried elsewhere. These other parts of the skeleton were buried as bundles in a burial ground, cemetery, or cave. Perhaps different bones of the same person would be further segregated and dispersed among several burial cave sites (Oliver 2003; Pagán and Oliver 2008; Rivera and Oliver 2005). For now it is not yet possible to archaeologically prove that minor bones of the *same* person were in fact dispersed and deposited into more than one burial cave site. Still, in the karst caves of the region of Utuado, Puerto Rico, I suspect that this was the case. I have entertained the hypothesis that such dispersion into key points in the landscape—namely, selected burial cave sites—would be linked to the deceased as a territorial domain. The dispersed bones of the (partible) individual were laid by descendants as markers for claiming the area covered between such key points of the sacred geography as "his" or "hers." The boundary linked by the caves would mark the lineage's traditional and ancestral territory of origin. Even if the bone parts of a dividual person were not dispersed and concentrated in a single cave, the fact remains that the singular cave marks the point of origin for the living descendants of that ancestor; if other ancestor bundles of the same family or lineage were buried in other cave sites, it would create a territorial boundary for the descent group. Since the other key parts of the ancestor would also be kept in houses (in cotton cemí idols or baskets) or in burial grounds in or around the residential settlements—such as, for example, demonstrated for the Cocal-1 site in Puerto Rico—that means that body dismemberment and dispersion function to articulate the living descendants with the various sacred points distributed in the landscapes (for Cocal-1 data, see Oliver 2003). These points would identify the origins of the descent group through the landscape.

Since in Taíno mythology the first protohumans emerged from a cave, it makes sense to argue that such localities in the landscape mark the points of origin (birth) and the localities where they will return upon death (Pané 1999:5–6). Translated into a sacred landscape, the bones of ancestors mark the ancestral, traditional geographic areas attached to each of the descent groups that comprise a community. By decomposing the partible person of the cacique and dismembering and segregating his skeletal parts as well as dispersing them throughout the landscape (Gell's [1998] distributed person), what is in fact accomplished is the opposite: the bringing together and the integration of the territory of origin and homeland of the descent group. The deconstruction of the ancestor, via bone dispersion, is what provides integration of the homeland and articulation among the living descendants. This is, of course, a hypothesis that would require much more archaeological testing (especially DNA) and outlays of research funds that are not easy to acquire. In this karst region, so many burial caves have been looted (by extraction of bat guano for fertilizer) that it is doubtful that a full picture of burial patterns could be obtained, thus discouraging grant agencies from investing in such risky propositions. However, it ought to be tried.

The practice of body desegregation and dismemberment after death dovetails with the notion of partible bodies *and* persons, with the various parts of the cacique's skeleton, in fact, inhabiting multiple locations: baskets, cotton and cemí idols kept inside houses, in the burial grounds in or near the village, and in one or several caves of the surrounding landscape.

One type of ancestor cemí idols that do *not* contain real skulls is the so-called Macorís type of stone head, which is to a large extent an anthropomorphic por-trait (Figures 3: e; 25), and when a zoomorphic personage is represented, it tends to be a bat-person—that is, an avatar of the dead souls. In contrast to the relatively flat guaízas, the stone heads are three-dimensional sculptures. The facial features of the stone heads depict large, round, and deep eye orbits, and prominent bony cheeks that suggest skeletal personages. Such skeletal features in stone heads are especially visible in the specimens from Hispaniola and Puerto Rico shown in Figures 3: e; 25.

José Juan Arrom (1975:85–92; Figure 25) identified these stone heads and other types of cemí icons as diverse representations of the mythical Maquetaurie Guayaba, the "Lord of the Nonliving" or "Lord of the Absent Ones," that Pané recorded for Hispaniola (Arrom 1975:79–80). This may be so, perhaps, but Arrom's identification is colored by western notions of art and the assumption of the indivisibility of both persons and art objects or subjects. Arrom views these and other cemí icons (e.g., in three-pointed stones, guaíza masks, stone collars) as being, literally, reproductions of the same mythical individual (Maquetaurie), or its avatar (the bat motif; see Figure 25: b), within a western and contemporary Christian tradition of iconographic interpretation (e.g., the many reproductions of an individual personage such as the Virgin Mary or Saint Francis).

The examples provided here (Figure 25) show facial features that are, by abductive reasoning (Gell 1998), the heads of ancestors, and repositories of the opía soul, hence imbued with sweet cemí potency. In a broad sense, these are trophy heads: they are still captives but not through war. They may refer to the mythical Maquetaurie Guayaba, as suggested by Arrom, but they may just as likely be the trophy heads of founding ancestors of specific descent groups. The stone head is like the skull of a cacique kept in a calabash or within a cotton idol but where the actual skull is not the required compositional element; the bone is replaced by stone. This is most obvious in the stone head of Figure 25: a.

Given that some caciques were also interred in direct, primary burials, making the skull inaccessible, it is possible that the cult to these caciques was "agencied" through his skull-head portraiture expressed in a different medium, a solid stone head. In contrast, if the funeral practice required evisceration, desiccation, body dismemberment, and skull selection, then the alternative process of cemíification would result in skulls being available for incorporation in the baskets or idols. Either as stone head, a skull in a calabash, or inside an idol, it seems that at least part of the deceased cacique's personhood was retained or kept among the living and thus had a direct engagement with and a physical presence among his heirs and descendants. It is worth stressing the significance of physical presence of not just ancestor but of all cemí idols. Recall that the cohoba ceremony taking place in the caney house or temple to summon and engage the potent cemís always involved the *physical proximity* between the idols and the cacique or shaman. If the invocation was for an ancestor cemí, then the physical proximity to the ancestor cemí idol would be likewise necessary for the proceedings to go ahead.

One might wonder why someone would bother sculpturing a stone skull or head when the real thing would seem to provide a much more direct link to the ancestor, even if it remained hidden within an idol or calabash. The substitution may be for various reasons. For instance, if the original skull of the cemíified cacique had severely deteriorated over several generations, then one way to preserve its iconic integrity would be to totally recompose it as a stone head. It could also be that some of these stone heads represented a remote, apical ancestor whose precise genealogical ties to living descendants had been lost in the mist of history. It may be that the funerary protocol to be followed, given the appropriate circumstance of death, required a primary interment of the full body. Therefore his or her descendants maintained physical proximity to their ancestor's potency by "capturing" his or her opía in a stone head. Certainly stone has the advantage of permanency over bone.

But not all stone-head cemís were necessarily kept among the living forever. There is at least one case where "a lithic Macorís [-type] face that . . . represented the face of the dead cacique" was found accompanying a full-bodied, primary burial site at La Cucama cemetery (Morbán Laucer 1979:36). It is the same burial already discussed earlier in connection to the rarity of burials indicative of a high-status individual. If the looter's description is correct, then there must have been specific circumstances when a stone head would be retired from circulation and buried, possibly with his descendant. The placement of an ancestral human skull next to a full-bodied interment has deeper historical roots in the Caribbean. From Elenan or Ostionan Ostionoid (ca. A.D. 900–1200) contexts at the Paso del Indio (Walker 2005:69) site, archaeologists have found three clear instances of a second adult male human skull placed with a complete adult male primary burial. This skull would be either held by or cradled in the arms of the three deceased, two male adults and one sub-adult (Crespo 2000:151–153, fig. 43; Walker 2005:71, fig. 2.5). Interestingly, no instances of females holding detached skulls were found at Paso del Indio. Finally, the craniums accompanying these full-bodied primary interments were determined by bioarchaeologist Edwin Crespo (2000:153) to "have been already *secos* [dry] when interred." There is thus a parallel between the earlier Paso del Indio and La Cucama, where a trophy head (skull or stone) accompanied the buried individual. Walker (2005:74) raises the question of whether the skull was of an enemy or a kin of the deceased, and suggests: "Solely on the basis of the positioning of the secondary skulls in the hands or arms of the primary individuals, I am willing to venture that these three pairs of burials are evidence of ancestor worship. The primary were positioned holding or cradling skulls close to their bodies—as if they were treasured and dear—not what I would expect to see when a man was buried with a trophy head of a mortal enemy" (Walker 2005:74).

Like Walker, and in agreement with Crespo (2000:152), I am inclined to think that these skulls at Paso del Indio, as well as the symbolic skull-as-stone-head (as a proxy) at La Cucama, are related by kinship to the deceased. I also agree with both authors that the final proof rests on the results of genetic proximity between the primary individuals and the secondary skulls, the results of which are not yet available. However, I disagree with Crespo's (2000:153) arguments that curated skulls at Paso del Indio are not related to a trophy-head cult. The skeletal stone heads at La Cucama were not considered in Crespo's dissertation, although he noted the skeletal (as well as the intentional cranial deformation) features of Macorís-type stone heads (Crespo 2000:228, fig. 65). It may well be that Crespo defines "trophy" head in a more limited sense (as war captives' or enemies' heads) than I do. Enemy trophy heads or skulls would perhaps have been treated more like the perforated human frontal bone pectorals, drilled teeth, and some of the hollow ceramic effigy heads found in Puerto Rico (as discussed by Roe 1991; Walker 2005:74). I agree with much of what Peter Roe (1991) considers to be enemy trophy heads (as opposed to those of ancestors). However, I disagree that guaízas, or flat face masks with drilled holes around the periphery, are "enemy" trophy heads. The term *guaíza* means "soul of the living," and thus I find it unlikely that these represent the trophy heads of enemies, unless one can prove that a guaíza specimen itself was taken as a trophy.

The cemíified stone-head idols or skulls-in-calabashes of caciques have direct links of descent with the living cacique and his kindred and, of course, define how the living relate (or not) to one another. These ancestor cemís, like all other cemí idols, have names and titles, ranks and status, and genealogy. They will also be subject to inheritance by descending generations of caciques of his lineage, although it is clear that under some circumstances these idols will also be interred along with their descendants. The circumstances under which some or most will be kept in the house or caney and others buried with a relative (the La Cucama, Paso del Indio cases) at some point in time are not known. Nonetheless, the curated cemíified ancestor idols (skulls) are the ones about whom areítos will chant in remembrance of the great deeds that the cacique accomplished in life, and to whom new deeds will be added henceforth in the afterlife. These would also likely be involved in the cohoba-induced consultations when important decisions have to be made. Perhaps these ancestor idols would be the focus of ritual when the issues at stake have to do with bride-giving, pregnancy, and marriage, and, in short, things to do with the well-being and future of the lineage members. If these ancestor cemí idols embody the lineage, as fractal, dividual persons, it would seem to me that they would rarely, if ever, be involved in bequests or gifted to foreign caciques, to groups outside the descent line. On the other hand, if areítos could be gifted (as attested by the cacique Guarionex case), then so too could these apparently inalienable "possessions." After all, the areíto is in many ways the rhetorical (speech) and dramatic (theater) realization of what the ancestor idols, as materials, elicit: the heroic, epic history of the living as well as the ancestor caciques who ruled the cacicazgo.

17 The Guaíza Face Masks
Gifts of the Living for the Living

If ancestor cemís, such as skulls in calabashes and cotton idols, were the physical links between the living cacique and his relative ancestors, mutually defining their personhood, then the guaíza (face) was the extension of the living cacique's soul to other living human beings. The Taíno term *guaíza* was given by Fray Bartolomé de Las Casas to refer to what the Spanish called *caratona* or *carátula*—that is, a "face mask," in Castilian (Las Casas 1929 [1]:361). Arrom (1975:84) correctly shows that this term is cognate with the term *wa-ísiba* (our face) used by modern Lokono (Arawak) of Guiana. Arrom (1975:84) suggested that the guaíza "is what individualizes and distinguishes a person when alive." But it is more than just a word for face or a mask, since Pané gave the word *goeíza* the meaning of "spirit or soul of the living": "When the person is alive, they call his or her spirit *goeíza*" (Pané 1974:33). In other words, the face of a being is the portal to or repository of the soul or spirit of a living human being. I disagree with Arrom only in his view of the human being as an indivisible, nonpartible person and, consequently, that the carved face masks are likewise individual, detached, and indivisible entities. Instead, these guaíza masks are extensions or parts that compose the living person. These face masks can thus be thought of as a visual synthesis of the head or face of the *living* cacique's spirit or soul that also contain that intangible potency and quality of having a living soul. If so, then they are quite distinct in concept from the skeletal sculptured stone heads or the skull heads of ancestors, whose soul is of a different nature: it is opía (also transcribed as *operito*).

A being is an operito, says Pané (in Arrom 1975:80), when living humans cannot find a navel in the body; *operito* means dead. The Island Carib language includes the cognate term *opoye-m,* meaning "spirit of the dead" (Arrom 1975:84). Spirits of the dead, however, can materialize as full-bodied persons, especially in the forests during nighttime, and their appearance is identical to a living human being except for the lack of a navel, the key anatomical part that connects the umbilical cord to the nurturing blood of the mother's placenta, and thus to life. These same beings can also materialize in different body forms: guava-eating bats or owls (Arrom 1988; Morbán Laucer 1988; Oliver 1998:73, 136–137; 2008b:figs. 37 and 38). The absence of a belly button denotes that the potency that animates the being is of a different source and nature: the nonliving spirit, the opía. Indeed, Pané's account makes the separation of living versus nonliving quite clear: any ordinary, living human being attempting to sexually interact with or apprehend an opía being is doomed to failure, as the opía always escapes; this interaction is barren and does not result in human reproduction or pregnancy. These potential encounters with opía-agencied beings (dead souls) are presented in myth as sexually alluring yet dangerous and unproductive. This is one reason the natives avoid going out into the forest during the night (Pané, in Arrom 1975:79–80). This digression is important to the discussion of guaíza in that it alerts us to the fact that both the opía and guaíza *animate* beings that can assume different bodies or parts of bodies that have physical presence in this world. Of course, the opía is a potency that animates the departed, former, or nonliving humans; guaíza is the power animating the still living humans. It is clear from Pané's account about native religious beliefs of death that the dead spirit beings activate at dusk and night, when the sun sets under the western horizon; by contrast, the proper yet ordinary time for living human activity is during daylight, from sunrise to sunset. This association of absence of sunlight (or night light) with the activation of the numinous is one reason for placing the cemí idols in the darkest recesses inside the caney or a cave, and why the cohoba ceremonies generally took place at dusk or night and in dark, enclosed places.

The guaíza is not simply an artifact that measures artisans' skill with a value translatable in just economic terms (quality of material + labor investment = value); rather, it is an item (an index; Gell 1998) that captivates and contains something valuable by virtue of its relation to its prototype: the cacique's living soul, which native believers locate in the face of a person. This value is not just in labor input and material output but much more on *who is* this living soul expressed or contained in this face mask. What a cacique is giving with a guaíza is a potent part of his personhood, his living soul. In contrast to the stone heads, for which there is not a single recorded instance of being used for exchange or trade, the guaízas are time and time again the favored high-value gifts to be given precisely to foreign caciques, including stranger ones like Christopher Columbus, whom the Taíno regarded as *guamiquina* (*wam[a]ikina*), a title meaning "our principal or first lord."

As Moscoso (1980:75–86) pointed out, these guaíza objects were the most ubiquitous of all gifts given by caciques of Hispaniola (Figure 27). They figured prominently in the exchanges between Guacanagarí and Caonabó with Christopher Columbus (Moscoso 1980; Tavárez María 2001; Wilson 1990). Even before Columbus disembarked on the domain of Marién, where Guacanagarí's settlement was located (near today's En Bas Saline, Haiti), the cacique "[s]ent him [Columbus] through a servant and ambassador, a sash (or belt) that instead of having a pouch it had a *carátula* [face mask] that had two large ears of hammered gold and also the tongue and eyes. This belt was made of very tiny beads made of white fish bones [i.e., shell], intercalated with red ones, as done in needlepoint" (Las Casas 1929 [1]:17).

Next day, on December 23, 1492, Columbus sent six of his men to reciprocate. Guacanagarí received the party, took them to his house, and ordered meals to be served. All the while the natives kept bringing the Spaniards "many items of cotton, woven and spun in bales" while the cacique offered them three fat ducks and gold nuggets. Afterward the Spaniards returned to their ships accompanied by natives in their canoes. Throughout all "that day came more than 120 canoes to the [Spanish] ships, all loaded with people. All had something to exchange with the Christians: bread and fish food, water in jars made of clay that were very well made and painted outside with iron oxide [red], and some seeds as spices"—namely, *ají* (*Capsicum sp.*; Las Casas 1929 [1]:18). Two of the most coveted Spanish items were the bronze or tin (*latón*) bells and *Mozarabic* glass beads.

After these initial and successful exchanges, Columbus resolved to meet Guacanagarí at his settlement in Marién, which is very likely the archaeological site known today as En Bas Saline (Deagan 2004). At midnight on December 25 the *Santa María* floundered on a coral reef or a sand bank (Figure 26: inset). It was thanks to Guacanagarí's command that the cargo (and sailors) of the *Santa María* were safely rescued and brought to his settlement. Las Casas (1929 [1]:276), in agreement with Columbus, noted that these caciques, "as judges or lords [of the señoríos], are all obeyed that is marvelous to see. And all these lords are of few words and elegant customs, and their command is, at most, given by making hand gestures which are then understood" by all. It is in this context that on December 26 Guacanagarí met Columbus on the ship *La Pinta* to reassure him that all the materials rescued from the *Santa María* were safe and to offer further assistance. In the meantime, canoes with natives from other settlements were also engaged in active trading, especially of gold nuggets "wrapped in cotton cloth" for the coveted cast tin bells and glass beads (Las Casas 1929 [1]:281; see Oliver 2000). Guacanagarí and the native traders told the Spaniards that the gold nuggets were coming from the rivers draining the Cibao mountain range (i.e., cacique Caonabó's Maguana region) and farther east.

After having a meal in the *La Pinta,* Guacanagarí invited the admiral to his settlement:

> [T]hey made him [Columbus] a great reception and honor, and he [Guacanagarí] took him to his house and he ordered drinks [consisting] of a mixture of three kinds of fruits, and fish and game, and other *viandas* [a mix of stewed tubers] that they had and [also] bread called *cazabi* [or cassava] to be served to the guests. He took him [Columbus] to see the very pretty *verduras* [greenery] and tree gardens next to the houses . . . and the King [Guacanagarí] already wore a shirt and gloves that the Admiral had given him, and what was most celebrated and feasted were the gloves. After dining, which took a long while, they brought him [Columbus] many herbs with

which he refreshed his hands . . . and then [they both] rinsed their hands with water. After the dinner he took the Admiral to the beach and [then] the Admiral sent for a Turkish bow and a bunch of arrows that he brought from Castile, and had a man from his company shoot them. And the King, as he did not know that these were weapons because they did not have them or use them, thought it was a great thing, all of this the Admiral said [Las Casas inserted comment]. [. . . Then] *they brought to the Admiral a great carátula that had large pieces of gold in the ears and eyes* and in other parts, which he gave along with other gold jewels, and the King himself put it on the Admiral's head and neck, and to the other Christians that were with him [Columbus], he gave many things of gold [Columbus's *Journal,* in Las Casas 1929 (1):282; my emphasis].

This passage narrated the first time ever that a native chief from Hispaniola engaged in full-scale diplomatic relations with the Spanish, and as such the protocols Guacanagarí followed had to be based on past experience, following strictly pre-Hispanic notions of reciprocity and exchange. As will be discussed later, Guacanagarí had an agenda behind such diplomacy: he was seeking to forge an alliance with Columbus to gain advantage over Caonabó and Behechio—two neighboring paramount caciques, whom he claimed had stolen or killed his women (see Tavárez María 2001). Columbus needed Guacanagarí's support if he was to leave his thirty-nine men at La Navidad (Figure 26: inset) and for them to explore the gold-bearing sources while he sailed back to Spain to organize a second, better-stocked expedition. He was, of course, aware that to explore the "eastern" gold sources in Cibao, the mythical Matininó island, and beyond (notwithstanding Columbus's confusion of mythical with natural geography), he would need a dependable infrastructural support and supply, especially of food, for his thirty-nine men and all the help he could get from Guacanagarí upon his return from Spain.

But before the admiral's departure, on December 30, 1492 (a day after the exchange described above), a final round of gift exchanges and diplomacy took place. This time not only Guacanagarí was present but also five other "kings," who Las Casas (1929 [1]:288) described as "his subjects":

[T]he Admiral left to eat on land and arrived at the same time that five Kings, all subjects of this great lord Guacanagarí, had arrived, all wore their crowns of gold on their heads, representing great authority, to such a degree that the Admiral said to the Kings [of Castile and Aragon], "Your Highnesses would have most pleasure to see their ways; it is to be believed that the King Guacanagarí sent for them to come to better display his greatness." And upon landing, the King came to receive him and took him by the arm to the same house of yesterday, where there was, the tribune [or platform] and the seats in one of which he [Guacanagarí] had the Admiral seat with great courtesy and respect. Then he took his [gold] crown from his head and placed it on the Admiral's. The Admiral took from his neck a necklace of good *alaqueques* [cornaline beads] and of beautifully colored beads that looked all around very well, and put it on him [Guacanagarí]. And then he [Columbus] gave him a cap of fine silk he was wearing that day and placed [it] on him [Guacanagarí] and he sent [also] for a pair of colored *borceguíes* [a type of shoe] and had him wear them. In addition he [Columbus] put on his [Guacanagarí's] finger a large ring made of silver . . . with these jewels the King found himself very rich and remained the happiest [man] in the world [Columbus's *Journal*, in Las Casas 1929 (1):288].

It is clear that the *carátulas* noted by the Spanish were items that formed a kind of buckle to hold a sash made of beads and cotton worn around the belt or hung as pendants from a stone necklace (Figure 27). However, some of these guaízas seem to also have been worn like diadems attached to a headgear or cotton band sewn together with multicolored beads and decorated with macaw (*papagayo*) feathers. I suspect that not all guaízas necessarily depicted an anthropomorphic face, but most archaeological samples have humanlike faces. Aside from the interesting details of the native Spanish protocols of diplomacy and reciprocity, the key point is that the guaíza of Guacanagarí was only gifted to what he correctly perceived to be the cacique of the Spaniards—Christopher Columbus; no other Spanish subordinate or emissary sent by Columbus was recipient of such a gift. For them, other items were given and exchanged. This pattern is repeated between Columbus and a Macorix-speaking cacique (Mayobanex) who resided in the northeastern territory marked as Hiabo (also Hyabo or Huhabo) in the 1516 map of Morales (see Oliver 2008a:72–73; Tavárez María 1996; Vega 1980, 1997; Figure 26). This is an example of the cacique giving his individual face or soul. This also means that his or her personhood was being distributed and extended to others.

The admiral left Marién and La Navidad sailing eastward along the north coast to ultimately go back to Spain. But he succumbed to the pressure to discover where the placer gold deposits were, and thus along the way he explored and stopped at various points on the northern and eastern coasts. He reached an area inhabited by the so-called Cigüayo Indians on what is today the eastern tip of Samaná Peninsula (Figure 26). Like the Macorix Indians found on the northeastern coast, the Cigüayos wore long hair "like women in Castile," gathered with nets and macaw feathers. The word "Cigüayo" refers not to an ethnic group as such but to this hairstyle. Neither the Macorix's nor Cigüayos' native language was Taíno (Las Casas 1929 [1]:305). Upon landing on the beach, the Spanish were confronted by some fifty-five natives with long bows and arrows, with whom they had a skirmish that resulted in the death of many. It was the first killing of natives in the New World, which Columbus commemorated by naming it the Golfo de Las Flechas (Gulf of the Arrows).

After news of the incident reached one unnamed Cigüayo chief or cacique, who lived far from the site, that cacique sent (on January 14, 1493) an envoy to Columbus, apparently in order to offer peace but also, I suspect, to appraise the admiral's forces and to entice him to negotiate some kind of agreement that both could live by. Hence the envoy of the unnamed cacique told the admiral that the next morning his chief would send a carátula of gold, and wisely let the admiral know that there was lots of gold in other islands to the east (e.g., the mythical Matininó and other real islands, like Boriquén). As Jalil Sued Badillo (1978) and others have noted, not only the Cigüayo chief, but ever since asking about gold in Cuba, the natives, too, tried to get rid of Columbus by sending him to the next region to the east—even his staunch ally Guacanagarí. In the event, the next morning the admiral and his men disembarked only to find out that the "king" did not show up, because his "village was far away," but had nevertheless sent an emissary with a "crown of gold, as promised," while the other natives came with gifts of "cotton, bread, *ajes* (sweet potatoes: *Ipomoea batatas*) and other edibles to eat, albeit all were armed with their bows and arrows" that were "as tall as those from England" (Las Casas 1929 [1]:308). The Cigüayo chief either had second thoughts—hoping that the gifts of appeasement would suffice—or in fact he genuinely lived too far away to make the trip. The Spaniards meanwhile exchanged the usual trinkets for gold and other items. Back on the ship, a canoe with four young natives arrived, possibly wishing to continue trading with the Spaniards. However, lamentably, Columbus decided to capture and take them to Castile against their will, because, argued Las Casas, of their valuable information on gold sources on other islands (he mentions San Juan; i.e., Puerto Rico) to the east. This was also the first act of enslavement of Amerindians. I suspect also that these Indians would be the hard evidence Columbus needed to convince the Spanish monarchs of the untold gold riches yet to be found, ensuring both the admiral's contract (his vice royalty) and the economic support he needed for the return voyage.

On his second voyage the admiral returned to the Bay of La Navidad on November 27, 1493. As is well known, the thirty-nine Spaniards left at La Navidad had been killed: a few by disease, others by fighting among themselves over native women, and still others had left La Navidad inland with their native mistresses to Maguana (Figure 26), the land of cacique Caonabó, "who killed all ten or twelve of them" (Las Casas 1929 [1]:361–363). And many days later Caonabó came with a large army and raided the La Navidad fortress and the houses. The seven Spaniards still in La Navidad had fled toward the sea, where they supposedly drowned. Guacanagarí confirmed the accounts given by the Indians to Columbus, and indeed he was still in his house nursing battle injuries. The previous night Guacanagarí had sent two envoys to Columbus's ship with magnificent "carátulas, that they call *guayças* [guaízas], very well made and with some gold . . . presenting them on behalf of King Guacanagarí." It ought not to be forgotten that Guacanagarí had an old score to settle against Caonabó for having kidnapped (or killed) two of his women. Therefore, the reason for the battle that doomed La Navidad is a complicated triangle starting with the old enmity between Guacanagarí and Caonabó, to which the Spaniards added fuel and the excuse for Caonabó to kill two birds with one stone. As Lesley Bird Simpson noted, "these men who went to Española in the first ten years were the choicest collection of riffraff ever brought together: ex-soldiers, broken noblemen, adventurers, criminals, and convicts. That there were some high-minded men among them does not appreciably alter the general picture" (Simpson 1966:7; see also Varela 2006; Varela and Gil 2008).

Francisco Moscoso (1980) discussed several other contexts in which cotton-made guaízas sewn in stone (known as *cibas*) or shell-beaded garments and decorated gold sheets were gifted to Admiral Columbus. These appear in the famous treasure list (Table 2), with some items revealing that these were taken from Caonabó's brothers (from the Maguana chiefdom) after their defeat in the 1495–1496 battles.

In addition to the key point that the carátulas (guaízas) were only gifted from caciques to the highest-ranked Spanish or native cacique, there is the important detail of *how often* the same type of item was gifted to the same person. Not one but at least three instances were recorded in which Guacanagarí gave Columbus his guaízas, and one occasion where it is clear that more than one guaíza were offered in the same transaction. Inevitably, this implies that a cacique had many such guaízas at his disposal, especially when compared to other different kinds of cemí idols. It seems reasonable to propose that *unlike* cemí icons, these face masks were not manufactured as a result of an uncanny encounter with cemí (as spirit) manifestations in nature. These items may or may not be imbued with cemí, but they do seem to have potency, since, after all, they are the guaíza—the living soul—of their cacique owners. In turn, the living soul of the cacique, what gives him his power and agency, is concentrated in the face. I think it is likely that the guaíza in the mask *and* in the human cacique are shared and extended parts of dividual entities: the guaíza is an extension of a part of the cacique, of the very core of his personhood: his soul. And also, the guaíza, having the cacique's living soul, will retain that part of the cacique wherever the guaíza goes. Although impossible to prove, it could well be that this condition of animacy (having a soul), of having potential and actual agency, is also encompassed by the notion of cemí.

In contrast to the ancestor cemí stone heads, the guaízas do not seem to have been the subject of any cult, or veneration, nor were they ever consulted or used in divination (via cohoba ceremonies). Rather, they seem to personify the political-religious potency and power of their original holder; hence the gift is one that is geared toward the public display of the greatness of the cacique, and hence it has

Table 2. A Selection of Columbus's Treasure List*

Region	Cacique	Guaízas	Cotton	Stone/Cibas	Gold/Caona
Maguana Hispaniola	Caonabo's brothers	11	11	11	1
		3	3	3	7
		2	—	—	—
		2	—	—	10
		1	—	—	4
		1	—	—	7
Hispaniola	Unknown cacique donors	5	—	—	8
		1	—	—	3
		3	—	—	11
		1	—	—	10
		5	—	—	15
		1	1	—	9
		4	—	—	21
		2	—	—	9
	TOTAL	42	15	14	115

* "Account of Gold Jewels and Other Things that the Admiral Obtained After the Receiver, Sebastián de Olaño, left this Island for Castile on the Year 95" [1495]. Archivo General de Indias, Patronato, Legajo 8, Ramo 12. Colección de Documentos Inéditos, Pacheco et al. Primera serie, Tomo 10, pp. 5–9 (Reproduced from Oliver 2000:table 10.1: A).

value for the receiver. To put it tritely, the donor's aura and prestige rub off onto the receiver. It is striking that while Guacanagarí gave the guaízas to cement and reinforce an advantageous alliance with Columbus, to hedge against his rival caciques Caonabó and Behechio, others like the Cigüayo cacique in Samaná had used them for quite the opposite, as a means to get rid of Columbus and his men, although perhaps he also sought some form of alliance or appeasement knowing the terrible consequences of a renewed armed conflict (i.e., the killing at Golfo de Las Flechas) with the Spanish. As the saying goes, if you can't beat them, you better join them—and if at all possible, with some advantages coming your way.

Also, unlike the sculptured stone heads or skull cemí idols, guaízas were highly visible gifts in alliance formations among foreign and even stranger caciques (as Columbus was in their eyes), and were given more than once between the parties, as Guacanagarí demonstrated. This repetition had to be a traditional, pre-Columbian practice of reciprocal exchange of guaízas. Columbus, of course, repaid in kind with other items, but I would expect that Guacanagarí's gifts of guaízas to native allied and foreign caciques would, on occasion, be repaid with similar guaíza icons.

If so, this could have very interesting consequences: many allied caciques would have often displayed in their regalia someone else's face mask, or soul, as their own! And this means that a good number of guaíza artifacts found at any given archaeological site are not likely to be locally made. While, of course, it was part of the symbolic and actual wealth of the local chief, the guaízas under his control would still retain such value and esteem by virtue of their relationship to their original cacique. I wonder what would happen to a guaíza given by a cacique who later would, for whatever reasons, kidnap his women (as was the Guacanagarí-Caonabó case). Would it be ritually destroyed, traded away, or buried in a midden?

Clearly guaízas cannot be comfortably classed as either alienable or inalienable possessions. On the one hand, they are inalienable in that a spiritual essence of the guaíza face, the living soul, is attached to and defined by the living cacique. On the other hand, they *are* gifted. I suspect that no matter who controlled the item after being gifted, it always retained that attachment to its original source and that this likely is one of the reasons such items were valued (perhaps even more) by foreigners or stranger chiefs, not the least because of their exotic aura. On the other hand, these are evidently and eminently alienable things, as the above cases amply illustrate. In practice, though, they are neither alienable nor inalienable simply because of the very notion of dividuality and partibility of persons or things; the object does not have to be physically kept, because in fact its essence, the living soul of the cacique, was never subtracted from or lost by him when giving the guaíza. This would not entail the dissipation or loss of part of the political-religious power held by the donor cacique.

One key conclusion can be made between guaízas and stone heads. The stone heads are all about ancestors, genealogical ties, history and, hence, memories; the emphasis is on vertical (deep time) relations involving relatives. By contrast, the guaízas are all about horizontal relations, about the here-and-now (shallow time) relations with non-kin, with potential partners and allies. Guaízas are gifts *for* the living; stone heads are gifts *from* the dead.

Given how prominent an exchange item the guaíza was, and that it was uniquely singled out as *the* item to be gifted to stranger and foreign caciques, it is not surprising that guaízas have a far wider geographic distribution than the stone heads (though not the skulls in baskets), elbow stones, and stone collars. Guaízas have been found from central-eastern Cuba as far south as the Grenadines (Figures 28, 30). And that only takes into account those guaízas made of resistant materials (especially shell); those made of cotton or wood only have not been preserved.

18 The Circulation of Chiefs' Names, Women, and Cemís

Between the Greater and Lesser Antilles

One of the motivations for the circulation of cemí idols and other valuables, including guaízas, was to strengthen and reaffirm political-economic support among caciques in the Greater Antilles. Funerary feasts of deceased caciques provided one context in which cemí idols cycled from generation to generation and from chiefdom to chiefdom. Establishing political alliances also involved other parallel or complementary exchanges, of which three others (besides cemí idols) are important. First is the gift of guaízas; second is the exchange of women as brides. The last one involved pacts cemented through the exchange of names, or guaitiao, and where women could also, but not always, be exchanged. The four together—cemí idols, guaízas, chief names, and brides—form complementary exchange systems in a network of chiefly alliances.

As Jalil Sued Badillo (1978:58–64; 2003:261) has aptly discussed, caciques in Hispaniola and Puerto Rico—at least at the time of the initial Spanish contact—were the only members of society identified by the Spanish chroniclers to be polygamous. Besides being a status marker, polygamy indeed was a useful political tool to extract and extend political alliances with neighboring foreign as well as subordinated caciques. Behechio, who in 1492 was arguably the most powerful cacique of Hispaniola, leading the Bainoa (Jaraguá) chiefdom, had thirty wives. He was already mentioned in connection with his funeral, involving the sacrificial interment of two of his wives. His rival and competitor, cacique Guacanagarí, ruler of the much smaller chiefdom around Marién, at one time had twenty wives (Sued Badillo 2003:261). Such polygamous households must have been potent units of social and economic production. Among other things, the chief's household commanded large areas of agricultural production that generated staple wealth (see Moscoso 1989), which is the one thing the Spanish relied upon to literally feed the conquerors and hence supported the whole colonial enterprise in the Greater Antilles.

Another mechanism to extend the network of political (and social) relations among caciques was through the ceremony of guaitiao, which, as noted earlier, includes the ritualized exchange of names between two parties. Sued Badillo (2003:261) defined it as a "pact of eternal friendship between the caciques and those visitors that the caciques consider their equals." Caciques also did more than decide on their own marriages. In extending their sphere of political alliances, the caciques also determined whom their female kindred (sisters, nieces, and daughters) should marry. As Sued Badillo (2003:261) noted, it is not known with total certainty whether guaitiao automatically entailed marital exchanges, but I concur with him that there are strong indications that such exchanges were implemented, albeit probably not on every occasion. Guaitiao was no doubt an effective mechanism for widening the kinship network "when consanguinity did not offer enough resources to meet the demands of production" of the extended chiefly household, or activated when "political commitment or commitments of other kinds" required it (Sued Badillo 2003:261–262). A guaitiao pact, along with the offering of one of the cacique's female kin, was precisely what cacique Agüeybana I did with Juan Ponce de León—whom he identified as his equal in rank and status—when he set foot in Boriquén, as we shall see later.

If bridal exchanges were a means to extend political influence and alliances, these women were also the targets of political competition and a source for (or symptom of) political tension that could lead to rupture and to war. According to Sued Badillo:

> Cacicazgos . . . held units of various social types in vassalage under them with ideological effects that were terribly confusing to the Spaniards. Intergroup discrimination such as that which occurred in the province of Guacayarima [southwestern Haiti, Figure 26] or with the Macorises [Macorix], the Cigüayos and Lucayos [natives of Bahamas], etc. were simply a reflection of the forced coexistence of groups that had historically been autonomous. It is possible that institutionalized violence represented in wars, or the raids carried out by caciques in order to kidnap women or steal other caciques' [cemí] idols, was resorted to in pursuance of these distinctions [Sued Badillo 2003:265].

Indeed, Sued Badillo (2003:265) cites the well-known example of kidnapping or killing women reported by Las Casas, Hernando Colón, and others in Hispaniola. The enmity and rivalry that existed between Guacanagarí, chief of the Marién chiefdom, and both Caonabó (of the Maguana chiefdom) and Behechio (of the Jaraguá/Bainoa chiefdom) came about because: "the other caciques were against him [Guacanagarí], particularly Behechio, because he had killed one of his wives, and Caonabó, who stole the other one. This is the reason why he begged [Christopher Columbus] to help him get her back and avenge him from these injuries" (Colón, cited in Sued Badillo 1978:59). It is this circumstance that led cacique Guacanagarí to seek a politically advantageous alliance with Christopher Columbus when he first reached this region and established the short-lived settlement of La Navidad, near En Bas Saline, Haiti (Figure 26; see Deagan 1995, 2004). Kidnapping or stealing women, like stealing cemí idols, surely signals competition between caciques, perhaps even factional rivalries among subordinated caciques within the chiefdom. And, of course, kidnapping and theft, as a last recourse, could and probably often did result in open, armed conflict between rival chiefs and chiefdoms. Such situations were thoroughly exploited by the Spanish, pitting chief against chief and changing the equation of native allegiances. It is likely that the theft of women, like that of cemí idols, was not a new tactic that developed solely in response to the Spanish, but a practice that almost certainly had been deployed in pre-Columbian times. In any case, the kidnapping of women, like that of cemí idols, took place in an environment of stress and pending, if not effective, political crisis.

The guaízas made of stone or shell have survived, but those made of perishable materials have not and are only known thanks to their description in ethnohistoric documents. The stone guaízas (Figure 27: m, n) are characteristic of Puerto Rico, whereas those made of shell are much less frequent (Figure 27: o), yet prevalent in Hispaniola and eastern Cuba. Some of the stone guaíza masks of Puerto Rico were clearly not made to be strung in a necklace or strapped in an armband, as they lack perforations. Instead, I think, the guaízas were probably for hand presentation and display; they could have also been wrapped in cloth (as the natives usually did with nuggets of gold when bartering with the Spanish in colonial times). But other guaízas, possibly of shell or cotton, were worn as pectorals, as clearly depicted in the petroglyph cemí of Caguana in Puerto Rico (Figure 27: r). By way of contrast, in Hispaniola and eastern Cuba (Figure 27: a-l) shell guaízas predominate, and thus were meant to be strung in necklaces (pectoral plaques) or sewn into belts, headbands, and armbands, as is clearly depicted in an anthropomorphic pendant from the Dominican Republic (Figure 27: p).

The shell-made guaízas have, thus far, the widest geographic distribution, reaching as far south into the Lesser Antilles as Île de Ronde (La Redonda) in the Grenadines. As discussed in the previous section, in Hispaniola guaízas were the gifts par excellence offered to stranger caciques and leaders—that is, to prominent individuals well outside the polity controlled or ruled by a cacique. The wider geographic distribution of all nonperishable guaízas (especially shell) makes sense given their primary function as symbolic gifts to foreign leaders. The guaíza gifts would probably be accompanied with name or bride exchanges if the circumstances merited further strengthening the pact of alliance. Before addressing the implications of the gift of the guaíza, a few words about the surviving guaíza artifacts are necessary.

Regardless of whether the guaíza was made of stone, shell, or cotton, or how it was worn or displayed, it is a part that identifies and forms the person of the cacique; to give it to others is to offer the receiving caciques the living soul that is represented by this object. Being a vital part that constitutes the cacique's personhood—his living soul—meant that giving guaízas was a means of extending a part of the cacique's person to the other, receiving person, a potential political ally or trade partner. The extension of the person of the cacique (or leader) via the guaíza is reminiscent of the heroic "divine kings" of Polynesia discussed by Marshall Sahlins (1991:63; but see critiques by Mosko 1992). These are lords "whose heroic capacities and actions summarize, unify, encompass and thus expansively *internalize* the relations of a society's members as a whole. Such figures are social-historical individuals" (Sahlins, quoted by Mosko 1992:698–699). Sahlins's view (as paraphrased by Mosko 1992:699) is that "persons of this magnitude personify their respective societies almost literally, that is, as 'heroic societies' . . . Sahlins said of the Polynesian chief that he lives the life of a whole tribe . . . stands in a certain relation to neighboring tribes and kinship groups, and . . . gathers the relationship to other tribes in his person." In this Polynesian model of heroic chiefs, their persons are built up to expansively encompass, internalize, and subsume all the relations of society in his persona. But in the case of the caciques in Hispaniola and Puerto Rico, to do so requires giving a part of their personhood, the guaíza (living soul materialized as an object), to other leaders and allies so that they *can be* encompassing.

Guaízas were unlike the three-pointers or ancestor stone heads examined earlier in that they appear not to be the subject of veneration and consultation in cohoba ceremonies but instead appear to be an essential component of the cacique's political-religious prowess and thus of his personhood. To use Walker's (1993) terms, the guaíza was personally "owned" but performed a very public function; it was displayed as part of the attire that signals his or her place, status, and rank in society. Interestingly, repeatedly giving guaízas also meant that any single cacique would have several other guaízas available, indicating even further partibility of his personhood. This form of distributed personhood parallels the guaitiao ceremony when names between the leaders were exchanged with not one but as many allies as was necessary. In parallel, the cacique would also give and take in marriage as many women as it would be wise to exchange. It is probable that each guaíza (like the other cemí idols discussed) bore the names, titles, and genealogy of its source: the living cacique.

I wonder what happened to the guaízas after the death of a cacique. And I mean both those he kept of his face (soul) and those that were gifted to him by others (someone else's soul). Here the archaeology is not very helpful, as most reports lack clear contexts. I know of no guaízas found in burial contexts, so again these were apparently maintained in circulation. However, in Cuba, Puerto Rico, and Hispaniola a few shell guaízas have been found in what seem to be midden deposits. Perhaps they lost potency once their current owners passed away, or maybe what we think of as "spent" items for garbage disposal were not so. A guaíza's disposal in a given midden may well respond to a ritual commemorative event, assuming that the guaíza never lost its potency. Probably there were regional variations as to what to do with guaízas after the death of a cacique, depending on factors such as whether the guaíza was his semblance (soul) or that of someone else (the giver of the guaíza). The fact is, we do not know with any degree of confidence. Another problem is that an adequate census of existing guaízas in the Caribbean needs to be carried out more fully. To date, only a very partial list totaling fifty-four specimens from the entire Caribbean has been compiled (by Angus Mol in 2007).

The differential distribution of shell versus stone guaízas is interesting. The prevalence of stone guaízas in Puerto Rico may indicate that as gifts to strangers these largely circulated among chiefs throughout Puerto Rico. However, the shell guaízas are spread wide throughout the Caribbean but are rare in Puerto Rico. Still, they are at least present in Puerto Rico, thus opening the possibility that some may have been circulated as gifts among chiefs in Hispaniola and elsewhere. First let us look at the nexus between Hispaniola and eastern Cuba.

A. The Nexus between Eastern Cuba and Hispaniola

The interconnectedness between eastern Cuba and Hispaniola is strongly indicated not only by the presence of shell guaízas in both islands but also by their strong similarities in ceramic styles and the presence of a range of sculptural art (cemí icons) that suggests a strong participation in what I have been calling Taínoness. Las Casas (1929 [2]:452) reported that some fifty years before the Spanish conquest of Hispaniola, natives from Hispaniola had migrated to Cuba. According to Cuban archaeologists, the interaction between eastern Cuban and Hispaniolan societies probably began as early as A.D. 800 and continued until the early years of Spanish conquest: these archaeologists recognize cultural variants or a spectrum of Taíno or Taínoan complexes, such as Pueblo Viejo, Baní, Maisí, Bayamo, and Damajayabo (Guarch Delmonte 1990; Rouse 1942; Valcárcel Rojas 1999, 2002a, 2002b). Other indigenous sites extended well into the Spanish colonial period, some apparently in relative isolation or marginated from European contacts (Los Buchillones), while others already display strong elements of syncretism and transculturation (e.g., Chorro de Maíta, Barajagua la Vieja, El Yayal, El Convento; Figure 28).

The Los Buchillones site, located in Ciégo del Ávila, on north-central Cuba, extended its occupation into the seventeenth century (A.D. 1295–1655) and retained in its material culture all of its aboriginal (i.e., Taínoan) heritage (Graham et al. 2000; Pendergast 1997, 1998; Pendergast et al. 2001, 2002; Figure 29). The necropolis at Chorro de Maíta (A.D. 800 or 900–1550), located farther east in the region of Banes, eastern Cuba, also retained an indigenous heritage into the middle of the sixteenth century, but European materials, including a Spanish skull interment and metals, were found in relative abundance (Cooper et al. 2008; Martinón-Torres et al. 2007; Rivero de La Calle et al. 1989; Valcárcel Rojas 1999, 2002a, 2002b; Valcárcel Rojas et al. 2003). Although the ceramic styles for these Taínoan cultural variants relate to what Rouse (1992) called the Meillacan Ostionoid or to the Chican Ostionoid series (see Figure 5), the materials that can be regarded as ceremonial paraphernalia show strong parallels with those of Hispaniola and even Puerto Rico (see Figures 29, 34). There are, of course, both similarities as well as differences in these materials. For example, Cuban wood duhos are of the same type as those in Hispaniola and the Bahamas, with raised backs for reclining, or as those in Puerto Rico, which are flat benches (see Ostapkowicz 1999). At sites like Los Buchillones, where wood has been preserved in astonishing abundance, miniature duhos were also found. While there are a number of wooden idols carved in the Chican Ostionoid style, they do seem to be local rather than imports from Hispaniola or beyond. As in Puerto Rico, there are no wood icons with the round platform to hold the cohoba hallucinogen. Most prevalent in eastern Cuba are the small, portable cemí icons (made from various raw materials) that are worn as body decorations or sewn into other objects (Figure 29). In the Banes–Maniabón Hill region (Figure 28; Rouse 1942) we find icons already familiar to us: a miniature three-pointed cemí, a pendant with the crouched personage, a fragment of a vomiting spatula, and the head portion of a medium-sized three-pointer, which only has close analogues in Puerto Rico, just to mention a few (Figure 29). The shell guaízas from eastern Cuba also show strong stylistic affinities to the Hispaniolan sample (see Figure 27). Given that guaízas were part of a system of gifts among stranger caciques, it is possible that some of the Cuban guaízas were manufactured in Hispaniola and vice versa. Shell, unfortunately, is a material that cannot be chemically analyzed or "fingerprinted" to gain information about provenience.

One of the interesting observations made by Las Casas (1929 [2]:460) about Cuba (based on memories of when he lived there in 1511–1514) is the presence of societies that he called *Ciboney,* no doubt a term that hides considerable variation. Nevertheless, in comparison to what he had experienced in Hispaniola and what he identified in Cuba as recent arrivals from Hispaniola, the Ciboney appeared to him simpler in their way of life and their material culture, and perhaps because their sociopolitical organization tended to show a more egalitarian ethos. He understood these "original" Indo-Cuban inhabitants to be subservient (though not slaves) to those natives he thought of as originating from Hispaniola. It is unclear the degree to which the Ciboneyes and the Taínoan Hispaniolans, who had been migrating to Cuba from much earlier, had culturally amalgamated with locals. Given Las Casas's comments, one might suspect that key differences remained despite coexisting as a plural yet well-articulated society. Thus, in eastern Cuba the religious ideology anchored in cemíism is materially well represented in the "Ciboney-Taíno" bricolage.

Such a phenomenon is not unheard of in ethnography, as, for example, the case of the Tukano of Piraparaná-Vaupés in northwestern Amazonia. There the Makú hunter-gatherers are incorporated to the agrarian Tukanoan society in the ceremonial (or specialist) role of "servants," while Tukano sib members are assigned to the roles of chiefs, warriors, dancers or chanters, and shamans (Hugh-Jones 1979:54–75). The latter specialist, ceremonial roles are fulfilled by closely related agnates (of a sib) for each simple or compound residential group that inhabits a *maloca* (longhouse). The Makú, despite their different ethnic-linguistic origins, are thus articulated with the Tukano, who, in addition to Tukanoan, are Arawakan speakers (used mainly in ritual or domestic contexts). This and other similar social mechanisms of articulation have been noted by scholars to also characterize many of the Arawakan-speaking societies, and indeed it is a key trait of "Arawakness." It is that capacity to include "Otherness" that is in part accountable for the huge geographic spread of the Arawakan stock of languages and the broad spectrum of cultural features displayed by these societies (for detailed arguments, see Heckenberger 2002, 2008; Santos-Granero 2002).

Shell guaízas, present on both islands, are good indicators of the importance of gift exchanges among leaders and chiefs in creating forms of both sociopolitical and personal articulation within and between eastern Cuba and Hispaniola. Following Sahlins's argument about heroic "kings" and of how they gather or subsume in their person what is in effect a plurality of social relations and ideologies (tribal lore, legends, rituals, icons), I am tempted to think that the articulation of the "Ciboney-Taíno" bricolage is in part facilitated and mediated through the gifts of guaízas, by the binding effect that giving his or her living soul to strangers or to others has.

B. Across Borders: Between Puerto Rico and the Windward Islands

Contributors to the edited volume *Late Ceramic Age Societies in the Eastern Caribbean* (Delpuech and Hofman, eds. 2004) have noted that during the earlier pre-Columbian period, between about 400 B.C. and A.D. 1200 or 1300, there were numerous close affinities and sustained contacts between the northeastern Leeward Islands and Puerto Rico–Virgin Islands (Figure 30). From A.D. 800 to A.D. 1200 or 1300 a period of growth was experienced almost everywhere in the Caribbean. This period was marked by very close correspondences of Elenan Ostionoid material cultures between Puerto Rico and the Virgin Islands, but also extended south to the northeastern Lesser Antilles (Knippenberg 2004). However, Samuel Wilson observed that "in later prehistory, by around A.D. 1300, it seems that an antagonistic relationship developed between the people[s] of the Windward Islands and Puerto Rico" (Wilson 2004:270; 2007:148, 175). He postulates, based on various lines of evidence, the existence of a buffer zone (Figure 30) ranging from Saba east to Nevis and quite probably also extending farther south and east to include Montserrat and Antigua. Wilson, however, is careful to note that the buffer zone was not totally but only relatively depopulated, "because people were probably going there to exploit particular resources, and there were likely temporary settlements" (Wilson 2004:271). He correctly points out that the ethnohistorical record for this region, starting in 1493 and through the sixteenth century, is difficult to interpret. Despite the broad cultural differences developing on either side of the postulated buffer zone, a few three-pointed stones of the large variety and shell guaízas have been recovered in the Lesser Antilles.

Wilson (2004:271) further hypothesized that perhaps the breakdown of relations on either side of the buffer zone correlates with the rise of political centralization (cacicazgos, or chiefdoms) in that island group. Although I do not see the kind of political centralization for Puerto Rico that Wilson assumes—certainly not in the earlier periods (A.D. 600–1100)—it is still plausible that competitive *peer* polities did consolidate around A.D. 1100 and matured by A.D. 1300, coincidental with the proliferation of Capá, Esperanza, and Maggens Bay–Salt River II (Chican Ostionoid) styles in Puerto Rico and the Virgin Islands. Farther west, across the Mona Passage in Hispaniola, it is safe to assume that there was a greater degree of political centralization than in Puerto Rico, and probably paramount chiefdoms were present there by A.D. 1300, if not earlier. I would agree with Wilson (2004:271) that by A.D. 1300, and certainly by early Spanish contact, the center of gravity in politics and demographics (though I would not include "cultural") in the Greater Antilles had shifted to Hispaniola (see also Curet 2003, 2006; Curet et al. 2004).

The interregional situation between A.D. 1300 and the early 1500s in the northeastern Caribbean is imperfectly understood. Nevertheless, as Wilson (2004, 2007) suggested, there is evidence of an "interest" by the natives of Hispaniola and Puerto Rico on the northernmost border of this frontier land. Chican Ostionoid materials in the Leeward Islands have been found at a limited number of sites as *complexes* rather than as isolated finds embedded in the local cultural complexes (belonging to the Suazan or Troumassan Troumassoid series). These sites are Kelbey's Ridge 2 on Saba, Sandy Hill on Anguilla, and Baie Rouge on St. Martin, all located *within* the proposed buffer zone (Hofman et al. 2007; Wilson 2004, 2007) and within the broader sphere of interaction, with Taínoan societies in the Greater Antilles. The Kelbey's Ridge 2 site on Saba (A.D. 1400s), however, did not yield guaízas or large, decorated three-pointed stones, but it *did* yield one small coral (*Porites spp.*) three-pointer, plus a small marine shell cohoba inhaler carved in the form of a fish—an unusual depiction to be found in Caribbean inhalers (Hoogland 1995:150–151, 193; Hoogland and Hofman 1993, 1999).

The limited number of guaízas recovered from the Lesser Antilles (Figure 30) are all made of shell and bear decorative motifs that are consonant with specimens from the Greater Antilles, especially Cuba and Hispaniola. A total of eleven samples are distributed as follows. In Anguilla there are two specimens from the Rendezvous Bay and Sandy Hill sites (Crock and Petersen 2004:151). In Antigua three specimens are reported, of which only one is known to be from the Indian Creek site, reported respectively by Fred Olsen and Douglas Bird (Mol 2007; see Figure 27: s). In Montserrat one specimen of unknown provenience was reported, also by Olsen (in Mol 2007). At La Désirade, a small island off the southeast coast of Guadeloupe, three guaíza shell specimens were recovered from the sites of Morne Cybèle and Morne Souffleur (de Waal 2006; Hofman et al. 2004:181; 2007). The first site has one calibrated date of A.D. 1440–1460. The second site is regarded as contemporaneous with Morne Cybèle (de Waal 2006; Hofman et al. 2004:166–167). Another shell guaíza was found on Marie Galante, just south of Guadeloupe (Hofman et al. 2004:181). The ceramic assemblages associated with Morne Cybèle and Morne Souffleur "seem to have no stylistic counterparts, bar some minor style elements, which look like Suazan" pottery (i.e., Suazan Troumassoid subseries: A.D. 800–1300 or 1500; Hofman et al. 2004:168).

Three other guaíza specimens remain. One was found by Ripley and Adelaide Bullen (1970) on St. Lucia, at the site of Lavoutte. This site's ceramic assemblages relate to the Troumassoid series (ca. A.D. 800 to 1400?); the specimen was collected from the surface. Interestingly, this guaíza was damaged and showed burn marks, but whether this was intentional (perhaps a ritual killing or desecration) or accidental cannot be determined (Mol 2007:130). On the Grenadines, at Union Island and Île de Ronde, respectively, two shell guaízas have been reported (see de Waal 2006; Hofman et al. 2007; Kaye et al. 2004). Of all these sites, only the shell guaízas from Rendezvous Bay and Sandy Hill in Anguilla are associated with a Chican (Taíno) component—that is, with social groups whose material culture and historical ancestry strongly displayed Taínoness. In any event, even if they are rare, guaízas have a very broad distribution throughout the Lesser Antilles and are embedded in cultural matrices that are clearly different (i.e., Troumassoid). The obvious question to ask is, why guaízas in particular? Why not other kinds of numinous, prestigious icons? I shall return to this question shortly.

The presence of three-pointed stones in some of the Windward Islands, regardless of how they got there (locally made, imitations, war booty, exchange, etc.) is more understandable, since the "faceless" (undecorated) miniature three-pointers go way back in time, to the Saladoid and possibly even pre-Arawak periods in the Lesser Antilles and Puerto Rico, and continued to be in production in post-Saladoid times (see Knippenberg 2004). For the later Troumassoid populations, the numinous attributions of triangular objects would be familiar to them. South of the Virgin Islands, the large three-pointed stones, provided with "faces" (i.e., visually coded identities), have been found in Anguilla, Guadeloupe, Dominica, and Carriacou of the Grenadines archipelago (see Clerc 1970). These larger, decorated specimens raise questions about whether they were locally made imitations or brought from abroad, and if so under what circumstances: alliances and exchange? Raid booty?

The earlier component at the Sandy Hill site in Anguilla yielded a ceramic assemblage comparable to the late Elenan Ostionan complexes found in Puerto Rico and the Virgin Islands, and it is in this context, with a date of A.D. 1070, that one shell guaíza was found, displaying Taínoan iconography. Two other surface fragments recovered before John Crock's excavation was conducted may well date to the last Chican Ostionoid phase (Crock and Petersen 2004). The latter two were described as "shell masks" and may relate to the later Chican Ostionoid component (Mol 2007:125). The temporal and cultural affiliations of the shell guaíza found at the Rendezvous site, however, remain uncertain but could date anywhere between A.D. 900 or 1000 to A.D. 1400 or 1500. At the Taínoan site of the Sandy Hill site in Anguilla (ca. A.D. 1200 or 1300–1500), the guaíza is further complemented by the presence of four larger, decorated three-pointed stones, albeit none quite as richly decorated as those commonly found in Puerto Rico and on the Virgin Islands (e.g., at St. Croix's Salt River site; Crock and Petersen 2004:fig. 7; Faber Morse 2004:fig. 10). All of the three-pointed stones are made of igneous porphyry. Since Anguilla is a limestone-coralliferous island, all four cemís had to be imported from islands with porphyry resources. At this juncture it is not known if Sandy Hill includes porphyry debitage that would suggest local manufacture. However, I am willing to bet that these were imported as finished products and that the most likely source would be somewhere between Puerto Rico and the Virgin Islands.

The presence of the guaízas at Sandy Hill would suggest that local leaders had been engaged in a guaíza exchange network. More specifically, whether this particular sample represented a gift received from another cacique or was instead his or her guaíza, it will always retain the potential for being given to a foreign cacique in, say, Puerto Rico, and hence for distributing and extending his or her living soul and power to foreigners or strangers. If one thinks of this guaíza as an uttered word rather than an object, the Anguilla's "big man" (or cacique, as John Crock would prefer) was speaking a language that was well understood in Puerto Rico, the Virgin Islands, and more so in Hispaniola and eastern Cuba, where shell guaízas are even more prevalent. If it was a gift from, say, allied chiefs in Puerto Rico or Hispaniola, the receiver of the guaíza would hence share in the extended person and identity of the giver; if it was his own (not yet given), then he or she would display the capability to potentially extend his or her living soul to other chiefs, or perhaps even to ritually exchange names and maybe arrange a few marriages. The presence of exotic porphyry three-pointed stones further strengthens the notion that these cemí-imbued objects were circulating, along with these guaízas, as part of an interinsular exchange system designed to create alliance networks between caciques.

That guaízas are present in Chican Ostionoid (Taínoan) sites is to be expected, but what of the others found to the south in clearly non-Chican (Troumassoid) sites? Here the explanations can be varied. If, as Samuel Wilson (2004) argues, there were antagonistic, bellicose relationships between the inhabitants of the Windward

Islands and those to the north of the buffer zone after A.D. 1300 or 1400 (especially Puerto Rico–Virgin Islands), then they could very well have been captured as war booty and appropriated by the victorious war leaders, much in the same way that rival caciques of Hispaniola stole prized cemí idols from one another. But politics being politics, some guaízas may also reflect the reinstatement of peace treaties. As already noted earlier, this is exactly what happened after Columbus's men attacked the Cigüayo natives in Puerto de Las Flechas, in Samaná, Hispaniola. The overture of the Cigüayo chief toward some form of peace agreement with Columbus was to send a guaíza gift. On the other hand, some of the guaízas could well be the result of mimicry, of emulating the symbols of power of foreign, potentially enemy, chiefs in the Greater Antilles.

Besides the four specimens from Anguilla, large three-pointed cemís have thus far been found in the Lesser Antilles (Figure 30), south of the proposed buffer zone: at the Anse à la Gourde site on Guadeloupe, at the Soufrière site on Dominica, and at the Grand Bay site on Carriacou—the southernmost spread of these relatively large three-pointed cemí idols (Clerc 1970:fig. 11; Hofman et al. 2007; Kaye et al. 2004: 85–86). Although present, these large three-pointers are very few in number. The samples from Guadeloupe, Dominica, and Carriacou, however, are as large as many in the Greater Antilles (23–30 cm long); both the Dominica and Carriacou samples are decorated as well. It is because these large icons are so rare that one may discount that they were the result of a local development (toward a larger size) in parallel to what occurred in southeast Hispaniola, Puerto Rico, and the Virgin Islands. The simplest explanation is that the Windward specimens were brought from the latter region. Again, the same explanations given for guaízas can be proposed for the presence in these islands of the large, three-pointed stone cemís. They could be war booty or the result of peace negotiations, however temporary, or mimicry. Most fascinating is the fact that the specimen from Guadeloupe shows evidence of decapitation: the head portion where the "face" was carved is missing (Hofman, personal communication 2006), a theme that has resonance in the Greater Antilles, too (see Figure 9). If this idol was captured in war, then the decapitation probably was a way to ritually kill the enemy's potent cemí icon. But others, such as the Dominica and the Carriacou Island specimens, are complete, which suggests that if these were also captured in battle from, say, Puerto Rico, they were added to the numinous icons of the local leaders; after all, the small faceless, undecorated three-pointed icons still held a religious significance that went back to Saladoid times.

An adequate analysis of the ethnohistoric data (1500s–1650s) for the Lesser Antilles to provide a framework in which to discuss the circulation of these rare cemí objects is beyond the scope of this book. It would require engaging in a long discussion to disentangle the many notions ascribed to the term *Carib* (and *caníbales*). I have avoided naming the native societies of the Windward Islands as "Carib" precisely so as not to raise in the reader's mind stereotypes of warlike, savage Carib versus civilized Taíno or Arawak. For those interested in the debates and problems brought about by the Carib label, I suggest consulting the works of Jalil Sued Badillo (1978, 1984, 1992), Peter Hulme (1992, 1993), and the articles in the volume *Wolves from the Sea,* edited by Neil Whitehead (1995). The most useful compilation of early Spanish documents referring to the so-called Carib raids in Puerto Rico and the Virgin Islands has been published by Alvaro Huerga (2006; see also Murga Sanz 1971) and, of course, one can also obtain valuable information by consulting the standard sixteenth-century Spanish and seventeenth-century French chroniclers (see Cárdenas Ruíz 1981; Sued Badillo 1978:bibliography).

The point is that whatever the ethnicity and languages of the peoples of the Windward Islands, their material cultures show far more differences than similarities with the spectrum of Greater Antillean Taínoan archaeological materials. Groups from Martinique, Guadeloupe, and Dominica in particular raided Puerto Rico often during the very early 1500s, and continued to do so for several decades. Not all of these raids were led by the so-called Caribs against the Taínos of Puerto Rico; indeed, some raids were organized by natives of Puerto Rico in alliance with those in St. Croix and the Virgin Islands (see Sued Badillo 1978). It cannot be assumed that this raiding pattern was an unchanging condition that existed unabated since A.D. 1300, as implied by the proposed buffer zone. No doubt, the interregional political situation was much more complex and variable. However, there is no question that natives were captured from Puerto Rico and the Virgin Islands and taken to the Windward Islands, just as I have no doubt that there also were natives fleeing the Spanish conquest in Puerto Rico seeking asylum in the Lesser Antilles. Perhaps these expatriates even participated in raids against the natives of Puerto Rico, particularly against those who continued to maintain loyalty to the Spanish.

Sued Badillo (1978:56–57) argued that the natives of Boriquén were fleeing from the conflicts generated by the Spanish conquest, and that they had sought and received asylum not just in Guadeloupe (Figure 30) but as far south as Trinidad. The implication is that there was some kind of a priori relationship or alliance that would obligate the hosts to undertake such a burden. This emigration began as early as 1511 and continued into the 1520s. There is a document dating to November 9, 1511, where King Charles instructed Lieutenant Governor Cerón and his magistrate Díaz (in Puerto Rico) with the following: "to go and search for the Indians of Boriquén that are under the power of the Caribs in the islands of Dominica, Matininó [i.e. Martinique], Santa Lucía [St. Lucia], San Vicente [St. Vincent], La Asunción, Barbados and Tabaco [Tobago]; bring them and have them as naborías [i.e., slaves] and be served by them as long as you dress them and [provide] the necessary things, as is customary" (Murga Sanz 1971:79). While Sued Badillo (1978) sees this as evidence that the Taínos of Boriquén had some sort of a priori alliance with Lesser Antillean natives that secured them asylum, others like Louis Allaire and Samuel Wilson (Wilson 2004:271) interpret that the Indians of Boriquén were taken as war captives by the Lesser Antillean Caribs.

What I do not agree with is the argument that *all* natives from Puerto Rico found in the Windward Islands were captives taken in raids by the so-called Caribs (see Huerta 2006; also Wilson 2004, 2007:ch. 5); some were also genuine refugees (see Sued Badillo 1978:56–57) who received asylum in the Windward Islands. But even by 1511, the intergroup and inter-insular geopolitics of the Caribbean natives had already changed so dramatically because of Spanish interference that it would be naïve to consider the later sixteenth-century Spanish and seventeenth-century French historical documents as a reflection of the ways in which natives interacted (in war and peace) in pre–Spanish contact times.

However, there is also evidence that kidnapping women from Puerto Rico by Lesser Antillean natives was probably a pre-Hispanic practice. On his second voyage, Admiral Columbus reached the island of Guadeloupe on November 4, 1493, for the first time (Figure 30; see Varela 1999:18, 205–224). The next day Columbus sent two boats to the island in order to gain information about its inhabitants and, in particular, directions to take him toward Hispaniola, as he was anxious to reach in the shortest possible time the thirty-nine Spaniards he had left at the settlement of La Navidad. The narration that follows was written by Hernando Colón, based on the admiral's lost *Diario* (*Journal*) for the second voyage and the documents (which have survived) of two witnesses, the learned physician Dr. Diego Álvarez Chanca (see Tió 1966) and Michele de Cuneo (1983 [1495]; see also Sued Badillo 1978:58–63).

> Each of these boats returned with magnificent young Indians. They agreed that they were not from that island but from another named Boriquén and now [named] San Juan [Puerto Rico], that the inhabitants of this island [Guadeloupe] were Caribes and they had captured them in their own island [in Boriquén]. Shortly thereafter, when the boats returned to pick up some Christians who remained behind, they [the mariners] found with them six women that had come to them running away from the Caribes and it was their will to embark on the [Spanish] ships. But the Admiral, to appease the people of that island, did not want to detain them in the ships, instead he gave them [the women of Boriquén] some glass beads and bells and had them taken to shore, against their will . . . after landing, the Caribes, in full view of the Christians, took away everything that the Admiral had given them. [Later] when the boats returned to stock up with drinking water and firewood, the said women returned to beg the mariners to take them to the ships, saying with signals that the people of that island were men eaters and that they had them for slaves [Colón 1985:166, ch. 57].

This incident suggests that the women from Boriquén were kept against their will on Guadeloupe, and that they fervently wished to be returned to their homeland. A raid to capture women on Puerto Rico at that early date (earlier than 1493) took place before the Spanish conquest and slave-raid armadas had time to radically alter the political scene in the Windward Islands. Therefore, Wilson (2004) has a valid point in suggesting that the pattern of raids from Guadeloupe to Puerto Rico go back to pre-Columbian times. At one point I wondered if the women were forced by their kinsmen in Puerto Rico to marry natives from Guadeloupe so as to establish far-flung alliances, which would explain the presence of guaízas and the few other Chican Ostionoid religious icons found in the Windward Islands. I imagined that alone and without the close support of their relatives, the plight of these women to be returned home made sense. Although I am no longer convinced of this argument, it ought to be kept subliminally in mind if only because politics is politics; relations of belligerence (raids, kidnappings, thefts) versus alliance and peace (guaitiao rituals, bride/groom exchanges, trade) can shift quickly and dramatically.

In conclusion, what seems to become clearer in examining the Lesser Antillean data is that some of the social dynamics that explain the distribution of guaízas and large three-pointers echoes that already discussed for the core area between the southeastern Dominican Republic, Puerto Rico, and the Virgin Islands: the gift of guaízas to foreign or stranger caciques and the circulation of three-pointers to cement alliances among leaders *and* its opposite, the theft or capture of cemí icons, guaízas, and women by raiding rival groups. The issue of mimicry or emulation by Lesser Antillean leaders, particularly involving guaízas, cannot be discounted.

The guaízas and three-pointed cemís examined in this section illustrate the complexities archaeologists are faced with in attempting to flesh out details of the entangled web of political-economic relations, especially when examining and contrasting the Greater Antilles with the Lesser Antilles. The role of these artifacts as symbols of power (but that translate into *effective* power relations) can best be assessed if one attempts to understand what each set of artifacts may have meant in the context of different kinds of transactions between individuals or groups. Although context in archaeological excavations is very important, it is only a small part of the story, as all it can provide is the very last context on what was probably (for the object and the peoples handling it) a more complex history of interaction and circulation.

What happened to the guaízas or the three-pointed cemí-imbued icons parallels that of other kinds of power relations, such as exchanging names or brides between caciques, or as targets for theft or kidnapping, even decapitation. The possible decapitation of the Guadeloupe three-pointer suggests the importance that faces, heads, and skulls had for both Greater and Lesser Antillean societies. Understanding the significance of the circulation of the potent three-pointed cemís and guaízas, rather than just economic goods, is particularly important because these are the objects where political power and prestige (centered on cemíism) focused. Their presence or absence can tell us a great deal about the natives' participation, exclusion, or meddling with Taínoness. These objects inform us about how natives dealt with those symbols of power and of Taínoness.

Part V of this book will return to the Greater Antilles to analyze the role of cemí icons in the context of war and battles between native caciques and Spaniards, between cemíism and Christianity. The analysis leads to two distinct results: one of belligerent native resistance against Catholic-Spanish hegemony; the other of the first steps toward transculturation and syncretism that would gradually result in the various constructions of the "ethnic" category of *Indio* through the Spanish colonial period and even into the twentieth century. Part V is thus about the issues of resistance versus compliance, rejection versus acceptance, and about the very early processes of syncretism or anti-syncretism that largely unfolded in a very brief period between A.D. 1503 and 1511. These historic events, the battles for and against the rule of the cemís, laid the foundation for the identities of the Indios that began to form and that continued to evolve and struggle for the next five hundred years in the Hispanic-speaking Caribbean.

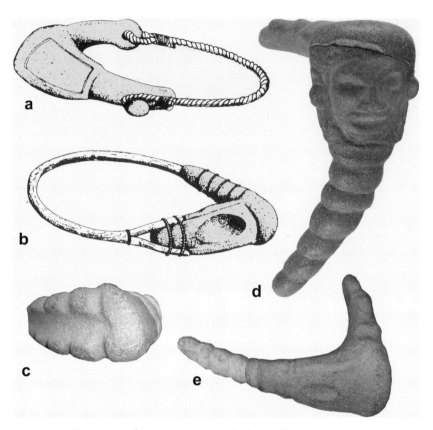

Figure 19. Elbow stones from Puerto Rico. The lithic elbow was tied up by (a) rope or *henquén* (vegetable) fiber or (b) bent wood to make a composite "collar"; (c) the groove or channel of an elbow stone for attaching wood; (d) elbow stone with an anthropomorphic head carved on its panel; (e) an elbow stone with simpler decoration (whiter color area is a reconstruction). Specimens c-e: ©Museo de Historia, Antropología y Arte–Universidad de Puerto Rico.

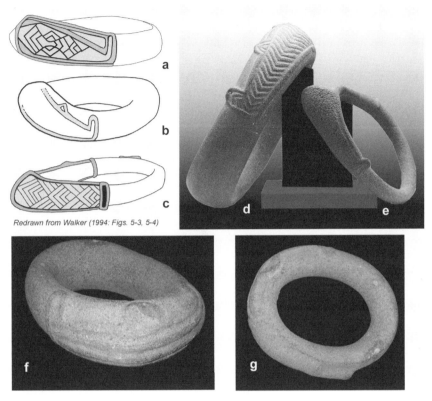

Redrawn from Walker (1994: Figs. 5-3, 5-4)

Figure 20. Stone collars from Puerto Rico. (a-d) Massive, bench-type stone collars with Headless-Fish motifs; (e) a slender, frame-type stone collar; (f-g) a decorated bench-type stone collar from Barrio Marín, Patillas, Puerto Rico. Specimens d-e: Fundación Arqueológica, Antropológica e Histórica de Puerto Rico (now defunct); specimen f-g, courtesy of Jaime and Arelis Pagán.

Figure 21. Slender stone collar from Puerto Rico: (A) view of the upper panel show-ing two pairs of opposing persons; (B) lateral right panel showing a bicephalous crea-ture with a single body with crossed arms, legs, and abdomen; (C) a frontal view of the notch or prominence; (D) lower lateral left panel. One of the four personages of the upper panel viewed from the top (*e*) and viewed laterally (*f*). The white chalk to fill in the grooves was added to enhance the design. Fundación Arqueológica, Antropológica e Histórica de Puerto Rico (now defunct).

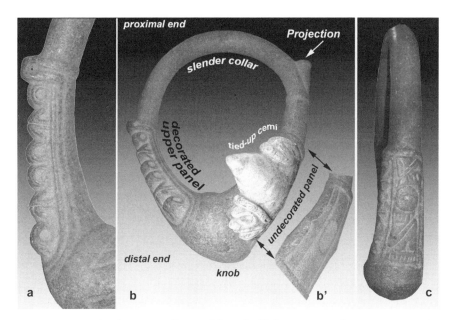

Figure 22. Two slender stone collars and "attached" three-pointer from Puerto Rico. (a) A detail of the upper decorated panel of stone collar b'; (b) stone collar with segment names; (b') the lateral undecorated panel where a three-pointed stone is theorized to be tied to the collar; (c) the decorated lateral panel of a different stone collar, showing abdominal circle and folded arms and legs. Fundación Arqueológica, Antropológica e Histórica de Puerto Rico (now defunct).

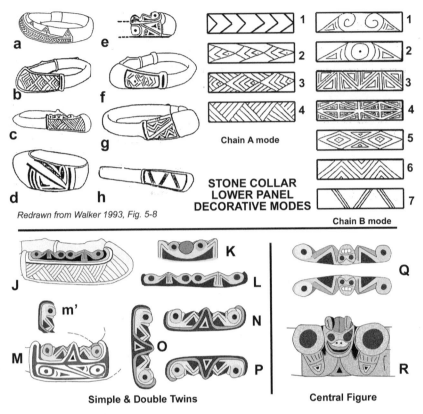

Redrawn from Walker 1993, Fig. 5-8

STONE COLLAR LOWER PANEL DECORATIVE MODES

Chain A mode

Chain B mode

Simple & Double Twins

Central Figure

Figure 23. Stone collars from Puerto Rico (a-h) showing two series (A and B) or chains of design modes (A: 1–4; B: 1–7) depicted on the lower panels of stone collars. The Simple-Twin personages mode (K) viewed from a lateral perspective. The Double-Twin personages viewed from a lateral perspective (J, L). The compound Bat-Winged personage (M) as central figure, with two eyes and a triangular nose in the upper decorated panel and wings folded in the lateral or side perspective. Rotation of one half of the Twin personage into vertical position (i.e., profile) reveals it in a kneeling position (m'); rotation of the upper panel with the Simple-Twin personages in lateral perspective with the base of the collar at the bottom (N), in vertical (O), and in inverted positions (P). Central figure of a bat personage in the upper panel in lateral view and in inverted position (Q), and another bat personage on the lateral lower panel (R).

Figure 24. A 75-cm-tall male cotton cemí idol from a cave site in
Maniel, Barahona, southwestern Dominican Republic. X-ray images
revealed the frontal segment of a human skull in the head area (teeth
visible) and an unidentified opaque object in the thorax-abdomen
area. ©Museum of Anthropology and Ethnography of Turin, Italy.

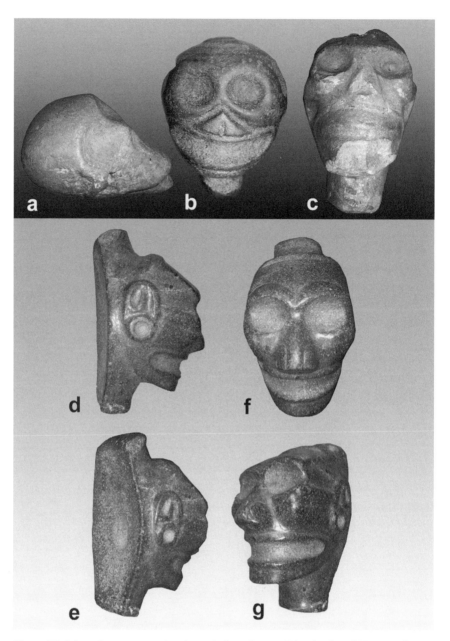

Figure 25. Macorís-type stone-head cemís from Puerto Rico (a-c) and Hispaniola (d-g). The skeletal features are noticeable in all examples. Specimens (a) and (c) are made of limestone; the rest are of various kinds of igneous rocks. All are anthropomorphic except specimen (b), which shows a nose motif reminiscent of a leaf-nose bat. The Hispaniolan example (d-g) shows fronto-occipital cranial deformation; the underside of this specimen (e) shows a dimpled base and also grinding (use-wear) marks. ©Museo de Historia, Antropología y Arte–University of Puerto Rico.

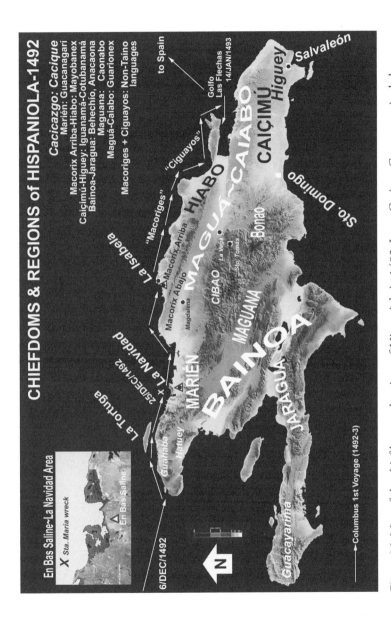

Figure 26. Map of the chiefdoms and regions of Hispaniola in 1492. Inset: Cacique Guacanagarí ruled over the small polity of Marién, where Columbus established La Navidad fortress after the Santa María sank (marked by an X).

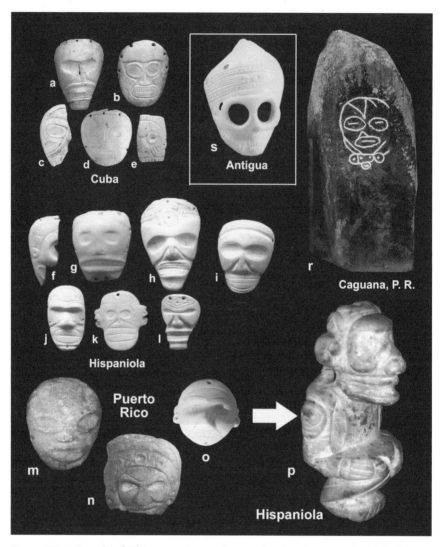

Figure 27. A Sample of Chican guaízas, or face masks. Specimens made of shell (*Strombus gigas, S. costatus,* or *S. pugilis*) from Cuba (a-e), Hispaniola (f-l), and Antigua (s). The Puerto Rican samples are more commonly made of stone (m-n) and less frequently of shell (o). Some were used as a plaque attached to a headband, as a pectoral pendant attached to a necklace, or as an armband. The central monolith of the main plaza of Caguana in Puerto Rico (r) displays an anthropomorphic head of a cacique with a guaíza resting on the chest. The stone pendant from Hispaniola (p) shows a guaíza worn as an armband (arrow). Specimens o-p: ©Museo de Historia, Antropología y Arte–University of Puerto Rico; a-e, courtesy of R. Valcárcel Rojas; f-l, Museo del Hombre Dominicano; e, courtesy of M. Hoogland.

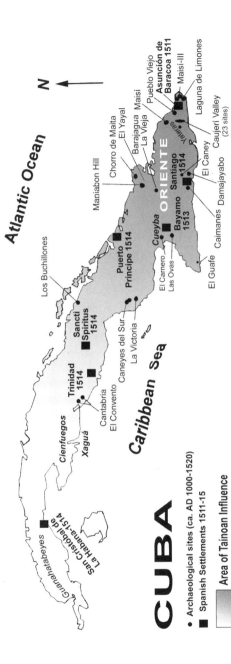

Figure 28. Map of Cuba showing the location of key archaeological sites and the first Spanish settlements. The area of Taínoan influence is shown in shades of gray; the darker the shade, the stronger the degree of Taínoness.

Figure 29. Cemí icons from the region of Banes in eastern Cuba. (a) A rare miniature decorated three-pointed stone; (b) an anthropomorphic stone pendant in the standard knee-bent pose; (c) a manatee-bone vomiting spatula with anthropomorphic head; (d) a necklace shell pendant with a three-pointed shape with birds, reminiscent of the ancient La Hueca vulture pendants; (e) shell button with dual inverted bird motifs, a design present also in the iconography of batey monoliths in Puerto Rico; (f) a truncated three-pointed stone cemí, a type that has been reported for Puerto Rico and eastern Hispaniola. Courtesy of R. Valcárcel Rojas.

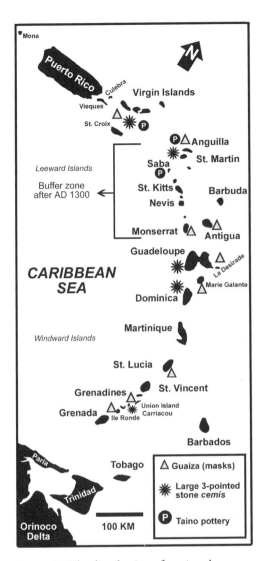

Figure 30. The distribution of guaízas, large three-pointed stone cemís, and Taíno (Chican Ostionoid series) ceramics in the Lesser Antilles. In the fourteenth century a buffer zone or frontier land, albeit not entirely depopulated, had developed in the northeastern Leeward Islands.

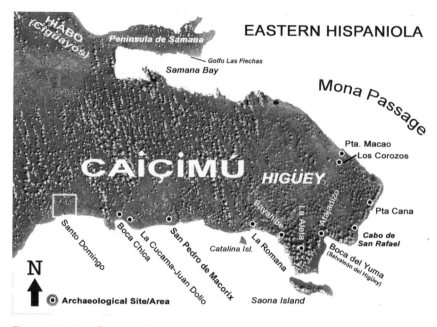

Figure 31. Map of eastern Hispaniola showing key archaeological sites and areas discussed in the text.

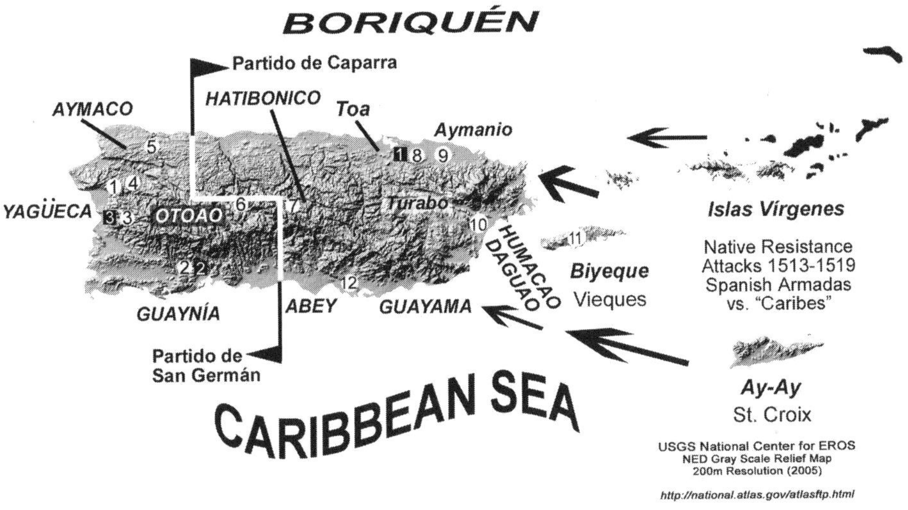

BORIQUÉN

Partido de Caparra
AYMACO
HATIBONICO Toa
Aymanio
5
1 4
YAGÜECA 3 3 OTOAO 6 7 Turabo
10
2 2 11
Biyeque
12 Vieques
GUAYNÍA ABEY GUAYAMA
Partido de
San Germán
CARIBBEAN SEA

Islas Vírgenes

Native Resistance
Attacks 1513-1519
Spanish Armadas
vs. "Caribes"

Ay-Ay
St. Croix

USGS National Center for EROS
NED Gray Scale Relief Map
200m Resolution (2005)

http://national.atlas.gov/atlasftp.html

LEGEND

Spanish Settlements (1508-1520)

1 Caparra
2 Villa de Tavora (Guánica)
3 Villa de Sotomayor - San Germán

Battles & Raids (1509-1520)

1 Urayoán drowns Salçedo
2 Agueybana attacks C. Sotomayor
3 Villa Sotomayor burned
4 Confrontation at Yagueca
5 Spanish attack Mabodomaca
6 Spanish attack Jayuya
7 Spanish attack Orocobix
8 Caparra Sacked & Burned
9 Cacica Yuisa Attacked by Taíno rebels
10 Caciques Daguao & Humacao attack Spanish
11 Cacique Cacimar of Biyeque Defeated
12 Native attack of the *salinas* (salt field) of Abey

Figure 32. Map of the battles for Boriquén, 1509–1520.

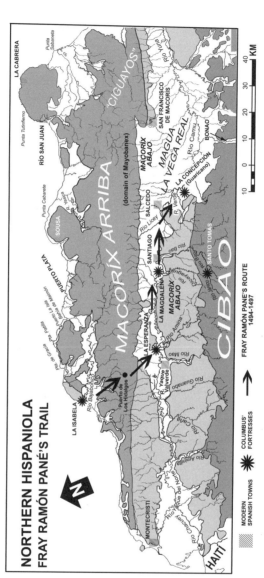

Figure 33. Columbus's fortresses and Fray Ramón Pané's trail in Hispaniola, 1494–1497.

Los Buchillones

CM ▮▮▮▮▮ cm

Figure 34. A wooden masculine cemí icon from the Los Buchillones site (ca. A.D. 1295–1655), north-central Cuba: (a) frontal view showing a typical flexed pose with hands tightly holding the knees; (b) dorsal view showing the vertebral column and rib cage, suggesting emaciation and millenarian age (ancestor cemí). Courtesy of Jago Cooper.

Figure 35: Left: A typical frame of a Virgin Mary icon devoid of all accoutrements (from Spain). The Vírgen de la Caridad del Cobre (right) is based on a similar frame, albeit the head portion is said to be made of vegetable material rather than wood. Left: Collection of Don Ricardo Alegría, Centro de Estudios Avanzados de Puerto Rico y El Caribe, Puerto Rico. Right: Courtesy of Lourdes Domínguez.

PART V

The Battles for the Cemís in Hispaniola, Boriquén, and Cuba

19 Up in Arms

Taíno Freedom Fighters in Higüey and Boriquén

This and the next section focus on two "Spanish-Taíno" battlefronts and their aftermath: the religious persecution and the destruction of native cemí idols. The scenario of the first two battles was the Higüey region in Hispaniola, a territory that was also designated as Caiçimú (literally, the "nose" or "beginning" of the land), in eastern Hispaniola (Figure 31). Sued Badillo (2003:264), citing the early chronicler Pedro Mártir de Anglería, noted that this land was governed by powerful caciques, including Cayacoa and, after his death, his wife, Inés de Cayacoa, and Cotubanamá. In another publication Sued Badillo (2001b:31), following Las Casas, highlights Iguanamá as the paramount chieftess of Higüey. The other battle-front opened up a few years later (at the end of 1510) in Puerto Rico, where cacique Agüeybana II led the Rebellion of the Caciques of Boriquén. From these events valuable insights can be gained about the inter-insular network of relationships between caciques. While the first battles grew as direct responses to the Spanish aggression (see Oliver 2008a; Varela and Gil 2008), they also suggest that the strategies of native warfare used were not all new but more likely were based on prior warfare experience and military traditions from pre-Hispanic times. From these conflicts one learns about the relationships between caciques of Higüey and Puerto Rico and, as well, of the role and function that cemí idols played, or might have played, during these crises of war.

The inferences to be made about the role of the cemís (as idols and as spirits) are, of course, predicated on accepting the arguments I have provided thus far on the personhood and identity of these objects, on the relationships of power they had with human caciques, and on how and why these (along with women giving and taking and name exchanges) circulated and changed hands to cement alliances and to front rival caciques and, of course, the Spaniards.

This is not a story about the "good" Taínos against the "evil" Spaniards. Native chiefs plotted with the Spanish to defeat their sworn cacique enemies; not all Spaniards were bent on the enslaving and murderous policies of the colonial elite. A minority were against such abuses against the natives, such as Friar Antón de Montesinos's and Bishop Las Casas's public indictments (see Fernández Buey 1995), or the initial noble, but failed, attempt by the Hieronymite order (1517–1519) to avert the ultimate decimation of the natives left in Hispaniola (Moya Pons 1987:141–162). In the balance, though, the Spanish colonial and exploitative policies, aided

by famine and pandemics like smallpox, led to the utter collapse of the natives'
way of life (Varela 2006; Varela and Gil 2008). Although their extermination was
not total everywhere, there is no doubt that the human cost was huge; hundreds
of thousands of Caribbean natives died or fled their homelands. No reliable demographic figures exist for the genocide. But in one estimate the native population in
Hispaniola was around 3.77 million inhabitants in 1492 (Moya Pons 1987:181–
189). In five years some 72,600 natives were killed, a ratio of 145 natives killed for
every Spaniard (of a total population of approximately 500) present in Hispaniola before the Ovando governorship. By 1510 the native population had declined
to about 33,500 (Moya Pons 1987:187), and in the census for the repartimiento
(distribution) of Indians taken by Alburquerque in 1514 (Moya Pons 1987:105-
passim), 26,344 souls were left to count, although this figure probably excluded
the *alzados,* or runaway, itinerant groups in the remote corners of Hispaniola. Still,
such a death toll is roughly on the order of 3.4 million, or 86 percent of the native
population, within just a dozen years—and it does not yet include the devastating
effects of the smallpox pandemic that spread five years later throughout Hispaniola, in January 1519 (Moya Pons 1987:161). Because the Spanish records are incomplete, Puerto Rican native demography is essentially unknowable, but again
there is no doubt that the cost in native life was also very high (Anderson-Córdova
1990, 2005; Sued Badillo 2000). This is not to argue that Taínos and other native peoples in some areas of Cuba, Hispaniola, Puerto Rico, and elsewhere did
not survive into the late seventeenth and even into the nineteenth centuries and
thus did not contribute (along with Spaniards, Africans, and other Amerindians)
to the emerging peasant social formation (e.g., the *jíbaro* in Puerto Rico; Rivera
and Oliver 2005), or that strands of pre-Columbian native genetic materials may
have survived in modern populations. It does mean that this demographic collapse
represented a severe rupture with the pre-Columbian social, cultural, and linguistic mosaic of the thirteenth to fifteenth centuries in the Greater Antilles.

Given what has been learned thus far about the role of cemí idols in the political-
religious life of natives in the Antilles, their persecution and destruction and their
eventual syncretic replacement (with Virgin Mary icons in some cases; see section
20) signaled the beginning of the end of a mosaic of traditions, configuring what
I call Taínoness, that was *at least* three centuries old, and some elements of it were
more than a millennium old. The persecution, indeed the murder, of cemí idols
for a society whose notions of personhood and even identity were dividual and
partible—and equally applied to human beings, other beings, and things—surely
meant that a part of their person had also been "killed," even when many native
human beings managed to survive. Alternatively, the eventual total replacement
of native icons for Christian ones, even when the latter may have been initially approached as cemís, as we shall see, led to a very different configuration: in places

natives became Indios, their sense of Taínoness (or whichever ethnicity) becoming ever more syncretized.

In chronicling the battles of Higüey and Boriquén, the early Spanish authors (and almost all modern writers) relegated the role played by cemí idols to obscurity (e.g., Alegría 1992). They instead focused on *human* beings as the cast of protagonists and antagonists in the conflict, and nearly always narrated from a Hispano-centric perspective. They failed to realize (or did not care) that the caciques' conducting war and deciding on other important political actions required the full engagement of these other partible and dividual nonhuman beings: the cemí idols. What happened or failed to happen throughout the conflicts was predicated not just on the caciques responding to his allies and the Spanish enemies, but also to the cemís, as idols *and* as spirits. As the narration of these events unfolds, it will become clearer that the cemí icons were never too far in the background. My task in the following two subsections is to fill in the gaps left, the things that were ignored or not written down by the Spanish chroniclers.

A. The Battle for Higüey in Hispaniola (A.D. 1503–1504)

The Higüey was the very last region to be conquered by the Spanish (Figure 31) in late 1503. Bishop Las Casas, who was a participant in the first battle, was of two minds in deciding if the Higüey region was a cacicazgo under the rule of a single paramount chief or, rather, a militarily driven confederation of several peer caciques, of which the one named Cotubanó, or Cotubanamá, was highlighted because of his prominent role in organizing and leading the military operations. Not just his prominence in battle leadership singled him out but also his outstanding physique. Las Casas could have very well been describing a Taíno version of Arnold Schwarzenegger! Cacique Cotubanamá was regarded by Spaniards as one who "*era también harto más esforzado que otros*" ["was also far more 'authoritative' (backed by the force of law) than others"] (Las Casas 1929 [2]:155–158). Cotubanamá, however, appears to have been one lord or cacique among several others, which included the female cacica Iguanamá (or Higuanamá) and another chieftess named Inés de Cayacoa. Las Casas observed that Cotubanamá was "one of the lords, and the bravest, for he was the most authoritative among them, and even though his persona announced who he was, [his prowess was] because of the great personality he had and the authority he represented" (Las Casas [2]:162).

Las Casas (1929 [3]:554–555) specifically stated that he was theorizing that Iguanamá was *probably* the "queen" of the Higüey and that the others were *probably* her subordinated caciques. He in fact noted that the Spanish generally did not take much care to note the different relative rank positions that caciques had with one another throughout Hispaniola, of which there were three vocative terms to address caciques, each with increasing distance and respect. The terms from highest to lowest were: *matunherí, baharí,* and *guaoxerí.* Another term for principal or first lord was *guamiquina* (our first or principal lord). These three terms of respect, however, do not necessarily translate into a two-level hierarchy of chiefs subordinated to a paramount chief. Writing many years after the events, Las Casas stated that he had the same difficulty as most Spaniards in distinguishing who was subordinated to whom or if these were actually peers rather than subordinates. He recalled that because in "the kingdom of Higüey, there were many señores, especially one named Cotubanamá . . . I will not be able to affirm whether or not the latter was a subject of queen Higuanamá" (Las Casas 1929 [3]:555). This, of course, is far from concluding that Iguanamá was necessarily a paramount chieftess, or that Cotubanamá was necessarily subordinated to her, or that the latter was paramount in his own right. This ambiguous situation with respect to a purported hierarchy of caciques is closely reminiscent to that described for the neighboring Boriquén, suggesting that there were strong similarities in their respective political structures.

For the Spanish, Cotubanamá certainly was "paramount" from a military point of view; it is clear that he was a well-respected chief among several other peers. He lived on a coastal settlement fronting Saona Island, perhaps near Boca del Yuma, maybe at the archaeological site of El Atajadizo, or perhaps on one of the known Boca Chica–affiliated archaeological sites around the La Romana area (Veloz Maggiolo et al. 1976). The first battle began midway through 1503, just a few months after Francisco de Bobadilla (1499–1502) was replaced by the *comendador mayor* de Lares, Fray Nicolás de Ovando, as lieutenant governor in Hispaniola. (A *comendador* is a knight who belongs to a chivalrous order and whose title is awarded by appointment and not inherited by birthright [Covarrubias Orozco 1995 (1611): 337]. *Mayor* implies high rank, and Lares is the town in Spain where he came from.) The summary that follows comes from Las Casas, who, as a participant, provided the most detailed account of this incident and the battles that followed in his *Historia de Las Indias* (Las Casas 1929 [2]:185–199, 157–163).

The immediate reason for the first battle was revenge. A peaceful, lively trade of manioc (cassava bread) between Santo Domingo and Saona Island existed. The cassava produced on orders of the cacique of Saona (Figure 31) was a major source of food that supported the recently established village of Santo Domingo, in effect the new seat of Spanish government and administration. On one occasion the Spanish unleashed a *mastín,* or mastiff (a dog trained to attack), onto the unnamed cacique of Saona, who was overseeing the loading of cassava bread made from yuca onto the barges. Las Casas was of the opinion (probably correct) that the mastiff attack was no accident, but that the dog was purposely egged on to kill—an act of sheer, senseless cruelty. Paraphrasing Las Casas, the dog bit the cacique's stomach and chewed his entrails, and as the cacique pulled away, the dog pulled the other way with intestines in his mouth. After the cacique died, the Indians took him for burial, "*dando gritos que ponían en el cielo, lamentando*" ["screaming to heaven and lamenting"] (Las Casas 1929 [2]:158). The Spanish and the dog fled back to the caravel. Unaware of the incident, in Santo Domingo Ovando had already ordered another caravel to set sail to scout, whose crew found a new settlement in Puerto Plata, on the north of the island. The ship stopped on Saona Island to stock up on cassava and other products needed for the expedition.

Word of the murder of the cacique of Saona had quickly reached Cotubanamá on the mainland, across from Saona. It is likely that such news spread like wildfire, reaching not just Cotubanamá but also Iguanamá, Inés de Cayacoa, and others. If Iguanamá was indeed a paramount chieftess, she may have ordered Cotubanamá to lead the revenge party; alternatively, Cotubanamá may have independently decided that he was under the obligation to avenge the dead cacique (perhaps as a result of a more direct alliance, such as a blood relative). Regardless, it was Cotubanamá who led the revenge attack and killed the eight unsuspecting Spanish sailors who landed in Saona.

The news of the revenge led by Cotubanamá reached Santo Domingo rapidly. Upon receiving the news, Nicolás de Ovando ordered the Spanish capitanes of each of the three other existing Spanish villages to gear up for arms and to recruit the Indians under their care to join the troops. The battle group, consisting of some three hundred troops, including Juan Ponce de León, was put under the overall command of Juan de Esquivel, a *caballero* (knight) and the future conqueror of Jamaica. Las Casas (1929 [2]:160–162) was quite certain that the prime motivation for the military expedition was not so much to punish but because it provided a great opportunity to enslave the Indians from Higüey. By killing the Spanish, the natives had inadvertently provided the Spanish with the legal recourse of *guerra justa* (just, fair war; see Fernández Buey 1995:87–93) and hence for enslaving them—thus, a greater economic incentive than the usual repartimiento of Indians for labor. While the latter is slavery in disguise (Rivera Pagán 2003:341–345), it still entailed rules, guidelines, and obligations emitted through *Cédulas Reales* (royal decrees) regarding the treatment of Indians that, should they be caught breaking them, they could potentially be held accountable, not because of breaking the law but because it provided a legal recourse for envious or aggrieved Spanish colonists who did not share as much the benefits of a given repartimiento of indigenous labor. Under the guise of "just war," however, slavery resulted in Indians becoming private property and owners being allowed to do with them as they pleased. The defeated could be chased in what the lingo of the time recorded as *cabalgadas* (horse raids), which could last many years after the battle ended.

I will not go into all the cruel details of the battle that ensued when the Spanish reached the Higüey region (see Las Casas 1929 [2]:160–162), but after an initial resistance and indeed acts of enormous individual courage by the native warriors of

Higüey, the natives were defeated. Many ran away to the hills, but many of those who were captured were cruelly executed, even by late Medieval Spanish standards; some were hanged; while others on the run, including women and children alike, were corralled and "slain and disemboweled as if they were sheep"; still others had their hands or feet amputated amid taunts; and others were beheaded or their bodies were cut in half. Some six hundred to seven hundred natives escaped to Saona Island to hide in caves, only to be imprisoned, taken to a large house and knifed to death, and then displayed in the plaza and finally body-counted as per orders of Juan de Esquivel. "In this manner, they left that island: destroyed and deserted, despite it being our breadbasket, as it was very fertile" (Las Casas 1929 [2]:162).

In the end, the *señores de los pueblos*—that is, the caciques of the settlements— sent messages of surrender to Esquivel, saying "that they did not want to fight any more and that they would serve them." Among these caciques, perhaps principally among them, was Cotubanamá, who agreed to the demands of surrender: they would prepare a large or great *conuco* (garden) of manioc to provide cassava bread, and also labor to build the (wood) fortress, near a "certain Indian settlement" close to the coast to house Captain Martín de Villamán and nine other Spaniards who remained behind. The Indians would attend to the Spaniards' needs and serve them. In exchange, the Spaniards' only offer was that the runaways could return to their villages without fear for their lives. The fortress was, in effect, built in or around what is today San Rafael del Yuma and where later (after the final battle) Ponce de León would build his stone-and-mortar house and an estate that was crucial in supporting the initial conquest of Puerto Rico (Murga Sanz 1971). The fortress-settlement would bear the name of Salvaleón (del Higüey). Years later, the Spanish would relocate the settlement farther inland and to the north, near the present-day city of Salvaleón, capital of La Altagracia district.

The surrender pact was ceremonially sanctioned by a guaitiao ritual between Esquivel and Cotubanamá, a custom that was by now familiar to the Spanish. The way Las Casas wrote it seems to suggest that it was Esquivel who initiated the ritual and "gave [Cotubanamá] his name, exchanging it for his [Esquivel]" (Las Casas 1929 [2]:162). If so, and not the reverse, it shows how well the Spanish understood and manipulated the power of guaitiao pacts. Las Casas goes on to explain: "This exchange [of names] in the common language of this Island was called guaitiao [meaning] 'me and the other, that exchanged names' and they so named each other. This was held as a great *parentesco* [fictive kin relationship] and as perpetual friendship and confederation . . . and so the Indians called the [Spanish] Captain, Cotubanamá, and the señor [cacique], Esquivel" (Las Casas 1929 [2]:162).

It is thus interesting that the pact cemented by the guaitiao ceremony could also be an act of submission or surrender demanded and expected by the victorious leader, although it is difficult to establish whether this was a Spanish reinterpretation of the ceremony as being an act of submission when traditionally, among native chiefs, it might have been an act made only between peers and potential allies.

As might be anticipated, Villamán and his nine men provoked the second and much broader battle of Higüey. Las Casas (1929 [2]:190–200) details not only the expected abuses but also hints at the rape of indigenous women being a cause for a renewed rebellion. Cotubanamá sacked and burned the fortress, with just one Spaniard escaping to Santo Domingo to raise the alarm. This new battle probably occurred early in 1504. Once again, Nicolás de Ovando ordered Esquivel to round up the armies from the three other Spanish villages, and also included hundreds of native Indians conscripted from the region of Ycayagua (Figures 26, 31: in perhaps Caiabó, or Hiabo), adjacent to Higüey. The Ycayagua indigenous troops were men of war and caused much damage among the rebel Higüey Indians (Las Casas 1929 [2]:188). As Sued Badillo noted (2003:280), there were various native reactions to the Spanish conquest. Some rival caciques sided with the Spanish to gain advantages or a military edge over their traditional competitors, and "many independent caciques saw in the arrival of the Europeans an opportunity to defend themselves against other, more expansionist caciques. And either by force or voluntarily, they joined the invaders' struggle."

The massacre of the rebel natives this time around was, if anything, much greater than before. Raids to both enslave and kill natives on the run were brutal. The Spanish-Ycayagua troops forced captive Indians to serve as spies to find the hiding places of the Higüey natives. At one point Las Casas (1929 [2]:189) noted that these captive guides, with a leash on their necks tied to their Spanish masters, were ordered by an unnamed cacique to throw themselves over the cliffs, thus dragging the Spaniards to death with them. Las Casas (1929 [2]:190–199) paints a bleak picture of utter disarray, despair, and desperation as the initial battle turned into raid, persecution, and execution. The natives also learned some lessons from the first battle, such as clearing false pathways on the thick, prickly *matorral* bush to entice Spanish horsemen into a trap. Other tactics were the traditional smoke messages to relay information and commands, and ordering women, children, and old men out of the settlements into hiding locations, especially along the cliffs that front the coast in many areas of the Higüey. But in the end, all of these military tactics were short-lived and unsuccessful. The defeat in this second battle truly marked the end of native-run cacicazgos in Hispaniola and resulted in the execution of Cotubanamá (Las Casas 1929 [2]:198). This is not to say that native resistance, now joined by the increasing black slave population, did not continue through the sixteenth century (Sued Badillo 2003:283–286).

The Spanish accounts, however, focused just on the Spaniards' roles, the battles, raids, and some confrontations between individuals. They did not witness or record all the ritual and ceremonial preparations for war and most particularly on the specifics of the rebel troops' chain of command. It is only when one examines the battles of Boriquén that the nature of inter-insular alliances and the relationships between caciques comes to light. It is in Boriquén that the Spanish chronicles offer insights about the role of ritual and ceremonies in which cemís were called upon in preparation of war. Furthermore, the data from Puerto Rico also provides grounds to suggest that the 1511 battle in Boriquén was not meant as an isolated event within the island, but as a broader front that would include, once again, the Higüey. Above all, it provides insights into the nature of the network of caciques through which the cemí icons, as well as other valuables, circulated.

B. The Rebellion of the Caciques of Boriquén (A.D. 1509–1519)

Barely five years after the decisive defeat of Cotubanamá and the allied chiefs of Higüey, Juan Ponce de León, who had participated as captain and economically benefited from the battles, set sail to colonize Puerto Rico (Murga Sanz 1971:33–*passim*). News about the potential gold riches to be obtained from the island of San Juan (today Puerto Rico) came to Ponce de León by way of the Indians of Higüey who were assigned to his household (Sued Badillo 2001b:37): "[Juan Ponce de León] had news from some Indians that served him that in the Island of San Juan, or Boriquén, there was plenty of gold, because being neighbors to the Indians of this province of Higüey they were the closest, and being the nearest landing from the Island of St. Juan, with no more than 12 or 15 leagues of distance, every day they went in their canoes or small boats from this island [Hispaniola] to the other one and those from that island [Boriquén] to this one, and they thus communicated. [This is how] ones and the others knew what was in the land of each other" (Las Casas 1929 [2]:290–291).

As several authors have noted (Alegría 1992:39–52; Anderson-Córdova 2005: 341–344; Murga Sanz 1971:48; Sued Badillo 2001b:36–37), previous short-lived explorations in Puerto Rico, such as those of Vicente Yáñez Pinzón and Martín García de Salazar (1504, 1505), also brought early news of the potential that Puerto Rico offered for gold and other resources, including an untapped Indian labor force. These resources were important as the availability of native labor in Hispaniola became increasingly critical as a result of the disruption of food production that followed on the heels of previous conquest battles (not just Higüey). The fall of food supplies stemmed from the fact that the natives who had been "liberated" by the rebellious Francisco Roldán (1497–1498) were no longer harvesting for Bartolomé and Diego Colón (the son, not the brother of the admiral), and the latter's men (see Oliver 2008a; Varela and Gil 2008; Wilson 1990).

It is possible that Ponce de León had also been to Puerto Rico earlier in 1506 (Anderson-Córdova 2005:342). The suggestion arises from a document titled *Probanza de Juan González* that included depositions by members of the Ponce de

León party. Their testimonies indicate that there may have been an earlier expedition in 1506. They noted that Ponce reached the south coast and stayed at the settlement of a cacique named Mabo El Grande (The Great), while Juan González (the son of Ponce de León and an expert interpreter of Taíno language) marched with some fifty men across the Cordillera Central toward the large bay (today Bahía de San Juan) that the natives had reported to exist on the north coast. Along the way they passed numerous villages and continued the pattern of gift (and perhaps name) exchanges (Anderson-Córdova 2005:343). Meanwhile, Ponce de León left Mabo's settlement and the domain of Agüeybana and sailed west and then north and east along the coast of Puerto Rico. As Karen Anderson-Córdova (2005: 342) noted, the date (1506 vs. 1508) may be just a confusion, but it is possible that Ponce de León had been there earlier for an initial exploration and to establish contacts with local caciques, such as Mabo El Grande, who may have been an ally or subordinate of Agüeybana the Elder. What is interesting here is that as the ground party crossed numerous settlements in the central mountains (Utuado, Jayuya, Orocovis), gift exchanges regularly took place between local chiefs and the Spaniards, which probably included name exchanges and also, I suspect, guaízas.

Ponce de León's own testimony is that he began preparations for the expedition in the late summer of 1508. Having obtained license from the governor, Comendador Mayor Fray Nicolás de Ovando (1502–1509), to officially explore Boriquén, Ponce readied for departure from Salvaleón del Higüey (today Boca del Yuma; see Veloz Maggiolo et al. 1976). But on August 3, 1508, a hurricane arrived, causing damages and delays. Ten days later, Ponce finally departed and foundered on Amona (today's Mona) Island, where he interviewed two caciques (Sued Badillo 2001b:41). That same day he arrived at a site somewhere along the southwest coast of Puerto Rico, a region controlled by an important cacique: Agüeybana I. This chief was regarded by the Spaniards as the ruler of a cacicazgo that later historiography labeled Guaynía, located on a broad stretch of the south coast more or less centered on today's city of Ponce (Sued Badillo 2001a; see also Las Casas (1929 [2]:291, ch. 46). Even though from the Spaniards' perspective Agüeybana was indeed "paramount," there is considerable disagreement among scholars on whether he was, indeed, a paramount chief ruling over second-ranked chiefs and their polities or even whether this polity was a chiefdom (in the classic anthropological sense; see Curet 2002, 2003). Seventy-three years later, a memorial sent to King Philip II and signed by Juan Melgarejo, then governor of San Juan, stated: "In this island there was no cacique that lorded over all of it, except that in each valley or principal river there was a cacique that had other capitanes as their lieutenants who served him and who were called in their language nitaínos" (Melgarejo, in Fernández Méndez 1973:116). This statement may be an exactingly accurate memory or, just as likely, a recollection of a past already marred by the encomienda system, in which any such paramount chiefs who might have existed had long since been forgotten. The archaeological data required to support or refute the presence of para-mount cacicazgos is simply not available yet (see Curet 2002).

For this first expedition to Puerto Rico, Ponce had specific instructions: (1) to leave with fifty men, (2) to speak with cacique Agüeybana on behalf of the king so as to establish large (plantation-size) conucos to ensure a subsistence base to support the Spanish colonists, and (3) to found a settlement (a *casa fuerte*, or fort house) and a port to be conveniently located to exploit and export gold (Murga Sanz 1971; Sued Badillo 2001b:41; see also Anderson-Córdova 2005:343; Thomas 2003:232).

The defeat of the caciques of Higüey was well known in Boriquén by the time Ponce de León met Agüeybana I in 1508, if not in 1506. Such knowledge no doubt affected the way in which both Agüeybana I and Ponce de León negotiated the terms for the Spanish presence in Boriquén. The battles in Higüey had apparently convinced Ponce de León that diplomacy and negotiation were better alternatives than outright conquest by arms, while Agüeybana, advised in no small way by his mother, also favored this diplomatic strategy of tolerance, given the disastrous con-sequences in the Higüey (Oviedo 1944 [3]:192). The sad news of the massacres of the Higüey—not to mention the prior collapse of the unquestionably powerful cacicazgos of Maguana, Caiabó, and Bainoa a few years earlier—had swiftly trav-eled across the Mona Passage.

Juan Ponce de León was received by Agüeybana I, his mother, and his foster fa-ther in his settlement near the mouth of the Coayuco River. As was customary among the natives, Ponce de León "was well received and feasted, offering him those things that the Indians have for their maintenance [food] and showing to him that he [Agüeybana] was pleased to know him and be a friend of the Chris-tians" (Oviedo 1944 [3]:199). Once the pact was in place, Agüeybana I exchanged his name with Juan Ponce, thus becoming guaitiao, "which was a signal among the Indians of these islands of perpetual confederation and friendship" (Las Ca-sas 1929 [2]:291). This pact was further solidified by Agüeybana's gesture of giv-ing Ponce de León "one of his sisters"—not, as Oviedo (1944 [3]:192) declared, as a "friend," but from Agüeybana's perspective, as a bride. On the third day, Au-gust 16, a second hurricane breached the island. While apparently this did not stop Ponce de León from pushing forward, the combined effects of back-to-back hurricanes on the agricultural fields must have been quite severe. The high pre-cipitation and flash floods that commonly follow hurricanes would have wiped out the conucos and perhaps even settlements, creating shortages in the food sup-ply (Anderson-Córdova 2005:343–344; Sued Badillo 2001b:41). Ponce, however, succeeded in getting Agüeybana and his allied (or perhaps subordinated) caciques to "sell [cassava bread] at a good price" to the Spaniards (Sued Badillo 2001b:61).

Hurricanes notwithstanding, Ponce and his fifty men, perhaps led by Agüey-bana himself, began to explore the south and east coasts searching for a convenient place to build the fort house close to gold-bearing rivers, such as Cibuco and Manatuabón. They finally reached the north coast, where he came upon a bay facing the mouth of the Ana River (possibly the Manatí River). The party stayed there for a month. From there they explored the land to the east as far as the Toa Valley. However, the Ana bay was subject to strong tidal changes, making it unsafe as a harbor. As a result, Ponce and fifteen of his men traveled by land to the south coast of today's San Juan Bay. Near the shore they finally established the tiny settlement of Caparra (1508). Caparra would shortly afterward be moved two kilometers inland from the southern shore of San Juan Bay (Alegría 1992:47–48). The settlement would later (1514) be sacked by the natives (conveniently labeled as *Caribes* by the Spaniards) and eventually relocated, in 1519, to the islet of Puerto Rico that is present-day Old San Juan (for contemporary documents, see Huerga 2006:59–66, 171–180). Farther west of Caparra, in the fertile Toa Valley, the Royal Hacienda of Toa was established for agricultural production in order to sustain the colonial gold-mining enterprise, served by hundreds of native laborers (Figure 32).

Cristóbal de Sotomayor, who became Ponce's alcalde mayor (or chief justice; from Anadalusian Arabic *al qalede,* meaning "to take charge of government"), arrived in early 1509 with license to establish a settlement somewhere in Boriquén. By October the Crown had recognized Diego Colón as the rightful heir and reinstated him as admiral and governor of the Indies, relieving Fray Nicolás de Ovando of his functions. Don Diego designated the brothers Juan and Martín Cerón as, respectively, alcalde mayor and alcalde (mayor or justice). Ponce de León decided to recognize the new appointments and yield the government to the Cerón brothers. It was Juan Cerón, in 1509, who ordered the first repartimiento of Indians of Boriquén among the Spanish colonists, an act that would directly lead to the noted Rebellion of the Caciques barely two years later.

By the end of 1509 Cristóbal de Sotomayor and his nephew arrived on the island. Sotomayor was a well-connected nobleman, having served (among other things) as secretary to King Philip "The Handsome" of the Hapsburg dynasty, and to whom Ferdinand "The Catholic" had already assigned lands and Indian laborers. Juan Cerón was keen to extend Spanish control to the south of the island, for which reason he ratified, with some amendments, Ferdinand's assignment of lands and Indians to Sotomayor. Among the assigned Indians was Agüeybana I, with whom Ponce de León had exchanged names in 1508.

Shortly upon arrival to Boriquén, Sotomayor founded the village of Tavora (or Távara, his maternal surname), possibly located near today's Guánica Bay on the south-central side of the island (Oviedo 1944 [3]:196; Sued Badillo 2001b:57–58). Sotomayor was a supporter of Columbus's interests and a political competitor of Ponce de León, who was favored by Nicolás de Ovando before Don Diego's appointment by King Ferdinand in 1509. Later, during the first months of 1510,

Sotomayor relocated the village to the west coast some four leagues distant, perhaps near today's Añasco, near the mouth of the Guaorabo River. The new settlement was renamed Villa de Sotomayor. According to Sued Badillo (2001b:57–58),
the change was made to gain better access to the gold resources and, more important, because of Sotomayor's persistent problems in getting the local caciques to
send him the native labor to work the conucos and mine for gold (Sued Badillo
2001b:62). Only a few months after Don Diego Colón named Juan Cerón as alcalde mayor, Juan Ponce de León received a royal decree from King Ferdinand re-
instating him as captain governor, with full civil and judicial jurisdiction of Boriquén and the authorization to appoint magistrates. Ponce took this opportunity
to imprison Juan Cerón and send him to Spain. Don Diego Colón, famously aggrieved by the intrusion of King Ferdinand in what he felt was his authority, con-
fiscated all of Ponce de León's assets in Boca del Yuma. Ponce de León, let us not
forget, was a business partner of the king in the Royal Hacienda in Toa, and his interests and loyalty were with the monarchs and not the Columbus family. Ponce,
however, mindful of Sotomayor's personal connections with King Ferdinand, had
designated Don Cristóbal de Sotomayor as alcalde mayor, despite the latter being favored by Don Diego Colón (see Alegría 1992; Murga Sanz 1971). Ponce de
León began to move toward more autonomy from Santo Domingo and the Columbus family: he requested and obtained permission to bring Franciscan friars to
evangelize the Indians and, perhaps more important, for the right to smelt gold in
Caparra. The Royal Hacienda in the Toa Valley just west of Caparra, with its Indian demora (labor period), supplied food for the colonial enterprise; some Spaniards also settled in the Toa and Cibuco Valleys to more comfortably exploit the
rich gold placers nearby.

The foundation of Villa de Sotomayor (1509) and the existing Caparra (and
nearby Toa in 1508) created two polar areas of Spanish colonial activities. In 1514,
following royal instructions, and after the Rebellion of the Caciques, the administration of the island was divided into Partido de San Germán (west) and Partido
de Caparra (east), each enjoying, for a while, a certain degree of autonomy (see
Murga Sanz 1971). The demarcation between the two *partidos* was established
by the course of the Camuy River on the northern coast to its headwaters, and
the Jacaguas River on the southern coast to its sources in the central highlands
(Figure 32).

On May 1, 1509, Ponce de León had to return briefly to Santo Domingo to deal
with his governorship appointment and to restock supplies to ship back to Puerto
Rico. He also "brought with him cacique Agüeybana, to see the things of the Island
of La Española" (Oviedo 1944 [3]:194). Whether or not this was Agüeybana's first
visit to Hispaniola, there is tentative evidence that he had relatives living there. In
the lists of the *Repartimiento de Indios* dating to 1514, there is one cacique named
Francisco de Agüeybana, from Saona Island (Figure 31), who was assigned to King

Ferdinand to work in the Royal Haciendas and gold mines: "For the estates and mines, and farms of the King, our lord, which he has in the city of Santo Domingo and its limits, he was assigned cacique Francisco de Agüeybana of Saona, which are seventy-seven men and eighty-six women" (Rodríguez Demorizi 1971:129). Las Casas (1929 [2]:10–11) also added that Agüeybana of Saona was "a great Cacique and Señor whose lands and señorío [fiefdom] was five or six leagues up the coast toward the east, and was named Agüeybana." He also noted that the admiral had ordered him to plant eighty thousand *montones* of crops, mainly cultivated with manioc. [The *montón* was an artificial mound of topsoil that had specific dimensions (nine to twelve feet on each side), which the Spanish adopted as a standard unit of measure in agricultural production (see Moscoso 1986:418)].

Given such a name, the Agüeybana of Saona Island *may* have been related to the two Agüeybanas of Guaynía in Puerto Rico, although this is speculative (but see Sued Badillo 2003:265). However, there is little doubt about another cacique from the Higüey region, named Andrés. He *was* a relative of the Agüeybanas of Boriquén. What remains unknown is precisely how cacique Andrés was related to the Agüeybana brothers. Was it by marriage or by blood? In any case, a binding connection between Higüey and Guaynía chiefs is documented. Archaeologist Miguel Rodríguez López (personal communication 2006) recalls coming across a copy of a Spanish-written document held or seen by Don Ricardo Alegría in which the following scene was described (paraphrased here): A Spaniard was supervising the assigned Indians doing labor in the fields somewhere in eastern Hispaniola. One of the natives, though, was hanging around just watching the activities. The Spaniard then approached the cacique in charge and asked him why that fellow was not working like the rest. The reply was that the native was a visiting cacique, a relative, from Boriquén. If this account could be confirmed, it would add significantly to the evidence of the close-knit relationships between the chiefs on both sides of the Mona Passage and of the frequent visits between them.

Whether they were marital alliances or blood ties between chiefs of Boriquén and Higüey, these relations underpin the proposed web—across the Mona Passage— through which the cemí idols and other economic goods, services (e.g., military support), and information flowed. The restricted geographic distribution of stone collars; elbow stones; large stone heads; and large, decorated three-pointed cemís is a reflection of these close relationships between the caciques, particularly if the Agüeybana blood-kin network across the Mona Passage was already several generations deep into the pre-Columbian past. The geographic distribution of cemí icons, especially the stone collars and elbow stones, and the three-pointers attached to the stone collars (see section 16), parallels the same spatial limits of the alliance or descent network of the historic caciques, the two Agüeybanas and Andrés. There are archaeological indicators that such chiefly alliances were forged several generations earlier. At the El Cabo site, near Cabo de San Rafael in the Higüey

(Figure 31), a fragment of a coarse (bench-type) limestone collar was found associated with Anadel or Transicional ceramic components (Hofman et al. 2007:100; Ortega 1978:fig. 18). Recent excavations at the El Cabo site yielded dates between A.D. 600 and A.D. 980 for the earlier Anadel (Ostionan Ostionoid) occupation and A.D. 980–1440 for the later Boca Chica component (Hofman et al. 2007; van der Plitch, personal communication 2006), and continued into the early sixteenth century as demonstrated by the presence of Majolica wares (Alice Samson, personal communication 2007). At this site two fragments of slender collars (the ring portion) made of exotic igneous stone were found associated with house structures and the late Boca Chica occupation, supporting Walker's seriation and evolution of the Puerto Rican collars (1993; see section 15). Furthermore, during the 2007 season a large, decorated three-pointed stone (anthropomorphic with legs and head on the lateral prominences) was also found in the house area (Samson, personal communication 2007). In contrast to the exotic stone collar fragments, the large three-pointed cemí was made of locally abundant limestone. Two simple (miniature) three-pointers were also found in and around the house area.

These iconic, emblematic, and potent objects worn and used by caciques are, in my view, a strong indication that the web of alliances via intermarriage or descent relations between chiefs (such as the historic Agüeybana and cacique Andrés) across the Mona Passage are indeed ancient, potentially going back to A.D. 600. What the research on stone collars, with their attached large, three-pointed cemí idols, also suggests is that the chiefs of Boriquén had produced a significantly greater number (and stylistic diversity) of these and with greater craftsmanship than the chiefs of eastern Hispaniola had. The dates point to between 450 and 800 years of sustained, intense relationships between the two areas, more than enough to create a fairly dense web of descent-related chiefly lineages. That being the case, the collars and attached three-pointers circulated only among these related chiefly lineages that had deep genealogical history between them. That the stone collars and three-pointers do not extend outside this region (i.e., Caiçimú-Higüey) indicates that, historically, the interaction of the chiefs of Boriquén and Higüey with other caciques in the rest of Hispaniola was likely to be perceived as one that engaged foreigners, perhaps even strangers—those chiefly clans and groups that had separate descent origins, such as is further suggested by the presence of different languages and ethnic groups of Hispaniola (e.g., the Macorix, Cigüayo, and the diverse mosaic of Taínos).

If the stone collars and the attached three-pointers are objects that *enable* chiefly political power, it is interesting that the polities on eastern Hispaniola and Boriquén in 450 (or a maximum of 800) years did not expand outside the Caiçimú-Higüey region or much beyond the Virgin Islands. In section 18 B, we already saw that the stone collars reached only some of the Virgin Islands, and that farther into the Lesser Antillean proposed buffer zone, large three-pointers embedded in Chican Ostionoid context extended only to Anguilla, but in absence of stone collars. For other caciques of Hispaniola and other political leaders further afield (Cuba, the Bahamas, Jamaica, and most of the Lesser Antilles), neither the stone collars nor the elbow stones were part of the arsenal or ensemble of potent objects of political-religious power. That the stone collars and three-pointers (attached or not) do not occur in, for example, the Bainoa, Marién, Magua, or Maguana-Caiabó chiefdoms also supports the idea that stone collars and elbow stones were neither stolen by these chiefs, nor would they be gifted to chiefly groups outside the deeply and historically intertwined web of chiefs of eastern Hispaniola and Boriquén. The circulation would have to be through inheritance by heirs, and *perhaps* as a bride's payments to her relatives; but mostly they would remain "in house," within the closely knit web of related chiefs. This does not preclude that internal factional competition among the closely knit chiefs could not occur and result in the theft of stone collars and attached cemí idols; with at least 450 years of time I would be surprised that such cleavages did not occasionally occur. I suspect that Oviedo's mention of bequests of the estate of a cacique to foreign caciques invited to the funerary feast would also apply to these caciques who shared generations of exchanging brides across the Mona and the Virgin Island Passages. Instead, with truly foreign (and stranger) caciques, other kinds of powerful cemí idols and potent icons, such as the guaízas, would be more likely exchanged.

This, I believe, is a powerful argument to speak *not* about a "Classic Taíno" culture but of different ways in which native actors participated in and defined their Taínoness. The web of relations proposed above is but one of various ways of defining Taínoness, this one operating in a circumscribed region (eastern Hispaniola–Puerto Rico–Virgin Islands, with the Anguilla outlier). But at the same time it is also important to emphasize that other networks did exist linking the natives of, say, the rest of Hispaniola, Jamaica, and the Bahamas. Taínoness, like ethnicity, is not a checklist of traits, but entirely a matter of different sets of interactions *simultaneously* operating with more or less intensity during a given span of time (thus, a consideration of the temporality of such relations is as important as its spatial extension).

Alas, peace would not last much longer in Boriquén after the arrival of Ponce de León and Sotomayor. In Shakespearean argot, 1510 was the "winter of discontent" in Boriquén. The caciques and natives assigned by King Ferdinand to the conquistadors had grown wary of their abuse and mistreatment, most specifically those assigned to Sotomayor and his men (Murga Sanz 1971:63–91). A royal decree from King Ferdinand had originally assigned Sotomayor the "best cacique" from Boriquén (Sued Badillo 2001b:57). This "best cacique" was Agüeybana I, the Elder. But Diego Colón, in his capacity as governor of the Indies (whose rights had just been partly reinstated in 1509), quickly modified Sotomayor's encomienda to replace the "best cacique" for another cacique, which turned out to be the brother of

Agüeybana I, and three hundred of his Indians (Sued Badillo 2001b:57). Agüeybana I was apparently reassigned to Ponce de León, but not for long; he died sometime in 1510. However, Sotomayor was unhappy and restless with Don Diego's change (via Juan Cerón) in his allotment of Indians. In keeping with native etiquette, this brother of Agüeybana I (i.e., the future Agüeybana II) and Sotomayor became guaitiao by exchanging names and also by Agüeybana's offering his sister to be Sotomayor's mistress (Oviedo 1944 [3]:194). In any event, it is clear from Sotomayor's subsequent actions that what he considered his right to extract labor was miles apart from what Agüeybana II and the other caciques understood the pact to entail. Sotomayor was unhappy that a number of the caciques who in his view were obligated to supply labor and goods (e.g., cassava bread) were refusing to do so. Things took a turn for the worse when both Agüeybana I and his mother, Doña Inés, died of natural causes sometime midway through 1510. As the brother of the dead cacique, Agüeybana II inherited the office. He was encomedado to Sotomayor while the latter still resided in the village of Tavora.

This second round of assignments involving natives of the south and southwest of the island was granted to the *vecinos* (settlers and neighbors) of Guánica by Diego Colón's envoy, the newly appointed lieutenant governor of Boriquén, Juan Cerón. It was this second repartimiento that truly sparked the first serious spate of troubles and confrontations that led to the general rebellion by the end of the year 1509 (Anderson-Córdova 2005:344–347; Sued Badillo 2001b:58).

> This second repartimiento caused great unrest among the caciques and the first violent skirmishes with the Spaniards . . . [For example,] Diego de Cuéllar, one of the original vecinos of Guánica, declared "that having Don Cristóbal ordered to round up and pacify certain caciques and bring them back to servitude, a cacique named Huyucoa, a principal person, defended himself, and fractured [injured] my left eye, for which reason I lost sight" . . . In a second inquest, Diego de Cuéllar . . . presented testimony [again restating] that "he was fighting in a war where his finger was broken and that after broken he tied his finger and hand to the sword and continued fighting; that it was public and notorious that cacique Utulloa fractured his eye with a *macana* [wooden war club] [Sued Badillo 2001b:62].

The relocation of the village of Tavora had been determined by the tense climate with the neighboring caciques resisting the encomienda, coupled with its inconvenient placement to access gold-bearing river areas (Sued Badillo (2001b:62). This settlement was renamed Villa de Sotomayor and established near the mouth of the Guaorabo River, in Añasco (see Figure 32). The tensions that accumulated through the year 1510 also included the importation of enslaved natives from the neighboring islands (Vieques, St. Croix, and the Virgin Islands). Not surprisingly,

Sotomayor was among the first to receive license to enslave these, the so-called Caribes, or *caníbales,* (Sued Badillo 2001b:62) from the Lesser Antilles, by now labeled as the *Islas Inútiles* (useless islands) in Juan de La Cosa's (1500) chart. The incident between Diego Cuéllar and cacique Huyucoa (or Utuyoa), apparently a subordinate of Agüeybana, was but one of a growing spate of such confrontations.

With the death of Agüeybana I (and his mother, Doña Inés) and the mounting troubles generated by the encomienda activities of Sotomayor and his men, the effects of the raids bringing captive Indians from neighboring islands to the east, the increasing competition between Ponce de León and Diego Colón and his lieutenants, not to mention the delayed effects of two seasons of hurricanes, the air was dense with resentment on all sides and primed for armed conflicts. There was, however, one matter that from the natives' perspective had to be resolved before they would fully commit to war against the Spaniards.

> From what the Indians of the Island of San Juan had heard of the conquests and wars that took place on this Island of Hispaniola . . . they believed that Christians could not have possibly conquered it had they not been immortal and incapable of dying from wounds or other disaster; and that since they had come from the direction of the sunrise, they fought the way they did; and that they were a celestial people and children of the sun, and Indians were powerless to hurt them. And when they saw that Christians . . . made themselves masters of the island, the Indians determined not to allow themselves to be subjugated by such a small number of persons. And thus, they wished to secure their freedom and not serve them, even though they feared them and thought they were immortal. And when the señores of the island had secretly assembled, they decided to put this question to a test and resolve their doubts, and to carry out an experiment on some stray Christian [Oviedo 1944 (3):210–211].

The secret war council meeting of the caciques was held in the winter of 1510, possibly in the settlement of Agüeybana II, most probably located somewhere near Villa de Sotomayor. As I see it, the question was not so much about the immortality of the Spanish but rather to investigate whether the Spanish experienced death in a way that was different from that of the caciques (recall the natives' multinatural perspective and partible, dividual personhood). Such a secret meeting falls squarely in the *cabildo* (council) type of meetings described earlier, where, in this case, an assembly of caciques would have gathered to perform a cohoba ceremony in order to consult with the cemís and divine about two major questions: Will we be victorious in war, and how can we be sure that the Spanish died? And "death" meant signs that showed a permanent change of state from living to nonliving, the mode of bodily corruption, and that the soul of the living is replaced by that of the dead (operito or opía). Given what has been learned about the crucial role of cemí idols and spirits in the process of such momentous decision making, I have no doubt that they *were* consulted and that a cohoba ceremony *did* take place, even though the chroniclers do not mention it. It is evident that the cemí supported their plan to ambush an unsuspecting Spaniard and test his manner of death, likely divining a favorable future outcome. This event highlights how important were the cemí idols and spirits, who made themselves present via cohoba hallucinogenic visions, in determining major policy decisions, and why caciques like Agüeybana II had to have those prestigious and powerful senior idols who could deliver positive results.

In that secret meeting it was resolved that cacique Urayoán, who commanded the region of Yagüeca located in western Puerto Rico, would carry out the test of mortality, whereas Agüeybana II would do much the same with Cristóbal de Sotomayor and his men. As it happened, Urayoán offered an unlucky young Spanish traveler named Salçedo some fifteen or twenty Indian porters to continue his voyage and, sure enough, he was drowned in the Guaorabo River (Figure 32). After the kill, Urayoán sent Indians every day for three days to verify the process of decomposition and on the third day went to witness the result himself (Oviedo 1944 [3]:211–212). The key factor was not that Salçedo was killed, but that his body was left to rot for three full days before he was declared "not living." I agree with Edwin Crespo (2000:125) that body putrefaction was the key indicator "of the undeniable fact of death" from the natives' perspective. The reality of the corruption of the Spaniard's body militated against the idea that all Spaniards somehow experienced a process of death, or of transformation of their guaíza (i.e., their living soul) into opía, in a fundamentally different manner than ordinary native human beings did.

It also seems that the same experiment was attempted at least once before the Yagüeca incident, by the cacique of the Aymanio region, in the autumn of 1510. The life of a Spaniard named Juárez was put up by the cacique as a price (or bet) in a ball game, with the right to kill him going to the victorious team (Oviedo 1944 [3]:197–198). However, Juárez was rescued at the last minute by Diego de Salaçar, thanks to the betrayal of a naboría Indian who was assigned to Juárez's service. As Juárez was tied up and imprisoned in a house, it is likely that this was an early but failed attempt to ritually execute a Spaniard and test his manner of death. But it could also have been a show of defiance and resistance against the *encomendero*, Juárez's father, who was one of Sotomayor's men. In any event, the miraculous and single-handed rescue of Juárez by the sword of Salaçar against so many Indians may even have lent credence to the general belief held by the Taínos that the Spanish somehow had a different and more powerful nature than theirs, hence the subsequent test by Urayoán, who indeed proved their fears wrong. I can imagine hearing them exclaim, "The Spaniards rot like we do!" I do not think the natives ever regarded the Spaniards as deities or divine entities; rather, the Spaniards, like the caciques or shamans, would be seen as having control over numinous things, like iron swords, harquebuses (a precursor of the rifle), glass beads, horses and so on, all of which were exotic things and beings that made them powerful. And because their physique alone would decidedly put the Spaniards in a category of "others," it is not surprising that questions arose about the nature of their persons (and their bodies), about how they were composed in life and decomposed death, and were recomposed in the afterlife. There is no indication that a Spaniard was treated as a cemí (i.e., a living divinity). The best data on this question comes from the engagement of the natives of Cuba (near Bayamo) and the Spaniards involving both native cemí icons and spirits and the Christian icons, to be analyzed in sections 20–22.

That the start of the military rebellion did not follow immediately after these initial tests demonstrates the great caution exercised by the caciques of Boriquén in facing the Spaniards. In any event, Agüeybana II, who was an important cacique, was the one who led the ultimate key test. This happened *"casi al principio"* ["almost at the beginning"] of 1511, and after the secret council meeting with the other caciques of Boriquén. The chroniclers did not say where that council meeting was held—perhaps in the Yagüeca region, or more likely in Agüeybana's territory of Guaynía. In any case, it is known that the failed attempt in Aymanio took place three months earlier than the execution of Sotomayor and his men ordered by Agüeybana II. This event either followed or was contemporaneous to the Juárez incident in Yagüeca.

Agüeybana II, like Urayoán, was also ready to test the mortality of Cristóbal de Sotomayor, who by then had evidently broken all of the expectations of reciprocity entailed by the pact cemented by name exchange and sister/wife-giving (Murga Sanz 1971:63–65; Oviedo 1944 [3]:200). Since during the secret council meeting the cemís had revealed their support and expectation of future success in battling the Spaniards, it is not surprising to find out that a major areíto ceremony was enacted to chant and dance in celebration of the death of Sotomayor, although he was (from our western perspective) still alive.

That he was regarded as good as dead before the fact was because the Yagüeca test had already been performed and had confirmed that Sotomayor's manner of death (body putrefaction) would be like that of any Indian, and because during the cohoba ceremony, in the mist of hallucinatory visions the cemís had confirmed to Agüeybana that Sotomayor and his men were "dead." But prior to the areíto ceremony, the life of Sotomayor was also ritually gambled, in absentia, in a rubber-ball game where the victorious players earned the right to ambush and kill the Spaniards. Despite Sotomayor being forewarned, he dismissed the warning as hearsay and departed with a number of Agüeybana's Indian porters toward Caparra: the ambush was set to go. Agüeybana II and his warriors reached the Spanish caravan at the Cauyo River (perhaps today's Yauco). There Sotomayor and his men were killed by blows from macanas and by arrows. Though not mentioned by Spanish chroniclers, it is likely that as in the Yagüeca incident, the Spaniards were left to rot for several days to check on the process of putrefaction. Sotomayor was later found by the Spanish sent by Juan Ponce de León to have been clumsily buried, feet exposed, next to the river. Sotomayor's death was quickly followed by the sacking and burning, at high noon, of the Villa de Sotomayor, marking the start of the island-wide rebellion.

> the Indians of this island rebelled on a Friday, almost at the beginning of the year one thousand five hundred and eleven . . . they saw that the Spanish [being few in number] were dispersed throughout the island, thus each cacique killed those that were in his [respective] house or land, so that they killed 80 Christians or more at the same time. And cacique Agüeybana, who was also named Don Cristóbal, as the most principal of them, ordered another cacique named Guarionex that he go as capitán, and gathered all the caciques to go and burn the new town called Sotomayor . . . and they attacked suddenly and immediately set the town on fire and killed some Christians (Oviedo 1944 [3]:196).

The sequence leading to general battle is clear. First, the decision to go to war depended on testing the nature of Spanish mortality, which would be acted upon only after a secret council meeting of the rebel chiefs involving a cohoba ceremony and consultation with the cemí idols and spirits supported such risky action. This was followed by a ball game, or *batey*, in which the lives of the Spanish targets would be played for in absentia. The game most likely decided which warrior-player teams earned the right to join the ambush team. Next, a war areíto feast celebrated both the death of the Spanish and the prowess and wisdom of the cacique Agüeybana and his cemíified ancestors. Only after all of these ceremonies were concluded was the actual ambush and execution carried out. The final phase involved the confirmation that the nature of mortality and bodily transformation from living to a nonliving being (and soul) was as expected; an advanced degree of putrefaction confirmed that this individual's soul had already departed to the land of the nonliving, to Coabey, the place where the dead souls resided (see Pané 1999). With these results in hand, each cacique, in their respective regions, would likewise order ball games and areíto ceremonies to celebrate the anticipated death of the Spaniards. Only then would they proceed to an island-wide rise in arms and battle against the Spaniards.

It is at this juncture, at the beginning of 1511, that the synchronized rise throughout Boriquén took place. Immediately before or in synchrony with the general rise to arms, Agüeybana II had sent cacique Guarionex (one of several known caciques in the Otoao, or Utuado, region [Oliver 1998:82–85]) as captain to round up all the caciques to join forces in order to attack and burn the village of Sotomayor. Sued Badillo (2001b:62) reports that thirty Cédulas Reales (royal decrees) against the rebel caciques were emitted, suggesting that at least that many caciques responded to Agüeybana's call for arms. Oviedo (1944 [3]:200–203) noted that in this first large battle, when the Villa de Sotomayor was burned, some three thousand Indian troops were deployed, resulting in the death of at least eighty Spaniards, which accounted for perhaps more than half of the island's Spanish population at that time. However, Diego de Salaçar and a few Spaniards were able to escape toward the Royal Hacienda of Toa, on the north coast, and alert Ponce de León.

The first Spanish reprisal took place on the mouth of the Coayuco River, "in the land of Agüeybana," who by then was supported by "many Indians, including Caribes and *flecheros* [who wielded bow and arrows tipped with poison] from the nearby islands who had joined" the battle (Oviedo 1944 [3]:212). It was the first defeat in battle for the rebel caciques. The second battle erupted in the region of Aymaco, to the northwest, where cacique Mabodomaca had assembled about 600 warriors. Sent ahead of the main troops commanded by Ponce de León, Diego Salaçar confronted Mabodomaca's warriors, resulting in the death of 150 natives (Oviedo 1944 [3]:213). A cacique, perhaps Mabodomaca himself, recognized by his guanín (tumbaga gold) pectoral (i.e., a guaíza), was killed by Salaçar, in hand-to-hand combat, which led to the surrender of the remaining natives. Another confrontation took place in the region of Yagüeca, where more than 11,000 native troops had assembled, possibly led by cacique Urayoán, against some 80 to 100 Spaniards. Here the troops were taunting each other, neither side committed to an all-out war, when a Spanish harquebus shot and killed an Indian, "and it was thought that he was a very principal man," because the native warriors, despite such numerical superiority, retracted and so did the Spanish.

A second round of raids and skirmishes erupted in 1513, in part fueled by Ponce de León leaving Caparra to explore Florida after Don Diego named first Cerón and then Moscoso as lieutenant governors. Spanish chroniclers recorded the term *postrera guerra* (posterior war) for that period following the 1511 uprise. It was in great measure fuelled because the Spanish administrative attention was fully on San Germán, the settlement erected on the ashes of Villa de Sotomayor (Partido de San Germán), while Caparra, the seat of the eastern insular jurisdiction (Partido de Caparra), was left unattended and exposed. Doubtless this was an opportunity for the rebellious caciques in the east and southeast. Caparra was sacked and burned by local rebels (Huerga 2006:172–179) who formed an alliance with natives from the northeastern Antilles (St. Croix and the Virgin Islands, perhaps even other islands farther south; see section 19 B). Even though the Spanish labeled many of these as "*Caribes*," most were probably natives of Puerto Rico in confederation with leaders from the Virgin Islands, perhaps including groups from the buffer zone of the northeastern Caribbean. Just days before the attack on Caparra, the rebels attacked a brigantine ship edging along the salt marshes of Abey (or Yabey) near modern Santa Isabel, in south Puerto Rico. In that period numerous dispersed Spanish farmsteads and homesteads throughout southeastern Puerto Rico were sacked by the natives and abandoned (cf. Huerga 2006:51–59; Murga Sanz 1971:86–87, 140–154). As well, there had been a punitive expedition led by cacique Caçimar of Bi[y]eque Island (today Vieques) against settlements of caciques who were loyal to the Spanish, resulting in the sacking and killing of chieftess Luysa of Aymanio, near today's village of Loíza (see Sued Badillo 2001b:64–65 and references within). After the incident, Governor Cristóbal de Mendoza persecuted the rebels all the way back to Vieques Island, "killing *cacique* Ya[h]ureibo, a brother of Caçimar. His village was ransacked and 12 canoes were destroyed. One [canoe] was so beautifully sculptured that the governor took it as a trophy for Admiral Diego Colón" (Huerga 2006:58).

While the Spaniards blamed the foreign "Carib" islanders, they nonetheless organized counteroffensive expeditions against local settlements in the eastern half of the island. In labeling the attackers from the east and the Virgin Islands as Caribes, the Spanish conveniently justified their enslavement. This meant that these natives would become private property and would be exploited at the owner's pleasure, unlike the case of encomienda or assignment, which despite abuses, still had royal "strings" attached. These raids to capture Indians as slaves, the famous cabalgadas, became a prevalent mode of pacification from 1513 until about 1519. For example, cabalgadas were directed against cacique Don Alonso of Otoao (near present-day Don Alonso district in Utuado) and cacique Orocovix in the central highland (a region today known as Orocovis), and even into as yet unexplored territories such as Daguao and Humacao, located to the southeast of the island (Murga Sanz 1971:86–87, 140–154; Sued Badillo 2001b:64–65). As Sued Badillo (2001b:65) noted, eventually a total of sixteen insurgent caciques "were exiled to Hispaniola without having any further information of their fate"; most were probably executed. Pockets of resistance throughout Boriquén and the ensuing punitive cabalgadas were to continue well into 1518. At that time reports were being received in Santo Domingo that still complained about the natives being on the run. The beginning of the end of the Rebellion of the Caciques began in January 1519, a fateful year, when smallpox spread like wildfire throughout Hispaniola and Puerto Rico. The pandemic broke down any armed resistance that the native rebels might have had in store. However, from the Windward Islands, natives did organize raiding parties to attack the Spanish in Puerto Rico through most of the sixteenth century, for which there are records for 1515, 1520, 1529, 1530, 1534, 1553, 1567, and 1578 (Huerga 2006). Contrary to Sued Badillo's opinion, the natives from places like Guadeloupe, Martinique, and Dominica were far removed from the shared social-cultural identity (Taínoness) of the native groups of Puerto Rico and the Virgin Islands. The Windward natives were not merely Taínos who had been branded as Carib for political reasons.

One of the consequences of the cabalgadas right after 1511 in Puerto Rico was that enslaved Indians and whatever war booty was publicly auctioned would be subject to taxation (the "royal fifth"). Some of these documents have survived, providing some tantalizing details of what was taken from the Indians and details about the enslaved. For instance, from the booty collected by Captain Salaçar there is a list of Indian slaves and items sold in auction that were taken from a *jagüey* (subterranean cave) belonging to cacique Mabo, which included among the items "*dos feguras de areyte*" ["two statues"] and "*una nagua de areyte*" ["one female loincloth"] sold for a total of seven *tomines* and fourteen *granos* (Murga Sanz 1971:286–287; for a discussion of monetary values, see Gelpi Baiz 2000:121–126). The first one undoubtedly refers to a pair of idols that the Spanish associated with areítos, perhaps suggesting that the cemí icons were publicly displayed in ceremonial areítos; the other item refers to the loincloths (*naguas*) worn by women participating in areítos. The auction of cemí idols is thus direct evidence of the capture of symbols of native religion and political power. This pair of figures must have been of enough value or curiosity to the Spaniards to end up in public auction rather than being destroyed. The fact that cacique Mabo had these and other items stowed away in a jagüey confirms that valuables, especially cemí icons, would often be hidden to avoid theft. In the five Spanish documents published by Vicente Murga Sanz (1971:279–289) listing the auctioned war booty, other goods included hammocks, fishing nets, cotton sashes and belts, *maos* (perhaps breastplates used in war), fool's gold or pyrite, and a stone necklace found "*en unos careyes*" (["in some (carapaces of) carey"]; *carey* is the loggerhead turtle, *Caretta caretta*).

It will not come as a surprise that the Rebellion of the Caciques of Boriquén, particularly in the early phases (1510–1511), spurred the caciques of the Higüey to once again conspire against the Spanish in their region. Friars of the Hieronymite order arrived in Santo Domingo on December 20, 1516, to evaluate and come up with solutions regarding the acute problems of the state of indigenous labor assignments, the political turmoil generated between the newcomer colonists and the grip on power by the veteran conquistador elite (gathered around Diego Colón), and the precarious state of food production on the island (Rodríguez Demorizi 1971:274). They acted as judges and were the powerful de facto governing body at least until 1519 (Moya Pons 1987:141–142). An inquest took place (reported in 1517) to evaluate "the opinions that were given [by the Spanish residents] about the manner in which the Indians of these islands should be [treated]," reorganized, and administered (Rodríguez Demorizi 1971:271). Opinion was sought among a select group of the conquistadors who had been in Hispaniola from the very early days. It is in this document where direct evidence of the links between caciques of

Higüey and the Agüeybanas of Boriquén can be found. One witness in particular, Marcos de Aguilar (a veteran conquistador), testified that:

> after this witness arrived to this island [Hispaniola] as a Magistrate, he knew about how a cacique [Agüeybana II] in the island of San Juan killed Don Cristóbal de Sotomayor and other Christians in a place called Jauca ["Cauyo" in other documents] in the island of San Juan. This was learnt later by cacique *Andrés, who now serves his Royal Highness, who was a relative of the other cacique who had killed Don Cristóbal.* The said cacique Andrés assembled in his house all the caciques and many peoples of this province of Higüey to celebrate with great feast and joy the victory that the Indians of San Juan had against the Christians. And when in such a state many caciques assemble, they, as usual, always discuss things against the Christians. They agreed among themselves saying that if Agüeybana killed the Christians in the island of San Juan . . . they should also do the same, because the Indians were already *manicatos,* which means *esforzados* [i.e., authoritative; backed by the force of law, according to Covarrubias Orozco's 1611 dictionary (1995:501)]" [Rodríguez Demorizi 1971:346–348; my emphasis].

Clearly the good news about Sotomayor and his men's mortality and the initial successes of the rebellion in Puerto Rico had rapidly reached Agüeybana's relative, cacique Andrés, in the Higüey. This prompted a meeting of caciques of the Higüey to celebrate the victory of their allies and relatives in Puerto Rico and also emboldened them to plot a conspiracy at home. In fact, it is not farfetched to assume that the message sent by Agüeybana II was a call to expand the battlefront from Boriquén to the Higüey and beyond throughout Hispaniola. Agüeybana II must have been aware of the benefits of cutting off the Spanish flow of supplies being shipped from Spanish port towns like Salvaleón (Boca del Yuma) and Santo Domingo. Be that as it may, the same witness, Aguilar, tells how the call for rebellion would be sent via messengers to the caciques quartered in their respective settlements in the Higüey region. The message consisted of a specific date when selected caciques would enter the village of Salvaleón, where they would start a fire into which a poison prepared by the *bohites* would arise as a toxic smoke and kill the inhabitants—indeed, evidence that natives knew about chemical warfare tactics! The plan also called for other caciques to simultaneously hit the city of Santo Domingo and other localities throughout Hispaniola. Sadly for the Taínoan freedom fighters, the plot was discovered by the Spanish and quashed before it even germinated.

The events in Boriquén recorded by the Spanish chroniclers have provided one context—warfare and acute political crisis—in which the cemí idols were invoked, consulted, and engaged by the military elite, primarily caciques, in secret council meetings. These icons, as well as the cemí as spirits (or as hallucinogenic visions), were instrumental in engaging the Spanish in battle, not the least of which involved the certification that the Spaniards experienced the process of death in a similar manner to the aborigines. The battles on both fronts also brought forth the nature of the alliances made between the caciques of the two islands through blood relations, intermarriage, or guaitiao pacts. It also showed the order of ceremonial and ritual protocols followed, from the cohoba to consult the cemí idols, to the ball games to select the warring parties, and then the areíto celebrating the victory predicted by the cemís.

The battles in Higüey and Boriquén bring to the fore the sociopolitical and inter-insular connections in which cemí icons of various kinds, and on occasion including those one might think of as inalienable, were exchanged and circulated. Part of the cemí idols circulating within and between the two insular regions went hand in hand with the exchange of wives, establishing political bonds between affine, who would also be guaitiao. With the death of caciques a result of the war, some of these icons would also be bequeathed to foreign caciques and allies. Given the close relationships among chiefs across the Mona Passage, these icons would also flow between Boriquén and the Higüey.

C. Idolatry, Religious Persecution, and the Destruction of Cemí Idols

The military battles in Hispaniola and Boriquén also entailed the religious persecution of the natives. In addition to the Spaniards' "legal and social disempowerment of the indigene peoples, came a religious persecution that entailed the destruction of idols and punishment for idolatry" (Sued Badillo 2003:279). Let us not forget the areíto figures listed among materials sold at auction in Puerto Rico immediately after the 1511 Rebellion of the Caciques. But the auction of religious paraphernalia as curios was probably not common; most of the idols that could not be hidden during the conflicts were almost certainly systematically destroyed by the Spaniards (see McEwan 2008). The hiding of cemí idols from the Spanish was done to avoid the capture and destruction of the very instruments of chiefly political-religious power. And hiding was done to avert pillage not only from zealot Spaniards, but also from the native caciques allied to the Spanish. The rebel caciques probably captured the cemí idols of caciques who were loyal to the Spaniards, although I would expect that rather than destroying them, they were put to the service of their cause.

A discrete set of events was recorded by Fray Ramón Pané (1999:33–38) while he was ordered by Admiral Columbus to go to live with cacique Guarionex, ruler of the cacicazgo of Magua-Caiabó around March 1495 (Oliver 2008a:89–90). These events exemplify the conflicts, struggles, and misunderstandings between Indians and the conquistadors, even pitting native brother against brother; they also high-light the role of religion and the power of images in a way that was disregarded by the chroniclers of the Higüey battles. The iconoclastic persecution to be de-tailed below is unique in that it is the only detailed written text providing an ac-count of the destruction of religious Christian imagery implemented by the Indi-ans rather than the other way around. It is once again thanks to Fray Ramón Pané (1999:30–38) that these events were recorded for posterity. Accompanying Pané was Fray Juan Leudelle (or de la Deule), nicknamed *El Bermejo* or *Borgoñés*. Born in the Bourgogne region, Leudelle was a Franciscan monk originating from a mon-astery in Hainaut, Belgium (Erraste 1998:25–29; Varela 2006). Fray Juan de Tisin ("El Francés"), another Franciscan also from Hainut may well have also accompa-nied Pané in his mission. Pané, on the other hand, hailed from the monastery of Sant Jeroni de La Murtra, in what is now Badalona, on the outskirts of Barcelona, in the province of Catalunya, in northeast Spain (Aymar i Ragolta 2008). It now seems likely that it was at Sant Jeroni that Columbus met the Catholic monarchs on his first return from Hispaniola and not at the Plaza Reial in Gothic downtown Barcelona (probably an invention of nineteenth-century Spanish Romanticism). Given that King Ferdinand, who favored the then-powerful Hieronymite order, had been at Sant Jeroni in April 1493 recovering from wounds received in a failed assassination attempt (precisely at the steps of the Plaza Reial), it is more than likely that Pané's name was suggested to Columbus by King Ferdinand himself or by the prior of the monastery of Sant Jeroni (Aymar i Ragolta 1993, 2007, 2008:43).

Pané and Leudelle accompanied Columbus on his second voyage to the Carib-bean. By January 2, 1493, Columbus had decided on La Isabela as the site for the new settlement after the fiasco of the La Navidad fortress. Fray Ramón Pané, who was a laic (i.e., not an ordained priest), was almost certainly at La Isabela (along with seven other clerics) for the first solemn mass conducted by Father Bernardo Buil (or Bernat Boyl; also a Catalan of the Benedictine order) on Epiphany Day, January 6. Pané and Leudelle (perhaps Juan de Tisin, too) left La Isabela for the land of cacique Mabiatué, about which neither Pané nor Leudelle left any informa-tion, but was probably within range of La Isabela on Macorix Arriba territory.

Pané wrote that at the beginning of 1495 he left La Isabela to reside in the for-tress of La Magdalena (Figure 33), where he lived for about a year under the pro-tection of Captain Luis de Artiaga. It was while in Magdalena that Pané, a na-tive Catalan speaker, learned the native language of Macorix, which, according to Las Casas, was a "strange, almost barbarian language" and unlike the "elegantly spoken" generalized Taíno language spoken in the rest of Hispaniola (see Erraste 1998:38). While the two friars were there, La Magdalena was attacked by the lo-cal cacique, Guatiguaná, and by other rebellious caciques under Caonabó's orders, but the fortress was soon liberated by Columbus's men. Toward the end of March 1495, Admiral Columbus ordered Fray Ramón Pané and Fray Juan Leudelle to move on to the village of cacique Guarionex, near another of the fortresses that Co-lumbus had ordered built next to El Verde River, named La Concepción (see Varela 2006:1–49).

Because the natives of the Macorix region spoke a different tongue than the gen-eralized Taíno language of Hispaniola, Pané and Fray Leudelle obtained permis-sion from Admiral Columbus to take "the best of the Indians" with him, including one named Guatícabanu, who was his most advanced catechumen, instructed in the Catholic faith (Pané 1999:33–34). Guatícabanu was one of sixteen intimate members of the household of cacique Guanáocobonel, who lived in the Macorix region, at a site or locality named Nihuirey (Deive 1976:140–141; Pané 1999:32). From there Pané and Leudelle traveled with seven catechumens, first back to La Isabela in the northwest and later returning to the southeast along the valley to-ward Guarícano (La Concepción; Figure 33). The natives around Guarícano (i.e., Guarionex's subjects) spoke Taíno; we know this because a large number of native terms in Pané's (1999) account are undoubtedly Taíno and closely related to other Caribbean Maipuran languages, as José Juan Arrom (1975; and in Pané 1999:xix-passim) has demonstrated. For the same reason, I also speculate that it was during his stay among Guarionex's people that Pané collected most of the myths and leg-ends contained in the *Relación*.

Initially, cacique Guarionex welcomed the clerics and the Macorix catechumens with grace, and even enrolled his own household in the catechism, convening twice daily to recite the Christian prayers (Pané 1999:35). At this stage Guarionex was still reticent to join in the anti-Spanish conspiracy being plotted by fourteen ca-ciques (Oliver 2008a:88–89; Wilson 1990:98–100). Thus the catechism lessons continued for about two years, from the spring of 1495 to near the end of 1497 or very early in 1498 (Varela 2006:36–37). Meanwhile, Bartolomé Colón was left in charge, as adelantado (i.e., an official with political-military functions who gov-erned an advance territory fronting the enemy), while Christopher Columbus was back in Spain from 1496 to 1498. Spanish-native conflicts in the entire region had reached a crescendo during the spring of 1497. Guarionex was under a lot of pres-sure from fourteen caciques (probably peers), who ultimately succeeded in con-vincing Guarionex that he had no choice but to renege on his strategy of tolerance with the Spaniards, because the latter had been usurping the land, carrying out at-tacks on them, and of course because of the extensive abuses in the gold-panning operations around the fort of Santo Tomás, near Xanique, in the Cibao Mountains (today's Jánico; see Figure 33), the land of cacique Caonabó—not to mention that the natives simply did not have the means to fulfill the required amounts of tribute in gold (for the full story, see Oliver 2008a:89-passim; Wilson 1990:97–108).

It is quite probable that a secret council and cohoba meeting was held, as it was in the case of Agüeybana II in Boriquén, where Guarionex and the fourteen ca-ciques met to deliberate on the best course of action. If so, upon receiving the appropriate signals from his cemí idols, Guarionex changed his policy of diplomatic tolerance for one of active resistance, joining the fourteen caciques. The plan was to take advantage of the day when the caciques paid the tributes (mainly gold) to the Spanish so as to gain access into the fortress and thus launch a surprise attack. Pedro Mártir de Anglería (1989:155; Wilson 1990:99) noted that Bartolomé Colón had learned beforehand that Guarionex had been chosen by the other caciques as their commander in chief to lead some fifteen thousand native troops to battle. It is very doubtful that such a decision would have been made without due invocation of, and assent by (via a cohoba ceremony), the appropriate contingent of cemí idols under the control of Guarionex and also those controlled by the other fourteen caciques.

Guarionex's decision was soon felt by Pané, resulting in his and the catechumens' hurried departure, if not ejection, from the Guarícano settlement. Pané headed toward the village of another "principal cacique" named Mabiatué (or Mahubiatíbire), "who has continued to be of good will [toward Catholic indoctrination] for three years now, saying he wishes to be a Christian, and who wants to have but one wife, although they usually have two or three, and the principal men have ten, fifteen and twenty" (Pané 1999:35, 38). The precise location of Mabiatué's domain is unknown; perhaps it was an area closer to the Magdalena–La Isabela region—or, more likely, to either the Bonao area or Santo Domingo—where Pané was deposed in an inquest against the Columbus brothers (Cristóbal, Bartolomé, and Diego) presided by Comendador Bobadilla.

Pané's whereabouts were unknown until Consuelo Varela (2006) recently located documents pertaining to the inquest against the Columbus brothers ordered by the Spanish monarchs and presided by the new governor, Comendador Francisco de Bobadilla, during the late autumn of 1500. Pané's deposition (Varela 2006:98–104, 203) is important because it shows that he was in either Bonao or Santo Domingo in 1500, and because his testimony contradicts some aspects of the text of the *Relación* that came down to the present through Hernando Colón (via Alfonso de Ulloa) and Pedro Mártir de Anglería. It is possible that either the imprisoned Columbuses or Bobadilla's envoys took Pané's famous *Relación* back to Spain, reaching Cádiz in November 1500 (giving Mártir a chance to read Pané's document). The key point of discrepancy is that Christopher Columbus had forbidden the natives to be baptized, contradicting the *Relación* (Pané 1999). The admiral made it very difficult for Pané and the other missionaries to accomplish their ultimate task of converting the natives. Columbus wanted them to first have the natives indoctrinated (taught the "Ave María," "Pater Noster," "Credo," etc.) but not baptized. The reason behind this was to exclude the native women from being legally recognized in marriage with Spaniards and to avoid the problems of *mestizaje* (i.e., the legal status of the offspring that results from Indian-Spanish sexual relations) at a time when the Crown forbade such unions. Equally important, natives who were not baptized and were captured in battle could be enslaved and sold in Spain. By 1500, Varela (2006:111–119) estimates that more than fifteen hundred "Indios" had been enslaved by Christopher Columbus alone. The accusation was very serious: Admiral Columbus was impeding the Indians from being converted to the Catholic faith, contravening Queen Isabella's express edict to convert them; she regarded them as her vassals (though the queen often wavered over the issue of vassalage versus slavery). Unfortunately, Pané's deposition (in Varela 2006:203) did not mention the incident of the desecration of Christian icons in Guarícano, Guarionex's town.

What happened in that incident is this. Frustrated because of Columbus's "no baptism" policy and because of Guarionex's joining the rebellion, Pané had left for Santo Domingo. He also left behind in Guarícano (ca. 1497) several of the catechumens from Guanáocobonel's household as custodians of the makeshift chapel (probably nothing fancier than a *bohío*) where the Catholic wooden images were kept for veneration. Guarionex then ordered six of his men to take the Christian idols by force. Once taken, the images were buried in a conuco, where the men then urinated on them while reciting "now your fruits will be good and great," which the Spanish interpreted as scorn and vituperation. Some native catechumens rescued the Christian statues from the conuco and hid them and then sent someone to inform Adelantado Bartolomé Colón of the incident. The adelantado captured the culprits and ordered them to be burned alive at the stake. Notwithstanding the execution, Guarionex ordered the Christians killed (four were killed), including Juan Mateo (Guatícabanu's Christian name), and also commanded that the Christian images be destroyed. Sometime later, the field where the images had been buried and urinated on was harvested and a large sweet potato in the shape of a cross was found. Both Pané and Guarionex's mother (whom Pané said was "the worst woman in these parts") took it for a miracle (Pané 1999:36–37).

These events show how the men sent by Guarionex interpreted and used Christian images as if they were cemí idols with analogous supernatural potency, as Arrom had originally suggested (Arrom 1975). At the same time, Guarionex also had to destroy the images, as they were equally interpreted as powerful beings that worked against the integrity of his polity: they were "feeding" the enemy by making crops grow. In reverse, the Spanish executed Guarionex's iconoclasts for heretics, and legitimized the righteousness of the Christian faith vested in these images by telling about the miracle of the cross-shaped tuber. Guarionex's mother *did* express wonderment, but perhaps not surprise, that the Christian "cemís" yielded what would be expected from the natives' three-pointed cemí idols.

Carlos Estéban Deive (1976), however, suggests an alternative motive for Guarionex's men urinating on the Catholic images. He suggests that it is also possible that it was a deliberate act of desecration: they did so to openly scorn the Spanish and deny the legitimacy of the imposed Catholic religion. He suggests that the whole doctrinal acquiescence by Guarionex and his people was a pretense, much in the same way that African slaves pretended to pray to Santiago (St. James) and other saints when in fact they were worshipping their native African *orichas* (deities), like Changó or Obatalá, whose icons were literally hiding behind the Catholic images or had "mounted" or entered the saint's body (Deive 1976:144–145; see also Brown 2003:121–127, 369–371). He asks, what other reason could there be for Guarionex's mother's surprise when she witnessed the miraculously cross-shaped sweet potato? Deive's view is plausible and depends on how one interprets the comment made by the natives while urinating (that it makes crops grow). It is either a direct, literal statement or one uttered with contempt and sarcasm. But even if the statement was one of scorn, it does not diminish my argument that it is almost certain that most natives saw and understood the Catholic images as the cemí analogues of the Spanish religious icons. The fact is that they *were destroyed,* suggesting a combination of scorn, contempt, and—yes—fear, because these Catholic images were undoubtedly seen as threat to the safety and integrity of their way of life.

Little has survived in the Spanish writings describing the destruction of cemí idols, but there is no question of their systematic destruction and persecution: the natives were hiding them anywhere they could (e.g., in caves, the forest, in jagüeyes) so that neither the Spanish nor the caciques allied with them could get their hands on their idols (see section 12).

This story encapsulates an iconoclastic struggle that, sadly, the native loyalists would not win. The destruction of powerful native cemí idols, along with the "decapitation" of entire chiefly lineages (and heirs), ruptured the web of political, economic, and military alliances and enmities that the caciques had spun for centuries; their daily life and routines were changed irrevocably. Whether in peace or in war, whether in alliances or competition, marriage exchanges, kidnapping women, playing ball games, or chanting and dancing, they did so under agreed and understood principles of right and wrong, justice and injustice, that were theirs to pursue and uphold, or not. From that first genocide in January 1493, at the Golfo de Las Flechas in Samaná, their destiny was no longer in their hands.

20 The Virgin Mary Icons and Native Cemís

Two Cases of Religious Syncretism in Cuba

Antonio Curet reminded me of yet another case of a clash of idols, but this time involving two native actors in Cuba: one wielding a native cemí and the other a Catholic image of the "Virgin Mother of God." A witness relayed the events to Pedro Mártir de Anglería in Spain. Mártir included the account in his famous *De Orbe Novo Decades,* in the sixth book of his Second Decade (Mártir 1989 [1514]:249–265), an epistle written to Pope Leo X.

The informant of the key event was Martín Fernández de Enciso—or *bachiller* Anciso, as Mártir identified him. (Here I use the former spelling, Enciso, except when quoting Mártir.) He was a firsthand informant. In Pedro Mártir's (1989 [1514]:255–256) own words: "I wanted, Beatific Father [Pope Leo X], to refer to You these details regarding the religion of the natives that I have learned not only from Anciso but also many other persons of authority so that Your Beatitude [may] understand how docile is this race of men and how easily is the road to instruct them in the rites of our religion." It is possible that when Mártir wrote the epistle, the story had been embellished so as to highlight the triumph of Christianity over paganism and to affirm to Pope Leo X that the native souls of Cuba were primed for conversion—a fact refuted later by Gonzalo Fernández de Oviedo y Valdés (1944 [3]:244–245).

The privileges of Christopher Columbus's son Don Diego were partly restored in 1509. Upon returning that year to Hispaniola, Don Diego named Alonso de Hojeda (also spelled Ojeda) and Diego de Nicuesa as governors of the fledgling Spanish dominions of Urabá and Veraguas in the Isthmus of Panamá-Colombia, respectively (Thomas 2003:243). The fame of Martín Fernández de Enciso was in connection to his involvement in the penetration and conquest of the Darién and the establishment in 1510 of Nuestra Señora de la Antigua, located next to the Atrarto River, Gulf of Urabá, in what is now Colombia (Thomas 2003:246). Because of factional competition, Vasco Núñez de Balboa expelled Enciso in the spring of 1511, because Enciso "had never been a friend since he had threatened to have Balboa placed on a desert island when he was discovered as a stowaway on his vessel to flee from creditors in Santo Domingo" (Thomas (2003:246–247). As a result, Enciso set sail for Santo Domingo that spring of 1511 but unknowingly veered into Cuba.

Around the time Martín Fernández de Enciso arrived, the situation in Cuba was taking a turn for the worse. In 1509 Sebastián Ocampo circumnavigated the area, confirming what most sailors in Hispaniola already knew: Cuba was an island (Thomas 2003:275). The conquest of Cuba began early in 1511 and was led, as well as financed, by Diego Velázquez de Cuéllar, a hidalgo. He was accompanied, among others, by his secretary, Hernán Cortéz (future conqueror of the Aztec empire); Fray Bartolomé de Las Casas (already ordained in 1508); and Juan Gonçález, the son of Juan Ponce de León, who had just left the battlefield of the 1511 Rebellion of Caciques of Puerto Rico. Velázquez set out to conquer Cuba from the makeshift wooden fortress in Baracoa, northeastern Cuba (see Figure 28). He cruelly defeated the local native resistance led by cacique Hatuey. This cacique had fled from what is today Haiti, where Velázquez had his estates, and organized the resistance in Baracoa. Legend has it that the captive Hatuey was burned alive at the stake for refusing Christianity: "he is supposed to have said that if Christianity meant that he had to spend eternity in the company of Spaniards, he would prefer not to be baptized" (Thomas 2003:277, using information from Las Casas 1929 [2]:469–488). Velázquez was then joined by Pánfilo de Narváez, just arrived from the conquest of Jamaica led by Juan de Esquivel—the same Esquivel who led the battle of Higüey, Hispaniola. As Velázquez moved across the Oriente Province, Narváez had already defeated the native resistance in Bayamo (claiming one hundred dead) led by a cacique named Caguax, who had replaced Hatuey. The Spaniards were persecuting the fleeing Indians toward Camagüey when they reached a settlement called Cueybá (or Cueibá), probably located between Manzanillo and Bayamo (Ulloa Hung and Lourdes Domínguez, personal communications 2007).

A. The Flemish Virgin Mary of Hojeda at Cueybá

It was at Cueybá where Narváez's men found the natives worshipping the image of the Virgin Mary (see map of Cuba, Figure 28). This statue of the Virgin Mary in Cueybá was left by Alonso de Hojeda on what was his last return trip from Urabá to Santo Domingo, where he died later in 1515. His ship did not make it and instead floundered in a large bay in the "province of Xaguá," where the city of Cienfuegos is today. In several nineteenth-century maps, this area was still called Bay of Xaguá, or Jaguá, and the region was known as Fernandina de Jaguá (Figure 28; Zayas y Alfonso 1931:228, 281). Hojeda and the Spaniards traveled some "100 leagues" (approximately 483 km) east toward Bayamo and the site of Cueybá (Las Casas [2]:339–341). Hojeda, noted Las Casas, "had in his rucksack an image of *Nuestra Señora* [Our Lady], exquisitely painted, made in Flanders, that the Bishop

Don Juan de Fonseca [secretary of King Ferdinand] . . . had gifted him" (Las Casas [2]:341). The Spaniards were in dire straits and lost for thirty days in a huge swamp, for which reason Hojeda at every opportunity "pulled out from his rucksack the image, placed her on a tree, and there he venerated her . . . begging her to remedy [save] them." By the time they reached Cueybá, already half of the seventy shipwrecked Spaniards had either drowned or died of hunger.

In Cueybá the local natives received the starved Spaniards with hospitality and nursed them back to good health. The local chief even sent a rescue party to the swamp in search of the rest of the survivors. Hojeda had made a solemn promise (*ex-voto*) that he would leave his statue of Our Lady in the first village where he could find succor. At Cueybá:

> He gave [the icon] to the señor of the village [and] ordered him to build an oratory or chapel with an altar, where he [Hojeda] put her [the statue of Our Lady], and offering some instruction to the Indians about God, as best as [he] could communicate, telling them that she was the Mother of God, that He was in Heaven, Lord and God of all the world, that she was named *Sancta María,* advocate of men. It was admirable to see the devotion and reverence they [Indians] had toward this image that they had henceforth, and how ornate the church was with clothes made of cotton, and how well swept and clean it was. They had couplets made in their language and accompanied with song and dance [Las Casas 1929 (2):342].

Las Casas said he and Narváez arrived a "few days later" after this event, in pursuit of the rebel cacique Caguax. And that brings up a second event relating to this image of Our Lady. Among Narváez's soldiers there were some of Hojeda's survivors who were devoted to this Virgin icon; they pressed on the padre (company priest) to recover the icon from this cacique. Although the padre had another image of the Virgin Mary, also sculptured in Flanders, the men were not as devoted to her as they were to Hojeda's Our Lady (Las Casas 1929 [3]:481). During a great meal prepared by the natives, the padre offered the cacique to exchange his Virgin Mary for theirs (i.e., Hojeda's). The cacique then "stood up, downcast" and pretended to hide his disappointment as best he could. At night he grabbed the icon and "took off to the hills with her." Next morning, as the priest readied for mass, he found out that the icon was gone and was informed by the natives that their cacique had run away to hide her, afraid the Spanish would take her away. Despite various attempts to entice the cacique to return, he refused. Indeed, "for the security of the icon," he did not return until the Spanish continued their colonizing expedition toward Camagüey (westward), still some twenty leagues (97 km) away (Las Casas 1929 [2]:482).

Las Casas marveled at the devotion these natives had to the Virgin of Nuestra

Señora (Our Lady), and that they composed couplets and songs and danced areítos in her honor. Led by Narávez, the expedition continued through several native villages and ended up in a settlement called Caonao. It is here that the events led to the massacre of around two thousand natives (see also Thomas 2003:278–279). This was the event that turned Las Casas from a conquistador and encomendero to the "Defender of Indians," even though at that time he was already ordained. In a short time Las Casas would follow the example of his Dominican brethren Fray Pedro de Córdoba and Fray Antón de Montesinos in denunciating the ill treatment of Amerindians (Thomas 2003:257–280; for an in-depth analysis, see Fernández Buey 1995).

By 1514 the Spaniards had already founded seven settlements, all in or adjacent to native villages (see Figure 28): Baracoa (1511); Bayamo (1513); Trinidad (1514); Sancti Spiritus; Puerto Príncipe, or Camagüey; Santiago; and San Cristóbal de La Habana in its original location on Batanabó Bay on the south coast (these last four also in 1514). The old Habana was relocated to its present location between 1519 and 1526 (Thomas 2003:280).

B. The Painted Virgin Image of Cacique Comendador

Martín Fernández de Enciso must have arrived in Cuba shortly after Hojeda, but it was probably at the same time as or earlier than Velázquez and Narváez began their push for colonization in 1511. Unlike Hojeda, Enciso did not suffer any travail while moving along the coast of Cuba. At some locality, perhaps between Camagüey and Bayamo, Enciso encountered a local chief or cacique who introduced himself as cacique Comendador. He liked and appropriated this Spanish title, which he had heard in reference to the former governor of Santo Domingo (Comendador Mayor Nicolás de Ovando). This appropriation no doubt says much about the importance of naming in relation to caciques. This method of name acquisition contrasts with guaitiao, the formal name exchange ritual already noted as taking place in Hispaniola and Puerto Rico, but it is consonant with titles of grandeur (usually celestial bodies or brilliant things, such as *turey* [sky]) with which prominent caciques were invested; see Oliver 2000).

Cacique Comendador told Enciso that a party of Spaniards had left a sick Spanish sailor in his care. Once recovered, in gratitude the sailor taught the cacique Comendador's troops new warfare tactics and helped them in their "usual" attacks against other native rivals—the reason they thereafter always came out victorious. The sailor was a pious devotee of the Virgin Mother of God. He always carried an image of her "beautifully painted in a piece of paper" (perhaps meaning a parchment or linen) and "sown to his chest" (Mártir 1989 [1514]:252). The sailor assured cacique Comendador that the reason for the victorious raids was because he was backed by the Virgin icon and he further added that "he counseled

[Comendador]," writes Mártir, "that he banish all his cemís to whom they rendered cult because they believed them to be nocturnal ghosts, voracious destroyers of souls." The sailor "persuaded them to adopt the blessed Virgin Mother of God, if they wished to secure their businesses in peace as well as in war" (Mártir 1989 [1514]:252). The cacique then "begged" the sailor to give him the garment with the Virgin sewn in it, and then he "consecrated a temple and altar." Although Mártir (1989 [1514]:252) says that cacique Comendador henceforth "disdained" the cemís venerated for so many generations, the statement seems to me to be an embellishment of either Enciso or, more likely, Mártir himself so as to curry the grace and favor of Pope Leo X, to whom he was writing. But if the report is accurate, this disdain for native iconography and its replacement by Christian iconography, even when both are still regarded as cemís and form part of cemíism, is a key turning point, as a significant and physical element of Taínoness had been rejected.

In any event, Comendador and his people, "of both sexes," entered the shrine, knelt down, and recited the "Ave María" over and over, as only very few had learned a few more words of this prayer. Upon Enciso's arrival, cacique Comendador took him by the hand and proudly showed the house where the Virgin painted on "paper" was kept. He pointed to the Virgin image, which was "surrounded by some *poyos* [original Latin: *podium,* a bench] where there were necklaces [and] ceramic vessels full of food and water: these are the offerings that instead of sacrifices they take to the Virgin, *reminiscent of the ancestral cult to the cemís.* They explained that the reason for such offerings was to avoid that the image, spurred by hunger, would find no food" (Mártir 1989 [1514]:252–253; my emphasis). The cacique told Enciso of yet another story involving the anonymous sailor. On one occasion when the sailor, wearing the Virgin image, was locked in combat, "the cemís of the enemies started to tremble" and "turned their faces" away from her, to which Mártir (not Enciso) inserted the comment that "it is known that both bands always have the cemís accompany them so that they help them" in these battles (Mártir 1989 [1514]:253). The natives affirmed Enciso that they were aided in battle not just by the image of the Virgin, but by "a beautiful Lady, full of life, elegantly attired with a white dress," whereas the enemies said that she was "a woman with a scepter who, with a menacing attitude, favored their opponents," and that upon seeing such an apparition "their hearts filled with terror" (Mártir 1989 [1514]:253).

C. The Ritual Contest between Virgin Mary and the Native Cemís

After the sailor had been rescued by the Spanish, cacique Comendador continued to engage in regular "bitter disputes" with a neighboring rival group on the issue of which of the cemís were more "saintly" and more powerful—the Virgin or the native ones? These arguments often ended in open, bloody conflicts. One day the two rival caciques made a pact to resolve their differences by selecting warriors from each band to engage in one-to-one combat at an agreed location. On that day, the hands of one young man from each band were tied behind his back. The victor would be the one whose tied hands were liberated, miraculously, by the power of his cemí. Each would loudly proclaim the superiority of his cemí. The cacique Comendador's opponents invoked their native cemí three times, and each time it failed to deliver. But when Comendador's warrior invoked the Virgin, a miracle occurred. The Virgin appeared "dressed in white, making the Devil [the opponent's cemí] run away, and then placing her scepter on the ligatures of her protected [warrior], he was suddenly freed in front of the eyes of the other, all the while the rope that was used to tie the Comendador's [warrior] moved on to his rival . . . so that the opponents found the opponent young man liberated while theirs was tied up with double ropes" (Mártir 1989 [1514]:254).

But there is more: Comendador's opponents thought there was some sort of trickery involved rather than any "divine" cemí power. So the challenge was repeated, this time with four men on each side, with the same result. After Comendador's rivals invoked their native cemís (e.g., Figure 34), the entire assembly saw the appearance of the "Devilish cemís, with their tails and enormous teeth, horns, similar to the ones [they have] represented in a hand-made effigy, who started to untie the man to whom each cemí was dedicated to" (Mártir 1989 [1514]:254–255). As this occurred, Comendador invoked the Virgin and she appeared as already described above. Her apparition resulted in the rival cemí fleeing the scene. And like before, the ropes tying Comendador's men ended up instead tying the hands of the rival combatants.

This victory of the Virgin Mary over the "devilish-looking" native cemís was such a notorious event throughout all neighboring groups in the region that as soon as word came that the Spaniards were on their way (Enciso and his men arriving in Cueybá), they sent messengers to seek "priests to baptize them" (Mártir 1989 [1514]:254–255). Again, here I am suspicious that Mártir (and/or Enciso) was embellishing the tale for the benefit of Pope Leo X. It is perhaps more likely that all were after the Christian cemí, a Virgin Mary or any other, in order to maintain political and military parity with cacique Comendador. The expanding reputation of Comendador's painted Virgin cemí confirms my previous arguments about how Taínoan cemí icons, once sculptured, begin to accrue a biography and reputation in coordination with the human trustee's actions. Their value as numinous and potent icons increases in the public eye.

D. Indo-Cuban Cemíism Compared

From the two events, the adoption and appropriation of Hojeda's Virgin Mary (a sculptured figure) and Comendador's use of Our Lady's image (a painted image), several inferences can be made. Let us begin at Cueybá with Hojeda's icon. This icon, made of wood and apparently polychrome-painted, was willingly adopted by the local cacique and treated as if it were a native cemí. One of the first things that the Cuban cacique did was to have the icon housed in a bohío structure that seems to have been exclusively devoted to the Virgin Mary icon. However, this does not imply that other cemí icons (such as shown in Figures 29: f; 34) were not also stored and honored in this bohío. I also suspect that other native cemí icons accompanied the Comendador's Virgin icon. I would be surprised if the cacique and the combatants did not also wear cemí icons as part of their attire, as body decorations (e.g., Figure 29: b-e), or carry the icons with them in, for example, a cotton bag, such as a miniature three-pointed stone (see Figure 29: a).

In terms of ritual, just like the natives of Guarícano in Hispaniola, the Virgin was given offerings of food, though it is not mentioned if such offerings were linked to a first harvest, as indicated in Pané's (1999) account for Hispaniola. The Virgin, like other cemís, was the focus of reverence and ritual invocation: couplets were sung and dances were performed in her honor. Like native cemís, the Virgin at the shrine in the bohío or out in ritual combat was apprehended from a multinatural and animistic perspective.

It can be surmised that the cacique of Cueybá received only the barest of Catholic instruction about who the Virgin Mary was, possibly learning formulaic phrases (probably in Latin), such as the ritualistic repetition of "Ave María, Ave María" in order to invoke her. Elements of the biography of the Virgin (as the Mother of God, etc.) would find resonance with other native feminine cemí idols (e.g., Attabeyra of Macorix or Magua in Hispaniola) and their biographies, as María Nelsa Trincado (in Portuondo Zúñiga 1995:61–65; 1997) has aptly noted (see also Arrom 1975:44–54). From the perspective of the Cueybá natives, the Virgin was, therefore, one more cemí incorporated into their ensemble of numinous icons controlled by their cacique. It did certainly help that the Cueybá natives witnessed the genuine, authentic devotion that Hojeda and his men had for the Virgin Mary icon, the fact that she was responsible for saving them from death in the swamps. The same processes seem to have been involved in the initial adoption of icons (saints or virgins) by Guarionex and his family, but the details of how they and other natives in Macorix and Magua venerated the Christian icons are unknown. It is also worth pointing out the importance of the exotic remoteness that the Christian images would have had; for the natives, the Virgin icons did really come from afar, a world beyond, thus adding to their value and desirability.

In other instances, as when Velázquez began the conquest of Cuba in earnest, it would also be evident to the natives that the Christian icons were powerful allies to have in warfare: much more often than not, the Spaniards emerged victorious. The icons that Pané gifted to Guarionex in Hispaniola were received when a number of caciques in the Macorix-Magua and Maguana regions had already been subjugated by the force of Spanish. But recall that Guarionex received them in a context where he still had not agreed to an alliance with the rebel caciques and may well have initially accepted the Christian icons for political, strategic reasons. The destruction of the Christian idols in Guarícano did not take place until Guarionex was forced to join the rebellion. In contrast, cacique Comendador and the cacique of Cueybá received the Virgin Mary "cemís" of their own free will, not under pressure.

Upon Narváez's arrival sometime later, the Spaniards, egged on by Hojeda's surviving companions, attempted to recover the Virgin icon. It is instructive to pay close attention to the Spanish side of the negotiation. The Spaniards wanted the original Virgin Mary back; it was that and not the other icon that performed the miracle of saving them. Seemingly, it did make a difference that Hojeda's Virgin was the authentic miracle performer; again, this is an instance of how a demonstrable reputation and building legendary status increases value and desirability. That the Cueybá cacique refused to exchange his Virgin "cemí" for another one like her (but of unknown reputation) is just as illuminating, but there could be other reasons for refusing. It may have to do with the etiquette of gift giving: it was a gift from Hojeda to the cacique, which may have made the cacique duty-bound *not* to exchange it for another icon even when it was of similar form (both Virgins were sculptured in the Flemish style). But I believe the key reason for the cacique's refusing the exchange is the fact that he already had proof of the potency and power of Hojeda's Virgin; the other Virgin was an unknown quantity. His reaction to the predicament was, I think, rather predictable. He ran away to hide the Virgin, much in the same way that the chroniclers said the natives of Hispaniola and Puerto Rico hid their cemí icons from their rivals and competitors, Spanish and natives alike.

One fascinating aspect of both the Cueybá and Comendador accounts is that when the caciques accepted the Virgin icon, she was *already sculptured or painted* and imbued with numinous power (i.e., cemí-like). This provides two instances where the cemís (the Virgins), along with their attached legends (Mother of God, etc.) were accepted from strangers like Hojeda or the sailor. By "accepted" I do not imply that the legend (and biography) was understood by the natives in the same terms as the Catholic Hojeda (or the sailor) understood it, inasmuch as Hojeda or the sailor may have also understood it differently from an expert theologian from the Vatican. These accounts lend credibility to the argument made earlier in this book: that at least in parts of Hispaniola and Puerto Rico *foreign* powerful cemí icons could and were accepted by the natives into their "pantheon," and that they "sat" comfortably in the company of all the local (non-foreign) cemís gathered in the caney. In the long pre-Columbian history, how often did such exchanges of foreign religious artifacts occur? What effects would such exchanges have had in formulating the varying expressions of Taínoness? The rivals of cacique Comendador displayed their already-made cemís in combat (as icons *and* as spirits or ghostlike apparitions).

E. Magic, Miracles, and Fetishism: To Believe or Not to Believe

The case of cacique Comendador reveals other aspects of native idolatry—namely, their beliefs about magic, miracles, and fetishism. Initially the Spanish sailor accompanied by the Virgin would invariably defeat Comendador's neighboring rivals in battle. The Virgin cemí icon was worn on the chest, not unlike the personal cemí icons (necklace pendants, etc.) worn by the natives (Figure 29: b, d). In contrast to Hojeda's Virgin icon, whose miracle was to protect people from dire circumstances, for Comendador and his men the painted Virgin icon's power was clearly associated with victory in battle, regardless of whatever else the sailor taught them about the Mother of God. It can be inferred that they believed it was through her magic power that the miracle of consistent victories was achieved.

What happened after the Spanish sailor was rescued by a passing Spanish vessel is the best available description of the role that some cemí icons played in native-versus-native warfare. The new warfare strategies learned from the sailor (and backed by the Virgin Mary cemí) gave a military edge over Comendador's neighboring rival caciques, thus creating a destabilizing atmosphere. This was amply demonstrated in real combat when the sailor commanded Comendador's warriors to repeated victories. This situation also generated what bachiller Anciso (in Mártir's account) described as a bitter argument over who had the most potent icons. Again this recalls the quote from Oviedo and other chroniclers about how caciques in Hispaniola bragged about having the best and most powerful icons, and vindicates my argument that one cannot continually brag without concrete favorable results. At some point the cacique will have to provide the evidence that backs up his or her claims. This is precisely what transpired in the case of Comendador and his rivals. Bragging had to be resolved with proof.

The disputes of the two rival caciques were wielded in the battlefield. However, it would seem that the warfare strategies Comendador learned were not as effective as they might have been in the absence of the Spaniard. This assumption is supported only by the fact that battle confrontations continued and went unresolved; there was no clear victor. Probably the loss of life had led both caciques to resolve conflict using a different tactic. The scale of the confrontation was reduced and, in this instance, brought under ritual control through personal combats. It is reminiscent of the varying degrees of managing conflict, from personal matches all the way to full-scale battle reported for many societies worldwide (e.g., the Yanömamö of Venezuela-Guiana-Brazil).

It will be recalled that the challenge was to have one's own hands untied by the *magical* power of the cemí (on magic, see Graeber 2001:239–254). The pertinent details are: (1) the confrontation of the rival men, each with their protector cemí icon; (2) the invocation of the cemí to untie the ligatures; (3) the magical apparition of the cemí envisioned as a spirit or ghost; and (4) the miracle of the ropes ending up in the rival's hands, double-binding him. Taken at face value, and suspending my westernized disbelief and agnosticism, it is clear that all present claimed they "saw the Virgin" icon and "the native cemí" in action and performing the miracle. Enciso and then Mártir were equally accepting of the magical and miraculous events performed by the numinous Virgin and native cemís, only for them the cemís were personifications of the devil. It is not clear who wore or held the icon of the Virgin—the combatant or Comendador. In any case, either the static icon must be understood as having some kind of spiritual double or ghostlike reflection, or it was "seen" as having become physically disembodied and performing the acts described.

Most fascinating is the issue of disbelief, not coming from me as a westerner, but coming from the Comendador's rivals. A second challenge was requested by the Comendador's rivals because of *their disbelief.* There was a suspicion that trickery (falsehood) was involved. As David Graeber astutely noted, what is interesting about such magic tricks is precisely that they call for the suspension of belief: "One reason why anthropologists don't really like the word 'magic' is that it is too closely allied to self-conscious illusions and tricks. It is no coincidence that when most people in America think of 'magic' nowadays they think of men in tuxedos pulling rabbits out of hats. I am suggesting though that this is precisely what's interesting about it" (Graeber 2001:245).

Graeber then adds that it is best to conceptualize magic around two features:

> First of all, that it is not inherently fetishistic, in that it recognizes that the power to transform the world ultimately goes back to human intentions. That is, even if alienated forces or invisible spirits of one sort or another are involved, the action always begins with some human intention and ends with some tangible result. Second of all, it always involves a certain degree of skepticism, a hesitation, between stating that the power involved is something mysterious and extraordinary and that it is simply a matter of "social effects," which in some cases means simply being aware that power is some sort of scam, but that it does not make it any less real or significant [Graeber 2001:245–246].

Just as Graeber (2001:246) notes that Maori (New Zealand) informants hesitated between a theological and a magical source for the hidden *mauri,* the source of cemí potency is called into question by the indigenous Cubans. Finally, the point made by Graeber in his analysis of Claude Lévi-Strauss's *The Sorcerer and His*

Magic (on Kwakiutl [Kwakwak'waka] shamans) is that whether it is a trick or not is ultimately irrelevant.

> While curers (for instance) can hardly help but know that much of what they are doing is a stage illusion [a performance], they also think that since it *does* cure people, on some level, it must be true. So again tricks are of no significance. . . . Curers, genuine or not, are clearly powerful and influential people. It means that anyone watching a performance was aware that the person in front of them *might* be one whose power was based only in the ability to convince others that they had it. And that, it seems to me, opens the way for some possibly profound insights into the nature of social power [Graeber 2001:243–244; my emphasis].

I think Graeber's arguments are just as applicable in apprehending precisely what transpired during the ritual combats. Despite initial disbelief, the rivals were overwhelmed by the second *performance* of Comendador (and his combatants) and his Virgin cemí. But it is not quite that the rivals where overwhelmed; their version of the events is not known. Rather, what is known is the version Comendador told to Enciso. To paraphrase Graeber, Comendador, as the influential leader of those men who watched the ritual combat, was the person whose power rested on his ability to convince the audience. Had not the Virgin icon led them to victory countless times? Yes, she did lead them to victory. Thus, whether Comendador was embellishing the event is not the crucial point, but rather his *performance* in retelling the story to Enciso is. It ought to be remembered that this event was narrated for the benefit of Enciso, who was not a witness but who readily accepted Comendador's account (performance), one that reached all the way to Pope Leo X in Rome. And that is power!

21 Religious Syncretism and Transculturation
The Crossroads toward New Identities

The events described by Pané during his missionary work in Hispaniola (see section 19 C) represent two responses to the advent of Catholic religion and, especially, of Christian icons: clearly some natives of the Macorix region were receptive, for whatever reasons, to catechism; but those in the Guarícano settlement in Magua, once cacique Guarionex joined the rebellion, rejected catechism and set out to destroy the icons. Native acceptance versus resistance is thus the key process involved. Resistance and rejection (e.g., at Guarícano) do not require further in-depth analysis, but the processes that are implicated in acceptance, adoption, appropriation, assimilation, and so forth, require further attention, because these are at stake in the genesis of new identities in Cuba as well as the rest of the Caribbean islands. And in these processes, the physicality of iconography and the sculptures of aboriginal cemís, saints, and virgins are as important as the performances—ritual theater—enacted by humans.

As Pané (1999) provided no detailed accounts of how such acceptance worked in northeastern Hispaniola, the two examples above from eastern Cuba provide useful insights. The acceptance of the sculptured (by the cacique of Cueybá) or painted (by Comendador) Virgin is a first step toward acceptance. It is clear, at least to me, that both caciques had adopted the Virgin icons and internalized selected elements of the icon's personhood (who she was) and legend (her powers). The way in which the Virgin was made to confront the traditional Indo-Cuban cemís can best be interpreted as an addition to the ensemble of native cemí icons that both caciques must have had, albeit their novelty and demonstrated powers catapulted the Virgin icons to the forefront. While such adoption and integration seems to be made within the ideological and religious framework of the Cuban natives, it nevertheless still points to the selective incorporation of elements from a different religious tradition. Her face, body, and attire were unlike anything they had seen before. Yet the ease with which the two Virgin icons were adopted by natives in Cuba suggests that there was no stigma attached or barriers to the acceptance of foreign religious elements. There is no sense of pollution or bastardization of their religion. In short, the argument is that just as these caciques accepted, in their own terms, foreign or stranger Virgin Mary (imbued with cemí) icons, so they would also be open to accept other stranger or foreign religious icons from Hispaniola, the Bahamas, and other aboriginal societies of the Caribbean with whom they interacted. Of course, the opposite is not true: Catholic dogma considers the adoption of foreign religious icons as sinful, a bastardization and pollution of the pure and true faith.

The processes implicated in the Indo-Cuban examples recall what Melville Herskovits (1937a, 1937b; Stewart 1999:47) famously subsumed under the concepts of *acculturation* (the "melting pot" ideal) through *syncretism,* and what the eminent Cuban scholar Fernando Ortíz (1973, 1995; Stewart 1999:48) redefined as *transculturation* in the first half of the twentieth century. Although the definition of all three concepts has since evolved (see Brown 2003:44–45), their essence still refers to the question of how and why societies resist or adopt elements or entire complexes of new and foreign ideologies, practices, or material cultures. The dyad of rejection/acceptance ought to be thought of as the endpoints of a *continuum of strategies* rather than an "either/or" proposition. Through syncretism, societies are continually being transformed into different entities that nevertheless still selectively and contextually display echoes of their diverse, multiple heritages. David H. Brown, quoting Karl Reisman, provides these illuminating thoughts on syncretism:

> In producing syncretisms, creative agents "remodel" or "reshape" the forms of symbols to resemble as closely as possible *both the historical source and the forms current in the environment* ([Reisman 1970:]131; emphasis added [by Brown]). Any "form that is retained (new or old) is likely to be one that can be interpreted in several ways, as related to a number of traditions" ([Reisman 1970:]132). In other words, syncretisms may not merely represent old wine in new bottles or new wine in old bottles—that is, masking or transvaluation, respectively. The historically situated performances of agents creatively change the shape of the bottles [e.g., cemís or Virgin idols] themselves into new "creole" forms, which "resemble," but do not reduce to, their "multifarious sources." In Reisman's terms, Afro-Cuban organizations "took on" and "remodeled" the iconography, status rankings, and processional style of encountered colonial forms . . . as well as elements of the slaveholders' material culture [Brown 2003:45].

Such dynamic processes (syncretism, acculturation, transvaluation, masking, and transculturation) have been used in various ways to construct, sometimes engineer, individual, regional, and national identities. The ineluctable visibility of the Spanish (white) and African (black) heritages led to a construction of identities from the sixteenth century onward in which the "Indian" heritage had been minimized, if not erased, from official history by the emergent, politically dominant oligarchies. Phenotypes (biological and cultural) of black and white led to prejudiced, racist, and Eurocentric categorizations ranging from white peninsular and white Criollos to varying admixtures of black and white. The category of Criollo in the Hispanic-influenced Caribbean, unlike the Creole of English and French colonies, did not carry the same negative connotations, albeit both are white-Eurocentric constructs (see Arrom 1951; Stewart 1999). Through the second half of the twentieth century, the Indian heritage has gradually been reinstated in the (re)construction of identities (from personal to national), most particularly in the Spanish-speaking Caribbean (e.g., Pérez Fernández 1999; Portuondo Zúñiga 1999; Trincado 1997). The key question here is, first, whether the initial seeds of religious syncretism between Spanish Catholicism and aboriginal cemíism exemplified by the two Indo-Cuban cases survived and continued to evolve into modern times, and, if so, what is the evidence.

Fernando Ortíz rejected Herskovits's focus on assimilation, which at the time in the United States was a highly encouraged but ultimately utopian goal of the "melting pot," which was to be replaced in the 1990s by multiculturalism, which in turn is now being questioned again (Stewart 1999). Ortíz famously likened *Cubanidad* or *Cubanía* (i.e., "Cubanity," or what it means to be Cuban) to the traditional *ajiaco,* a stew of meatballs, vegetables, and ají pepper: "The characteristic thing about Cuba . . . is that since it is an *ajiaco,* its people are not a finished stew, but a constant [process of] cooking. . . . Hence the change of its composition, and [the fact] that *Cubanidad* has a different flavor and consistency depending on whether one tastes what is in the middle [of the pot], or at its surface, where the foods (*viandas*) are still raw, and the bubbling liquid still clear" (Ortíz, quoted in Stewart 1999:48; Stewart's clarifications in brackets).

In the 1990s Ortiz's culinary metaphor had been updated by performance artist Guillermo Gómez-Peña: "[The] bankrupt notion of the melting pot has been replaced by a model that is more germane to the times, that of the *menudo* chowder. According to this model, most of the ingredients do melt, but more stubborn chunks are condemned to float" (Gómez Peña, quoted in Stewart 1999:48).

Syncretism, as I see it, minimally refers to the processes by which separate religious ideologies and practices are amalgamated to form yet another distinct or separate coherent system. This is an important concept because it is all about *cultural mixture,* and debates around this concept underpin precisely the same ones raised in section 2 C in connection with Taíno (as a "pure," unmixed tradition) and Taínoness (a spectrum of social entities resulting from diverse cultural heritages and face-to-face interactions). Syncretism is a powerful concept in (re)constructing past Caribbean societies. For example, the centerpiece of Dominican archaeologist Marcio Veloz Maggiolo's (1976, 1977, 1980, 1985) rejection of Rouse's normative, homogenous (i.e., "pure") cultures rests on his concept of hybridization, albeit cushioned in the language of Marxism and historical materialism. Hybridization is, in this case, another way of bringing to the fore syncretism. Reniel Rodríguez Ramos's (2007) and my use of the term Taínoness implicitly alludes to syncretism as well as multilinear heritage (see section 2 C). I find Charles Stewart's (1999:40) deceptively simple description of syncretism, "an inquiry into cultural mixture," as the essence of its definition. But it still needs further conceptual fleshing out.

The above narrative of Catholic–native Cuban relations (via religious iconography and ritual) is precisely about cultural mixing, syncretism. But syncretism is a loaded concept that has had both negative and positive implications ever since Plutarch came up with the notion, the definition of which, since Roman times, has had many conceptual revisions (see Brown 2003:43-*passim*; Stewart 1999). To paraphrase Stewart (1999:57), most definitions of syncretism require the fusion of disparate and disharmonious elements that contravene the tenets of one or several of the "initial" religious systems. Carsten Colpe (in Stewart 1999) provided a veritable arsenal of analytical concepts for distinguishing syncretism and for comprehending its processes: synthesis, evolution, disintegration, absorption, amalgamation, equivalence, bricolage, and so on. "One might almost contemplate," writes Stewart (1999:58), "adopting a vocabulary of chemistry, where compounds, mixtures, and colloids are all objectively distinguishable . . . [but,] obviously, religions and cultures are too complex and fundamentally subjective phenomena to be tamed by objective analytical vocabularies, however subtle." Given the premise that there is no such thing as a pure culture or religion, an anthropology of syncretism "must comprehend how zones of purity and hybridity come into being"; its heuristic value exists in that it focuses attention on "accommodation, contest, appropriation, indigenization, and a host of other dynamic intracultural and intercultural transactions" (Stewart 1999:55). This is exactly the point made by David Brown in the quote above, where he used the shape and content of "bottles" as a metaphor to illustrate the process of syncretism.

Stewart (1999:57–58) argued that we should not be concerned with the issue of whether this or the other religion is or is not syncretic, as *all* religions are a mixture of different traditions. Instead, syncretism should: (1) study "the various arguments made for or against the notion of religious mixing"; (2) "be concerned with competing discourses over mixture, whether syncretic or asyncretic"; and whenever syncretism occurs (3) it should consider "the commentary and registered perceptions of actors as to whether amalgamation has occurred and whether this is good or bad," since a purely objective perspective "could never be sufficient." Of the three, of course, the last one is the most difficult to examine with only a recourse to sixteenth-century chronicles. Stewart (1999:58) suggests that scholars should proceed with the broadest definition of syncretism ("the combination of elements from two or more different religious traditions").

The previous analyses of the Virgins in the hands of Cuban natives followed the spirit of Stewart's methodological steps. They were examined as competing discourses over the nature of the Catholic and Indo-Cuban "mixture" and have explored how it may have been perceived from various perspectives: native-Spanish, native-native, and Spanish-Spanish, and one can at least imagine whether this initial syncretism was bad or good from these various perspectives (but with my personal bias toward understanding the natives' viewpoints). But the two Indo-Cuban examples are essentially snapshots framing short temporal spans. Because syncretism of any kind is an ongoing dynamic process, it stands to reason that gazing at a longer temporal span would provide greater insights into its varying trajectories and social effects. How did this initial syncretism, made largely in Indo-Cuban native terms, unravel through time?

I will not dwell on the now well-known fact that for the next 450 years the natives (Indios), not just in Cuba, were excised from history and denied having any contribution to the formation of an emerging Cuban society. The myth of the rapid and total extinction spurred by the dominant white oligarchy led to identities that acknowledged only the multiple and diverse African heritage represented by slaves and their descendants, in large measure because "blackness" was all too visible for the white class to sweep under the carpet of history; all shades (mixtures) between whiteness and blackness were recognized, but on a sliding scale of white (positive) to black (negative) racist values. This history has been critically analyzed by a plethora of scholars with far greater insights and detailed knowledge than I could do justice to in this section.

The analyses of the Vírgen de la Caridad del Cobre by Olga Portuondo Zúñiga (1995) and María Nelsa Trincado (1997), and of the Vírgen de Guadalupe de El Caney de San Luis by Rolando Pérez Fernández (1999) present tantalizing evidence for syncretism originating in the kind of cemíism illustrated in the case of the cacique Comendador. The icon of the Virgen de la La Caridad del Cobre (Figure 35: b) probably arrived from Illescas in Spain sometime between 1599 and 1613, nearly a century after the cacique Comendador's events in 1511 (Arrom 1971; Trincado 1997). It was first the local Virgin patron of the copper-mining settlement of Las Minas del Real (now El Cobre) not far from Santiago, then the administrative center of Oriente Province (see Figure 28). Soon, though, a legend developed of how the statuette of the Virgin appeared miraculously over the sea that with time (up to present day) has spun several versions. The earliest written documents of the legend date to 1701 (now lost), with two additional documents from 1766 and 1783 that include consequent editorial changes (Portuondo Zúñiga 1995:30; see Trincado 1995). This Virgin is today a symbol of Cubanía ("Cubanity"), but in the early seventeenth century the cult was more localized and in the hands of the Indios of the Oriente Province (see Figure 28).

The essence of the Vírgen de la Caridad legend is as follows. The Virgin icon appeared to two native Indios, Rodrigo and Juan de Hoyos, and to a ten-year-old black boy named Juan Moreno. All three were residents of Barajagua La Vieja, a settlement of Indios located inland and southwest of Nipe Bay (see Figure 28). They had left Barajagua to gather salt destined for the mining town of El Cobre.

As they were at sea, a storm gathered and soon turned violent. Amid the waves the three "Juanes" (as they are traditionally called) saw an object floating that turned out to be the actual icon of the Virgin (not an apparition as in most other Marian legends, such as that of the Vírgen de Guadalupe de Tepeyac, Mexico). They also found a floating wood plaque that announced the Virgin's name (de la Caridad, or Charity). They then prayed for her help, and the Virgin enveloped them with a shining light protecting them from the storm; all the while, the weather began to calm and the boat miraculously eased its way to the coast. The icon was first taken to Barajagua, where a chapel was built by the Indios. The Virgin, however, disappeared mysteriously several times from the chapel only to miraculously reappear. The Indios took this to mean that the Virgin wanted to be moved elsewhere and, with sadness, the Virgin was moved to the mining town of El Cobre. Eventually, as the Virgin's cult spread, it was moved to the regional capital city of Santiago, where it remains today. The story of the movements of the Virgin icon as her cult gained popularity, of course, hides a process of appropriation by the Church and Spanish civil hierarchy, removing the Virgin from Barajagua, a town dominated and controlled by Indios.

The key ingredients of syncretism proposed by Olga Portuondo Zúñiga (1995) and María Nelsa Trincado (1997) revolve around a number of observations of varying merits. First is the fact that two Indios and an Afro-Cuban child were the protagonists of the legend and, second, the three boys were residents of a small settlement whose population was almost entirely composed of Indios. It was thus a cult initiated by Indios and Afro-Cubans (freed and enslaved) in the largely Indio town of Barajagua. The authors point to some intriguing features. Although the icon seems to have in fact come from Illescas (between Madrid and Toledo), there are parts of the icon that appear to be of local manufacture (e.g., the head is made of a vegetable paste and is painted over; Figure 35). Both of the two authors indicate that by this late date (early 1600s) the religion of the Indios or Indo-Cubanos must have already been substantially syncretized: aborigines from Yucatán (i.e., post-classic/colonial Maya), from the coast of northern South America, and from other regions had been enslaved or indentured to labor in the Cuban fields, especially in the copper mines. In spite of this cultural mixture, what both authors point to as specifically aboriginal Indio syncretism (i.e., of Taíno heritage) are the conceptual similarities shared between the Virgin and one of the cemís of Hispaniola. Pané (1999) stated that there was a cemí that had five names: Attabeyra Yermao Guácar Apito Zuimaco. Pané (1999:3–4) also said that Attabeyra was the "mother" of a high-ranking masculine cemí called Yocahú Guamá Bagua Maorocoti, who "is in heaven and is immortal, and that no one can see him and that he has a mother." José Juan Arrom (1975:47) translated the first name, Attabeyra, as "Mother (atté) of the Lake Waters (itabón)" and speculates that Guácar (wá-kar) may mean "Moon" or "menstruation." Arrom concludes that at least these names suggest a "feminine deity" (her other three names have not been deciphered). The latter cemí personage is translated by Arrom (1975: 20–21) as the "Manioc (*yuca*) Lord (*-hú*) of the Ocean (*bagua*)" and "Without (*ma-*) Grandfather (*órocoti*)." Elsewhere I have argued that it is possible that his first name is *not* Yocahú but, following Alfonso de Ulloa's original Italianized transcription (1571) of Pané's (1974 [1494–1497]) *Relación*, it could be *Luku-* or *Loko-hú*, in which case it would mean "Person (*loko*) Lord (*-hú*)"—that is, "Person-Lord of the Ocean" (Oliver 1998).

The allusion to a "Mother of the Lake Waters" cemí who is the mother of the high-ranked masculine cemí personage who also lords over or comes from the waters is taken by Portuondo Zúñiga and Trincado as a strong point for the adoption of a Virgin Mary icon who is the Mother of God and also is linked to the waters. Syncretism came about because of the shared features of mother and water. I am less convinced that this necessarily constitutes proof of a uniquely Taínoan contribution, as the same notions of waters and motherhood invested in icons can be found in many parts of the world, including African and Afro-Cuban icons. We do not know how Hojeda's Virgin icon was interpreted by the cacique at Cueybá, but we do know that the painted Virgin held by Comendador was strongly linked to war and had, as far as can be judged, no bearing on water or motherhood. The Attabeyra example was also cited by Portuondo Zúñiga and Trincado as possible evidence of the syncretic processes that led to the adoption of the Virgin of Guadalupe (more on this image below). One also must be careful in drawing analogies with legends and biographies of cemís specific to the Macorix-Maguá region in Hispaniola.

Trincado (1997) also points out that the cult of this Virgin led to replications of her icon by *eremitas,* or *ermitaños* (i.e., hermits), who typically lived in isolation and in small structures that were both their residence and chapel. Trincado (1997) points to documents purporting that the eremitas devoted to the Virgin of the Caridad (a replica of the original) were discovered in the remote caves in the Sierra Maestra highlands. She argues that because worship in caves was also an aboriginal practice, syncretism must have taken place. But again, worship in caves is just as true of Catholic and Orthodox hermits in the Mediterranean as it is in Europe in general.

I am not arguing that syncretism did not take place, or that there are no aboriginal religious elements of cemíism, but that the demonstration or proof is not conclusive. These are just possible points of coincidence that *may* be indicative of syncretism. If scholarly research is to disentangle elements of the cult, legend, and iconography of the Vírgen de la Caridad de El Cobre, it will inevitably turn into a frustrated exercise unless every single step of the syncretic process is exhaustively (ethnographically) documented: that gap between 1511 and the early 1600s is too vast, especially with the influx of so many other Amerindian and Old World peoples into this region. In sum, as I commented earlier, following the strands to a particular "pure" source of religious belief, practice, and materiality (iconography) leads the scholar to adopting for analysis a conceptual approach like that of chemistry—of figuring out how to objectively disentangle compounds, mixtures, colloids, and so forth; or how to define the ingredients of a stewing ajiaco, to use Ortíz's culinary metaphor. As Charles Stewart (1999:58) cautioned, religion is far too complex to apprehend it with such utopic objectivity. To comprehend where zones of aboriginal "purity" and "hybridity" come into being requires, as I have insisted, much more ethnohistoric or ethnographic documentation for the relevant period. What can be said with certainty is that after some eighty to one hundred years of colonialism, a new Indio identity had emerged—one that is at once a conscious self-designation (by Indios themselves) and imposed by the colonial elite. The construction of Indio no doubt has multiple sources, but it also could have emerged only in opposition to other categories created by the colonial experience (e.g., white, black, *Criollo, Mestizo,* etc.).

The other case, that of the cult of the Vírgen de Guadalupe of El Caney de San Luis, just northeast of Santiago, in many ways parallels the arguments wielded for the Vírgen de La Caridad del Cobre (Fernández Pérez 1999). The cult was introduced from Mexico to Cuba, with the first icon of the Virgin taken to Santiago in 1664. El Caney was constituted as an Indio community in the sixteenth century. The Indios of El Caney found out about the Amerindian origin of the Vírgen de Guadalupe of Tepeyac, Mexico (she appeared in 1531 to an Indio: Juan Diego Cuauhtlatoatzin). With such an Amerindian origin, the Indios of El Caney adopted the Vírgen de Guadalupe cult as their own. The official cult in the parish of El Caney was that of San Luis, for which there was a church. By 1690 a small chapel dedicated to the Vírgen de Guadalupe was erected by the Indios next to the "big" church of San Luis de El Caney. By 1835 the city councilors, all Indios, had requested that the Virgin be relocated to "the big parochial church" and displayed prominently, as befitted the "great Lady whom this town had always regarded for Patroness Protector of all the Indios" (1838 document, cited in Fernández Pérez 1999:66). The ecclesiastical authorities in Santiago permitted the relocation but, as Fernández (1999:67) pointed out, with an air of prepotency and with disregard to a variety of petitions made by the Indio councilors—specifically, that the Vírgen de Guadalupe be placed in a lateral altar rather than in the central altar, where the icon of San Luis remained. "As can be appreciated from this episode," says Fernández, "the popular religiosity of these natives was neither taken into account (barely meriting a certain disdainful tolerance by the authorities [in Santiago]) nor were they given any power to decide for themselves in the affairs that directly affected them" despite the fact that in 1821 "a Royal Decree had proclaimed the equality of all free persons born or resident in the Spanish colonies" (Fernández Pérez 1999:67). The old native chapel was demolished by the authorities so as to give the "big" church a clear view from the plaza.

By the last decade of the 1700s the thirst for land ownership by the dominant white peninsular and white Criollo oligarchy (with whom Church authorities were identified) had become critical. In theory, a vast swath of the rural land in Oriente and Cuba was held in ownership by the Crown. Such lands were called *tierras realengas* (royal lands), and any freed subject of the Crown could reside and settle there as long as it was cultivated or kept in production. Between 1758 and 1796 a barrage of lawsuits inundated the courts as a result of illicit and dubious encroachments on the Indios' rural settlements and farmsteads, coupled with accusations of sedition, which resulted in Indian rebellions against the oligarchs, not just in El Caney but throughout the region. By the 1840s, a few years after the Vírgen de Guadalupe was moved to the marginal altar, King Charles IV, having received complaints "from those natural Indians," intervened with a series of instructions and decrees that, in Fernández Pérez's (1999:67) words: "would finally lead to the dispossession by the colonial authorities of the lands held by the community, under the pretext that the aboriginal [Indian] race was extinguished; and likewise in the subsequent abolition of the Indian *Ayuntamiento* [town council], whose foundation went as far back as 1629 . . . from that time [1850] the community identity with Indio would begin to disappear, melting into the great stream of national identity. A clear symptom of this is the generalized adoption of the Vírgen de la Caridad del Cobre, Patroness of Cuba."

Regardless of how many or how few elements of cemíism can be identified in this last case, what does matter is that both Virgins were held as the key symbols of Indio identity and solidarity, and at least the Vírgen de Guadalupe de El Caney was held in stark contrast and opposition to the icon of San Luis, expressing quite blatantly the marginated social and political position held by all those who were seen by others as Indios (often in a deprecatory sense) and those who proudly identified themselves with their "Indianness." The Vírgen de Guadalupe is thus wielded out in the struggle for respect and identity, for fairness and humanity, against oppression and abuse of power, clearly implicit in the subordinated position that this icon held in relation to San Luis, who represented the interests and impositions of the dominating white class. These two case studies make one pause and think there are some universal features that are distinctive of the ideological struggles and "war of religions" where icons are engaged, because seen in its most irreducible structural relation it is precisely what had led to the ritual competition and battles between cacique Comendador and his rival; it is at the heart of why native (Taínos) stole one another's cemís or sought to control those that they thought would bring power and thus protection to them.

Although, as I have said, the strands leading from these Marian cults to aboriginal cemíism (and Taínoness) as it was in pre-Columbian to early Spanish contact (1490s–1510s) are still difficult to isolate, there are other kinds of evidence that point to native heritage. Manuel Rivero de La Calle (University of Havana) and

Milan Pospisil (Yale University) as well as Richard Gates (1954) have conducted bioanthropological studies among the communities of Yateras (Figure 28), north of Guantánamo, in the late 1960s (Pospisil 1971; Rivero de La Calle 1966:55–60; 1978). Although the studies are based on somatic features, hemoglobin tests, and anthropometric measurements, rather than DNA, the statistical and qualitative results strongly favor an Indo-Cuban (aboriginal, Amerindian) population that is significantly different from the rest of the population in Cuba. The studies also point to a strong degree of endogamy, given the pattern of inherited pathologies and other somatic features that almost certainly have a genetic basis. The collected genealogies of the Yateras region inhabitants (e.g., Tiguabo settlement), along with other historical documents, show that some (e.g., with surnames such as Rojas and Ramírez) had emigrated from El Caney in the 1750s (Fernández Pérez 1999:65; Rivero de La Calle 1978:154–155). Rivero (1996:59) points out that the Rojas surname in Yateras, Tiguabo, San Andrés, and El Caney is ultimately derived from Manuel Rojas, a nephew of the conquistador Diego de Velázquez (1510–1520s), who had natives in encomienda as well as slaves (hence they adopted the master's surname), or in the case of the surname Ramírez, the source is traced to Bishop Miguel Ramírez (1528), who was designated "Protector of the Indians." Obviously, the bioanthropological studies of the 1960s–1970s did not have the sophisticated technologies that are available today, and thus can best be treated as encouraging possibilities of ancient, native heritage lines. These connections will require additional research, albeit such studies would be difficult, given all the ethical implications that any study connecting genetics to social and cultural identity has, especially in regard to potential redefinitions of "Indio" or "Indo-Cuban," and given that apparently many of these Indio communities have gradually disappeared.

The other arena to further elucidate the question of heritage and ancient aboriginal cultural ancestries lies squarely in archaeology. The Cuban authors cited in this section repeat ad nauseam the large number of archaeological sites with evidence of pre-Columbian Taíno and European assemblages, and rightly so (e.g. Domínguez 1991). I mentioned earlier the case of Los Buchillones in Ciégo del Ávila (see Graham et al. 2000; Pendergast 1997; Pendergast et al. 2001, 2002) as an instance of a native settlement persisting into the mid-1600s that retained what can only be regarded as a Taínoan aboriginal material culture, ranging from types of house structure to the portable artifacts, particularly the ubiquitous cemí icons engraved in a variety of items, including anthropomorphic figurines (Figure 34). The paraphernalia that are most likely related to cemíism (and Taínoness) at Los Buchillones strongly indicate a resistance to syncretism with Christian, African, and other Amerindian religious iconography (e.g., colonial Maya immigrants); however, if there was any move toward syncretism, it has most certainly remained invisible in the archaeological record. This site alone, and assuming that the date range (A.D. 1295–1655) obtained from the wood beams of the house reflects the actual age range of the occupation (see Pendergast et al. 2001), strongly argues for the continuity of natives and the native way of life (Taínoness) from pre–Spanish contact times to well into the Spanish colonial period. This site was occupied at the time when the cult of the Vírgen de la Caridad del Cobre began to emerge (early 1600s).

The village to which the Vírgen del Cobre was taken, Barajagua La Vieja, has archaeological remains that span the period before and following the Spanish contact. It was excavated by José Guarch Delmonte (cited in Portuondo Zúñiga 1995; Trincado 1997), but I have not been able to obtain the reports. Many more sites in the Maniabón Hills, Banes, Mayarí, Bayamo, Baracoa, Guantánamo, and Santiago areas in the Oriente Province have yielded plenty of sites straddling the Spanish contact period, for which there are generally few published references (e.g., for recent references, see the journal *El Caribe Arqueológico,* issues from 1995 to 2006). One of the problems of the reports I have read is that a good number of them describe the assemblages in typological terms in order to define each "pure" population (i.e., what is aboriginal versus Spanish or Old World). Their coexistence in strata or contexts does suggest, of course, interaction (exchange, trade, etc.) with different degrees of intensity and frequency. But what the coexistence of such a mixture implies in terms of identities, social dynamics, and politics is not as well explored (or published). It is assumed, with good reason, that such findings imply that syncretism and transculturation are present or eventually will take place, but the content of the processes involved in syncretism and transculturation have been neglected. It is not enough to assume or to note syncretism; the process and the materials that document it need to be analyzed and described in relation to what they can inform about social, political, and religious arenas where the syncretic and anti-syncretic processes are at play in the construction of new identities, such as Indio, Mestizo, Criollo, Negro, Indo-Cubano, Afro-Cubano, and so forth. The same critique applies to other Greater Antillean islands (but see Deagan 1995, 2004; Deagan and Cruxent 2002).

One way archaeologists can approach the data to build the evidence that interests me in this book is by focusing on precisely what is happening to the native religious icons and iconography (art style) vis-à-vis those of Christian or Afro-Caribbean authorship. When did the native cemí icons stop being produced in favor of adopted or locally crafted Virgins or other Christian imagery? When did the personal body adornments depicting cemí icons (e.g., pendants, statuettes) become accompanied by and then substituted with, for example, tin medallions, pins, or *estampas* (cards with images) of the Vírgen del Cobre? What can be deduced when both Christian icons and Indian cemís are found together or in the same contexts? In what ways do local (native, popular) manufactures of Christian icons reflect elements of continuity with the official Church dogma? Are the deviations reflective of syncretism? Although it is evident that aborigines (e.g., Cueybá) and later Indios (Barajagua) constructed shrines (*adoratorios*) and chapels, there is still a notable absence of archaeological data on such structures. It is important to find and focus excavations on these to determine when and how *both* native cemís and Christian iconography and paraphernalia occupied the same space, as we know it did in 1511. Such archaeological excavations would contribute a plethora of new insights about ritual behavior that Enciso's and Mártir's 1514 accounts ignored. What happened to these native shrines, chapels, and their religious paraphernalia over time? When and why were native icons replaced by Christian forms? How did these chapels differ from domestic household shrines? How did village shrines or chapels compare and relate to other loci of religious performance, such as the caves later used by the hermits? Burials are critical spaces of the analysis of syncretism and anti-syncretism, because icons, votive offerings, interment practices, and place- ment of burials in relation to one another (social markers of class, age, gender, etc.) and in relation to shrines or chapels can provide invaluable data as to what sorts of social-religious behaviors and attitudes can be inferred from the mix of aborigi- nal, Christian, African (black Creole), and other Amerindian groups. Such stud- ies have already produced fascinating results at Tipu, a post-classic/colonial Maya site in Belize (Graham 1991). Much can be learned by comparing the Caribbean situation with Hispanic-Amerindian "Mission Archaeologies" across Hispanic- occupied (or -conquered) territories in the Americas (see Graham 1998:49–52).

It is not enough to know that, for example, at Chorro de Maíta (ca. 1000– 1550s) a Spaniard's detached skull was buried at the feet of a Taíno native, or that some of the natives had offerings made of tin cylinders or tin plaques via Spanish trade (Cooper et al. 2008; Martinón-Torres et al. 2007), or that Majolica wares intermingled with Pueblo Viejo (Chican Ostionoid) aboriginal ceramics, and cow and pig bones were mixed with native *hutía* (a rodent of the Capromydae family) bones, and then say that this is syncretism in the works (Rivero de La Calle et al. 1989; Valcárcel Rojas 1999, 2002a, 2002b). We need to focus on the processes of syncretism, the spectrum of strategies that range from anti-syncretism (that which is rejected or resisted) at one end to syncretism (e.g., adoption, mimicry, transcul- turation, etc.) at the other. The cases of Cueybá, of cacique Comendador in Cuba, and the events at Guarícano in Hispaniola or the sale of areíto icons as trophies of war (by Spaniards) in Puerto Rico provide glimpses of the endpoints of such a continuum of strategies, but archaeology is what is now left to fill the gaps in the record.

I wish to conclude this section by reiterating what I think is a very impor- tant point. There is something of a profound loss in cultural diversity (in blatant analogy to biodiversity) when the physical and visible symbols and materials of re- ligious beliefs and practices are gone forever. As I read the cases of the Cuban Vir- gins of Charity and Guadalupe, the most striking feature is the absence, or the loss, of the cohoba ceremony—the inhalation of the magic hallucinogenic substances that allow ordinary human beings to invoke, dialogue, and negotiate with the cemís. The other notable feature is that from the mid-seventeenth century onward there were no longer images and icons made that figure the cemí personages that were revealed through the cohoba, whose physicality and formal features visually expressed Taínoness. The diverse cast of cemí personages had been curtailed or replaced by a different-looking cast of Christian personages. None of the Christian cemí Virgins or saints were to function as the cemíified ancestors of caciques or leaders; all of these are significant losses.

Even if the shift was at first superficial (such as Mary, the Mother of God of Cueybá or that of Comendador) and regarded as another, albeit quite different-looking cemí icon in the 1510s, by the middle of the seventeenth century the choices of ritual performance and paraphernalia were quite different from those of the cacique of Cueybá or Comendador. If at first these were not always imposed upon natives by the conquistadors (e.g., as in the cases of Hojeda and the anonymous sailor), I have little doubt that as the century progressed, Christian iconography was the only choice available to the Indios, as much as saints and Virgins (as *orichas,* or Lucumí deities) were also the only choice available to the African slaves and their descendants. (Of course, in regard to Afro-Caribbean societies I am simplifying it here; see Brown [2003] for a detailed, nuanced discussion). Still, the native resistance did go on for much longer than what was assumed by the official histories in the Hispanic Caribbean, as the site of Los Buchillones suggests, but ultimately colonialism would create the Indio; his or her social and religious identities would be transformed beyond the recognition of any of their pre-Columbian ancestors.

PART VI
Conclusions

22 Final Remarks

This study is in many ways an extended essay. In its original Latin sense, the noun *exagĭŭm* means "weight." Its verb form ("to assay") refers to the action and effects of probing and recognizing (i.e., weighting, evaluating, testing) something before using it (*Diccionario de la Real Academia de la Lengua Española* 1992:596). As Karen Sykes (2005:8) noted, "the essay continues to find full expression" in anthropology, "because the form continues to utilize the skeptical stance to the best advantage of making a critical contribution to wider knowledge. *An essay is a try at explanation—no more and no less—and that can be quite enough*" (my emphasis).

Such as they are, the conclusions I have reached in various sections of this book are an attempt at explanation. The book began with a healthy skepticism about currently held notions of Taíno, cemí, cemíism, and of the individuals and persons involved. The explanations and conclusions present a logical argument based on the analysis of Spanish ethnohistorical documents but also informed by archaeological data and anthropological theory. Certainly these conclusions will need to be independently tested by further archaeological research that for now is not as rich as I would wish, especially for the set of cemí artifacts (idols and other potent icons) that forms the material evidence of this work. On the other hand, I am encouraged that the theory on caciques and cemí idol interactions (agent-patient relations and personhood) presented here were productive and generative in a Popperian sense. They provide a baseline and coherent argument against which future archaeological research on native religions and their material correlates can be assessed and, hopefully, will stimulate an all-out debate about how we, as western scholars, think about the natives as human beings and as agents. The arguments are constructed so as to force us to think about the consequences stemming from the relationships of humans with powerful and potent religious artifacts, and finally, on how these relations contribute to the construction and deconstruction of Taínoness as well as new identities, such as the Indios of Spanish colonial times. I have purposely skirted the economic dimensions of the analyses and instead focused on the political-religious dimension that ideologically underpins economy. However, the economic implications are silently implicit in much of this work.

In order to identify the peoples, agents, and actors engaged in cemíism and cemí idolatry, I started with a critical overview of the cultures constructed through archaeological and ethnohistoric research, leading to the conclusion that the Taíno people and culture as a "pure," homogeneous, and identifiable entity was an illusory, idealistic construction emerging from normative approaches in culture history. Instead, I have unabashedly borrowed Reniel Rodríguez Ramos's (2007) notion of Taínoness to express the spectrum, even mosaic, of societies that the notion of "a Taíno people" (e.g., Rouse 1992) could not express. The Taínoness that characterizes some of the native populations and societies of the Caribbean, I argued, arises from multiple and diverse lines of heritage, and its cultural contents are, at any time, contested and negotiated and always in the process of becoming. This dynamic process of contestation and negotiation found resonance with the concepts of syncretism and transculturation when later I analyzed the impact of Hispanic Christianity and its iconography on native cemíism. I have made an effort not to use the classifier "Taíno" (not an easy thing to do) in my discussions, in large measure to accomplish one principal objective: to instill in the reader the idea that the focus of analysis is not on the *labels* that social groups could be given but rather on the nature of the *relations* among various social groups and their material cultures, specifically cemí idols and icons. For this reason, I stuck with the use of "natives," "Indians," and their geographic locus (of Hispaniola, etc.) or "Taínoans." The overview of the archaeological record, taking as an example Puerto Rico, supports the notion of the plurality of ancestries and the diversity of expressions that gave rise to Taínoness. Taínoness, I concluded, is expressed variably among the inhabitants of the Greater Antilles. Having discussed Taínoness as a variable spectrum of peoples and cultures, the analysis of the caciques and their cemí idols (iconography) could proceed within a framework that is focused on the dynamics of individual agents and patients: caciques and their cemí idols.

In this book I focused on caciques and their interaction with idols and other icons and things imbued with cemí supernatural potency. I strived to make sense out of the web of interactions spun by native rulers in eastern Hispaniola (Caiçimú-Higüey), Puerto Rico (Boriquén), and further afield in Cuba and the Lesser Antilles. I addressed the questions of what motivated and sustained the web through which cemí idols and potent objects flowed and humans interacted. I closely examined the nature of the face-to-face (agent-patient) interactions between human beings and cemís. In doing so, I have taken what I think is a fresh, new outlook for the Caribbean on how to fruitfully approach and appraise these interactions. I particularly made it a point—intentionally repeated ad nauseam—that the underlying nature and significance of the cemís can only be understood in terms of the various social contexts in which human beings and these idols engaged as patients and agents, and doing so by positing that both the artifacts (cemís) and human persons are conceived not just as individual entities, but also as dividual and partible. Cemí idols, like people, are multiauthored and exhibit different context-dependent natures (multinatural); they have properties of personhood that are owed, attached, or extended to and incorporated by other human and nonhuman beings that are also dividual and partible. Personhood and identity are not all about dividuality: individuality is also displayed in, for example, their names or unique biographies. These human–cemí idol relationships are framed in a worldview where nature *is* multinatural and where other beings and things are animated (an animistic cosmos). This approach I have taken for analysis and interpretation is thus a departure from current Caribbean scholarship, where the western and modern views of peoples and other beings and things are still largely anchored on the premise that natives and their material culture are indivisible and individually conceived.

In the course of this study I moved from the very intimate relations between a human and the first manifestation of cemí in nature to the broader network of extended relationships that humans had with them, focusing on inheritance, bequests, and gift exchanges with foreign and stranger caciques, and also the theft of cemís. I have concluded that cemí idols are dividual persons and do have personal yet partible identities that are partly defined by the string of caciques ("owners") entrusted with them; the idols have names, titles, and ranks, and they also acquire biographies and reputations around which legends are built. And all of these features of identity and personhood, including the legends and biographies that justify their prestige, are created and re-created—composed, decomposed, and recomposed—in the web of relationships with equally partible and dividual human beings (caciques, shamans, etc.). I have shown that effective governance is not in the hands of caciques alone but could only be implemented in concert with a panoply of potent cemís, as idols and as spirits.

Inevitably, the analysis of this socially driven interaction, the web through which beings (human or otherwise) and animated things circulate or flow, led me to study the most fundamental of the driving force of sociality, which rests upon the principle of reciprocity, of gift giving and taking. Cemí idols of various types were examined in light of how they, as dividual, partible entities—as persons—were given and taken, and explored what such exchange meant (values, motivations). The issues of the alienability and inalienability, of "keeping-for-giving" and "giving-for-keeping," in regard to cemí idols, were confronted against the ethnohistoric data and nurtured by current theoretical discussions in sociocultural anthropology emerging largely from Melanesian and Polynesian ethnographic analyses. I pointed out that when seemingly inalienable possessions (a powerful three-pointer or an areíto, for example) were exchanged, they most likely could be gifted, because regardless of physical separation they would always retain in their personhood a quality or feature shared or derived from the originators (the donors). In this study I concluded that because of the dividual, partible nature of the agents and patients (caciques and idols), there were circumstances in which seemingly inalienable icons were in fact gifted, and that these often also involved both exchanging names (guaitiao) between caciques, and the heroic genealogies of caciques and their ancestors chanted in areítos. Taking a clue from Alfred Gell's distributed person and Marshall Sahlins's encompassing, heroic persons (kings, chiefs, and their cemís), I suggested that "extendability" perhaps is a more productive conceptual property than the segregating character of the inalienable versus alienable dichotomy. This concept is not too far from the notion of "*galactic*" relations proposed by Michael Heckenberger (2005, 2008) to describe the extended configuration of chiefly power and relations across the Xingú landscape in Brazil and also into their ancient history via ancestors.

I identified the all-stone and fiber/wood and (elbow) stone collars as a distinct and complex class of powerful chiefly objects/cemís that circulated only within a tightly knit set of related (via intermarriage) caciques who were geographically circumscribed to Caiçimú-Higüey and Boriquén to areas of the Virgin Islands—involving bridal exchanges that had deep historical roots, going back at least four and a half centuries and possibly more. Such objects were evidently not traded outside these closely related chiefly lineages and polities. I also argued that some cemí idols, specifically the ancestor cemís (cotton idols, skulls in baskets, or stone heads), would rarely circulate in reciprocal exchange systems and hence were more likely to remain within the descent group of the cacique. By way of contrast, of all the icons analyzed here, the guaízas, or face masks, that embody the living soul of the cacique were the ones selected for far-flung exchanges among foreign caciques. The guaízas and the three-pointed cemís were most informative in regard to the complicated relations between Greater Antillean and Lesser Antillean leaders and caciques. In late pre-Columbian times the extent of the guaízas could be followed to Anguilla–St. Martin and reflected a web of relations that orbited toward Greater Antillean Taínoness. Beyond, into the Windward Islands, the same icons could have been captured by belligerent societies that the Spaniards lumped as "Caribs." Alternatively, I also suggested that some of the large three-pointed stones or shell guaízas reached the Windwards through exiled natives who brought them as they fled the battles and slave raids that raged in the Greater Antilles, and who sought and received asylum in islands such as Guadeloupe, Carriacou, or La Dèsirade.

For me, one of the fascinating aspects of the circulation and flow of cemí idols was to discover how closely it parallels the exchange of brides/women and the ritual of the reciprocal name exchanges (guaitiao) between caciques. The women offered as brides, the names of caciques offered in guaitiao pacts, and the cemí idols (as persons) are partible components of personhood that are reciprocally exchanged to establish bonds of alliance and cooperation. The motivations for giving or taking cemí idols/persons are not substantially different from those for exchanging women (as brides) and names (guaitiao) between groups. I concluded that to exchange one's name is to give to another a part of one's identity at both a personal level and a group level (the name is that of the cacique's lineage). To give one's sister, daughter, or niece is not just a personal exchange of brides, but one that takes on her descent group as a whole body—that is, as a fractal person: the betrothal is never just between two persons, but is also between two corporate kin groups, each as distinct bodies (persons), linked as affine. To bequest or give cemí idols, or guaízas, also entails giving and receiving dividual persons, parts of which remain attached to their original string of trustees, but that also provide new opportunities for developing relations, the stuff of which generates legends, biography, and, in a word, history. I also showed that the same persons, the cemís and women, are sources of conflict as much as cooperation: they both could be and were stolen or kidnapped, therefore leading to the rupture of the principle of reciprocity. Cemís and women were agents and patients, in promoting factional competition and conflict as much as in building cooperation and alliances.

I have also compared the ancestor stone heads with the guaízas, a contrast that can be aptly characterized as vertical/temporal versus horizontal/spatial relations. The skeletal stone-head cemís as well as the cotton idols and human skulls placed in higüeros involve the connections and veneration of the living to cemíified ancestors, hence they are about vertical relations, genealogical history, and memories. Instead, the guaízas involve connections between living humans (caciques, leaders) who, in addition, are not initially connected by descent or by marriage: they are initially gifted to strangers, such as Columbus or to "native-others" in the Caribbean. I concluded that the emphasis in guaíza exchanges is not on the past (ancestors, genealogical-historical depth) but on the present and the future (i.e., allies to be), with the emphasis being on spatially and socially *expansive* relations, hence they are horizontal.

In examining the cemí-cacique relationships, one principal concern was in clarifying how the religious beliefs invested in these icons and on the cacique translated into political power and everyday action. It became clear that cemí idols are equally engaged in the making and breaking of caciques and cacicazgos. The key points made were that all cemí idols are powerful and numinous from conception, but that their reputation as effective agents (beneficial social production and reproduction) is not necessarily isomorphic with that of their human partner. Pairing potent cemís with powerful humans—those with high rank, status, seniority, or antiquity—was the most effective combination. In other words, there is symmetry of power between high-ranked caciques and high-ranked, legendary cemí idols that allows for effective negotiations and desirable outcomes. But if the cacique was newly installed, then the relationship was asymmetrical in regard to power. Only time and experience could shift the power relations to a more symmetrical stance.

The battles of Higüey and the Rebellion of the Caciques in Puerto Rico provided the scenarios of crisis in which to evaluate the shape(s) that the relationships took between cemí idols, other powerful objects, allied caciques, and Spaniards (enemies). The context is one of war, battle, skirmishes, and raids, and of strife, misery, and death. Such is the time when religious faith is always put to its ultimate test. The division of loyalties among native caciques, initially motivated by older, pre-Hispanic conflicts and enmities, prevented a united resistance front against the Spanish conquistadors and ultimately contributed to the collapse of Taínoness and of traditional ways of living and interacting.

These battles provided details of the relationships that existed between caciques in Boriquén and eastern Hispaniola, and a framework to understand the consequences of warfare when religion is ineluctably drawn into it, specifically in regard to the cemís and cemíism. The Spanish conquest spurred intense rounds of stealing cemí idols between different competing caciques. The death in battle or by execution of caciques, or their imprisonment, along with the elimination of members of the cacique's lineage and household, led to a severe crisis of accession to the office of chief. The heirs to the office were often not the preferred ones or the most able ones and would most likely lack the proper contingent of legendary, reputable cemís to effectively carry on the duties of a political (and military) leader. These political crises, with different degrees of severity, were likely to have occurred in the pre-Columbian past; the cemí theft was not just a new strategy that the natives developed specifically to respond to Spanish aggression. The same scenario of battle and warfare also helps to understand how caciques and military leaders of Puerto Rico and the Virgin Islands maintained (or ruptured) alliances with other diversely assembled ethnic groups and societies (including those homogenized as Caribs, Island Caribs, etc.) beyond their sphere of direct, hegemonic political control, extending into a region described by Samuel Wilson (2004, 2007) as a buffer zone, a frontier land "in flux."

The analysis of battles in Hispaniola and Boriquén provided evidence about the religious and iconoclastic persecution of the natives—specifically, the destruction of their cemí idols and, in some instances, the confiscation of these potent cemís and their sale in public auction, as curious or even war trophies, as was the captured luxurious canoe from native rebels in St. Croix. The destruction of cemí idols and other symbols of political-religious power by the Spanish, and also by caciques allied to the Spanish, led to the hiding of many of these images in the forest—especially in caves, which is where most of the museum-quality specimens have been found. This was exactly what the cacique of Cueybá in eastern Cuba did with his newly adopted Virgin cemí icon. The destruction of cemí idols was more than killing an icon in the eyes of the natives; it was in effect killing a part of the cacique's personhood, negating his or her potentiality as an extended, distributed person and thus his or her capacity to rule.

The case of the destruction of Fray Ramón Pané's Catholic idols in Guarícano, in the Magua-Caiabó chiefdom in Hispaniola, is a stark reminder that the "war of the idols" was carried out for the survival of the native way of life. It is the first recorded instance in the New World in which natives took the initiative to destroy the Spanish Christian power, and not the usual reverse situation. It reminds us that both the Spaniards and natives understood the power (not necessarily the theology) of each other's idols and religious symbols (Virgins, saints, cemís), realizing that the ultimate defeat or success of their respective traditions depended on wiping out each other's religion as much as it did on killing and driving away the enemy.

I argued that the clash of cultures led to a continuum of strategies regarding religion and its iconography. At one end of the spectrum is resistance, rejection, repudiation, and, in a word, anti-syncretism. At the opposite end is acceptance, adoption, mimicry, and, ultimately, syncretism and transculturation, perhaps in some cases even assimilation. I concluded that in the seventeenth to eighteenth centuries the syncretic processes (still imperfectly documented and understood) had led to a significantly different religious complex in Cuba that would have been quite unfamiliar to their pre-Columbian (Taínoan) ancestors. The processes of syncretism and transculturation, coupled with masking and transvaluation (Brown 2003; Reisman 1970; Stewart 1999), went hand in hand with the construction of new identities, of what it was to be and to feel like a native—an identity that crystallized in the simultaneously racist and self-designated term *Indio*. The suppression of the ancient cohoba rituals, I argued, was a substantial loss—one that was not syncretized. Its suppression by Spanish authorities was precisely because the cohoba ceremony was the key institution of governance, of political and military decision making. The primary and most fundamental mode of engaging cemís as icons or spirits was lost. Cemíism without cohoba is no longer cemíism. Even if initially superficial, the intrusion of, and eventual replacement by, the figures of the Virgin Mary and other saints of Christian iconographic art (the idols' faces, bodies, garments, and other accoutrements), no matter how much conceptual syncretism underpinned these images, is a drastic shift from a religion and imagery suffused with Taínoness. The stories of the native/Christian icons of Cuba and Hispaniola are paradigmatic examples of the political and religious conflicts and resolutions that were soon to follow in continental America as the conquistadors pushed forward in their quest for gold, glory, and the souls of Amerindians (see Graham 1998).

Despite stark differences in their respective notions of what constituted victory in battle, the wars in Higüey and especially Boriquén demonstrate that the natives did engage to kill and harass the Spaniards and those natives allied to the Spaniards. The ultimate destruction of Taínoan cemí idols and the cohoba ceremony closes a key chapter of effective native rulership and control over their future destinies. The decapitation of the rebel native leadership stratum (caciques, behiques, and even nitaínos), coupled with religious persecution of their instruments of power (the cemí idols and the cohoba ceremony), effectively ended the native political order and certainly decimated a huge block of knowledge about native religion; as Pané (1999:20; see also Erraste 1998:50) noted, it was the caciques and shamans (behiques) who held the unswerving faith in and deep knowledge of religion. The remaining native population was decimated not only by the wars but also by the repartimiento and encomienda regimes, slavery, diseases, and by periodic but severe famines. The survivors, against all odds, as the case of Cuba suggests, managed to create and reformulate new identities (subsumed under "Indios") and to preserve at least echoes of the ancient idolatry (as defined by Alfred Gell) and cemíism. Still, far more archaeological work needs to be done to track down the substance and character of the processes involved—be these syncretism, transculturation, or assimilation—and to flesh out the new webs of relations that emerged, not to mention of how persons were constructed and deconstructed. I suggested that whatever the specific content and character of syncretism in various regions may turn out to be, religious practices (cohoba rites, and of icon forms) available to the aboriginal populations were severely curtailed.

It is a well-known fact among Caribbean archaeologists of all theoretical persuasions that there is a lack of material evidence for social stratification that is independently supported by archaeological data. Among other things, this is because there is severe paucity of well-documented household units, of clear stratification between households and mortuary practices, of evidence of differential accumulation of prestige and wealth items throughout a site (much less groups of sites), and of differential control over the distribution and redistribution of commodities and other resources. This paucity of archaeological data conspires against resolving pressing questions about the emergence and functioning of Greater Antillean chiefdoms, or even of what kind of chiefdom were the cacicazgos of the so-called Taínos. Almost all of what has been written on the topic of chiefdoms has had no choice but to rely on what Antonio Curet (2003) and others call the "tyranny of ethnohistory."

Allen Johnson and Timothy Earle (2000) have emphasized the importance of a political-economic framework to address the causal processes that led to the general evolution as well as the particular historical development of chiefdoms or so-called middle-range polities. One of the key objectives is, essentially, to ascertain who controls what, and how, in order to financially sustain that polity, and when such controls came into operation, and for how long it was before these changed. Once this is defined and archaeologically documented, then one can ask questions about how and why a chiefdom developed a particular kind of *configuration* (a word I am stealing from the great Alfred Kroeber). Johnson and Earle (2000) identified two fundamental modes of financing a preindustrial polity, both defined in terms of wealth. One is staple wealth, which involves modes of controlling the production, storage, and (re)distribution of food supplies. The other is prestige wealth, typically centering on items deemed to be of high symbolic, ideological, and economic value (Graeber 2001).

In this study, prestige, or symbolic, wealth includes the cemí idols in the form of elaborate three-pointed stones, stone heads, stone collars, elbow stones, wood and cotton idols, and guaízas. To these one could also add duhos (seats), *caona* (gold), guanín (copper-gold-silver alloy), ciba (stone) shell or coral beads making up necklaces, and elaborate belts and sashes. By analyzing the behavior and patterning of the two kinds of wealth from secure archaeological contexts, one ought to be able to characterize the essential features of the economy that sustained a polity and identify who controls the wealth, who produces it, and how these are put to use (or consumed), distributed, and, of course, exchanged. And by comparing these patterns with preceding ones or others that might follow in time, one ought to be able to address questions about causes for change as well as persistence.

One of the results of this study is to raise the alarm and caution as to how archaeologists identify and then weigh or measure the usually polysemic values (in the sense given by Graeber [2001]) of objects to be classified as prestige wealth. If this is the first step in identifying inequality (leading toward social stratification), then we must ensure that the reasons for inclusion as wealth are defensible. Strictly economic arguments alone will not do in the case of cemí idols. The very elaborate three-pointers, wood idols, and stone collars, for example, would indicate that although the raw materials are not necessarily rare (in fact, they are abundant), their manufacture entails considerable investment of time and labor: they would be expensive to make and thus in an economic sense valuable. However, at least in the case of the three-pointers and carved (cohoba-related) wood and stone figures, I have demonstrated that they have differently ranked values that are unrelated to the cost of manufacture. Two exact replicas of the same cemí icon will have different values owing to the reputations they have accrued during their lifetime as a result of different relationships with their human trustees. Although from conception each cemí icon is potent and powerful, they materialize as idols with different ranks and, hence, values that will not be apparent to us by looking at raw materials, size, decorative complexity, or by calculating manufacturing costs (man-hours). And, of course, there is also the question of their antiquity, the increased prestige value that these idols acquired as they circulated through generations of heirs or through a line of different caciques. Therefore, it is more than probable that there were examples of simpler and less elaborate cemí idols whose value by far surpassed that of other more costly-to-produce idols. In this regard I am not surprised that some of the archaeological contexts in which elaborate cemís have been found do not necessarily point to elite households, and instead were found in what amounts to a run-of-the-mill farmstead settlement (all with their single batey, or plaza), as demonstrated in the Caguana area, in sites such as Utu-20, Cag-04, Utu-44, or Utu-27. I am not arguing that prestige value should exclude the cost of labor or time, but it is clear that this is not the only variable to consider in attaching to it a prestige value and wealth. Seniority, antiquity, can be ascertained archaeologically if and when we are able to demonstrate that the objects themselves have been curated: the wood idol is significantly older than all other artifacts and materials associated with it in a given stratigraphic context.

Finally, there are some basic steps that would be useful to take in the near future. A detailed Caribbean-wide study of the formal variability and changes through time of all the three-pointers would be invaluable to chart the evolution of cemí ideology from its humble beginnings involving small, private, personal religious icons to the much larger public ones of later pre-Columbian times. Precise analyses of the raw materials used could help in identifying quarry sources and areas of origin (as Knippenberg [2004] did for the pocket-sized calcirudite three-pointers in the Lesser Antilles); while stylistic, formal analyses would shed light on the natures, personhoods, and identities of the sculptured cemí beings. Secure archaeological contexts for these objects should be made public. I strongly believe that many of the large, still unresolved questions regarding the nature of caciques and cacicazgos (e.g., hierarchical or heterarchical; centralized or decentralized) are dependent on how archaeologists appraise and evaluate the cemí idols as prestige wealth.

I am optimistic that as long as we, as archaeologists, do not lose sight of *who* the persons (human and otherwise) behind social action are, and how they relate to others, to their material cultures, and to their world, we will be on the right track.

References Cited

Alegría, Ricardo E.

1979   Apuntes para el Estudio de los Caciques de Puerto Rico. *Revista del Instituto de Cultura Puertorriqueña,* No. 85.

1983   Ball Courts and Ceremonial Plazas in the West Indies. *Yale University Publications in Anthropology,* No. 79. Department of Anthropology, Yale University, New Haven.

1986   Nuevas Interpretaciones en Torno a la Parafernalia de los Jugadores de Pelota en las Antillas Mayores. *La Revista del Centro de Estudios Avanzados de Puerto Rico y El Caribe* 3:31–42.

1992   *Descubrimiento, Conquista y Colonización de Puerto Rico: 1493–1599.* Colección de Estudios Puertorriqueños and Editorial Corripio, San Juan–Santo Domingo.

Alegría Pons, Francisco

1993   *Gagá y Vudú en la República Dominicana.* Ediciones El Chango Prieto, San Juan–Santo Domingo.

Altos de Chavón—Catalog

n.d.   *Catálogo Conmemorativo Vto Centenario.* Museo Regional de Arqueología, Altos de Chavón, Fundación Centro Cultural Altos de Chavón, La Romana.

Anderson, David G.

1994   *The Savannah River Chiefdoms: Political Change in the Late Prehistoric Southeast.* University of Alabama Press, Tuscaloosa.

Anderson, Martha G., and Philip M. Peek

2002   Introduction: Charting a Course. In *Ways of the River: Arts and Environment of the Niger Delta,* edited by M. G. Anderson and P. M. Peek, pp. 25–35. UCLA Fowler Museum of Cultural History, Los Angeles.

Anderson-Córdova, Karen F.

1990   Hispaniola and Puerto Rico: Indian Acculturation and Heterogeneity, 1492–1550. Unpublished Ph.D. dissertation, Department of Anthropology, Yale University, New Haven.

2005   The Aftermath of Conquest: The Indians of Puerto Rico during the Early Sixteenth Century. In *Ancient Borinquen: Archaeology and Ethnohistory of Native Puerto Rico,* edited by Peter E. Siegel, pp. 337–352. University of Alabama Press, Tuscaloosa.

Arrom, José Juan [also see Pané, Fray Ramón]

1951   Criollo, Definición y Matices de un Concepto. *Hispania* 34:172–176.

1971   *Certidumbre de América: Estudios de Letra, Folklore y Cultura.* Editorial Gredos,
[1959] Madrid.

1975   *Mitología y Artes Prehispánicas de las Antillas.* Siglo XXI Editores, México, D.F.

1988   La Lechuza: Motivo recurrente en las Artes Taínas y el Folclor Hispanoamericano.
        In *El Murciélago y la Lechuza en la Cultura Taína.* Fundación García Arévalo,
        Santo Domingo.

Aymar i Ragolta, Jaume

1993   Colom a Sant Jeroni de La Murtra. In *Colom i El Mon Català,* edited by R. Dal-
        mau, pp. 213–223. Centre D'Estudis Colombins–Generalitat de Catalunya, Bar-
        celona.

2007   El Primer Evangelizador de América Salió de Barcelona: Fray Ramón Pané, Monje
        de La Murtra. Electronic document, http://www.catalunya-america.org/español/
        primerevangelizador.htm. Accessed November 30, 2007.

2008   Fray Ramón Pané, Primicia de América. In *El Caribe Precolombino. Fray Ramón
        Pané y el Universo Taíno,* edited by J. R. Oliver, C. McEwan, and A. Casas Gil-
        berga, pp. 34–55. Co-edition of the Ministerio de Cultura, Museu Barbier-
        Mueller d'Art Pre-Colombí, and Fundación Caixa Galicia, Barcelona.

Ball, Philip

1999   *The Self-made Tapestry: Pattern Formation in Nature.* Oxford University Press,
        Oxford.

Bennett, John P.

1989   An Arawak-English Dictionary with an English Word-list. *Archaeology and An-
        thropology* 6 (1–2). Walter Roth Museum of Anthropology, Georgetown, Guyana.

Bercht, Fatima, Estrellita Brodsky, John A. Farmer, and Dicey Taylor (editors)

1997   *Pre-Columbian Art and Culture from the Caribbean.* Museo del Barrio, Monacelli
        Press, New York.

Betancourt, Obed

2007a   Peligra Tesoro Arqueológico [PO-29]. *El Vocero de Puerto Rico.* Electronic docu-
        ment, http://www.vocero.com/noticias.asp?s=Locales&n=101446, San Juan. Ac-
        cessed October 19, 2007.

2007b   Contradicen Informe sobre Yacimiento [PO-29]. *El Vocero de Puerto Rico.* Elec-
        tronic document, http://www.vocero.com/noticias.asp?s=Locales&n=101889,
        San Juan. Accessed October 23, 2007.

Brinton, Daniel

1871   The Arawak Language of Guiana in Linguistic and Ethnological Relations. In
        Transactions of the American Philosophical Society of Philadelphia, Vol. XIV, n.s.,
        pp. 427–444. Macalla and Stanley Printers, Philadelphia.

Brown, David H.

2003   *Santería Enthroned: Art, Ritual, and Innovation in an Afro-Cuban Religion.* Uni-
        versity of Chicago Press, Chicago.

Bullen, Ripley P., and Adelaide K. Bullen

1970   The Lavoutte Site: A Carib Ceremonial Center. In *Proceedings of the 3rd Inter-
        national Congress for the Study of Pre-Columbian Cultures of the Lesser Antilles,*

St. Georges, Grenada, edited by R. P. Bullen, pp. 61–86. Florida State Museum–University of Florida, Gainesville.

Cabello Carro, Paz

2008   Colecciones Españolas del Caribe: Viajes Científicos e Inicios de la Arqueología en las Antillas (Siglos XVIII y XIX). In *El Caribe Precolombino: Fray Ramón Pané y el Universo Taíno,* edited by J. R. Oliver, C. McEwan, and A. Casas Gilberga, pp. 202–221. Co-edition of the Ministerio de Cultura, Museu Barbier-Mueller d'Art Pre-Colombí, and Fundación Caixa Galicia, Barcelona.

Callaghan, Richard T.

1995   Antillean Cultural Contacts with Mainland Regions as a Navigation Problem. In *Proceedings of the 19th International Congress of Caribbean Archaeology,* edited by M. Rodríguez López and R. A. Alegría, pp. 181–190. IACA, San Juan.

2003   Comments on the Mainland Origins of the Pre-Ceramic Cultures of the Greater Antilles. *Latin American Antiquity* 14(3):323–338.

2008   Patterns of Contact between the Islands of the Caribbean and Surrounding Mainlands as a Navigation Problem. In *Islands in the Stream: Inter-island and Continental Interaction in the Caribbean,* edited by L. A. Curet. University of Alabama Press, Tuscaloosa, in press.

Callaghan, Richard T., and Warwick Bray

2007   Simulating Prehistoric Sea Contacts between Costa Rica and Colombia. *Journal of Island Archaeology* 2:4–23.

Cassá, Roberto

1974   *Los Taínos de La Española.* Editora de la Universidad Autónoma de Santo Domingo.

Cárdenas Ruíz, Manuel (compiler and translator)

1981   *Crónicas Francesas de los Indios Caribes.* Compiled, translated, and annotated by M. Cárdenas Ruíz, with an introduction by Ricardo E. Alegría. Editorial Universidad de Puerto Rico and Centro de Estudios Avanzados de Puerto Rico y El Caribe, Río Piedras.

Caygill, Marjorie

2002   *The Story of the British Museum.* 3rd ed. British Museum Press, London.

Chanlatte Baik, Luis

1991   *El Hombre de Puerto Ferro.* Museo de Antropología, Historia y Arte–Universidad de Puerto Rico, Río Piedras.

Chanlatte Baik, Luis, and Yvonne Narganes Storde

1984   *Arqueología de Vieques.* Universidad de Puerto Rico, Editorial Corripio C. por A., Santo Domingo.

Chanlatte Baik, Luis, and Yvonne Narganes Storde (editors)

2005   *Cultura La Hueca.* Museo de Historia, Antropología y Arte–Universidad de Puerto Rico, Río Piedras.

Chapman, John

2000   *Fragmentation in Archaeology: Peoples, Places, and Broken Objects in the Prehistory of South Europe.* Routledge, London.

Clerc, Edgar
1970   Recherches Archéologiques en Guadeloupe. *Parallèles* 36/37:68–88.

Cody, Ann K.
1993   Distribution of Exotic Stone Artifacts through the Lesser Antilles: Their Im-
        plications for Prehistoric Interaction and Exchange. *Proceedings of the 14th In-
        ternational Congress for Caribbean Archaeology,* Barbados, edited by A. Cum-
        mings and P. King, pp. 204–226. IACA, Museum and Historical Society, Bar-
        bados.

Colón, Hernando (Ferdinand Columbus)
1985   *Historia del Almirante.* Edition of Luis Arranz, Información y Revistas, SA. Se-
[1571] rie Historia No. 16, Madrid. [First published in Italian by Alfonso de Ulloa in
        Venice, 1571.]

Cooper, Jago, Marcos Martinón-Torres, and Roberto Valcárcel Rojas
2008   American Gold and European Brass: Metal Objects and Indigenous Values in
        the Cemetery of Chorro de Maíta, Cuba. In *Crossing the Borders: New Methods
        and Techniques in the Study of Archaeological Materials in the Caribbean,* edited by
        C. L. Hofman, M. L. P. Hoogland, and A. L. van Gijn, pp. 34–42. University of
        Alabama Press, Tuscaloosa.

Covarrubias Orozco, Sebastián de
1995   *Tesoro de la Lengua Castellana o Española,* editor in charge F. C. R. Maldonado,
[1611] revised by M. Camarero. Nueva Biblioteca de Erudición y Crítica, Editorial Cas-
        talía, Madrid.
2001   *Suplemento al Tesoro de la Lengua Española Castellana,* editors in charge G. Dopico
[c. 1611] and J. Lezra. Ediciones Polifemo, Madrid.

Crespo Torres, Edwin F.
2000   Estudio Comparativo Biocultural Entre Dos Poblaciones Prehistóricas en la Isla
        de Puerto Rico: Punta Candelero y Paso del Indio. Unpublished doctoral disserta-
        tion, Universidad Nacional Autónoma de México, Facultad de Filosofía y Letras,
        División de Estudios de Postgrado, Instituto de Investigaciones Antropológicas,
        México, D. F.

Crock, John G., and James B. Petersen
2004   Inter-island Exchange, Settlement Hierarchy, and a Taino-Related Chiefdom on
        the Anguilla Bank, Northern Lesser Antilles. In *Late Ceramic Age Societies in
        the Eastern Caribbean,* edited by A. Delpuech and C. L. Hofman, pp. 139–156.
        British Archaeological Reports International Series 1273, Paris Monographs in
        American Archaeology 14. Archaeopress, Oxford.

Cuneo, Michele (Miguel) de
1983   Narraciones Sincrónicas de Las Noticias de las Islas del Océano Occidental
[1495] Recopiladas para Don Cristóbal Colón, Genovés. Carta a Geronimo Annari,
        15–18 de octubre, 1495, Savonna, Italia; prologue by Bernardo Vega. *Boletín del
        Museo del Hombre Dominicano* 9(18):239–256.

Curet, L. Antonio
2002   The Chief Is Dead, Long Live . . . Who? Descent and Succession in the Protohis-
        toric Chiefdoms of the Greater Antilles. *Ethnohistory* 49(2):259–280.

2003   Issues on the Diversity and Emergence of Middle-Range Societies of the Ancient Caribbean: A Critique. *Journal of Archaeological Research* 11(1):1–41.

2005   *Caribbean Paleodemography: Population, Culture History, and Sociopolitical Processes in Puerto Rico.* University of Alabama Press, Tuscaloosa.

2006   Missing the Point and an Illuminating Example: A Response to Keegan's Comments. *Ethnohistory* 53(2):393–398.

Curet, L. Antonio, Lee A. Newsom, and Susan D. deFrance

2006   Prehispanic Social and Cultural Changes at Tibes, Puerto Rico. *Journal of Field Archaeology* 31:23–39.

Curet, L. Antonio, and José R. Oliver

1998   Mortuary Practices, Social Development, and Ideology in Precolumbian Puerto Rico. *Latin American Antiquity* 9(3):217–239.

Curet, L. Antonio, Joshua Torres, and Miguel Rodríguez

2004   Political and Social History of Eastern Puerto Rico: Ceramic Age. In *Late Ceramic Age Societies in the Eastern Caribbean,* edited by A. Delpuech and C. L. Hofman, pp. 59–85. British Archaeological Reports, International Series 1273, Paris Monographs in American Archaeology 14, Archaeopress, Oxford.

Deagan, Kathleen A.

2004   Reconsidering Social Dynamics after Spanish Conquest: Gender and Class in Culture Contact Studies. *American Antiquity* 69(4):597–598.

Deagan, Kathleen A. (editor)

1995   *Puerto Real: A Sixteenth-Century Spanish Town in Hispaniola.* University Press of Florida, Gainesville.

Deagan, Kathleen A., and José M. Cruxent

2002   *Archaeology at La Isabela: America's First European Town.* Yale University Press, New Haven.

Deive, Carlos Estéban

1976   Fray Ramón Pané y el Nacimiento de la Etnografía Americana. *Boletín del Museo del Hombre Dominicano* 6:133–156.

1979   *Vodú y Magia en Santo Domingo.* Ediciones del Museo del Hombre Dominicano, Santo Domingo.

Delpuech, André, and Corinne L. Hofman (editors)

2004   *Late Ceramic Age Societies in the Eastern Caribbean.* British Archaeological Reports, International Series 1273, Paris Monographs in American Archaeology 14. Archaeopress, Oxford.

Descola, Philipe

1996   Constructing Natures: Symbolic Ecology and Social Practice. In *Nature and Society: Anthropological Perspectives,* edited by P. Descola and G. Palsson, pp. 82–102. Routledge, London.

de Waal, Maaike

2006   Pre-Columbian Social Organisation and Interaction Interpreted through the Study of Settlement Patterns: An Archaeological Case Study of the Pointe de Châteaux, La Désirade, and Les Iles de la Petite Terre Micro-region, Guadeloupe, F.W.I., Ph.D. dissertation, University of Leiden.

Diccionario de la Real Academia de la Lengua Española
1992   *Diccionario de la Lengua Española.* Real Academia Española, Espasa, Madrid
Domínguez, Lourdes
1991   *Arqueología del Centro-Sur de Cuba.* Ediciones Academia, La Habana.
Drewett, Peter L.
2000   *Prehistoric Settlements in the Caribbean: Fieldwork in Tortola, Barbados, and Cayman Islands.* Barbados Museum and Historical Society. Archetype Publications, London.
Drewett, Peter L., and Bill Bates
2001   Casting a Long Shadow: Ritual Activity at the Belmont Site, Tortola, British Virgin Islands. In *Proceedings of the 18th International Congress for Caribbean Archaeology,* Vol. 2:13–20, St. Georges, Grenada. International Association of Caribbean Archaeology and Conseil Régional de la Guadeloupe, Mission Archaeologique, Basse Terre, Guadeloupe.
Dunn, Oliver, and James E. Kelley Jr.
1988   *The Diario of Christopher Columbus's First Voyage to America, 1492–1493.* Abstracted by Bartolomé de Las Casas. University of Oklahoma Press, Norman.
Ekholm, Gordon F.
1961   Puerto Rico Stone "Collars" as Ball-game Belts. In *Essays in Pre-Columbian Art and Archaeology,* edited by S. K. Lothrop, pp. 356–371. Harvard University Press, Cambridge.
Erraste, O. F. M., Mariano
1998   *Los Primeros Franciscanos en América: Isla Española, 1493–1520.* Serie Investigaciones No. 8, Fundación García Arévalo, Santo Domingo.
Espenshade, Chris T., and Peter E. Siegel
2007   Detailed Phase II Archaeological Testing and Data Recovery Planning: Site PO-29, Portugues Dam and Pool, Puerto Rico. Unpublished report on file at the U.S. Army Corps of Engineers, Jacksonville, Florida, and the Oficina Estatal de Conservación Histórica de Puerto Rico [PR-SHPO], San Juan.
Faber Morse, Birgit
2004   At the Onset of Complexity: Late Ceramic Developments in St. Croix. In *Late Ceramic Age Societies in the Eastern Caribbean,* edited by A. Delpuech and C. L. Hofman, pp 183–193. British Archaeological Reports, International Series 1273, Paris Monographs in American Archaeology 14, Archaeopress, Oxford.
Fernández Buey, Francisco
1995   *La Gran Perturbación: Discurso del Indio Metropolitano.* El Viejo Topo, Barcelona.
Fernández Méndez, Eugenio
1973   *Crónicas de Puerto Rico: Desde la Conquista hasta Nuestros Días (1493–1955).* Editorial Universitaria, Río Piedras.
Fewkes, Jesse W.
1907   *The Aborigines of Porto Rico and the Neighboring Islands.* 25th Annual Report of the Bureau of American Ethnology to the Secretary of the Smithsonian Institution, 1903–04, pp. 1–220. Government Printing Office, Washington, D.C.
1922   *A Prehistoric Island Culture of America.* 34th Annual Report of the Bureau of

American Ethnology to the Secretary of the Smithsonian Institution, 1912–13. Government Printing Office, Washington, D.C.

Firth, Raymond

1959   *The Economics of New Zealand Maori.* R. E. Owen. Wellington, New Zealand.

Fowler, Chris

2004   *The Archaeology of Personhood: An Archaeological Approach.* Routledge, London.

García-Arévalo, Manuel

2005   La Frontera Tipológica entre los Objetos Líticos de la Cultura Taína. *Proceedings of the 15th International Congress for Caribbean Archaeology,* Santo Domingo, edited by G. Tavárez María and M. García Arévalo, pp. 264–272. Museo del Hombre Dominicano and Fundación García Arévalo, Santo Domingo.

Gates, Richard R.

1954   Studies in Race Crossing: The Indian Remnants of Eastern Cuba. *Genetics* 27: 65–96.

Gell, Alfred

1993   *Wrapping Images: Tattooing in Polynesia.* Clarendon Press, Oxford.

1998   *Art and Agency: An Anthropological Theory.* Clarendon Press, Oxford.

Gelpi Baiz, Elsa

2000   *Siglo en Blanco: Estudio de la Economía Azucarera en Puerto Rico, Siglo XVI.* Editorial de la Universidad de Puerto Rico, Río Piedras.

Gillespie, Susan

2001   Personhood, Agency, and Mortuary Ritual: A Case Study from Ancient Maya. *Journal of Anthropological Archaeology* 20:73–112.

Godelier, Maurice

1999   *The Enigma of the Gift.* Polity Press, Oxford.

Godelier, Maurice, and Marilyn Strathern (editors)

1991   *Big Men and Great Men: Personifications of Power in Melanesia.* Cambridge University Press, Cambridge.

Gordon, Raymond G. Jr. (editor)

2005   Language Family Trees. In *Ethnologue: Languages of the World.* 15th ed. SIL International, Dallas. Electronic document, http://www.ethnologue.com/show_family.asp?subid=90534. Accessed June 24, 2008.

Graeber, David

2001   *Toward an Anthropological Theory of Value: The False Coin of Our Own Dreams.* Palgrave, New York.

Graham, Elizabeth

1991   Colonial Period Life at Tipu, Belize. In *Columbian Consequences: The Spanish Borderlands in Pan-American Perspective,* edited by D. H. Thomas, pp. 319–335. Smithsonian Institution Press, Washington, D.C.

1998   Mission Archaeology. *Annual Review of Anthropology* 27:25–62.

Graham, Elizabeth, Jorge A. Calvera, and M. Juan Jardines

2000   Excavations at Los Buchillones, Cuba. *Antiquity* 74:263–264.

Guarch Delmonte, José (editor)

1990   *Taíno: Arqueología de Cuba-Historia Aborigen de Cuba según Datos Arqueológicos.*

CD-R for Windows Format. Centro de Diseño de Sistemas Automatizados, Ministerio de Ciencia, Tecnología y Medio Ambiente, La Habana. Published by Centro Nacional de Discos Compactos (Cenedic), University of Colima, Mexico.

Hague, Per, and Mark S. Mosko
  1998 Austronesian Chiefs: Metaphorical or Fractal Fathers? *Journal of the Royal Anthropological Institute* 4(4):786–795.

Heckenberger, Michael J.
  2002 Rethinking the Arawakan Diaspora: Hierarchy, Regionality, and the Amazonian Formative. In *Comparative Arawakan Histories,* edited by J. D. Hill and F. Santos-Granero, pp. 99–122. University of Illinois Press, Urbana.
  2005 *The Ecology of Power: Culture, Place, and Personhood in the Southern Amazon,* A.D. 1000–2000. Routledge, New York.
  2008 Amazonian Mosaics: Identity, Interaction, and Integration in the Tropical Forest. In *Handbook of South American Archaeology,* edited by H. Silverman and W. H. Isbell, pp. 94–961. Springer, New York.

Herskovits, Melville J.
  1937a *Life in a Haitian Valley.* Knopf, New York.
  1937b African Gods and Catholic Saints in New World Negro Belief. *American Anthropologist* 39(4):635–643.

Hofman, Corinne L., Alistair J. Bright, Arie Boomert, and Sebastian Knippenberg
  2007 Island Rhythms: The Web of Social Relationships and Interaction Networks in the Lesser Antillean Archipelago between 400 B.C. and A.D. 1492. Manuscript accepted for publication in *Latin American Antiquity.* Cited with permission by the authors.

Hofman, Corinne L., and Menno L. P. Hoogland
  2004 Social Dynamics and Change in the Northern Antilles. In *Late Ceramic Age Societies in the Eastern Caribbean,* edited by A. Delpuech and C. L. Hofman, pp. 47–57. British Archaeological Reports, International Series 1273, Paris Monographs in American Archaeology 14. Archaeopress, Oxford.

Hofman, Corinne L., and Menno L. P. Hoogland (editors)
  1999 Archaeological Investigations on St. Martin (Lesser Antilles): The Sites of Norman Estate, Hope Estate, and Anse des Peres. *Archaeological Studies Leiden University* No. 4, Leiden.

Hofman, Corinne L., Menno L. P. Hoogland, André Delpuech, and Maaike S. de Waal
  2004 Late Ceramic Age Survey of the Northeastern Islands of the Guadeloupean Archipelago. In *Late Ceramic Age Societies in the Eastern Caribbean,* edited by A. Delpuech and C. L. Hofman, pp. 159–181. British Archaeological Reports, International Series 1273-Paris Monographs in American Archaeology 14, Archaeopress, Oxford.

Hofman, Corinne L., Menno L. P. Hoogland, José R. Oliver, and Alice V. M. Samson
  2007 Investigaciones Arqueológicas en El Cabo, Oriente de La República Dominicana: Resultados Preliminares de la Campaña de 2005. *El Caribe Arqueológico* 9:95–106.

Hoogland, Menno L. P.

1995 The Settlement of Saba, N.A. In *Proceedings of the 16th International Congress for Caribbean Archaeology,* Vol. 2:156–167. IACA, Conseil Régional de la Guadeloupe, Mission Archéologique et du Patrimoine, Basse-Terre, Guadeloupe.

Hoogland, Menno L. P., and Corinne L. Hofman

1993 A 14th-Century Taíno Settlement on Saba, Netherlands Antilles. *Analecta Praehistorica Leidensia* 26:163–181.

1999 Expansion of the Taíno Cacicazgos toward the Lesser Antilles: The Case of Saba, N.A. *Journal de la Société des Américanistes* 85:93–113.

Huerga, Alvaro

2006 *Ataques de los Caribes a Puerto Rico en el Siglo XVI.* Academia Puertorriqueña de la Historia, Centro de Estudios Avanzados de Puerto Rico y El Caribe and Fundación Puertorriqueña de Las Humanidades, San Juan.

Hugh-Jones, Christine

1979 *The Palm and the Pleiades: Initiation and Cosmology in Northwest Amazonia.* Cambridge University Press, Cambridge.

Hulme, Peter

1992 *Colonial Encounters: Europe and the Native Caribbean, 1492–1797.* Routledge, London.

1993 Making Sense of the Native Caribbean. *New West Indian Guide/Nieuwe West-Indische Gids,* n.s. 67(3–4):189–219.

Ingold, T.

2000 Totemism, Animism, and the Depiction of Animals. In *The Perception of the Environment: Essays in Livelihood, Dwelling, and Skill,* pp. 111–131. Routledge, London.

Insoll, Tim

2005 *Archaeology, Ritual, and Religion.* Routledge, London.

Insoll, Tim (editor)

2006 *The Archaeology of Identities: A Reader.* Routledge, London.

Johnson, Allen W., and Timothy Earle

2000 *The Evolution of Human Societies: From Foraging Group to Agrarian State.* 2nd ed. Stanford University Press, Stanford.

Joseph, Joseph W.

2007 Open Letter to the Archaeological Community of Puerto Rico, Ref.: New South Associates' Archaeological Excavation of Site Ponce-29. Dated November 7, 2007, 6 pp. Electronically disseminated open letter, on file at the Consejo Para La Protección del Patrimonio Arqueológico Terrestre de Puerto Rico (San Juan) and the U.S. Army Corps of Engineers, Jacksonville, Florida.

Joyce, Rosemary

1998 Performing the Body in Pre-Hispanic Central America. *RES: Anthropology and Aesthetics* 33:147–165.

2001 *Gender and Power in Pre-Hispanic Mesoamerica.* University of Texas Press, Austin.

2005 Archaeology of the Body. *Annual Review of Anthropology* 34:139–158.

Kaye, Quetta, Scott Fitzpatrick, and Michiel Kappers
  2004   A Preliminary Report on the Excavation and Grand Bay, Carriacou, West In-
          dies, June 28th–July 31st, 2004. *Papers from the Institute of Archaeology,* Vol. 15:
          82–89.

Keegan, William F.
  2006   All in the Family: Descent and Succession in the Ethnohistoric Chiefdoms of the
          Greater Antilles: A Comment on Curet. *Ethnohistory* 53(2):383–392.

  2007a   Benjamin Irving Rouse. Unpublished electronic article posted by Yale University
          Archaeological Studies at http://www.yale.edu/archaeology/rouse/about.html.
          Accessed July 3, 2008.

  2007b   *Taíno Indian Myth and Practice: The Arrival of the Stranger King.* University Press
          of Florida, Gainesville.

Keegan, W. F., and Morgan D. Maclachlan
  1989   The Evolution of Avunculocal Chiefdoms. *American Anthropologist* 91(3):613–
          630.

Keegan, William F., Morgan D. Maclachlan, and B. Byrne
  1998   Social Foundations of Taíno *Caciques.* In *Chiefdoms and Chieftancies in the
          Americas,* edited by E. M. Redmond. University Press of Florida, Gainesville.

Kennedy, Hugh
  2004   *The Court of the Caliphs.* Phoenix, London.

Kerchache, Jacques (editor)
  1994   *L'Art des Sculptureurs Taïno: Chefs-d'oeuvre des Grandes Antilles.* Musée du Petit
          Palais, Editions des Musées de la Ville de Paris.

Kessing, Roger M.
  1984   Rethinking "Mana." *Journal of Anthropological Research* 40(1):137–156.

Knippenberg, Sebastian
  2004   Distribution and Exchange of Lithic Materials: Three-pointers and Axes from
          St. Martin. In *Late Ceramic Age Societies in the Eastern Caribbean,* edited by
          A. Delpuech and C. L. Hofman, pp. 121–138. British Archaeological Reports
          International Series 1273, Paris Monographs in American Archaeology 14, Ar-
          chaeopress, Oxford.

Las Casas, Fray Bartolomé de
  1929   *Historia de Las Indias,* Vols. I-III. Editorial M. Aguilar, Madrid.
  [1552–
  1561]

Lathrap, Donald W., and José R. Oliver
  1984   The Caribbean as Positive Space: Vieques and Long-Distance Trade Networks in
          the Circum-Caribbean. Unpublished research proposal. Copy on file with the ju-
          nior author.

Leis, Philip E.
  2002   Preface: Cultural Identity in the Multicultural Niger Delta. In *Ways of the River:
          Arts and Environment of the Niger Delta,* edited by M. G. Anderson and P. M.
          Peek, pp. 15–23. UCLA Fowler Museum of Cultural History, Los Angeles.

Lévi-Strauss, Claude
1974   *From Honey to Ashes.* Harper-Torchbooks, New York.

Lewis-Williams, David
2002   *The Mind in the Cave: Consciousness and the Origins of Art.* Thames & Hudson, London.

McEwan, Colin
2008   Colecciones Caribeñas: Culturas Curiosas y Culturas de Curiosidades. In *El Caribe Precolombino: Fray Ramón Pané y el Universo Taíno,* edited by J. R. Oliver, C. McEwan, and A. Casas Gilberga, pp. 222–248. Co-edition of the Ministerio de Cultura, Museu Barbier-Mueller d'Art Precolombí, and Fundación Caixa Galicia, Barcelona.

MacGaffey, Wyatt
1993   The Eyes of Understanding: Kongo Minkisi. In *Astonishment and Power: The Eyes of Understanding and the Art of Renée Stout,* W. MacGaffey and M. D. Howard, pp. 20–103. National Museum of African Art, Smithsonian Institution Press, Washington, D.C.

Malinowski, Bronislav
1992   *Argonauts of the Western Pacific.* Dutton, New York.
[1922]

Mann, Charles, C.
2000   Earthmovers of the Amazon. *Science,* n.s. 287(5454):786–789.

Mañón Arredondo, Manuel, Fernando Morbán Laucer, Aída Cartagena Portalín, and Manuel García Arévalo
1971   Nuevas Investigaciones de Áreas Indígenas al Noroeste de Guayacanes y Juandolio. *Revista Dominicana de Arqueología y Antropología* 1(1):81–135. Universidad Autónoma de Santo Domingo, República Dominicana.

Martinón-Torres, Marcos, Roberto Valcárcel Rojas, and Thilo Rehren
2007   Metals, Microanalysis, and Meaning: A Study of Metal Objects Excavated from El Chorro de Maíta, Cuba. *Journal of Archaeological Science* 34(2):194–204.

Mártir de Anglería, Pedro (Pietro Martyre D'Anghiera, Peter Martyr)
1989   *Décadas del Nuevo Mundo.* With an introduction by Bernardo Vega (pp. 3–6),
[1493– a biographic study by Edmundo O'Gorman (pp. 9–44), and bibliographic re-
1525]   search by Joseph H. Sinclair (pp. 45–71). Sociedad Dominicana de Bibliófilos, Inc., Santo Domingo.

Mauss, Marcel
1990   *The Gift: The Form and Reason for Exchange in Archaic Societies.* Foreword by
[1925] Mary Douglas. Routledge Classics, Abingdon.

Menocal, María Rosa
2002   *Ornament of the World: How Muslims, Jews, and Christians Created a Culture of Tolerance in Medieval Spain.* Back Bay Books, New York.

Meskell, Lynn, and Rosemary Joyce
2003   *Embodied Lives: Figuring Ancient Mayan and Egyptian Experience.* Routledge, London.

Métraux, Alfred

1972   *Voodoo in Haiti.* Schocken, New York. [First published in 1958 in French with
[1958]   the title *Le Vaudou Haitien*].

MHAA-UPR Catalog (Museo de Historia, Antropología y Arte–Universidad de Puerto
Rico)

2006   *Culturas Indígenas de Puerto Rico/Indigenous Cultures of Puerto Rico. Colección
         Arqueológica.* Museo de Historia, Antropología y Arte–University of Puerto Rico,
         Impresos Universitarios–UPR, Río Piedras.

MHD Catalog (Museo del Hombre Dominicano)

1977   *Arqueología Taína de Santo Domingo.* Exposición Presentada por el Instituto de
         Cultura Hispánica en el Centro Cultural de la Villa de Madrid 15 Mayo–15 Sep-
         tiembre 1997. Ediciones Cultura Hispánica, Madrid.

Mol, Angus A. A.

2007   Costly Giving, Giving *Guaízas*. Towards an Organic Model of the Exchange of
         Social Valuables in the Late Ceramic Age Caribbean. Unpublished M.Phil. dis-
         sertation, Faculty of Archaeology, University of Leiden.

Morbán Laucer, Fernando

1979   *Ritos Funerarios: Acción del Fuego y Medio Ambiente en las Osamentas Precolom-
         binas.* Academia de Ciencias de la República Dominicana, Editorial El Taller, C.
         por A., Santo Domingo.

1988   El murciélago: Sus Representaciones en el Arte Rupestre y la Mitología Precolom-
         bina. *Boletín del Museo del Hombre Dominicano* 15(21):37–57.

Morey, Nancy

1975   The Ethnohistory of the Colombian and Venezuelan Llanos. Unpublished Ph.D.
         dissertation, Department of Anthropology, University of Utah, Salt Lake City.
         University Microfilms International [#BWH75–29890], Ann Arbor, Michigan.

1976   Ethnohistorical Evidence for the Cultural Complexity in the Western Llanos of
         Venezuela and Eastern Llanos of Colombia. *Antropológica* 45:41–69.

Moscoso, Francisco

1980   Las Guaízas: Apuntes para el Estudio del Trueque entre los Taínos. *Boletín del Mu-
         seo del Hombre Dominicano* 14:75–86.

1986   *Tribu y Clases en el Caribe Antiguo.* Universidad Central del Este, Vol. LXIII, San
         Pedro de Marcorís.

Mosko, Mark S.

1992   Motherless Sons: "Divine Kings" and "Partible Persons" in Melanesia and Poly-
         nesia. *Man,* n.s. 27(4):697–717.

1995   Rethinking Trobriand Chieftainship. *Journal of the Royal Anthropological Institute*
         1(4):763–785.

2000   Inalienable Ethnography: Keeping-While-Giving and the Trobriand Case. *Jour-
         nal of the Royal Anthropological Institute* 6(3):377–396.

Moya Pons, Frank

1987   *Después de Colón: Trabajo, Sociedad y Política en la Economía del Oro.* Alianza Edi-
         torial, S.A., Madrid.

Murga Sanz, Vicente
1971   *Juan Ponce de León.* Editorial Universidad de Puerto Rico, Río Piedras.
Myers, Kathleen A.
2007   *Fernández de Oviedo's Chronicle of America: A New History for a New World.* With translations by Nina M. Scott. University of Texas Press, Austin, Texas.
Navarrete, Martín Fernández de
1922   *Viajes de Colón.* Calpe, Madrid.
Newsom, Lee A., and Elizabeth S. Wing
2004   *On Land and Sea: Native American Uses of Biological Resources in the West Indies.* University of Alabama Press, Tuscaloosa.
Noble, Kingsley G.
1965   Proto-Arawakan and Its Descendants. *International Journal of American Linguistics,* Publication No. 39; 31(3):1–129.
Oliver, José R.
1980   A Cultural Interpretation of the Iconographic Art Style of Caguana's Ceremonial Center, Puerto Rico. Unpublished Master's thesis, Department of Anthropology, University of Illinois at Urbana–Champaign.
1992   Taíno Iconographic and Spatial Symbolism at the Caguana Ceremonial Center, Puerto Rico. Unpublished paper presented at the 91st Annual Meeting of American Anthropological Association, held in San Francisco, in the symposium "Model Building and Validation in South America," Papers in Honor of Donald W. Lathrap.
1997   The Taíno Cosmos. In *Indigenous People of the Caribbean,* edited by Samuel Wilson, pp. 140–153. University Press of Florida, Gainesville.
1998   *El Centro Ceremonial de Caguana, Puerto Rico: Simbolismo Iconográfico, Cosmovisión y el Poderío Caciquil Taíno de Boriquén.* British Archaeological Reports, International Series No. 727, Archaeopress, Oxford.
1999   The La Hueca Complex in Puerto Rico and the Caribbean: Old Problems, New Perspectives, Possible Solutions. In *Archaeological Investigations on St. Martin (Lesser Antilles): The Sites of Norman Estate, Hope Estate, and Anse des Peres,* edited by C. Hofman and M. Hoogland, pp. 253–297. Archaeological Studies Leiden University No. 4, Leiden.
2000   Gold Symbolism among Caribbean Chiefdoms: Of Feathers, Cibas, and Guanín Power among Taíno Elites. In *Pre-Columbian Gold in South America: Technology Style and Iconography,* edited by C. McEwan, pp. 196–219. British Museum Press, London.
2003   An Interpretative Analysis and Discussion of the Río Cocal-1 Community of Sabana Seca, Puerto Rico. In *Archaeological Survey and Evaluation of Sites at NSWC Sabana Seca,* Vol. IV, Pts. I–II: Evaluation of Prehistoric Site Río Cocal-1 Site, authored by R. C. Goodwin, J. R. Oliver, D. D. Davis, J. Brown, S. Sanders, and M. Simmons, pp. 337–402. Submitted by R. Christopher Goodwin & Associates to the United States Department of the Navy, Atlantic Division, Naval Facilities Engineering Command, Norfolk, VA.

2005   The Proto-Taíno Monumental Cemís of Caguana: A Political-Religious Mani-
        festo. In *Ancient Borinquen: Archaeology and Ethnohistory of Native Puerto Rico,*
        edited by Peter E. Siegel, pp. 230–284. University of Alabama Press, Tuscaloosa.

2006   Cemís and Human Agency; or, Religion and the Making of Taíno Political His-
        tory. Unpublished paper read at the 71st Annual Meeting of the Society for Ameri-
        can Archaeology, in the symposium "Enduring Motives: Religious Traditions in
        the Americas" (in *71st SAA Abstracts,* 2006:304) organized by Warren DeBoer.

2008a   Tiempos Difíciles: Fray Ramón Pané en La Española, 1494–1498. In *El Caribe
        Precolombino: Fray Ramón Pané y el Universo Taíno,* edited by J. R. Oliver, C.
        McEwan, and A. Casas Gilberga, pp. 72–95. Co-edition of the Ministerio de
        Cultura, Museu Barbier-Mueller d'Art Precolombí, and Fundación Caixa Gali-
        cia, Barcelona.

2008b   El Universo Material y Espiritual de los Taínos. In *El Caribe Precolombino: Fray
        Ramón Pané y el Universo Taíno,* edited by J. R. Oliver, C. McEwan, and A. Casas
        Gilberga, pp. 136–201. Co-edition of the Ministerio de Cultura, Museu Barbier-
        Mueller d'Art Precolombí, and Fundación Caixa Galicia, Barcelona.

Oliver, José R., Colin McEwan, and Anna Casas Gilberga (editors)
2008   *El Caribe Precolombino: Fray Ramón Pané y el Universo Taíno.* Co-edition of the
        Ministerio de Cultura, Museu Barbier-Mueller d'Art Precolombí, and Fundación
        Caixa Galicia, Barcelona.

Oliver, José R., and Juan Rivera Fontán
2006   Bateyes de Viví (U-1). Final Report: Nomination to the National Register of His-
        torical Places. Document on file at the Puerto Rico State Historic Preservation
        Office in San Juan and the United States National Park Service, Atlanta.

Oliver, José R., Juan Rivera Fontán, and Lee A. Newsom
1999   Arqueología de Barrio Caguana, Puerto Rico. *Trabajos de Investigación Arqueo-
        lógica: Tercer Encuentro de Investigadores,* edited by J. Rivera Fontán, pp. 8–26.
        Publicación Ocasional de la División de Arqueología–Instituto de Cultura Puer-
        torriqueña, San Juan.

Ortega, Elpidio
1978   Informe sobre Investigaciones Arqueológicas Realizadas en la Región Este del
        País, Zona Costera desde Macao a Punta Espada. *Boletín del Museo del Hombre
        Dominicano* 11:77–105.

Ortíz, Fernando
1973   *Los Negros Brujos.* Ediciones Universal, Miami.
[1906]

1995   *Cuban Counterpoint: Tobacco and Sugar.* 2nd English ed. Duke University Press,
[1940] Durham.

Ostapkowicz, Joanna
1999   Taíno Wooden Sculpture: Rulership and the Visual Arts in the 12–16th Century
        Caribbean. Unpublished Ph.D. dissertation, Center for the Visual Arts, Univer-
        sity of East Anglia, Norwich.

Oviedo y Valdés, Gonzalo Fernández de
1944   *Historia General y Natural de la Yndias, Yslas y Tierra Firme del Mar y Océano.* Pro-

[1535–   logue by J. Natalicio González, footnotes by José Amador de los Ríos. Editorial
1548]   Guaranía, Asunción del Paraguay.

Pagán Jiménez, Jaime, and José R. Oliver
2008   Starch Residues on Lithic Artifacts from Two Contrasting Contexts in North-
         western Puerto Rico: Los Muertos Cave and Vega de Nelo Vargas Farmstead.
         In *Crossing the Borders: New Methods and Techniques in the Study of Archaeo-*
         logical Materials from the Caribbean, edited by C. L. Hofman, M. P. L. Hoog-
         land, and Annelou van Gijn, pp. 137–158. University of Alabama Press, Tusca-
         loosa.

Pagán Jiménez, Jaime, Miguel A. Rodríguez López, Luis A. Chanlatte Baik, and Yvonne
Narganes Storde
2005   La Temprana Introducción y Uso de Algunas Plantas Domésticas, Silvestres y
         Cultivos en las Antillas Pre-Colombinas. *Diálogo Antropológico* 3(10):7–33. Also
         available as an electronic document, http://www.dialogoanthropologico.org/05/
         html/sitio/index.html. Accessed July 3, 2008. Comments by J. R. Oliver and R.
         Rodríguez Ramos and reply by Pagán et al. follow in the same issue.

Pané, Ramón [annotated version of J. J. Arrom]
1974   *Fray Ramón Pané: Relación Acerca de las Antigüedades de los Indios.* Nueva versión
[1497–   con notas, mapa y apéndices por José Juan Arrom. Siglo XXI Editores, México,
1498]   D.F.
1990   *Fra Ramon Pané: Relació sobre les Antiguitats dels Indis.* Nova versió amb notes i
         apèdixs per José Juan Arrom. Translated to Catalan by Nuria Pi-Sunyer. Gener-
         alitat de Catalunya-Comissió Amèrica i Catalunya-1992, Barcelona.
1999   *An Account of the Antiquities of the Indians.* A new edition with introductory study,
         notes, and appendices by J. J. Arrom, translated into English by S. C. Griswold.
         Duke University Press, Durham.

Pauketat, Timothy R.
1994   *The Ascent of Chiefs: Cahokia and Mississippian Politics in Native North America.*
         University of Alabama Press, Tuscaloosa.

Payne, David L.
1991   A classification of Maipuran (Arawakan) Languages based on Shared Lexical Re-
         tentions. In *Handbook of Amazonian Languages,* Vol. 3, edited by D. C. Derby-
         shire and G. K. Pullum, pp. 355–499. Mouton de Gruyter, Berlin.

Pendergast, David M.
1997   Up from the Shallows. *Rotunda: The Magazine from the Royal Ontario Museum*
         30(2):28–35.
1998   The House in the Water. *Rotunda: The Magazine from the Royal Ontario Museum*
         31(2):26–31.

Pendergast, David M., Elizabeth Graham, Jorge A. Calvera, and M. Juan Jardines
2001   Houses in the Sea: Excavation and Preservation at Los Buchillones, Cuba. In *En-*
         during Records: The Environmental and Cultural Heritage of Wetlands, edited by
         B. A. Purdy, pp. 71–82. Oxbow Books, Oxford.
2002   The Houses in Which They Dwelt: The Excavation and Dating of Taíno Wooden
         Structures at Los Buchillones, Cuba. *Journal of Wetland Archaeology* 2:61–75.

Pérez Fernández, Rolando A.

1999   El Culto a la Guadalupe. *Del Caribe* 29:62–73, Santiago de Cuba.

Pérez y Mena, Andrés I.

1998   Cuban Santería, Haitian Vodun, Puerto Rican Santería: A Multiculturalist Inquiry into Syncretism. *Journal for the Scientific Study of Religion* 73(1):15–27.

Pink, Thomas

2004   *Free Will: A Very Short Introduction.* Oxford University Press, Oxford.

Plazas, Clemencia, Ana M. Falchetti, Juanita Sáenz Samper, and Sonia Archila

1993   *La Sociedad Hidráulica Zenú: Estudio Arqueológico de 2.000 Años de Historia en las Llanuras del Caribe Colombiano.* Museo del Oro-Banco de La República, Bogotá.

Portuondo Zúñiga, Olga

1995   *La Vírgen de La Caridad del Cobre: Símbolo de Cubanía.* Editorial Oriente, Santiago de Cuba.

Pospisil, Milan F.

1971   Physical-Anthropological Research on Indian Remains in Eastern Cuba. *Current Anthropology* 12.

Rafinesque, Constantine Samuel

1836   *The American Nations; or, Outlines of Their General History, Ancient and Modern: Including the Whole History of Earth and Mankind in the Western Hemisphere; the Philosophy of American History; the Annals Traditions, Civilizations, and Languages, etc.* Philadelphia. 2 vols. in 1. (For "The Haytian or Taino Languages Restored, with Fragments of the Dialects of Cuba, Jamaica, Lucaya, Borinquen, Eyeri, Cairi, Araguas. Grammar roots and comparative vocabularies"; see Vol. 1:215–259.)

Rainbird, Paul

2007   *The Archaeology of Islands.* Cambridge University Press, Cambridge.

Rasmussen, Susan

1995   *Spirit Possession and Personhood among the Kel Ewey Tuareg.* Cambridge University Press, Cambridge.

Reddish, Paul, producer

1996   *Spirit of the Jaguar Series: Hunters of the Caribbean.* VHS Film of the Natural History Unit, British Broadcasting Corporation (BBC), Bristol.

Redmond, Elsa, and Charles Spencer

1994   The Cacicazgo: An Indigenous Design. In *Caciques and Their People,* edited by J. Marcus and J. F. Zeitlin. Anthropological Papers No. 89, pp. 189–221. Museum of Anthropology, University of Michigan, Ann Arbor.

Reichel-Dolmatoff, Gerardo

1978   *Beyond the Milky Way: Hallucinatory Imagery of the Tukano Indians.* Latin American Center Publication, University of California Los Angeles.

1979   Desana Shaman's Rock Crystals and the Hexagonal Universe. *Journal of Latin American Lore* 5(1):117–128.

1988   *Goldwork and Shamanism: An Iconographic Study of the Gold Museum.* Compañía Litorgráfica Nacional, S.A., Medellín, Colombia.

Reisman, Karl
   1970   Cultural and Linguistic Ambiguity in a West Indian Village. In *Afro-American Anthropology: Contemporary Perspectives,* edited by J. F. Szwed and N. Whitten, pp. 129–142. Free Press, New York.

Rivera Fontán, Juan
   2002   Batey Delfín del Yagüez: Un Asentamiento Arqueológico del Barrio Quemado, Mayagüez. In *IV^{to} Encuentro de Investigadores: Trabajos de Investigación Arqueológica.* Publicaciones Ocasionales, División de Arqueología del Instituto de Cultura Puertorriqueña, San Juan.
   2005   Informe Técnico: Proyecto Arqueológico del Barrio Quemado, Sitio Batey del Yagüez (Pts. I & II). Unpublished technical report on file at the Programa de Arqueología y Etnohistoria of the Instituto de Cultura Puertorriqueña and the Consejo Para La Protección del Patrimonio Arqueológico Terrestre de Puerto Rico, San Juan.

Rivera Fontán, Juan, and José R. Oliver
   2005   Impactos y patrones de ocupación histórica jíbara sobre componentes taínos: El sitio "Vega de Nelo Vargas" (Utu-27), Barrio Caguana, Municipio de Utuado, Puerto Rico. In *Proceedings of the 20th International Congress for Caribbean Archaeology,* edited by Glenis Tavarez María and Manuel García-Arévalo, pp. 1–14. Published by Museo del Hombre Dominicano and Fundación García-Arévalo, Santo Domingo.

Rivera Pagán, Luis N.
   2003   Freedom and Servitude: Indigenous Slavery and the Spanish Conquest of the Caribbean. In *General History of the Caribbean,* Vol. I: "Autochthonous Societies," edited by J. Sued Badillo, pp. 316–332. UNESCO Publishing, Paris.

Rivero de La Calle, Manuel
   1966   *Las Culturas Aborígenes de Cuba.* Editora Universitaria, Habana.
   1978   Supervivencias de Descendientes de Indoamericanos en la Zona de Yateras, Oriente. In *Cuba Arqueológica I,* pp. 149–176. Editorial Oriente, Santiago de Cuba.

Rivero de La Calle, Manuel, César Rodríguez, and Minerva Montero Díaz
   1989   Estudio del Cráneo Europoide Encontrado en el Sitio Aborígen de El Chorro de Maíta, Yaguajay, Banes, Provincia de Holguín, Cuba. *Revista de Historia* 3(2–3).

Rodríguez Demorizi, Emilio
   1972   *Los Dominicos y las Encomiendas de Indios de la Isla Española.* Academia Dominicana de la Historia, Vol. 30. Editora del Caribe, S.A., Santo Domingo.

Rodríguez López, Miguel
   1997   Excavaciones en Maruca, Puerto Rico. Informes y Documentos (1995–1997). Unpublished report submitted to the Consejo Para la Protección del Patrimonio Arqueológico Terrestre de Puerto Rico, San Juan.
   2004   Informe Final: Excavaciones en el Yacimiento Arcáico de Maruca, Ponce. Unpublished final report submitted to the Programa de Arqueología, Instituto de Cultura Puertorriqueña and the Consejo Para La Protección del Patrimonio Arqueológico Terrestre de Puerto Rico, San Juan.

Rodríguez Ramos, Reniel

2001   Lithic Reduction Trajectories at La Hueca and Punta Candelero Sites, Puerto Rico. Unpublished Master's thesis, Department of Anthropology, Texas A&M University, College Station.

2005a   The Crab-Shell Dichotomy: The Lithics Speak Out. In *Ancient Borinquen: Archaeology and Ethnohistory of Native Puerto Rico,* edited by P. E. Siegel, pp. 1–54. University of Alabama Press, Tuscaloosa.

2005b   El Utillaje Pétreo de La Hueca. In *Cultura La Hueca,* edited by L. Chanlatte Baik and Y. Narganes Storde, pp. 73–76. Museo de Historia, Antropología y Arte, Universidad de Puerto Rico, Río Piedras.

2006   From the Guanahatabey to the Archaic of Puerto Rico: The Non-Evident Evidence. *Ethnohistory.* Accepted for publication, 2007. Cited with author's permission.

2007   Puerto Rican Precolonial History Etched in Stone. Unpublished Ph.D. dissertation, Graduate School of the University of Florida, Gainesville.

Rodríguez Ramos, Reniel, and Jaime Pagán Jiménez

2006   Interacciones Multivectoriales en el Circum-Caribe Precolonial: Un Vistazo desde las Antillas. *Caribbean Studies* 34(2):103–143.

Rodríguez Ramos, Reniel, Joshua Torres, and José R. Oliver

2008   Rethinking Time in Caribbean Archaeology. In *Island Shores, Distant Pasts: Archaeological and Biological Approaches to the Pre-Columbian Settlement of the Caribbean,* edited by S. Fitzpatrick and A. H. Ross. University Press of Florida, Gainesville, in press.

Roe, Peter G.

1991   The Best Enemy Is a Killed, Drilled, and Decorative Enemy: Human Corporeal Art, Belt Ornaments, Carved Humeri, and Pierced Teeth in Pre-Columbian Puerto Rico. *Proceedings of the 13th International Congress for Caribbean Archaeology,* A. Ayubi and J. Haviser, editors, pp. 854–873. IACA, Curaçao.

1993   Cross-Media Isomorphisms in Taíno Ceramics and Petroglyphs from Puerto Rico. *Proceedings of the 14th International Congress for Caribbean Archaeology,* A. Cummins and P. King, editors, pp. 637–671. IACA, Barbados.

Rouse, Irving (Ben)

1942   Archaeology of Maniabón Hills, Cuba. *Yale University Publications in Anthropology,* No. 26. Department of Anthropology, Yale University, New Haven.

1948   The Arawak. In *Handbook of South American Indians,* Vol. IV: "The Circum-Caribbean Tribes," edited by J. H. Steward, pp. 507–546. Bulletin No. 143, Bureau of American Ethnology, Washington, D.C.

1952   Porto Rican Prehistory. In *Scientific Survey of Porto Rico and the Virgin Islands,* Vol. 23, Pts. 3 and 4. New York Academy of Sciences, New York.

1965   The Place of "Peoples" in Prehistoric Research. *Journal of the Royal Anthropological Institute of Great Britain & Ireland* 95(1):1–15.

1985   Ceramics and Religious Development in the Greater Antilles. *Journal of New World Archaeology* 5(2):45–55. UCLA.

1992   *The Taínos: The Rise and Decline of the People Who Greeted Columbus.* Yale University Press, New Haven.

Ruthven, Malise

2000   *Islam: A Very Short Introduction.* Oxford University Press, Oxford.

Sahlins, Marshall

1991   The Return of the Event, Again; with Reflections on the Beginning of the Great Fijian War of 1843 to 1855 between the Kingdoms of Bau and Rewa. In *Clio in Oceania: Toward Historical Anthropology,* edited by A. Biersack. Smithsonian Institution Press, Washington, D.C.

Santos-Granero, Fernando

2002   The Arawakan Matrix: Ethos, History, Language, and History in Native South America. In *Comparative Arawakan Histories,* edited by J. D. Hill and F. Santos-Granero, pp. 25–50. University of Illinois Press, Urbana.

Saunders, Nicholas J., and Dorrick Gray

1996   Zemis, Trees, and Symbolic Landscapes: Three Taíno Carvings from Jamaica. *Antiquity* 70:801–812.

Siegel, Peter E.

1996   Ideology and Power and Social Complexity in Prehistoric Puerto Rico. Ph.D. dissertation presented to the Graduate School, Department of Anthropology, State University of New York, Binghamton. University Microfilms International, Ann Arbor.

1997   Ancestor Worship and Cosmology among the Taíno. In *Taíno: Pre-Columbian Art and Culture from the Caribbean,* edited by F. Bercht, J. A. Farmer, and D. Taylor, pp. 106–111. Monacelli Press, New York.

1999   Contested Places and Places of Contest: The Evolution of Social Power and Ceremonial Space in Puerto Rico. *Latin American Antiquity* 10(3):209–238.

Simpson, Lesley Byrd

1966   *The Encomienda in New Spain: The Beginning of Spanish Mexico.* University of California Press, Berkeley.

Stevens Arroyo, Antonio M.

1988   *Cave of the Jagua: The Mythological World of the Tainos.* University of New Mexico Press, Albuquerque. [A 2nd edition with a new auhtor's preface is published by University of Scranton Press, Scranton, 2006].

Steward, Julian H.

1948   The Circum-Caribbean Tribes: An Introduction. In *Handbook of South American Indians,* Vol. IV: "The Circum-Caribbean," edited by J. H. Steward, pp. 1–41. Bulletin 142. Bureau of American Ethnology, Smithsonian Institution, Washington, D.C.

Stewart, Charles

1999   Syncretism and Its Synonyms: Reflections on Cultural Mixture. *Diacritics* 29(3): 40–62.

Strathern, Marilyn

1988   *The Gender of the Gift.* University of California Press, Berkeley.

Sued Badillo, Jalil

1978 *Los Caribes: Realidad o Fábula.* Editorial Antillana, Río Piedras.

1979 *La Mujer Indígena y su Sociedad.* 2nd ed. Editorial El Gazir, Río Piedras.

1984 Another Version of the Carib Affair, and Bartolomé de Las Casas, the Caribs and the Problem of Ethnic Identification. *Homines* 8(1):199–208.

1985 Las Cacicas Indoantillanas. *Revista del Instituto de Cultura Puertorriqueña* 24(87): 17–25.

1992 Facing up to Caribbean History. *American Antiquity* 57(4):599–607.

1995 The Island Caribs: New Approaches to the Question of Ethnicity in the Early Colonial Caribbean. In *Wolves from the Sea,* edited by N. Whitehead, pp. 62–89. KITLV Press, Leiden.

2001a La Formación Cacical en el Sur de Puerto Rico. In *Culturas Aborígenes del Caribe,* edited by Federación Internacional de Sociedades Científicas, pp. 61–74. Banco Central de La República Dominicana, Santo Domingo.

2001b *El Dorado Borincano: La Economía de la Conquista, 1510–1550.* Ediciones Puerto, San Juan.

2003 The Indigenous Societies at the Time of Conquest. In *General History of the Caribbean,* Vol. I: "Autochthonous Societies," edited by J. Sued Badillo, pp. 259–291. UNESCO Publishing, Paris.

Sykes, Karen

2005 *Arguing with Anthropology: An Introduction to Critical Theories of the Gift.* Routledge, London.

Tanodi, Aurelio

1971 *Documentos de la Real Hacienda de Puerto Rico. Vol. 1 (1510–1519).* Centro de Investigaciones Históricas, Universidad de Puerto Rico. Editorial NOVA S.A.C.I., Buenos Aires, Argentina.

Tavárez María, Glenis

1996 Límites Territoriales de los Aborígenes de la Isla de Haití a la Llegada de Los Españoles. In *Ponencias: Primer Simposio de Arqueología del Caribe,* edited by M. Veloz Maggiolo and A. Caba, pp. 34–47. Museo Arqueológico Altos de Chavón, Organization of American States, Santo Domingo.

2001 La Figura de Guacanagaríx, Cacique de Marién, en los Primeros Encuentros Aborígenes en La Española. In *Culturas Aborígenes del Caribe,* edited by Federación Internacional de Sociedades Científicas, pp. 39–48. Banco Central de La República Dominicana, Santo Domingo.

Taylor, Douglas MacRae

1977 *Languages of the West Indies.* Johns Hopkins University Press, Baltimore.

Thomas, Hugh

2003 *Rivers of Gold: The Rise of the Spanish Empire.* Weidenfield & Nicolson, London.

Tió, Aurelio

1961 *Nuevas Fuentes Para la Historia de Puerto Rico.* Universidad Interamericana, San Germán.

1966 *Dr. Diego Álvarez Chanca.* Instituto de Cultura Puertorriqueña, San Juan.

Torres, Joshua M.
2005 Deconstructing the Polity: Communities and Social Landscapes of the Ceramic-age Peoples of South Central Puerto Rico. In *Ancient Borinquen: Archaeology and Ethnohistory of Native Puerto Rico*, edited by Peter E. Siegel, pp. 202–229. University of Alabama Press, Tuscaloosa.

Trincado, María Nelsa
1997 El Aborigen y La Caridad del Cobre. *El Caribe Arqueológico* 2:114–120.

Ulloa Hung, Jorge
2005 Approaches to Early Ceramics in the Caribbean. In *Dialogues in Cuban Archaeology*, edited by L. A. Curet, S. L. Dowdy, and G. La Rosa Corzo, pp. 104–146. University of Alabama Press, Tuscaloosa.

Ulloa Hung, Jorge, and Roberto Valcárcel Rojas
2002 *Cerámica Temprana del Centro-sur del Oriente de Cuba*. Viewgraph-Taraxcun, S.A., Santo Domingo.

Valcárcel Rojas, Roberto
1999 Banes Precolombino: Jerarquía y Sociedad. *El Caribe Arqueológico* 3:84–89.
2002a *Banes Precolombino: La Ocupación Agricultora*. Ediciones Holguín, Cuba.
2002b Reporte de Composición Metálica de Objetos Asociados a Entierros en el Sitio Arqueológico Chorro de Maíta. Ms. on file, Departamento Centro Oriental de Arqueología, Holguín.

Varela, Consuelo
1999 *Cristóbal Colón y los Cuatro Viajes-Testamento*. Alianza Editorial, Madrid.
2006 *La Caída de Cristóbal Colón: El Juicio de Bobadilla*. Edición y Trascripción de Isabel Aguirre. Marcial Pons Historia, Madrid.

Varela, Consuelo, and Juan Gil
2008 La Española a la Llegada de Ramón Pané. In *El Caribe Precolombino: Fray Ramón Pané y el Universo Taíno*, edited by J. R. Oliver, C. McEwan, and A. Casas Gilberga, pp. 56–71. Co-edition of the Ministerio de Cultura, Museu Barbier-Mueller d'Art Precolombí, and Fundación Caixa Galicia, Barcelona.

Vega, Bernardo
1971– Descubrimiento de la Actual Localización del Único Zemí de Algodón Antillano
1972 que Aún Existe. *Revista Dominicana de Arqueología y Antropología* 2(2–3): 88–110.
1980 *Los Cacicazgos de la Española*. Ediciones Museo del Hombre Dominicano, Santo Domingo.
1997 *Les Caciquats de l'île de Quisqueya*. Preface by Federico Mayor and Geraldo Cavalcanti; translated by Françoise Mironneau. UNESCO-Union Latine, Paris.

Veloz Maggiolo, Marcio
1976 *Medioambiente y Adaptación Humana en la Prehistoria de Santo Domingo*, Vol. 1. Colección Historia y Sociedad No. 24. Universidad Autónoma de Santo Domingo, Editora Taller, Santo Domingo.
1977 *Medioambiente y Adaptación Humana en la Prehistoria de Santo Domingo*, Vol. 2. Colección Historia y Sociedad No. 30. Universidad Autónoma de Santo Domingo, Editora Alfa y Omega, Santo Domingo.

1980   *Las Sociedades Arcáicas de Santo Domingo.* Museo del Hombre Dominicano/
        Fundación García Arévalo, Santo Domingo.
1985   *La Arqueología y la Vida Cotidiana.* Biblioteca Taller No. 181. Ediciones de Taller,
        Santo Domingo.
Veloz Maggiolo, Marcio, Elpidio Ortega, and Plinio Pina Peña
1974   *El Caimito: Un Antiguo Complejo Ceramista en las Antillas Mayores.* Museo del
        Hombre Dominicano, Serie Monográfica No. 30. Ediciones Fundación García
        Arévalo, Santo Domingo.
Veloz Maggiolo, Marcio, Elpidio Ortega, Renato O. Rímoli, and Fernando Luna Calderón
1973   Estudio Comparativo y Preliminar de Dos Cementerios Neo-Indios: La Cucama
        y La Unión, República Dominicana. *Boletín del Museo del Hombre Dominicano*
        3:11–52.
Veloz Maggiolo, Marcio, Iraida Vargas, Mario Sanoja, and Fernando Luna Calderón
1976   *Arqueología de Yuma (República Dominicana).* Ediciones Taller, Santo Domingo.
Vitebsky, Piers
1993   *Dialogues with the Dead: The Discussion of Mortality among the Sora of Eastern
        India.* Cambridge University Press, Cambridge.
Vivieros de Castro, Eduardo
1996   Cosmological Deixis and Amerindian Perspectivism: A View from Amazonia.
        Journal of the Royal Anthropological Institute 4:469–488.
Voguel, Susan M.
1997   *Baule: African Art in Western Eyes.* Yale University Press, New Haven.
Wagner, Roy
1991   The Fractal Person. In *Big Men and Great Men: Personifications of Power in Mela-
        nesia,* edited by M. Godelier and M. Strathern, pp. 159–173. Cambridge Univer-
        sity Press, Cambridge.
Walker, Jeffrey B.
1993   Stone Collars, Elbow Stones, and Three-Pointers and the Nature of Taíno Ritual
        and Myths. Unpublished Ph.D. dissertation, Department of Anthropology,
        Washington State University.
1997   Taíno Stone Collars, Elbow Stones, and Three-Pointers. In *Taíno: Pre-Columbian
        Art and Culture from the Caribbean,* edited by F. Bercht, E. Brodsky, J. A. Farmer,
        and D. Taylor, pp. 80–91. Museo del Barrio, Monacelli Press, New York.
2005   The Paso del Indio Site, Vega Baja, Puerto Rico: A Progress Report. In *Ancient
        Borinquen: Archaeology and Ethnohistory of Native Puerto Rico,* edited by Peter E.
        Siegel, pp. 55–87. University of Alabama Press, Tuscaloosa.
Watters, David R.
1997   Maritime Trade in Prehistoric Eastern Caribbean. In *Indigenous Peoples of the
        Caribbean,* edited by S. Wilson, pp. 88–89. University Press of Florida, Gaines-
        ville.
Watters, David R., and Richard Scaglion
1994   Beads and Pendants from Trants, Monserrat: Implications for Prehistoric Lapi-
        dary Industry of the Caribbean. *Annals of Carnegie Museum* 63(3):215–237.

Weiner, Annette

1985 Inalienable Wealth. *American Ethnologist* 12: 210–227.

1992 *Inalienable Possessions: The Paradox of Keeping-while-Giving.* University of California Press, Berkeley.

Whitehead, Neil L. (editor)

1995 *Wolves from the Sea.* KITLV Press, Leiden.

Willey, Gordon R., and Jeremy Sabloff

1974 *A History of Archaeology.* Freeman & Sons, San Francisco.

Wilson, Samuel

1990 *Hispaniola: Caribbean Chiefdoms in the Age of Columbus.* University of Alabama Press, Tuscaloosa.

2004 Linking Prehistory and History in the Caribbean. In *Late Ceramic Age Societies in the Eastern Caribbean,* edited by A. Delpuech and C. L. Hofman, pp. 269–272. British Archaeological Reports International Series 1273, Paris Monographs in American Archaeology 14, Archaeopress, Oxford.

2007 *The Archaeology of the Caribbean.* Cambridge World Archaeology Series, Cambridge University Press, Cambridge.

Wilson, Samuel, Harry B. Iceland, and Thomas R. Hester

1998 Preceramic Connections between Yucatán and the Caribbean. *Latin American Antiquity* 9(4):342–352.

Zayas y Alfonso, Alfredo

1931 *Lexicografía Antillana.* Diccionario de Voces Usadas por los Aborígenes de las Antillas Mayores y Algunas de las Menores y Consideraciones acerca de su Significado y Formación. Tipos-Moliana y Cía., 2nd ed. Habana.

Photo Credits and Copyrights

I am indebted to several museums, institutions, and individuals for their generosity in making their archaeological specimens available for publication in this book. Copyrights and credits follow in alphabetical order.

Institutional (Copyright)

Museum of Anthropology and Ethnography of Turin (Italy)
With kind permission by Dr. Emma Rabino Massa, Director
Photographer: Dr. Joanna Ostapkowicz (retouched with Adobe Photoshop by J. R. Oliver)
Figure 24—Cotton Cemí. Catalog number not available.

The Trustees of the British Museum
Great Russell Street, London WC1B 3DG
Photographer: Figures 11, 18, Front Cover—J. R. Oliver (retouched with Adobe Photoshop)
Photographer (British Museum): Figures 16 and 17—Ivor Kerslake (Head of the Department of Photography); Jonathan Williams, Dave Agar, and Michael Row, photographers
Front Cover: Cat. No. Am 1977.Q1 (Isaac Alves Rebello Collection)
Figure 11: a—Cat. No. Am 1977.Q1 (Isaac Alves Rebello Collection)
Figure 11: b—Cat. No. Am 1997.Q793 (Donated by James Theobalds, 1757)
Figure 11: c—Cat. No. Am MI.168 (William Wareham, Christy Collection)
Figure 16—Cat. No. Am 1977.Q2 (Isaac Alves Rebello Collection)
Figure 17—Cat. No. Am 1977.Q3 (Isaac Alves Rebello Collection)
Figure 18—Cat. No. Am 1949.22.118 (D. K. Oldman Collection)

Museo de Historia, Antropología y Arte–University of Puerto Rico
Universidad de Puerto Rico, Recinto de Río Piedras. P.O. Box 21098
For specimens lacking catalog numbers, see MHAA 2006 in References Cited.
Photographers: Víctor González and Jesús Marrero (only figures 3: d, e, 19: d); J. R. Oliver (retouched with Adobe Photoshop)
Back Cover: No catalog number available
Figure 2: l, m, m'—No catalog number available

Figure 3: a—No catalog number available

Figure 3: d—Cat. No. 10,004

Figure 3: e—Cat. No. 15,357

Figure 6: B, C—Old Cat. No. 163 (formerly Dr. A. L. Oliver Collection, donated 2007)

Figure 7: A, B, D—No catalog number available

Figure 19: c—Cat. No. 11,053

Figure 19: d—No catalog number available

Figure 19: e—Cat. No. 11,051

Figure 25: a-c—No catalog number available

Figure 25: d-g—Cat. No. 15,358

Figure 27: m, n—No catalog number available

Figure 27: p—No catalog number available

Other Copyright Photos

New South Associates–David Deiner

With kind permission by Joe Joseph, Vice President, New South Associates; and David McCullough, U.S. Army Corps of Engineers, Jacksonville, FL.

New South Associates, 6150 East Ponce de Leon Avenue, Stone Mountain, GA 30083

Photographer: David Deiner (9: b—retouched with Adobe Photoshop by J. R. Oliver)

Figure 9: a, b

Institutions and Foundations (Copyrights waived)

Centro de Investigaciones Arqueológicas, Universidad de Puerto Rico, P.O. Box 22603

Courtesy of Luis Chanlatte Baik, Director

Photographer: J. R. Oliver (retouched with Adobe Photoshop)

Figure 6: A

Centro de Estudios Avanzados de Puerto Rico y El Caribe

Courtesy of Miguel Rodríguez López

Photographer: J. R. Oliver (retouched with Adobe Photoshop)

Figure 35 (left)—from the collection of Don Ricardo Alegría

Museo Adolfo de Hostos–Fudación Antropológica, Arqueológica e Histórica de Puerto Rico

(closed in the late 1970s; c/o Wilfredo A. Géigel)

Photographer: J. R. Oliver (retouched with Adobe Photoshop)

Note: Photographs were all taken between 1973 and 1974 while on loan to the
    Museo. The sample in Figures 22: a, b is probably from the Latimer Collection,
    Smithsonian Institution, Washington, D.C.
Figure 20: d, e
Figure 21: A-D
Figure 22: a, b (stone collar, Latimer Collection #AO 17095?)
Figure 22: c

Museo de la Fundación García Arévalo
Embotelladora Dominicana, S.A., Santo Domingo, República Dominicana
With kind permission by Manuel García Arévalo
Photographer: J. R. Oliver (retouched with Adobe Photoshop)
Figure 7: C, F—#1692 (from La Cucama site)
Figure 13: a-i—No catalog numbers available
Figure 15: a, b—No catalog numbers available
Figure 27: f-l—No catalog numbers available

Museo del Hombre Dominicano
Plaza de La Cultura, Henríquez Ureña, Santo Domingo, República Dominicana
With kind permission by Carlos Hernández Soto (Director in 2006) and Glenis
    Tavárez María (Assistant Director)
Photographer: J. R. Oliver (retouched with Adobe Photoshop)
Figure 2: a-i—No catalog numbers available
Figure 3: c—No catalog numbers available

NASA WorldWin (public domain satellite images)
Retouched with Adobe Photoshop by J. R. Oliver
Figures 26, 31

Peabody Museum of Natural History, Division of Archaeology, Yale University
Courtesy of Prof. Richard L. Burger, Head of the Department of Anthropology
Photographer: J. R. Oliver (retouched with Adobe Photoshop by J. R. Oliver)
Figure 3: b—Cat. No. 145191–6203 La Parguera. P.R. stone collar (detail).

USGS National Center for EROS (public domain satellite images)
Retouched with Adobe Photoshop by J. R. Oliver
Figure 32

Individual Credits (Private)
Dr. Jago Cooper and Roberto Valcárcel
University of Leicester, U.K.

Photographer: Jago Cooper (retouched with Adobe Photoshop by J. R. Oliver)
Figure 34—Los Buchillones, Cuba

Prof. Lourdes Domínguez
La Habana, Cuba
Photographer: Unknown (retouched with Adobe Photoshop by J. R. Oliver)
Figure 35 (right)

Wilfredo A. Gégiel, Esq.
Gallows Way, St. Croix, USVI
Photographer: J. R. Oliver (retouched with Adobe Photoshop)
Figure 14—Three-pointed stone from Turabo Valley, Caguas
Figure 22—Three-pointed cemí (white "marble")

Drs. Menno P. L. Hoogland and Corinne L. Hofman
University of Leiden
Photographer: Menno P. L. Hoogland
Figure 27: s—This specimen is either from the Antigua Historical Society or the
    Fred Olsen Collection (now at Yale University–Peabody Museum of Natural
    History, Division of Anthropology)

Miguel A. Oliver (private collection)
Photographer: J. R. Oliver (retouched with Adobe Photoshop)
Figure 10—formerly Dr. A. L. Oliver collection

Juan Rivera Fontán
Photographer: Juan Rivera Fontán
Figure 12: g—Bateyes del Delfín de Yagüez, Puerto Rico

Jaime and Arelis Pagán Jiménez
With kind permission by Arelis Pagán, San Juan, P.R.
Photographer: Jaime Pagán Jiménez
Figure 19: f, g—Stone collar from Marín, Patillas, Puerto Rico

Robinson Rosado
Ciales, Puerto Rico
Photographer: J. R. Oliver (retouched and reconstructed with Adobe Photoshop)
Figure 8: e—Inhaler and winged vomiting spatula

Roberto Valcárcel Rojas
Photographers: Roberto Valcárcel, Jago Cooper, and other members of DCOE
    (retouched with Adobe Photoshop by J. R. Oliver)

Departamento Centro Oriental de Arqueología, CISTAT-CITMA, Holguín, Cuba
Figure 27: a-e—Specific site location not provided: Eastern Cuba
Figure 29: a-f—Banes, Cuba

Dr. Jeff Walker
Caribbean National Forest
Río Grande, Puerto Rico
Drawings by J. R. Oliver after illustrations by J. Walker (1993)
Figure 19: a-c—from Walker 1993 (figs. 5–3, 5–4)
Figure 23—from Walker 1993 (figs. 5–8)

Index

Abey, Puerto Rico: salt marshes of, 212; salt mines of, 41. *See also caciques* (chiefs) of
aboriginal, xv, 114, 161, 232, 234, 237, 238–43, 254
aborigines, 82, 215; Yucatán 237, Cueybá, 242
achira (*Canna sp.*). See *gruya* (*Achira sp.*)
Acrocomia media. See *corozo* palm trees (*Acrocomia media*)
adelantado, 219; definition of, 107, 217
adoratorios. *See* shrines
adversario. *See* opponent
affine, 30, 41, 104, 215, 251
Africa, xvi, 28, 33, 50, 59
African: black Creole, 243; icons, 238; idols, xvi; heritage, 233, 236; *orichas* (deities), 220; religion, 241; slaves, 33, 39, 220, 244
Afro-Cuban (Afro-Cubano), 233, 237–38
Afro-Caribbean, 242, 244
agency, 112; and sociality 113; as causality 47; of *cemís* 115; concentrated in the face, 154; human, xv; human-*cemí*, xiv; seminal, 133; social, 70; repositories of, 70
agriculture, 9, 134; *montón* system, 203
Agüeybana I (*cacique,* chief), 38–39, 108, 138, 158, 199–202, 205–6
Agüeybana II (*cacique,* chief), 39, 191, 206–10, 214, 217
Agüeybana, Francisco de (*cacique* of Saona Island), 203
Aguilar, Marcos de, 214
ajes (*Ipomoea batatas*), 153
ají (chili peppers, *Capsicum* sp.), 150, 234
alaqueques (cornaline beads), 152
Alburquerque, Alfonso de, 102
alcalde, 201;
alcalde mayor, 202
Alegría Pons, Francisco, xv

Alegría, Ricardo, 23, 80, 89, 121, 126, 129, 188, 193, 198, 201–3
alienability, 82, 109–17, 249; as a category 112; gifts (can be given), 110; things, 44, 156; moveable 113; possessions, 108, 111, 122, 156; vs. inalienable wealth, 106, 250
Altagracia Province or district of Hispaniola, 128, 196. *See also* Higüey
Alvarado, Pedro, 127
Álvarez Chanca, Dr. Diego, 6, 169
alzados. *See* runaway, itinerant groups (*alzados*)
Amerindian, 48–49, 51, 53, 59, 238, 239, 241, 243
Ana River. *See* Manatí River, Puerto Rico
Anacaona. See *caciques,* names of
Anadel style or complex, 9, 18, 128, 142, 204
Anadenanthera peregrina (*cohóbana* tree), 13, 14. See also *cohoba*
Añasco, region of Puerto Rico, 202, 206
Añasco, Luis de, 38
ancestors: apical, 146; bundles of 144; *cemís,* idols, 52, 82, 67, 112, 141–45, 147–48, 154, 207; cemíified 22, 52, 141; of chief/s or *caciques,* 81, 137, 143, 147; direct link to, 146; kept in, 144; physical presence of 145; personages, 22, 136; stone heads, skulls, 147, 154, 160, 250–51; veneration, 133, 143; worship, 106
ancestral: Cedrosan Saladoid source, 9–10; chiefs 108; community, 126; cult to the *cemís,* 235; culture, 8, 23; histories, 27; style 8; human skull, 126; line 18; semicircular villages, 22; sources, 48; territory, 144
Anciso. *See* Fernández de Enciso (or Ancisco), Martín
Anderson, David, 24, 79